The Company Store

J.B. McLachlan and the Cape Breton Coal Miners

1900–1925

Open Thy Mouth, Judge Righteously,

and Plead the Cause of the Poor and Needy

—*Proverbs* 31:9, engraved on
J.B. McLachlan's gravestone

The Company Store is John Mellor's gut-wrenching telling of Labour's battles in Cape Breton Island, 1900–1925. The company store is a powerful symbol for the system against which coal miners and steelworkers fought—the system wherein the company owned the mines, the steel plant, the homes, the stores, controlled most newspapers and even ministers and priests—with the goal of profits for shareholders and keeping workers in line. And when all this failed, provincial and federal governments sent in troops against the workers!

Through it all, J.B. McLachlan served as a leader, an inspiration, and a symbol for the resistance and strategies of the workers, as they went on strike again and again in the face of wage cuts, poor housing, and a system determined to deny them any control, even if it meant evictions, police brutality, and murder.

Were this not a true story, it would be unbelievable.

To my wife Pamela—
my most ardent critic, mentor,
and a tower of strength
in the face of adversity

The Company Store

J.B. McLachlan and the Cape Breton Coal Miners 1900–1925

John Mellor

Breton Books

Editor: Ronald Caplan; production assistant: Bonnie Thompson; graphic coordinator: Fader Communications

Front cover illustration by Steve Marchesi.

Back cover photos: J.B. McLachlan's promotional photo during an election campaign, signed "Yours in the fight." Soldiers behind barbed wire at the Caledonia Mine during the 1909 strike. Cape Breton Coal Miners: Back Row, left to right: Jim Wadden, Peter Jobes, Tim Wadden. The shift has just finished and they have changed to street clothes. The young men in the front row, left to right: Tius Tutty, Fred Wadden, Bill MacKenzie and, standing, F.K. Wadden. Off to the left is Allie MacKenzie. Allie will go on to become one of Canada's finest football and baseball players. His picture will hang in the Hall of Fame in Halifax. And Allie will die at thirty in a gas attack in the First World War. But when this picture was taken, Allie was nine years old and had already worked three months as a trapper boy in Caledonia Colliery. All photos courtesy Cape Breton Miners' Museum, Quarry Point, Glace Bay, Nova Scotia.

We acknowledge the support of the Canada Council for the Arts for our publishing program.

Canada Council for the Arts Conseil des Arts du Canada

We also acknowledge support from Cultural Affairs, Nova Scotia Department of Communities, Culture & Heritage.

NOVA SCOTIA
Communities, Culture and Heritage

We acknowledge the financial support of the Government of Canada through the Canada Book Fund for our publishing activities.

Canadä

Library and Archives Canada Cataloguing in Publication

Mellor, John, 1922–2007

The company store : J.B. McLachlan and the Cape Breton coal miners, 1900–1925 / John Mellor.

Includes bibliographical references and index.

ISBN 978-1-926908-10-6

1. McLachlan, J.B. (James Bryson), 1869–1937. 2. Labor unions—Nova Scotia—Cape Breton Island—History—20th century. 3. Coal miners—Nova Scotia—Cape Breton Island—History—20th century. 4. Strikes and lockouts—Coal mining—Nova Scotia—Cape Breton Island—History—20th century. 5. Working class—Nova Scotia—Cape Breton Island—History—20th century. I. Title.

HD5329.M615M45 2012 331.88'122334'097169 C2012-903165-8

Printed in Canada

Introduction

by Bill McNeil

The company store in a one-company town was symbolic of everything that was wrong in a system where the company had it all and the workers had nothing. The company had total power over the people it employed, telling them who would work, where they would work, when they would work, how much they would be paid, where they would live, and, through the company store, how well they would live. Everything a worker needed for his family and himself to stay alive was contained within the four walls of the company store—food, clothing, and other supplies. The company store sold on credit and collected its money directly from the workers' wages.

The store itself was chock-full of things that the workers couldn't afford on the subsistence wages they were paid, and these things were always of the highest quality and price, the idea being to entice a man into debt so that he would be forever bound to the company. The temptation of giant hams, beef roasts, fruits, and nuts of all kinds to a worker who could barely afford oatmeal was tremendous. The sight of silk and satin dresses to a wife used to cotton was irresistible, as was the sight of warm clothes for the children and good things to eat. "Charge it." "Put it on my bill." It was so easy to say such things, and the company store was only too willing to oblige. One more man in debt. One more worker caught in the company's web for life. That's the way things were in the Cape Breton of John Mellor's *The Company Store*, the Cape Breton where I grew up and where one company, Dosco, had the power of life and death over its employees and, indeed, over the towns where they lived.

Dosco owned the mines where virtually everybody worked, the

houses they lived in, and the stores that supplied the necessities of life. Dosco was *the* company in all of the one-company towns of Cape Breton, and its influence was all-powerful and all-pervasive, extending out to the provincial and federal governments, and even to the churches. Everybody, even those who didn't actually get their cheques from the company, depended on the company—the doctors, lawyers, churchmen, small storekeepers, town employees—everybody.

When the wheels on the bankhead at the coal mine weren't turning or bringing coal out of the pit, the whole town suffered. In the town of Glace Bay where I was born into a coal mining family, we all watched the wheels at the pit and listened every day for the six o'clock whistle. One long blast meant that there would be work tomorrow. Two blasts meant no work, and during the Depression years of the thirties, it was two blasts more often than one. Those were my growing-up years, and even though I was young, I fully understood that the company was the aggressor and "we, the people," were the oppressed. It was "we" and "them." The company couldn't be loved because, as it had proved many times in the past, it didn't love us.

My child's ears had absorbed my mother's oft-told tales of the terrible strike of 1909 when soldiers with machine guns came in to keep order in the town, but they were really there because an obliging government had sent them in to protect the company's property. My mother's own family was evicted from a company-owned house in the dead of winter, and her sick father was carried out, bed and all, and placed on the sidewalk among the tangle of tables and chairs. That was his folly and his crime because he was a striker. Mother, who was fourteen years old when this happened, never could forget that terrible day, and she could never, even in her old age, tell the story without breaking down in tears.

Then there were stories about young boys who were accidentally electrocuted on the power-filled fences which the company had strung around their mines to keep the strikers out. There were stories about goon squads brought in by the company from the Montreal waterfront to control the striking miners with big sticks, fists, and guns. There were stories of strikers being run down by company police on horseback and of strikers being killed by these same company police. There were stories of children too hungry and ill-clothed to attend school and stories of whole families evicted from homes, living in tents in the cruel Cape Breton winter. There were one or two stories of victory too, such as the one about the starving miners in the 1925 strike storming the well-stocked company store and rolling home barrels of food for their families.

The whole history of the labour movement in Cape Breton is one of warfare between a company obsessed with profit at any cost and a labour force trying to escape the bonds of slavery, for that's what it was—slavery pure and simple. I think you might agree with this terminology as you read John Mellor's absorbing account of a shameful and sordid period in Canadian history.

This is a story I would like to have written, but am glad I didn't. I was, and still am, too emotionally involved. John Mellor came in from the outside as a professional and dispassionate reporter. He had no axes to grind and no unhealed hurts, as I do. He just wanted to set the records straight. He researched the facts, talked with the old people who still remembered those times, and made his own assessment. It took seven years of his life to produce *The Company Store*, and in my opinion it's the kind of work that gives real meaning to one man's life. It's a shocking narrative which proved to me that all those tales my mother told me were just too true. I thank him for it.

Bill McNeil
"Voice of the Pioneer"
Canadian Broadcasting Corporation
Toronto

Preface

by John Mellor

Coal mining, with all its many hazards, was for hundreds of years a sad history of backbreaking toil rewarded by pitiful wages and a complete disregard for even the most basic safety measures. But the coal mining industry began with the discovery of coal miraculously formed millions of years before man with all his frailties ever walked the surface of the earth.

Often described romantically as "Buried Sunshine," coal was created from the luxurious vegetation that abounded in the hot, humid, primeval forests covering much of the earth's land mass some 300 million years ago. As dense layers of leaves and spores fell to the swampy ground, they were buried, compressed, and dehydrated for countless aeons of time until the greenery of long-dead forests was converted into rich, brown peat deposits, one above the other, some no thicker than a man's arm, others six, ten, and even forty feet or more in depth, each layer representing an age hundreds or even thousands of years apart.

Countless ages passed as through a long, slow process of fossilization, the peat beds were pressed into hard, brittle deposits of carbon known as coal. Millions of years went by, but the process was sure and continuous until, eventually, rich, black seams of bituminous coal were miraculously formed, each seam representing a separate age when nature had captured the warm, life-giving rays of the sun, stored them inside fallen vegetation, and reserved them for the future in the form of fossil fuel.

Many more millions of years passed and vast land masses were formed or separated through continental drift. As each continental mass joined the other, folding and faulting occurred to throw up great mountain chains all along the ocean seaboards of the world.

The enormous forces generated by the folding and faulting action applied varying degrees of pressure to form fields of coal. Off the coast of Cape Breton Island on the Atlantic seaboard, the Sydney coalfield—one of the richest coal deposits in the world—was formed. It extended east under the Atlantic Ocean from the shores of Cape Breton towards Newfoundland.

The last and perhaps the most dramatic of the geological changes occurred a mere million years before man was created. For countless ages the northern hemisphere had enjoyed hot, humid, equatorial weather conditions, but then gradually, the weather changed. Winters became longer and more severe; vast areas of Canada became cooler, more temperate zones, and then over a time period of thousands of years, the whole northern portion became a frozen waste where snow and ice lay on the ground all year round. Successive snowfalls and fierce blizzards followed, and the snow became a blanket hundreds of feet thick. As temperatures plunged, the lower levels turned to ice, and in a slow, imponderable movement lasting many more thousands of years, the ice, which had been transformed into huge glaciers one and even two miles high, began to move down from the mountains into the plains below.

The ice was so thick and heavy that its very weight depressed areas hundreds or even thousands of feet below the surface of the earth. The coal beds were forced deeper into the earth by the awesome weight of the glaciers, but the added weight served to speed the long gradual process of dehydration and hardening of the bituminous coal. Impossible to halt, the glaciers swept all before them. In Canada, vast areas of land on the Atlantic seaboard were stripped clean. Trees, bushes, even the very topsoil so vital to future agriculture, were wiped clean from the land and dumped into the Atlantic Ocean, leaving the ancient Precambrian bedrock polished and scored clean.

The intense cold transformed so much seawater into ice that the oceans were lowered for hundreds of feet to expose vast areas of the continental shelf, and as the mighty glaciers continued their advance to the south, huge gullies were gouged out of the land. The northern tip of Nova Scotia was separated from the mainland by one such gully, known at a later date as the Strait of Canso.

And then after another twenty thousand years, the mighty glaciers halted their imponderable advance to the south and began to withdraw slowly over a period of many more thousands of years. Some regions benefited during the withdrawal as the glaciers dumped rich deposits of topsoil scraped from other areas during the advance southward. Nova Scotia and its northern tip were not so fortunate. The precious topsoil was not returned in any great quantity, leaving the land barren and rocky for the most part.

With the withdrawal of the glaciers and the attendant increase in temperature, the oceans returned to their normal levels to cover the rich coal beds lying off the eastern coast of Nova Scotia. The rising seas flooded the Strait of Canso to isolate the northern tip of Nova Scotia from the mainland and form the island of Cape Breton. The isolation of the newly created island from the rest of the Canadian land mass was to have far-reaching political and sociological effects on its residents many millions of years hence.

The loss of the island's topsoil and the inability to grow life-supporting crops were also to have adverse effects in a future age—especially during times of industrial strife when famine stalked the land.

The land may have been left devoid of much of its topsoil, but the mineral wealth was enormous. Stretching out from the eastern shores of Cape Breton Island, the Sydney coalfield reached out for many miles, one rich seam above the other, sloping down from the shoreline to a point hundreds of feet below the ocean floor to form submarine coalfields unique in North America.

Complementing the huge coal deposits off Cape Breton Island was a never-ending source of iron ore at Wabana, Newfoundland, and a plentiful supply of limestone—all within easy reach of each other and close to the great, natural harbour of Sydney—to provide cheap and easy transportation to any country in the world. Coal (to be converted into coke), iron ore, and limestone, the three main ingredients used in the manufacture of steel. But that day was in the far distant future. As yet, no man had set foot on earth.

The coal could have remained hidden and undetected for millions of years after man's arrival, but many of the rich coal seams sloping under the ocean from the shores of Cape Breton Island became exposed as the ever-restless seas pounded and eroded the rocky cliffs guarding its eastern shores. Sharp-eyed entrepreneurs, recognizing the worth of the black, glistening seams threading through the cliffs, made haste to mine the coal for personal profit during the eighteenth century. Others, more enterprising, prevailed upon the authorities to grant a monopoly and exclusive mining rights over all the coalfields within their jurisdiction.

Nature had been cheated. Her precious gift of fossil fuel intended for the use of all mankind, especially the poor and needy, was now to be exploited to make vast profits for a privileged few. Lowly workingmen would be used to mine the coal as beasts of labour, born to suffer and to die deep beneath the ocean floor, victims of a rigid class system that denigrated them and denied them the basic human rights of freedom of expression and dignity.

For many generations the history of coal mining was a sad chronicle of man's inhumanity to man, a continuing saga of exploitation, oppression, and persecution by companies motivated solely by greed and swollen profits built through the suffering of low-paid miners and disregard for even the most basic safety measures. The toll in blood and suffering brought demands for regulatory measures and a change in the structure to bring a more equitable sharing of the great wealth workers had helped create. But blind protests and uncoordinated action by workers to force such a change were easily met and contained through brute might and the introduction of punitive anti-labour laws. Without leadership and organization, miners were doomed to a serf-like existence, forced to live and work under intolerable conditions little short of slavery.

As each generation of miners succeeded the other, they learned that work stoppages and slowdowns were poor weapons at best, and that political representation through the election of workingmen was the only sure method of redressing their grievances and improving their miserable lot in life. But to their consternation they found the path blocked by a lack of formal education. As child workers forced to enter the mines at nine or ten years of age, most of them had entered manhood illiterate and lacking the valuable attributes of articulate speech and the ability to read and write well. Without formal education they were as putty in the hands of unscrupulous coal operators.

A select few did succeed in overcoming the odds to gain an education through great sacrifice and denial of leisure hours after the long day's work was done. It was men such as these who became leaders. Men of this calibre, recruited from the ranks of low-paid workers and subject to the same degrading labour practices and working conditions as their fellows, had all been created from the same potter's mould but with a difference. They were militants, and to them the formation of the first trade unions and the initiation of political labour movements in Great Britain and North America must be credited.

Before the turn of the twentieth century, men, women, and children were forced to toil like beasts of the field from dawn to dusk, six and seven days each week for a few miserable coins and a place to sleep. In Cape Breton, Nova Scotia, they worked in the submarine coal mines extending for miles under the floor of the Atlantic Ocean. Hard, dangerous work, which earned them the worthy sobriquet—"Men of the Deeps."

Living in company houses, forced to buy food and other necessities of life from company stores through an iniquitous checkoff system, Cape Breton miners were like slaves in a feudal system where everything, even body and soul, was owned by the company. The militants began by questioning existing institutions and practices, found them seeping with injustice and tyranny, and began to agitate for reform and an end to social evils that held them in bondage. But many of them became martyrs for the cause. Any attempt to organize fellow miners to bargain for better working conditions inevitably led to blacklistings and forced eviction from company houses, often in the depth of winter. Denied the opportunity to work for a living, the "undesirables" and their families faced starvation, for social services such as unemployment insurance and relief were dreams of the future. Hundreds of blacklisted miners were forced to leave the island of Cape Breton and seek work in the United States or western Canada, far from the baleful influence of coal and steel barons who had been granted exclusive mining rights by the provincial government of Nova Scotia through an iniquitous system of leasing for periods of up to ninety-nine years.

Some of the blacklisted miners remained in Cape Breton to continue the struggle and encourage their fellows to free themselves from the yoke of servitude. Through their untiring sacrifice, miners were organized into a union to demand better working conditions, but for their efforts they were vilified by the press, persecuted by federal and provincial governments, the judiciary and the courts, the more affluent segments of Canadian society, and even the clergy. During the turbulent strikes of the 1920s, ministers of all denominations openly sided with influential coal and steel producers in Cape Breton at the expense of starving, evicted miners, even to the extent of waving Union Jacks from their lofty pulpits as they solemnly warned their flocks of the danger of Bolshevik infiltration by godless atheists posing as union leaders.

The struggle continued in Cape Breton through a series of crippling strikes, each worse than its predecessor. Hundreds and then thousands of men, women, and children suffered famine and sickness as federal and provincial governments refused to intervene or even afford a small measure of relief in food or money. Many died, but the government's only response was to send in armed troops and machine guns to intimidate striking miners and force them to return to work under the coal company's harsh, punitive terms, which included wage slashes and further discrimination.

Cape Breton miners suffered for over twenty-five years under abominable working conditions and intimidation before the flames of violence and rebellion swept from one end of the island to the other. Burning and looting became the order of the day, with the forces of law and order, long accustomed to protecting coal company interests at the expense of starving miners and their families, retreating in fear and disarray.

During these early years of struggle when it was considered sacrilegious or even traitorous for workers to demand wage increases or improved working conditions, the Cape Breton miners were led by James Bryson McLachlan, a Scottish immigrant miner who landed on the shores of Cape Breton at the turn of the century after being blacklisted for union activities in the Scottish coalfields.

Destined to lead miners in their age-old struggle to free themselves from the yoke of servility and to gain decent working conditions, McLachlan was vilified by his opponents, who labelled him a dangerous Soviet, a communist insurgent intent only on the overthrow of the capitalist system and state. For many years he continued his crusade to organize miners and lead them through a series of painful strikes and confrontations with the coal companies, but in his unending struggle to end oppression and gain a decent standard of living for his fellows, he was to suffer greatly

This is the story of the Cape Breton miners, and of J.B. McLachlan—who led them, and encouraged them to fight fire with fire, and ruthlessness with even greater ruthlessness, to force the powerful coal barons to bargain in good faith for better wages and working conditions. It is a story of great suffering, but it is also a story of greatness—of the nobility of man.

1

Whitney, Coal and the Steel Boom

Many early miners in Cape Breton Island had arrived as penniless immigrants from lands across the sea. They had looked to the "Mecca" of North America as the ultimate goal of freedom and democracy only to find on arrival their lot had worsened rather than improved. For many years only passive resistance was offered against the deplorable working conditions and wages provided by the multitude of small coal mining companies operating in the province, but with the amalgamation of the small private companies into one vast consortium, conditions deteriorated still further.

The rebellion of the Cape Breton miners during the 1920s can be traced directly to the granting of an exclusive provincial charter under a ninety-nine-year lease to the Dominion Coal Company.

A Sydney businessman, A.C. Ross, is credited with being the first to visualize the enormous advantage of an amalgamation of many of the small unproductive coal mining companies operating throughout the island of Cape Breton, Nova Scotia. With keen insight, Ross had realized the potential of a rail link connecting the Sydney coalfield to the ice-free port of Louisbourg, twenty miles to the south. During the winter months when the harbours at Sydney and Glace Bay were icebound, coal mining companies had been forced to suspend operations and lay off thousands of Cape Breton miners until the spring thaw. If the coal could be transported by rail to Louisbourg to be loaded into ships bound for the United States and Europe, every coal mine throughout the

Sydney coalfield could continue mining operations through the cruel Canadian winter to accrue much greater profits and maintain full employment.

Ross approached a Boston businessman, H.W. Whitney, who was known to have extensive interests in the United States which required large amounts of good, bituminous coal for manufacturing operations.

With Whitney's enthusiastic endorsement, the plan for an amalgamation of coal companies was presented to the Honourable W.S. Fielding, premier of the province of Nova Scotia in 1891. As expected, it was not a difficult task to persuade Fielding and his cabinet to add their own support for the ambitious project. With declining output of coal from the many unprofitable coal mines in Cape Breton, a mere seventy thousand dollars had been fed into hungry provincial coffers the previous year from royalties paid at the rate of ten cents per ton. With an amalgamation of all small companies and a large infusion of foreign capital to modernize mining equipment and build an efficient transportation system, the output of coal could be enormously increased to add greatly to provincial royalties.

Leases for a period of ninety-nine years, renewable on expiration for an additional twenty years, were granted by the Nova Scotia provincial government in 1894 to the new company, which was to be known as the Dominion Coal Company. The exclusive monopoly for coal mining was confined to the island of Cape Breton, with the mainland of Nova Scotia excluded from the agreement. With little additional persuasion, the provincial government agreed to a request from the new consortium for a heavy subsidization of costs for the new railway to be constructed from Sydney and Glace Bay to the town of Louisbourg, but in partial payment they demanded an increase in royalties from the previous ten cents to twelve and a half cents per ton of mined coal.

Thus, in one swift stroke of the pen, the enormous natural resources of Cape Breton had been confiscated from the citizens and handed over to an international consortium of doubtful reputation. The few critics who opposed the granting of the ninety-nine-year lease and an exclusive charter to mine Cape Breton's rich minefields realistically pointed out that any development the new company brought to the industry was founded upon a thousand and one considerations, not one of which was in the interest of the people of Nova Scotia. The most outspoken critic, George Forrest, a member of the legislature for Cumberland County, declared solemnly they were selling the precious raw resources of the province to foreign interests for a mere pittance:

> Is it reasonable to believe that a foreign corporation will use our raw materials to manufacture goods to compete with them in the markets they are striving to obtain for themselves?... This measure [exclusive mining rights] provides machinery whereby in this little Nova Scotia of ours, a monopoly could be created in a product for which there is no substitute and which is essential to our success as a manufacturing centre. If we jealously guard this commodity, the day may yet dawn when Nova Scotia will become to the Dominion of Canada what Manchester is to Britain.

George Forrest's warning sounds prophetic today as strenuous efforts are being made to export every last ounce of Canada's natural resources in spite of serious unemployment and a decreasing world market for its finished products, but in 1894 the prospect of increased markets for Nova Scotia coal seemed a godsend to many people.

Without delay, the Dominion Coal Company took over a large number of unprofitable coal mines in the Sydney coalfield and, with a large outlay of capital, the output was boosted tenfold. Much of the coal was sold to Whitney's New England interests after piers had been built at Boston to allow easy unloading of coal-carrying vessels obtained on charter. Loading facilities at the ports of Sydney and Louisbourg in Cape Breton were also greatly improved.

By the year 1900, Whitney's efforts were bearing fruit. The company prospered and the work force grew by leaps and bounds. The towns of Glace Bay, Reserve Mines, and Bridgeport grew around the collieries owned by the Dominion Coal Company. Over thirty-five hundred miners were employed initially. A number of unproductive mines were closed but six remaining mines owned by the company were modernized to increase their output—

a modernization that did not include improved safety measures to avoid frequent catastrophic accidents with their inevitable toll of dead and crippled miners.

All six mines were located in or near the town of Glace Bay and within easy access of the newly constructed Sydney and Louisbourg Railway, owned by the company and financed through the benevolence of the Nova Scotia provincial government. And then to supplement the fleet of chartered, oceangoing vessels carrying Dominion's coal to Boston, Halifax, and Montreal, the Black Diamond Steamship Line was formed as a subsidiary of the coal company. Five modern steamships were built in addition to a number of tugs, barges, and other vessels, and by the year 1901, exports of coal had boomed. The port of Montreal received over one million tons of coal in the first year's operation, coal that had been mined in the Sydney coalfield and loaded from piers at Glace Bay and North Sydney.

So rapidly did the output of the Dominion Coal Company's mines increase that it soon became evident that another major industry could be supplied without sacrificing existing markets. As a result of experimentation, it was found that the bituminous coal mined from the Sydney coalfield was well suited to the manufacture of good quality metallurgical coke, used in the making of steel. This discovery directed attention to the possibility of erecting extensive iron and steel mills in the Sydney area to use coke derived from Dominion coal. Limestone was available in large quantities locally and an ample supply of iron ore was obtainable from nearby Bell Island, where another company, Nova Scotia Steel and Coal Company, owned huge deposits.

Whitney then approached the provincial and federal governments for financial assistance in the form of liberal bounties to stimulate the growth of what he hoped would be a vast steel industry in Cape Breton, which would create thousands of new jobs for the unemployed and provide a source of lucrative royalties for government coffers. Both levels of government agreed eagerly and plans went ahead for the construction of a new iron and steel complex to be located along the shores of Sydney harbour. With tongue in cheek, Whitney then approached the city of Sydney for assistance in obtaining a free site for the new works with exemption from municipal taxes for a very lengthy period. The city fathers, delighted with the prospect of having a huge steel complex built within the boundaries of Sydney to employ many of its citizens, readily acceded to both requests and granted the new company, Dominion Iron and Steel Company, 480 acres of prime industrial land coupled with a tax exemption for the next ninety-nine years —a period reduced to thirty years after strenuous objections had been raised by some aldermen.

A provincial charter was granted to Dominion's new venture the same year, but the share capitalization left a great deal to be desired. In Ottawa, the Canadian Prime Minister, Sir Wilfred Laurier, was reported to have been greatly disgusted by manoeuvers in the organization of Dominion Iron and Steel Company. Neither government—federal or provincial—saw fit to question the legality of launching a company through the use of watered stock and paper assets.

The introduction of watered stock in the financial structure of Dominion's companies was to become a familiar pattern in the years ahead. Dividends paid on watered stock could be obtained only through reduction of operating costs, especially through wage reduction.

Construction of the new steel mills began immediately and almost overnight the site became a hive of industry, with construction giving an added impetus to the commercial and industrial life of Cape Breton as the demand for construction workers increased. Carpenters, bricklayers, masons, machinists, and labourers flooded into the island from all parts of Canada and the United States. Many native Nova Scotians who had been forced to seek work outside the province during hard times were encouraged to return home to share in the unprecedented boom that was providing work for so many. The future had never looked brighter.

The first blast furnace was fired on December 19, 1900, and was immediately placed into production to fill a huge backlog of orders from all over the world. The proximity of iron ore, limestone, and coal added to the undoubted advantages of low-cost water transportation made the finished product extremely competitive in world markets.

The future of Sydney and its new steel plant may have appeared bright and promising to the city fathers and the directors and shareholders of Dominion Iron and Steel Company, but unfortunately, cost figures for raw materials and transportation did not include one other important reason for the low, competitive price of the finished product, and that was the cost of labour. Thousands of workers had been hired to work in the steel mills for twelve and fourteen hours a day, six days and even seven days each week, for a wage that put them far beneath the poverty level.

Dark clouds were beginning to form on the bright horizon. Low wages and intolerable working conditions were already sowing the seeds of mutiny and discontent.

If steel was king in Sydney, coal reigned supreme in the nearby town of Glace Bay, which was merely a collection of small villages and settlements mining coal on a small scale prior to the take-over by the Dominion Coal Company. With the influx of new capital, the town of Glace Bay rapidly became the most important mining settlement in Cape Breton. Its growth, which was equally as rapid as that of its neighbour Sydney, resulted from an increased demand for coal for industrial and domestic use. The hungry furnaces at the Sydney steel mills, plus the coke and gas conversion in Boston, had created an incessant demand for first-rate bituminous coal from the Sydney coalfield. An ever-increasing demand for coal necessitated a continuous-shift operation of the mines, so that night and day, six days a week (no self-respecting Scot would work on the Sabbath), summer and winter, the mines in and around the town of Glace Bay spewed the black gold out of the bowels of the earth for cheap transportation to Sydney, Louisbourg, and foreign ports throughout the world.

The incessant demand for coal and steel was also responsible for the mass recruitment of miners from England, Scotland, Ireland, and Wales. By boat and train they flooded into the boom towns of Glace Bay and Sydney, anxious to share in the wealth from the mushrooming industries that had created so many jobs. Some came to seek their fortune—others to work for their daily bread and provide for their families. Sydney's population jumped almost overnight from three thousand to ten thousand, while Glace Bay and its outlying districts doubled that of Sydney.

The unprecedented boom created serious accommodation shortages in Glace Bay and other colliery districts. Contracts were awarded by the Dominion Coal Company for the erection of a thousand double miners' houses. Two new towns sprang up—Dominion No. 2 and Dominion No. 4—complete with company houses, streets, town halls, and company stores. Of necessity, each new town was built around one of the mines owned by the Dominion Coal Company.

But while all these buildings were being erected, men were arriving daily by the hundreds. To give them shelter, large boardinghouses—or "shacks" as they were known locally—were hurriedly built, each accommodating a total of seventy-two men, with each bed shared by two men on a shift basis. Forty cooks were employed by the company to feed the multitude of workers, but the price of each meal was deducted from pay envelopes at the end of the week. Thousands of other workers "squatted" in crude, homemade shanties constructed out of rough boards and tar paper, while every private house in the area was reported to be stuffed to the rafters with boarders. Some six-room houses were rumoured to have as many as twenty boarders. Men were living everywhere!

Inevitably, there were problems, some of a serious nature. Sanitary matters were far from satisfactory, but this problem was resolved when the waters of a nearby lake were gravity-fed to the town's water supply. Electric lights were introduced for the first time, and after the streets had been improved, an efficient tram service was operated. A fire department, a police force, and a town hall followed shortly after. A hospital was built and operated with contributions from thousands of miners. Children by the hundreds attended school after several primary schools were built and teachers engaged, and by the year 1901, a town council and a mayor had been elected.

The town of Glace Bay was beginning to take on a decidedly prosperous appearance, but it was a prosperity not shared with low-paid miners, for the town was owned, lock, stock, and barrel, by the Dominion Coal Company. The first mayor of Glace Bay, D.M. Burchell, sought to have his new town incorporated as a properly constituted borough in the Dominion of Canada, and his prophecies regarding his town, preserved in the municipal records, indicated a bright and prosperous future:

> During the past two years we have had in proportion to our population, as great a boom as Sydney has experienced.... While coal is King and the basis of the industrial prosperity of this country and the world, we have every reason to feel that at no distant date, Glace Bay will take its place among the leading cities of Canada.... There is employment for everyone willing to work, wages are good and good order is maintained.
>
> Our people are law abiding, hospitable and progressive!

Mr Burchell's prophecies and hopes for the future of Glace Bay were sound, and if things had gone according to plan, the future of the town and its many inhabitants might indeed have been promising. Unfortunately, markets for coal and steel were not to remain constant, yet dividends to stockholders would have to remain lucrative if the company was to survive. The company had been launched on a shaky foundation, using watered stock, paper assets, and a great deal of bluff. With falling markets lowering profit margins, costs of production would have to be reduced drastically, and cost reduction would be directed against miners' and steelworkers' wages, which were already far beneath the poverty level. Wage reductions would eventually lead to strife and violence. Strikes and constant work stoppages would shatter the "storefront" facade of prosperity in Sydney and Glace Bay and lead to unprecedented suffering and cruelty. The thin veneer of prosperity masked the debt each worker was accruing at the company store through an easy credit system and wage checkoff. Daily, the debts piled higher and higher as inadequate wages forced workers to purchase food, clothing, and even their mining tools and explosives from the company store.

The early pioneers of the trade union movement in Canada came from many different lands and cultures. At the turn of the century when coal and steel companies were moving into Cape Breton, leaders of radical factions demanding reform of archaic labour laws and an improvement in the intolerable working conditions and wages were, in the main, British immigrants. Living and working under dreadful conditions, they had emigrated to Canada hoping to improve their lot and give their offspring an opportunity for education and to achieve a better standard of living in the New World. To their dismay, they found on arrival in the "promised land," working and living conditions worse than those they had fled. Disillusioned, angry, and bitter against the company agents who had recruited them for overseas employment with golden promises of full employment, good wages and working conditions, they began to question existing orders that treated working men and women as objects deserving little sympathy or consideration. Realizing that strength lay in numbers, they joined combinations and protective associations to demand better treatment from employers holding them in bondage.

Before the turn of the century when miners were flooding into Cape Breton to seek work with the new Dominion Coal Company, many were persuaded to join a protective association known as the Provincial Workmen's Association. Formed secretly in August 1879 in a lonely forest clearing outside the tiny mining community of Springhill, Nova Scotia, by angry, desperate men, it was known originally as the Provincial Miners' Association. This first miners' association in North America was formed a mere thirty years after Scottish immigrant miners had been slapped in irons for striking against intolerable working conditions at Fort Rupert in the province of British Columbia, eleven years before the giant United Mine Workers of America was formed, and only four years after the infamous Masters and Servants' Act had been amended in Canada to provide for a fine of one hundred dollars in place of a mandatory jail term for striking workers.

The PWA was destined to influence the growth of labour unions throughout Canada and the United States for the next hundred years. According to C.B. Wade's *History of District 26, United Mine Workers of America*, its stated aims were better wages, reduced hours of work, the securing of political support for the improvement of labour laws, and to "improving the condition of members morally, mentally and socially." The terminology may have sounded somewhat flowery, but its sincerity was unquestioned—at least initially. How the leaders of the PWA planned to achieve these lofty plateaus remained somewhat obscure, however, for even the most ardent backers of the new association stated they had no intention of using militant means to reach their goals; rather they prided themselves on "getting along with the coal companies on a friendly, man to man basis."

In Nova Scotia and Cape Breton, thousands of working men, women, and children, long accustomed to working under a feudal system for ten and twelve hours each day at starvation rates of pay, saw in the new association a glimmer of light and a hope for the future and, overnight, the membership grew by leaps and bounds. But behind the scenes, opposition was mounting. Coal companies operating in the province were determined to oppose demands for wage increases and improved working conditions. To avoid costly labour stoppages and decreased profit margins, efforts were made to suborn the leaders of the Provincial Workmen's Association through favoured treatment in the mines where they worked.

Disillusioned with the PWA and its leaders, many workers began to agitate for a new, more forceful organization to represent them, but as yet, none existed. Working conditions in Canada at the turn of the century may have been oppressive, but they were no worse than in the United States—especially in the coal mining industry, where miners were not represented by a union until 1890. According to UMWA records, President Baer of the American Coal Producers' Association indicated his undying opposition to organized labour at this time when he publicly stated: "The rights and interests of the labouring man will be protected not by the labour agitator, but by the Christian men and women to whom God in his infinite wisdom has given control of the property interests of this country."

In Canada, Baer's words were echoed by Robert Dunsmuir, ex-premier of the province of British Columbia and owner of a coal mine at Wellington in that province, after his miners had gone on strike in protest against a wage cut: "There is an impression in the community that we are obligated to accede to miners' demands; but for the benefit of those it may concern, we wish to state publicly that we have no intention of asking any of them to work for us again at any price!"

Forceful evictions from company houses at the point of a bayonet, intimidation, and blacklisting were but a few of the weapons used by unscrupulous employers in their battle to keep out unions. All too often their cruel tactics were backed by the power and majesty of the law and corrupt government.

Prejudice breeds rebellion. Downtrodden workers began to look for more militant ways to right their grievances and to improve their miserable lot in life. In Nova Scotia and Cape Breton, the coal and steel barons, fully aware of workers' hopes and ambitions for the future, made haste to suppress rebellious factions and outlaw those who preached sedition and revolt.

2

The Company Store and the Two Unions

Living in company towns and company houses, forced to buy food and other necessities of life from company-owned stores, worshipping in churches where the collection was deducted along with other debts from their weekly pay envelopes, miners and steelworkers in Cape Breton felt they were in grave danger of being subjugated into a medieval form of serfdom that could eventually prove as oppressive as that experienced by the lower classes in Britain during the Middle Ages.

In Glace Bay and its outlying districts, the Dominion Coal Company had inherited a number of company stores along with the mines it had purchased from the small private companies when it had been given its provincial charter for exclusive mining rights in 1894. As the company expanded its operations and built new mines, it erected new company stores—usually close to a local mine and the company houses clustered around it. Thus the greater portion of the retail trade in groceries, clothing, and a thousand other domestic items was controlled by the all-powerful company in every mining community throughout Nova Scotia.

All company stores were constructed alike—two storeys high, complete with basement and loading dock at the rear—and, like the company houses, built of wood. Large double windows at the front entrance displayed good quality furniture, toys, and clothing to tempt miners' wives to buy them on credit. All credit purchases were recorded, using the old "McCaskey" system of bookkeeping, before being debited to each miner's check number.

Inevitably, during hard times, many miners' wives used up their full amount of credit on non-essential items only to run out of staple foodstuffs before the week was out, forcing their families to go hungry. As retired miner Gordon MacGregor told it: "To my mother there was a kind of blight, in a way, for everybody to deal there. She had a fear of it. Lots of women did. Because once they got a grip on you, God help you."

The company store may have held miners and their families in bondage, but all are agreed that the quality of merchandise was excellent. Butter—fine quality creamery butter—was sold in large square wooden boxes (margarine had not yet made an appearance); cheddar cheese in huge rounds was just as delicious. Flour, the most important staple food, was kept in huge barrels, although most people preferred to purchase smaller quantities, made up in 24-, 48-, and 96-pound cotton bags. Flour bags, which were of excellent quality, were utilized by thrifty miners' wives as material for underwear and dresses for their many children during hard times.

Hanging in the cool basement of each store were huge slabs of bacon, sides of beef and mutton, and whole carcasses of pork. Stacked up to the low ceiling were hundreds of bags of flour, barrels of wet salted cod, turbot, mackerel, and herring, boxes of apples and biscuits, hogsheads of pure molasses, crates of eggs, and a great multitude of foodstuffs to be sold in bulk. Not listed in the inventory were the ubiquitous rats and mice, the population of which was kept rigidly controlled by three or four store cats.

Most retail business was conducted on the ground floor, where smartly attired store clerks served customers from behind long wooden counters. Fresh groceries were contained in glass-fronted drawers beneath each counter. Bacon, cheese, and plug tobacco were sliced, weighed, and wrapped expertly on the countertops by clerks who were well trained, efficient, and for the most part, pleasant to deal with.

Ready-made clothes, dressmaking materials, bolts of cloth, and all the paraphernalia of home sewing—reels of cotton, scissors, needles, buttons, and paper patterns—were readily available from counters at the other side of the room, while clerks at a rear counter sold clay pipes, combs, hardware, nails, small tools, coal oil lamps, and a hundred other knickknacks of every description.

In a back storeroom on the main floor, great flitches of bacon, slabs of dried codfish, cooked hams, and long strings of bologna were suspended from the roof in a seemingly endless chain—enough food to satisfy every living soul for miles around—providing they could pay for it or had sufficient credit.

The company had thought of everything. A shed at the rear of each company store contained bales of hay and foodstuffs for horses, cattle, and pigs for those fortunate enough to own livestock, while the top floor of the main building contained boots and shoes, house furnishings, furniture, bedding, linoleum, cutlery, crockery, and hundreds of other household items. The merchandise was of excellent quality, but beyond the reach of people who had been subjected so long to a deliberate policy of slow starvation.

There was one last item of merchandise sold in the company store that is worthy of mention. To tempt children's palates, large, prominently displayed glass bottles contained moderately priced, succulent candies, crispy chocolates, nutty bars, and packets of mouth-watering humbugs, while "penny goods"—small chocolates, jelly beans, suckers, peanut brittle, and fudge—were sold at the more economical price of two or even three for one cent! Most miners' wives found they had willing helpers when they made their weekly visit to the company store. With luck, an enterprising boy or girl could be rewarded with a nutty bar or a packet of jelly beans for carrying the family's groceries.

When Nova Scotia miners formed the Provincial Workmen's Association in 1879, their leaders had warned that the company stores and their iniquitous system of extended credit would eventually be used as a means of forcing miners to accept wage cuts and a below-poverty-level existence. A miner deeply in debt to one company store found it impossible to gain credit at another until the debt was paid. With credit extended and little hope of repaying debts, the price of goods, especially foodstuffs, was greatly increased to delinquent miners and their families. Without ready money to purchase food, they were unable to deal at a private grocery store, and after long years of inadequate wages, the evil multiplied until their debts stretched far into the distant future without even the remotest hope of repaying them.

It is worthy of note that the practice of overcharging was not due to methods employed by the store clerks, most of whom were the sons or daughters of miners. In fact, the reverse seems to have been the case, according to many old miners who insisted they had always been given a break as far as quantity, with the scales weighted in their favour. It was considered a plum job for miners' children employed at the company store, and in many cases, the experience gained in working there was used to advantage at a later date when they ventured into business themselves. Miner Dan "Dancer" MacDonald of Glace Bay was most emphatic on this point:

> What you got at the company store was quality and quantity. A private merchant might cut off a few ounces, but there in the company store it was our own flesh and blood—our daughters and sons of miners. If there were any breaks, you got it. And everything was first class. Clothes, furniture, grub, was the best of everything. But it created a way of life which wasn't good. You know, there were men that died and were still owing to the company store.

At the end of every work week, they received pitifully small wages along with an account known as a "Bob-tailed Sheet," which showed the total amount of deductions for rent, coal, light, water, doctor, hospital, church, blasting powder, and company store purchases of food and dry goods. More often than not, they were left with little or no wages after deductions, especially when employed on short time with only two or three days' work each week. Their weekly pay sheets were dubbed Bob-tailed Sheets because of the company practice of cutting off the tail end to show that a miner had no wages due after he used up all his earnings at the company store in credit during the week. The company stores were dubbed "Pluck Me Stores" for the same reason. Years before, it was said, when one Cape Breton miner was handed his wage packet and Bob-tailed Sheet to find his sum total of earnings after deductions was nil, he turned to his mates and shouted, "Christ, they've plucked me!" And the name stuck.

The company store, besides being a profit-making venture,

served the purpose of feeding and clothing miners and their families during the winter months when coal mines were forced to suspend operations. Upon the reopening of navigation in the spring, miners were heavily in debt to the company, but with sufficient work, could pay off all their debts through a checkoff system during the remainder of the year.

The company store thus became a form of vassalage, binding the men to remain in the employ of one company and one mine. Evidence given by the "miners' friend," Dr Arthur Kendall, to the Duncan Royal Commission in 1925 was to the effect that "If a man got into debt at one colliery it was arranged by the manager that he would not be able to shift from one colliery to another. He had to stay there. In cases where men were in debt to the company store and could not get out of debt, the prices charged were higher than those charged the other men."

It is important to realize also that such social benefits as unemployment insurance or relief benefits from local authorities were nonexistent in Canada at the turn of the century, forcing miners and their families to take advantage of their employer's doubtful "charity." The danger remained that the company could and did use the company store credit system as a weapon during a strike.

This contentious issue eventually led to another serious rift among the executive of the Provincial Workmen's Association. According to Wade's *History of District 26*, some of its officers held that company stores should be abolished and miners forced to pay cash for their goods, while others held that they should be retained but only under government supervision and regulation. The controversy over this additional problem split the executive into two separate factions and eventually the discontent spread from the executive down to the members, who began to leave the PWA in droves. By 1902, twenty-three years after its formation, only one lodge remained on the mainland of Nova Scotia plus another two on the island of Cape Breton.

For a short period in 1902, the PWA seemed on the verge of extinction, but with a change in the executive, the association tried to renew its old vigour. The election of John Moffatt as grand secretary, and Stephen B. MacNeil as grand master, convinced members that great things were expected of the Provincial Workmen's Association in the future.

In the summer of 1902, a tramp steamer arrived off the island of Cape Breton to discharge her cargo of immigrant miners recruited in Great Britain by the Nova Scotia Steel and Coal Company. One of the immigrants, James Bryson McLachlan, who stepped ashore at Christie's Wharf, was a man destined to change the political and labour history of Nova Scotia and Canada in his lifelong battle for decent wages and working conditions for Nova Scotia miners.

To the casual observer there seemed little in McLachlan's physical appearance to distinguish him from any of the other recent arrivals to Cape Breton. Of small stature, a legacy of starvation wages and a life of toil and suffering, he looked exactly what he was—a miner who had spent his entire working life digging for coal in the bowels of the earth. Born in the tiny Scottish Lowland village of Ecclefechan in 1869, James Bryson McLachlan, or "J.B." as he was affectionately called, first saw the light of day in a humble, whitewashed cottage adjacent to the famous "Arched House," where the immortal poet and essayist Thomas Carlyle had been born. Forced through economic circumstances to enter the local coal mine at Wishaw, in the Lanarkshire coalfield, at the tender age of ten, McLachlan had, like thousands of other child miners of his day, learned the true price of coal, a price paid in blood and suffering—occupational hazards that countless generations of miners and their families had been forced to accept in the earning of their daily bread.

First elected union secretary at the age of fifteen, McLachlan had been blacklisted from the Scottish coalfields after answering Keir Hardie's strike call in 1887—a strike that had caused widespread suffering and starvation before miners returned to work beaten. Forced to travel to seek work to support his wife and four children, he found like many others before him that his reputation as a militant union organizer had spread far and wide. Work was denied him in even the remotest coal mine. The blacklisting had marked him as a troublemaker and a radical outside the pale of working-class society—a pariah shunned by every employer throughout Scotland.

In 1902, agents for the Nova Scotia Steel and Coal Company toured the Scottish coalfields recruiting miners for work in the new mining boom towns of Glace Bay and Sydney Mines in Cape Breton, Nova Scotia. Beyond the undeniable fact that the recruits were experienced miners, the agents knew little or cared little about the reasons for the mass blacklistings. McLachlan was signed on and provided with a passage to Cape Breton without delay. Directed to a cramped berth in steerage, McLachlan was joined by several old friends blacklisted like himself in the disastrous 1887 coal strike: the brothers George and Tom Mulholland, Charles Kernick, Jamie Thomson, the Robertsons and the Taylors. Together they sailed from the shores of Scotland bound for the New World and a fresh start in life.

At the time of McLachlan's arrival, the town of Sydney Mines, like its neighbours Glace Bay and Sydney, was in the throes of a frenzied expansion. Nova Scotia Steel and Coal Company had imported thousands of men to work in their Princess Mine and the nearby steel mills. Anxious to share in the trade boom created by Dominion's new coal and steel companies, they had embarked on an ambitious program of expansion, which included the building of new piers at the nearby port of North Sydney and the enlargement of their industrial holdings. In the town of Sydney Mines, hundreds of new company houses and boarding houses were erected around the Princess Mine to accommodate the horde of workers pouring in daily.

But the facade of prosperity was merely a repeat of the Glace Bay story. Wages paid by Nova Scotia Steel and Coal Company were much lower than those paid by Dominion. Even the highest-paid miner or steelworker found his weekly wage insufficient to rear a family and to pay for the bare necessities of life. Vast profits were being made, but only at the expense of workers.

Since his arrival in Cape Breton, J.B. McLachlan had been employed at the old Princess Mine. True to form, he immediately became involved in the PWA, even to the extent of becoming president of the Drummond Lodge. But his undoubted talents as a union organizer went unrecognized by Grand Secretary John Moffatt and Grand Master Stephen B. MacNeil, who had already begun to dampen the renewed enthusiasm for the PWA by cooperating with the coal and steel companies at the expense of rank and file members who were seldom consulted or asked for a determining vote.

At the time of McLachlan's arrival in Cape Breton, the PWA executive had signed agreements with the companies without a vote from the membership—thus taking control of the association out of their hands and creating a serious split in the organization. This individual dealing on the part of the PWA executive became a very sore point with the members, especially after Moffatt had publicly stated he was opposed to strikes and did his utmost to prevent them.

McLachlan, with his reputation as a radical union organizer, was regarded as Moffatt's antithesis who must be prevented from rocking the boat at all costs.

In truth, Moffatt and his top executives had adopted a passive attitude to the coal and steel companies because they were out of their depth. The Provincial Workmen's Association could, and did, deal very successfully with individual small companies, but a provincial association with its limited budget was completely ineffectual in attempting to force its will on a rich, powerful organization such as the Dominion Coal Company or Dominion Iron and Steel Company. For the moment, the association appeared to be holding its own, even at times successfully arranging for minuscule raises for its members, but what the attitude of Moffatt would be if an actual wage reduction was proposed or enforced by the giant corporation was anybody's guess.

Any misgivings the men may have had regarding their Provincial Workmen's Association headed by Moffatt were temporarily shelved after Dominion Iron and Steel Company reduced steelworkers' wages, which were already at a pitiful level. The first cut took place on December 1, 1903. The reason given by the company was "on account of the state of the market."

Too late, Moffatt and his peace-loving executive realized they had been duped into a passive frame of mind by ruthless marketeers anxious to squeeze additional profits from their venture. The PWA, faced with massive protests by its members, demanded a return to the previous wage scale, but the company refused, forcing Moffatt to adopt a more militant policy in his dealings with company executives, and on June 1, 1904, six months after Dominion Iron and Steel Company had arbitrarily imposed its wage cut, the total work force of fifteen hundred men walked out on strike from the Sydney steel plant.

In retaliation, the company answered the strike call by "*a general suspension of work until the market improves*," but the shutdown, which was an obvious attempt to intimidate workers and force them to return to work, did not have the desired effect, for the workers stood firm and refused to submit to threats of any kind. When the company tried to resume operations later, in July, using supervisory personnel and imported scab labour, violence broke out on the picket lines. The disturbances, though minor in nature, then provided the necessary excuse for the company to approach a sympathetic provincial government asking that troops be sent into the strike area to control the situation, and charging that local and company police forces were inadequate and unable to maintain order. Without delay, the provincial government acceded to Dominion's request for armed military troops to protect its vested interests, which had been heavily subsidized by the federal and provincial governments and the city of Sydney. Little sympathy was wasted on striking workers and their families, who were already beginning to suffer from hunger and want.

In 1900, a federal Department of Labour had been formed and a Conciliation Act known as the Industrial Disputes Investigation Act (IDI) passed into law in 1907 to allow unions and employers to apply for the services of a government-appointed Conciliation Board empowered to listen to both sides of a dispute before issuing a majority report which then had to be ratified by both union and employer. Either side in the dispute could add a minority report if in disagreement with the recommendations of the majority.

The Sydney Board of Trade now applied for the services of

a federally appointed conciliator to protect its investment in the Sydney steel mills, but for a considerable length of time, the application was not supported by the Provincial Workmen's Association on the grounds that the presence of troops had greatly incensed its members, who believed a fair compromise would be impossible while the plant remained under what was virtually martial law. Eventually, however, the PWA was forced to agree to the request for a Conciliation Board under the terms of the IDI Act. Severe malnutrition and privation were taking their inevitable toll among the young and the old as the strike continued.

The matter was deemed sufficiently important for the Deputy Minister of Labour, William Lyon Mackenzie King, to travel to Cape Breton to attempt to end the work stoppage. His efforts were successful and the PWA called off the strike on July 22, 1904, after the company solemnly pledged there would be no discrimination practised against workers and their leaders once they returned to work.

When work was resumed, however, several hundred steelworkers were immediately fired and blacklisted by the company, forcing them to move out of the province with their families to seek work elsewhere, far from the company's baleful influence. Strikebreakers hired during the dispute replaced them.

The strike and its aftermath hurt the PWA, which had gone heavily into debt to pay strike benefits for each week its members had been out of work. In truth, the strike would have been settled even without the intervention of the Minister of Labour, for the depleted strike funds would have forced the workers to return to work under any terms. The association's capitulation and the return to work without gaining any raise in wages did much to convince its members that the PWA was a weak, ineffectual organization—totally unsuited to engage in a dispute with a large international corporation. Leaders such as McLachlan preached that they must seek further afield for a stronger, more militant organization if future strikes were to be won.

The defeat did have one positive effect, however. It made workers realize that their only hope lay in political representation as a labour group. The lessons learned at great cost by their forefathers in Britain were about to be repeated in Cape Breton. Under the auspices of a much chastened Provincial Workmen's Association, an Independent Labour Party was formed in Cape Breton, and when a federal election was called later the same year, Stephen B. MacNeil, grand master of the PWA, was nominated as the candidate for the new labour party. When the votes were counted, however, MacNeil had been soundly beaten by his Liberal opponent. The people of Cape Breton were not yet ready to accept a labour Member of Parliament to represent them in the House of Commons in Ottawa.

Although the disastrous steel strike and the political setback caused a serious blow to the PWA, they did result in its complete reorganization. Reverting to its original concept, formed at Springhill in 1879, the Grand Council decided to restrict membership to coal miners and to remain strictly a coal mining union.

After their ignominious surrender to Dominion Iron and Steel Company in 1904, miners and steelworkers were forced to accept a punitive three-year contract extending from 1905 to 1908 with wages remaining unchanged in spite of the rapidly rising cost of living.

The Dominion Coal Company, owned by the same financial consortium, was beginning to flex its muscles. After the recent fiasco at Sydney, the company felt confident that any future labour dispute—justified or not—could be dealt with in similar fashion. If blacklistings and threats did not suffice, bayonets and armed might would.

Within the ranks of the PWA, the first signs of rebellion were beginning to show. J.B. McLachlan, leader of Drummond Lodge, representing miners from the old Princess colliery at Sydney Mines, had become rapidly disillusioned with the PWA and its executive. As a union leader of long experience, he was convinced that coal miners would have to seek a more militant and powerful organization to represent them if future battles were to be won.

In the west of Canada, just such an organization had gained a foothold. The United Mine Workers of America, an international union representing miners in the United States and western Canada, had already shown its worth by winning two strikes in 1906, at Lethbridge in Alberta, and Fernie in British Columbia, where working conditions and wages had been equally as bad as—if not worse than—in Nova Scotia.

In 1907, with the support of some of the more militant Cape Breton miners, McLachlan contacted the United Mine Workers of America through its international headquarters in Indianapolis in the United States. A series of letters followed before arrangements were made for a senior union official to make a preliminary survey of the Nova Scotia coalfields and report back to John Mitchell, international president of the UMWA.

This first emissary, Peter Patterson, was a fellow Scot who had himself worked in the Nova Scotia coalfields before moving to western Canada, where he had eventually been appointed international board member for the United Mine Workers of America, District 18, covering the western provinces. Using a great deal of diplomacy and tact, Patterson approached John Moffatt and his PWA executive board to request that he be allowed to address the Grand Council of the PWA when it convened in September of 1907 in Halifax, the provincial capital. His request was granted, albeit somewhat unwillingly, but his proposal for an amalgamation of the two union organizations representing miners in the province—PWA and UMWA—was not met with any measure of enthusiasm by Moffatt and his colleagues, who wished to retain their exclusive monopoly of union control.

Although the Dominion Coal Company and its competitors had their past differences with the PWA, they remained keenly aware of the advantages of dealing with a small, provincial association as opposed to its international rival, which had a vast membership in the United States and a very substantial treasury with which it could easily finance a long and protracted strike. Behind the scenes, Dominion Coal Company was frantically making preparations to keep the American-based union out of the province of Nova Scotia. The company had determined to use every possible means—legal or otherwise—to achieve its ends.

John Moffatt and the members of the Grand Council of the PWA gratefully acknowledged the company's preference and favour, and from then on, the PWA became almost a company union, subservient to the wishes of Dominion Coal Company.

Moffatt's new allegiance was soon put to the test. In December 1907, as the three-year agreement forced on the PWA by the coal companies back in 1905 was drawing to a close, the Dominion Coal Company informed Moffatt it wished to renew the contract under exactly the same terms as before—without any increase in wages to compensate for the cost of living, which had risen 20 percent since 1905. But Moffatt, faced by strident demands for a firmer stand in his dealings with Dominion, refused to agree to a continuation of the agreement.

The company promptly retaliated with a notice of wage reduction. The PWA, stung into action at last, countered with its own demand for a wage increase with the threat of strike action, but as the company well knew, the threat was but a bluff. After the disastrous steel strike in 1904, the PWA strike fund had remained pitifully low and totally inadequate to support a strike.

In a last-ditch attempt to salvage the situation, the Provincial Workmen's Association now applied to the federal Labour Department for a Conciliation Board to force the company to negotiate in good faith. As their representative, the PWA chose Dr Arthur Kendall, a local doctor, well known and respected in labour circles. The company chose Dick Fraser, son of a prominent steel manufacturer. The government appointed Dr Adam Shortt, an economist, as chairman.

Evidence given to the Board by James Ross, president of the Dominion Coal Company and G.H. Duggan, general manager, emphasized that the company could not afford to pay a wage increase at this time due to the poor state of the market, which had reduced profits to an all-time low. They were followed by Dr Kendall, who recalled in 1925 to the Duncan Royal Commission the circumstances surrounding his appointment: "I was asked by the workmen to represent them on the board, and after some hesitation I did. I told them I didn't know much about coal mining and they said 'Never mind, we know all about coal mining and we will prompt you on these matters.... We want you because we do not think you can be bought!'"

Their faith in Dr Kendall's integrity proved to be fully justified, for after the hearings he told of an attempt by the Dominion Coal Company to bribe him and suppress vital testimony that could be damaging to its case:

A few days before we sat, I received a telegram from a friend of mine in Montreal, asking me if I would meet him at the Halifax hotel on a certain date. I was lying in bed smoking at the time, and I passed over the telegram to my wife and said—"James Ross proposes to buy me." She begged me not to go, but I said—"I must see what is inside the cup." I shall not mention who the man was, but if anyone is curious he can look up the old register of the hotel and see what night I registered and who registered the following morning.... Well there are more ways of killing a cat besides choking it with butter and there are more ways of bribing a man than offering him a package of thousand dollar bills. I met the man and he said—"Dr Kendall, down in Cape Breton you have the reputation of being able to assay the amount of timber on an acre of land very well, and we would like to hire you from today. We have recently purchased a thousand square miles of timber land in New Brunswick and Quebec and we would like to hire you for the next three months." I then told him—"The people who put me where I am will never have to reproach me or my children for having disappointed them...." I refused the bribe!

When the Board began its hearings, it became increasingly obvious that its members (with the exception of Dr Kendall) were biased against the workers and strongly in favour of the company's case for a reduction in wages. After the third day, Dr Kendall wrote a letter to the chairman of the board, urging that the provisions of the IDI Act be followed to the letter to determine the truth about the company's ability to pay a wage increase in spite of sworn evidence to the contrary. If necessary, Dr Kendall pleaded, time should be allowed to bring engineers and financial experts from England—men not under the influence of the Dominion Coal Company—to give evidence to the Board after conducting a private audit of the company's books.

Dr Kendall's letter had an immediate effect on the negotiations. The following day, General Manager G.H. Duggan remained closeted for many hours with the Board chairman. The same evening it was announced that a settlement had been reached. The wage reduction had been withdrawn and a wage increase offered in its place.

The offer was presented to the men and accepted by a narrow margin after a pithead vote. The new contract, which was signed on March 23, 1908, provided a small increase in wages for most classes of mineworkers but it still excluded many workers from any wage increase whatsoever—some even received a wage decrease!

Considering the rapid escalation in the cost of living since the last contract had been signed in 1905, many rank and file members of the PWA believed the wage increase totally insufficient. The dissatisfaction, added to the growing demand for a stronger organization to represent Nova Scotia coal miners, and the influence of recent British immigrants, accustomed to a more vigorous type of unionism, began to have an effect on those wishing to leave the PWA.

Many of the men felt they had insufficient control over the executive and officers of the PWA, who had been elected by the votes of delegates rather than by a democratic election in which each member of the association could make a free choice. Others believed the association's financial plight revealed inherent weaknesses. Additional grievances included the slow progress of improved labour legislation to better the lot of working men and women. Employers such as the Dominion Coal Company had steadily opposed all improvements to the Mines Regulation Act and Workmen's Compensation bill, and the delays in improved legislation for the betterment of their working conditions convinced Nova Scotia miners they were denied privileges willingly conceded elsewhere.

An amalgamation of the PWA and the UMWA could have provided the necessary strength to oppose the giant Dominion Coal Company, but all efforts towards amalgamation had failed, mainly because of the intransigence of John Moffatt and the Grand Council of the PWA. To leaders such as McLachlan, it seemed obvious that those wishing to be represented by the United Mine Workers of America should set up their own branches throughout Nova Scotia and be recognized as a union district by the international headquarters in the United States.

In the summer of 1908, a motion was made by J.B. McLachlan, president of Drummond Lodge of the PWA, to invite the international president of the United Mine Workers of America to visit Nova Scotia to explain the advantages of an amalgamation to the individual lodges belonging to the PWA. The invitation was accepted and the message must have been convincing for agitation for an amalgamation between the two labour organizations continued long after the president's return to the United States.

Under pressure from PWA members, Moffatt and his Grand Council now agreed to allow lodge delegates to hold a referendum on the controversial subject of amalgamation, and after the votes had been counted, they were shocked to find that the delegates had voted overwhelmingly in favour of an immediate amalgamation. Waiting until the delegates had departed, Moffatt then called a special general meeting, attended by a majority of his supporters, to vote on a motion to put aside the recent vote on the grounds that the meeting had been unconstitutional and illegal because the delegates had voted in favour of an amalgamation without receiving instructions from the individual members of their lodges to authorize such action.

On a devious technicality, Moffatt and his Grand Council had effectively shelved the thorny issue of amalgamation, but in setting aside the referendum they were denying the wishes of the rank and file membership of their organization. To add to the controversy, the Grand Council then passed a resolution condemning McLachlan and his supporters. The condemnation was accompanied by a threat of expulsion for any lodge continuing the campaign for amalgamation with a "foreign" union such as the United Mine Workers of America.

McLachlan and his fellow rebels reacted to the threat by applying for a court injunction to prevent Moffatt and the Grand Council from using the funds of the association until the matter had been resolved by democratic means, but with the help of political influence, the injunction was removed. McLachlan, refusing to acknowledge defeat, then laid a charge of perjury against

Moffatt, but the charge was dismissed later in the year, in spite of overwhelming evidence to the contrary, through the efforts of the giant Dominion Coal Company working with a judicial system loaded in favour of private enterprise and financial institutions.

The year 1908 drew to a close in an atmosphere of bitter acrimony and distrust. Sides were being drawn up as the Provincial Workmen's Association split into two separate factions—the Moffatt men, wishing to retain the PWA as their sole bargaining agent, and the McLachlan men, who had voted to replace the ineffectual PWA with the stronger, more militant, United Mine Workers of America. In a move calculated to inflame the situation further, the Grand Council then disbanded five local lodges whose members had refused to bow to the autocratic edict issued earlier by Moffatt and his colleagues.

Union war was about to be declared. At Springhill, birthplace of the PWA, miners disbanded their local PWA lodge and replaced it with the first Nova Scotia branch of the United Mine Workers of America. Miners at Bridgeport immediately followed suit, and by the end of 1908, eight more Cape Breton lodges had renounced the PWA and formed local branches of the UMWA.

Past history had shown that the Dominion Coal Company was not above using bribery and corruption to achieve its ends—especially across the bargaining table from the union. Now, through the medium of a sympathetic press, it began a vigorous campaign of hatred and vilification against the UMWA, charging that it was part of an American conspiracy to take over the Canadian coal industry. Headlines in the popular press neglected to remind readers that the Canadian coal industry in Cape Breton and Nova Scotia had already been taken over by American capitalists aided by an international consortium of businessmen and financiers whose primary interest lay not in the welfare of Canadian coal miners, but in quick profits extracted at minimum cost.

Peter Patterson, international board member for District 18, UMWA, remained in Nova Scotia. Now, actively encouraged by J.B. McLachlan, Patterson travelled all over Nova Scotia visiting the many different PWA lodges to seek converts to the UMWA. His efforts were successful, for by the spring of 1909, about twenty-six hundred of the forty-five hundred miners employed by Dominion Coal Company had signed union cards with the UMWA. Almost every miner employed by other coal companies at Springhill and Inverness had joined the ranks to bring the total membership of miners joining the United Mine Workers of America up to forty-eight hundred. The figure was impressive, but it was less than one half of the total number of miners employed.

In March 1909, forty-nine delegates from the newly formed branches of the UMWA throughout Nova Scotia met in Sydney to organize a district federation. It was at this meeting that District 26 was born.

As the first president of the district, delegates chose Dan MacDougall, a miner from Glace Bay and a well-respected town councillor. The vital post of secretary-treasurer was filled by Jim McLachlan, while another Glace Bay miner, James D. MacLennan, was made international board member, representing the new District 26 on the executive council of the UMWA at its headquarters in Indianapolis. It was an impressive group of officers. All were well known and respected in miners' circles as men of honour and integrity. In selecting them, Nova Scotia miners had chosen wisely, but in the months ahead, the executive officers would require a large measure of courage in addition to their other outstanding qualities.

Coal companies operating in Nova Scotia were not taking the emergence of the new international union lightly. They decided to unite and fight the United Mine Workers of America before the remaining PWA members could be swayed into joining the militant organization posing a threat to their uncontested control of the rich coalfields of Nova Scotia.

Within one week of the launching of District 26, UMWA, representatives of all the major coal companies met in Truro, Nova Scotia, to plan their future strategy. At the end of the meeting, a motion was passed to strike back at the new "foreign" union and force it to disband. *The Labour Gazette* wrote:

> It is unanimously resolved by all the coal companies attending this meeting...that the agitation being carried on by the organization known

as the United Mine Workers of America to gain control of labour at the mines is fraught with much danger to the Nova Scotia industry and is likely to result in the loss of a large part of our trade to the Americans. It is further resolved that the attempt of a foreign organization to control our mines should be resisted in every possible manner and a course of action agreed upon.

The solemn resolution must surely have been made with tongue in cheek. The largest coal operator in Nova Scotia, the Dominion Coal Company, had been formed and financed by those same "foreign" interests in the United States. The owners also feared that a strong union would destroy the advantage Nova Scotia coal operators enjoyed in American markets because of their comparatively low labour costs. The extremely poor wages and excessive hours of work of the Nova Scotia miner had allowed coal operators to sell coal to customers in the United States at a price much below that of American coal, which had been mined for higher wages and shorter hours due to hard bargaining and threat of strike action by the UMWA. If an American union took control of Nova Scotia coal miners, there was a very real possibility that Nova Scotia miners would demand parity with their American brothers, and coal exports from Nova Scotia into the United States would then lose their competitive edge—an advantage based on suffering.

On the local scene, the Dominion Coal Company did not waste any time in following the "course of action" that had been decided at the meeting of coal operators at Truro. More and more miners were finding themselves on the street after losing their jobs. At the Dominion No. 2 plant, which supplied electricity to all surrounding collieries owned by the Dominion Coal Company, the chief mechanic, anxious to have only what he termed "dependable" men working under him, asked each of his workers if he would remain at work in the event of a strike. Those answering in the affirmative retained their jobs while the remainder were immediately fired [Eugene Forsey, *Economic and Social Aspects of the Nova Scotia Coal Industry*]. By coincidence, every one of the men so fired was a member of the UMWA. By another strange "coincidence," the chief mechanic was himself a master workman of a PWA lodge.

The power plant was not the only instance of victimization and firings. In every mine owned by Dominion, the witch-hunt continued day after day, but the company's supervisory staff avoided the discriminatory question, "Are you in favour of the UMWA or the PWA?" In all cases, they insisted the men had been fired because they were not dependable!

Every meeting of the UMWA was attended by company police and spies complete with note pads to list names and record conversations to hand to management the following day. Those not fired outright were victimized in many other ways. Job location was one. Miners who had previously worked rooms where the coal face was a lucrative five feet in height were now forced to work in wet, low locations where their daily tonnage of coal was but a fraction of that mined previously. With the wages of miners strictly controlled by the amount of coal mined and weighed at the bankhead, many found their pay drastically reduced.

Almost overnight, a black cloud of suspicion and hatred began to form over the mining communities of Cape Breton, as the towns of Glace Bay, Dominion, Sydney Mines, New Waterford, and Inverness suffered under the policy of discrimination and intimidation. Everywhere, at work or at play, company spies and pimps listened with open ears to every conversation between miners, recording anti-company or anti-PWA sentiments. Men who had been friends and workmates all their lives now began to avoid each other openly, even to the point where they walked on opposite sides of the streets. No PWA man would speak to a UMWA man and vice versa. The hatred spread even into the homes of miners. Wives and children of one faction battled verbally against the other, with many children forced to "run the gauntlet" on their way to school.

In such an atmosphere of gloom and suspicion, it must have been obvious to even the most uninformed that trouble was brewing and that the battle was about to commence.

In March 1909, District 26, the United Mine Workers of America, applied for another Board of Conciliation to avoid an open conflict with the Dominion Coal Company. The federal Minister of Labour, MacKenzie King, complied by appointing a chairman, Judge W.B. Wallace; the company refused to appoint a representative so the minister appointed a well-known industrialist, G.S. Campbell, while the union named their own district president, Dan MacDougall.

At the hearings, company witnesses had to be subpoenaed and forced to give evidence—much of it distorted and untruthful. Most of the testimony heard by the Conciliation Board was given by members of the UMWA as they described how they had been discriminated against or dismissed because of their union affiliation.

In summing up, spokesmen for the UMWA asked for an immediate cessation of the company's discrimination policy, for the company to recognize the UMWA as the official bargaining unit for half its workers, and for a union dues checkoff to be forwarded to District 26, United Mine Workers of America. (Up to this time, the company had continued to deduct union dues from the pay envelopes of UMWA men, but the money had been paid into the PWA's bank account against the wishes of the men.) Finally, the UMWA asked the Conciliation Board for an increase in wages and better working conditions, including shorter working hours, in a new contract to take effect after the existing contract expired on January 1, 1910.

The majority report, which had been signed only by board chairman Judge Wallace and company representative G.S. Campbell —Dan MacDougall filed a minority report totally disagreeing with the views of the other board members—was published on April 14, 1909.

Dealing first with the charge that men had been discriminated against or threatened because they had signed union cards with the UMWA, the majority report "*found that this charge was not substantiated by the evidence*" and that the charges laid by the UMWA regarding the use of spies and company police to attend union meetings for the purpose of reporting the names of men who were members of the UMWA, and of intimidating their members, was "*not substantiated.*"

Dealing with a question submitted to the Board for judgement concerning the thorny problem of the company's giving preference to PWA men, the majority report, which surely must have been written in a state of blind euphoria, stated:

> Without dealing with the question of whether a company has the right under ordinary circumstances when engaging workmen, to show a preference for the members of one labour union to those of another, in the present case there were special circumstances which made the preference a natural and reasonable one.... The Board believes that no foreign body should be allowed to exercise power over industrial disputes in Nova Scotia.... The company was amply justified in refusing to recognize any organization which could exercise such a dangerous and continually menacing power. Foreign officials sitting in Indianapolis should not have the power or the right to decree that Nova Scotia miners, even when they are without a grievance, should stop working and thereby cripple a great Nova Scotia industry.

Dealing with the UMWA's charge of intimidation, the majority report declared that "*there had been no intimidation*"!

With the report, the Board of Conciliation in which the miners of Nova Scotia had placed their blind trust dismissed all charges against the company in spite of voluminous evidence to the contrary. The general manager of the Dominion Coal Company, G.H. Duggan, who had contemptuously ignored the Board's request to appoint a company representative, appeared only on the last day of the hearing, and in spite of the company's intransigent attitude toward the Board and its refusal to testify unless its witnesses were subpoenaed, the chairman insisted on hearing Duggan's testimony as, with Bible in hand, he swore that no man had been blacklisted or refused employment because of his affiliation with the UMWA. He readily admitted under questioning, however, that men had been discharged from the power plant and from other key jobs, but insisted that his company had been perfectly justified in doing so to protect its own interests.

Dan MacDougall's minority report differed on every point. He insisted that there had been hundreds of proven cases of discrimination and firings against men whose only offence had been to belong to an international union.

Unfortunately, MacDougall's minority report carried little

weight with the federal government and the Minister of Labour, and throughout the mining communities of Nova Scotia, the majority report was regarded with disgust. It had been padded with inconsistencies, distortions of the truth, and inaccurate platitudes—all designed to favour the company at the expense of the men. The company had shown "preference" but it had not discriminated; the company had shown no harshness towards UMWA men, they had merely put them on the street because their affiliation with an international union proved they could not be relied on in the event of a strike against the company! Never again would miners of Nova Scotia place their faith in government-appointed conciliation boards.

The release of what miners considered a scandalous majority report unleashed a new wave of terror and intimidation throughout the mining communities of Nova Scotia. It was almost as though the coal companies had been given a mandate to crush the "foreign" union by any means—fair or foul, legal or illegal.

By April 23, only nine days after the report had been released, every UMWA leader, including McLachlan and MacDougall, had been fired, along with over a thousand miners whose only crime had been to declare their loyalty to a new, more progressive union. To replace them, hundreds of out-of-work transients and waterfront alcoholics from the ports of Halifax and Montreal were sought and recruited by company agents. Miners from many countries overseas were also recruited with the promise of a better life in a new land and lucrative wages—some of the company's agents even going as far as Bulgaria. [Forsey]

And then at the last hour, as all the mining communities throughout Cape Breton stirred with an ugly unrest, Dominion Coal Company, anticipating trouble, requested permission from the Cape Breton County Council to appoint 625 special constables from the ranks of company officials and "loyal" miners belonging to the rival PWA. County Warden H.C. LeVatte and the members of the county council readily agreed to the request after General Manager Duggan offered to pay the salaries of each of the specials. The request was accompanied by a long list of PWA men and company officials, headed by Duggan and John Moffatt, grand secretary of the Provincial Workmen's Association, who were to be made constables.

The county council was also requested to approve the appointment of a special county sheriff, who would be allowed to take on his duties only in the event of a strike against the Dominion Coal Company. This request was also granted, with the choice of a suitable applicant left to Duggan's discretion. Duggan then appointed one—James Campbell—to the post. The fact that Campbell had recently been jailed for drunkenness was not mentioned or taken into consideration—in point of fact, Campbell's past record may have been noted as one of the prime requisites for the job in light of his conduct at a later date.

In approaching the county council for permission to appoint his special constables and sheriff, Duggan deliberately bypassed the proper channels of communication. The mayor and council of Glace Bay should have been approached initially. Constitutional authorities had long emphasized that the overriding of civil power and authority was a serious matter. Once a municipality's authority had been subjugated to another authority—one not elected through the proper democratic process of elections—a state of emergency existed and martial law had to be declared.

But Duggan, fully aware of Mayor Douglas' sympathy for striking UMWA men, made plans to use political patronage through the Liberal Party of the province to influence Warden LeVatte and his county councillors. The provincial government was determined to continue the flow of coal royalties into its treasury—strike or no strike.

Obviously the person or persons selected to replace the authority of a duly elected mayor and town council had to be a person beyond reproach with an impeccable character, someone generally respected throughout the community, but at this stage, Dominion was not looking for character references. It now had a willing tool in a position of authority—a person who would carry out the company's bidding without question.

To back up the authority of the Dominion Coal Company's sheriff, a special magistrate, Stewart McCawley (an official of the Dominion Coal Company), was then appointed from the ranks of "loyal" company employees by General Manager Duggan with the advice of Warden LeVatte. With the help of Duggan, Moffatt, 625 other special constables, Magistrate McCawley, and Sheriff Campbell, Dominion Coal Company saw little difficulty in controlling unruly miners in the event of a strike.

Meanwhile, over a thousand miners walked the streets after being fired by the Dominion Coal Company. Each man received a small measure of relief from the international headquarters of the UMWA in Indianapolis, but the amount was insufficient to support a man and his family.

Wholesale evictions had begun to take place everywhere as company police moved in to eject unemployed miners and their families from company homes. Once a man had been fired, the company ordered him to vacate his company-owned house immediately, and if the order was not obeyed without delay, brutal company goons threw furniture and personal possessions onto the street. Pregnant women, little children, grandparents, it made no difference. Suffering was viewed with complete indifference.

As tensions mounted, the collieries took on a new, martial appearance. High fences were erected to enclose the bankhead and surface buildings, and then behind the protection of fences, rows of barrack-like huts were erected to house the flow of "scab" labour being shipped in from a hundred different melting pots around the world. Once the defence preparations had been completed, the coal company then added what must have been the worst infamy of all. The high wooden fences surrounding each colliery were topped with strands of electrified barbed wire to trap the unwary and deter the curious. Three small boys were electrocuted before the fences were torn down.

Meanwhile, in contrast to the scenes of warlike preparation, the new District 26 executive of the UMWA was trying desperately to avert a strike. In spite of all manner of provocation, every possible avenue of negotiation and compromise was approached to try to reach an honourable settlement with the coal companies.

McLachlan, with his long experience of coal strikes in Scotland, knew full well that a miners' strike in Cape Breton had little chance of succeeding, even when backed by a powerful international union, if only 50 percent of the work force walked out on strike to support their demands.

Firmly allied to the coal company's cause, the Liberal press, which had often been described as the official mouthpiece of federal and provincial governments, was whipping itself into a frenzy as it published editorial after editorial condemning the United Mine Workers of America for its actions, which, they claimed, had led to the present impasse and the very real possibility of a province-wide strike. Piously they warned rebel miners belonging to the UMWA that their actions would be fought with all the forces under the command of government and municipal authorities. The Sydney *Post*, May 14, 1909: "This lunacy is wrong in principle and against the wishes of the great majority of people whose only desire is to live in peace.... They should be allowed to prosper in the bountiful care of the company, living in company houses, fed from company stores and steadily employed in the mines at 'good rates of pay.'"

Towards the end of May 1909, the international headquarters of the UMWA decided to lend a little weight to the fruitless negotiations being conducted at the District 26 level. Accepting an invitation from District President MacDougall and Secretary-treasurer McLachlan, the newly elected international president of the union, Thomas L. Lewis—not to be confused with John L. Lewis, president at a later date—visited Nova Scotia to discuss the tense situation with the district executive before travelling to the provincial capital at Halifax to confer with Premier George H. Murray. Nothing concrete was resolved at this meeting—Murray and his cabinet knew they held all the cards—they had already made the secret decision to support Dominion and the other coal companies in their forthcoming struggle with a "foreign" union.

Lewis returned to Cape Breton from Halifax to discuss the situation with prominent businessmen, clergy, and the mayor and councillors of Glace Bay, where the major confrontation would take place, but efforts to arrange a meeting with Duggan, general manager of the Dominion Coal Company, were in vain. Duggan flatly refused to meet the international president of the union or to establish any contact whatsoever.

Having exhausted all possible avenues of conciliation, the

District 26 executive now decided to hold a mass meeting in Glace Bay on the evening of June 4, when Thomas L. Lewis would address all UMWA miners. It was reported that the meeting, held at the Alexandra Ice Rink, was attended by six to seven thousand people, jammed into every corner of the vast building. Prior to the mass meeting, a huge parade of coal miners, twenty-five hundred strong, marched through the streets of Glace Bay, brass bands playing lustily and Union Jacks held proudly aloft to proclaim their allegiance to Canada and the king.

Significantly, the Liberal press denounced the march the following day, claiming it was "a communist inspired mob, waving red flags, determined to overthrow the forces of law and order!"

On the same day, Thomas L. Lewis gave an interview to the Halifax *Herald* in which he intimated that unless the coal companies recognized the right of their employees to join any labour union they wished, it could lead only to one result, and that was the suspension of mining operations in Nova Scotia, even though the UMWA was opposed to strikes as a means of settling labour disputes.

Lewis returned to Indianapolis, his mission for a peaceful settlement a failure. The decision to strike or not to strike was now left to the discretion of the District 26 executive on the local scene.

It was an extremely difficult decision to make. District 26 had tried every possible means to settle their grievances with the coal companies in a peaceable manner. But it had been refused recognition as an official union with bargaining rights for its members. Wholesale firings and other forms of discrimination had followed. The international president of the UMWA had offered his own goodwill to settle the dispute, but the coal operators spurned his offer. Now, the District 26 executive had been forced into a corner and left with the possibility of a strike to enforce their just demand for recognition.

The executive knew that if the threat to strike was withdrawn at the last hour, the UMWA would undoubtedly lose prestige; the men would in turn lose faith in the new organization and resign en masse; the district charter would then be withdrawn by the international union and the Provincial Workmen's Association would continue to represent Nova Scotia miners in its boot-licking role as a company-controlled union for the next twenty years or more without gaining any significant increases in wages to combat the spiralling cost of living, which was steadily depleting the miners' already meagre incomes.

On June 23, 1909, the District 26 executive made one last effort to reach a settlement. Over the signature of its president, Dan MacDougall, a letter was sent to all coal companies in the province of Nova Scotia requesting a meeting to reach a peaceful settlement of the dispute and try to avert a possible strike. The letter makes interesting reading today in light of the many charges levelled at a later date against the union for its so-called militant attitude. The letter contained such phrases as:

> You are respectfully invited to attend a conference of the representatives of the operators and miners of Nova Scotia to be held in Sydney, July 2nd, 2 p.m. at the Y.M.C.A. Hall.... The object of this meeting will be to discuss the situation and endeavour to arrive at an understanding mutually beneficial to the mine owners and mine workers of Nova Scotia.... There is no reason why we should have a serious disagreement.... We sincerely desire that you be present and we again extend to you an invitation and respectfully urge you to give the question your careful and favourable consideration. [Records, UMWA, District 26]

Hardly the words of fanatical revolutionaries or radical socialists as they had been described by the popular press and the coal companies. If anything, the letter shows a sincere desire to avoid a strike.

The union's polite request for a meeting was ignored. The spirit of the Truro meeting with its "course of action" continued to govern the conduct and tactics of the coal companies, which felt that by even acknowledging a letter or a request from a "foreign" union they were partially recognizing its existence.

Now, with the latest refusal to meet with them, the union was being forced to take action. A district convention of the UMWA was held in Glace Bay on July 2, 1909, to consider the whole situation and reach a final solution. The delegates regretfully decided at this meeting to give notice to the Dominion Coal Company that unless it agreed to meet with District 26 representatives on July 5 to discuss grievances and reach some form of settlement, they would be forced to instruct all members of District 26, the United Mine Workers of America, to cease work the following day, July 6, 1909.

This time there was an immediate response from Dominion Coal Company. General Manager Duggan contacted the Sydney *Post* to state there was not the slightest possibility of his company meeting with District 26 representatives on Monday, July 5, and that therefore the much heralded strike would be expected by the company on the following day.

The gauntlet had been thrown down and the union openly challenged to do its worst. To follow up the challenge, a notice signed by Duggan was posted at every colliery owned by the Dominion Coal Company. Threat followed threat; persecution, eviction, wholesale firings, and blacklistings were all promised with gusto:

> The company gives notice that under the terms of the I.D.I. Act, 1907, it is illegal for men to go on strike without thirty days notice.... Every man in contravention of the Act is subject to a fine of from ten to fifty dollars a day while on strike.... The company will proceed at once to fill the places of men refusing to work and loyal men remaining at work will have first consideration in the allotment of places, so that when the strike is called off, a man at work will not lose his place to a man who has been on strike.... Men on strike will be treated as no longer in the employ of the company as regards houses, coal or any of the other privileges they may now enjoy.... Any man not reporting for work on Tuesday morning is liable to be regarded as a striker and treated as such.
>
> G.H. Duggan, General Manager

The same day Dominion Coal Company informed the press it had been in touch with coal companies in England, Scotland, and Wales and that they had promised to send as many men as would be required in fill strikers' places in the mines. This dubious strategy had been decided at the Truro meeting of coal companies. Trade unions may have been legalized thirty-seven years previously in 1871, but the hiring of strikebreakers was still perfectly legal.

To their everlasting credit, most miners approached by coal company agents in Great Britain declined after McLachlan sent telegrams to his old friend Keir Hardie and the Miners' Federation of Great Britain begging for support in the forthcoming struggle and requesting them to discourage their union members from accepting "blackleg" jobs, which would no doubt be offered them when the Nova Scotia coal strike commenced.

Initially, the strike was to be called against only three coal companies: the Dominion Coal Company operating the Sydney coalfield on the east coast of Cape Breton Island, Inverness Railway and Coal Company on the west coast of the island, and Cumberland Railway and Coal Company at Springhill on the mainland of Nova Scotia.

To consolidate Duggan's pithead ultimatum, a statement was then issued from Dominion's head office in Montreal by Vice-president F.L. Wanklyn: "We have the right of the matter and are not going to give in to a bunch of American agitators. If the miners go on strike we will fight them to the bitter end!" [Montreal *Star*, June 5, 1909]

In making such derogatory statements regarding foreign control of unions in Canada, the coal companies knew they were on safe ground. The federal government of Canada had long been of the same mind. A bill introduced in the Senate in 1903 would have made it a criminal offence for anyone not a British subject to incite or induce workmen by any act or means to leave their employment or go on strike. [R.H. Coats, 1914]

On the eve of the strike, the town of Glace Bay lost its usual carefree atmosphere and optimism for the future. With muted voices, groups of men congregated at street corners to discuss the tense situation. Everywhere, in bars, on the streets, or at impromptu union meetings, men gathered to glean the latest news or the choicest rumours, many of which were false and deliberately planted by company spies and informers mingling freely with honest workmen, listening with Judas-like ears while outwardly shouting encouragement and enthusiasm for the forthcoming strike.

At a higher level, last-minute telegrams between government and union were being dispatched in a final attempt to avert a strike, while coal companies throughout Great Britain sent further telegrams pledging support for Nova Scotia coal companies and a never-ending supply of emigrant miners to break the strike.

The 625 special constables had been duly sworn in and now stood menacingly before the gates of every beleaguered colliery, their defensive weapons including loaded revolvers, long-handled billy sticks, and pick handles topped with ugly, murderous spikes.

As dawn approached, lights still burned in company and union offices as plans were made for the opening day of the strike.

The real test would be the amount of coal mined and shipped during the strike. Almost half the total work force had signed union cards with the United Mine Workers of America and were about to strike, but if the company could still maintain a profitable output using its remaining labour force and imported strikebreakers, the strike would undoubtedly fail and the UMWA would be banished from Nova Scotia.

The battle lines had been drawn as last-minute preparations were made to commence one of the most bitter and prolonged strikes in the history of Canadian labour. It was to be a strike destined to split families, to turn father against son, brother against brother. It was to be a battle between members of the new United Mine Workers of America and members of the old Provincial Workmen's Association, who had been ordered to remain at work by their leaders during the strike. Most important, it was to be a battle to force coal companies to recognize the United Mine Workers of America, District 26, as the official bargaining agent for those miners who had signed union cards and who wished to renounce the company-controlled PWA.

In some ways, it was to be an unjust fight, for many of those remaining at work did so in the honest belief that their own cause was just and that the PWA had been right in joining hands with the coal companies to resist the entry of a union that was considered, rightly or wrongly, a "foreign" union and therefore dangerous.

The costs would be heavy, the burden great, but no one could deny that all those who took part in the great 1909 strike did so in the belief that their own cause was just. Like their forefathers who had rebelled against persecution in other lands across the sea, they willingly accepted the premise that a price had to be paid if they wished to retain their liberty and dignity—democratic freedoms forever lost if they bowed to cruel and insensitive employers, who with the blessing of a benign provincial government and a ninety-nine-year lease, had assumed the mantle of medieval barons.

3

J.B. McLachlan and the 1909 Strike

The next day, July 6, 1909, the morning whistles sounded as usual at seven, calling miners from all the surrounding districts to report for work. Coal company officials stationed at the gates of each colliery anxiously counted heads to ascertain the strength of the work force and to direct operations of company police and special constables blocking every gate in a brute show of strength.

The District 26 executive of the UMWA, not to be outdone, had appointed its own officials to direct strike operations at each mine and to control pickets, who were posted in long lines outside the gates to dissuade those reporting for work.

The real test was expected to be at the Dominion No. 2 mine, located in the New Aberdeen district of Glace Bay. It was the largest and the best-equipped mine owned by the Dominion Coal Company, employing over two thousand miners, most of whom owed allegiance to the Provincial Workmen's Association. The battle for supremacy between the UMWA and PWA could therefore be determined at this one location. If the rival UMWA could succeed in closing down this PWA stronghold, it would help establish its claim that the great majority of miners were in favour of belonging to the new union and of fighting under its colours. Here at the No. 2 mine, Secretary-treasurer McLachlan and President Dan MacDougall of the UMWA joined the picket line to provide the necessary leadership in this most crucial test.

Many men must have been influenced in their decision to

report for work by the proclamation that the company had issued the previous day. The threat to force striking miners and their families to vacate company houses meant that every UMWA supporter could be without a roof over his head that same night. To meet this contingency, the international headquarters of the UMWA had provided over two thousand Bell tents, which were beginning to spring up like mushrooms in fields all around the colliery districts—they were a poor substitute for houses but they would give some measure of shelter to evicted families. Most of them were without occupants, but subsequent events soon changed that.

Since dawn, hundreds and then thousands of striking miners had been quietly leaving their homes to congregate outside the gates of each colliery owned by the Dominion Coal Company before the whistle sounded at seven. As the oncoming shift of PWA men came through the gate, they were greeted by cries of "Scab" accompanied by hisses and boos from a crowd estimated to be in excess of three thousand men and women.

The Sydney *Record* reported that the men going to work were met by an extremely hostile crowd:

> The fears of some sections of the community were realized this morning. As the men desiring to work approached the mine at Dominion No. 2, they found all the approaches surrounded by thousands of excited men, jeering, shouting and attempting to prevent the resumption of work.... Mr Duggan, general manager of Dominion Coal Company, placed himself at the head of the newly appointed special constables and exhorted the strike leaders to disperse their men but to no avail. It was at this point that Mr Duggan was viciously assaulted by a striking miner, but the assault was not serious.

It would be an understatement to say that the Sydney *Record* was not in favour of labour unions, especially mining unions. Reading their reports today, one sees not merely a bias but an outright distortion of the facts as they occurred. Many witnesses to the so-called "vicious attack" on Duggan reported the assault took place after he had led his "specials" into battle against unarmed men, women, and children. Mounted on a great black charger, "Constable" Duggan rode alongside another special constable—John Moffatt, grand secretary of the Provincial Workmen's Association—a union leader throwing his full support behind the company in a bullying attempt to crush striking miners who had, until recently, worked alongside him, deep beneath the ocean floor, sharing common dangers and enjoying the rare camaraderie that binds miners together like blood brothers. The incident that provoked retaliation was a particularly vicious attack on a woman. Duggan had slashed her across the face with a rawhide whip. Cries of outrage were followed by a concerted attempt to drag him down from his horse.

It was at this point that Jim McLachlan, secretary-treasurer of District 26, UMWA, stepped forward with a tongue-in-cheek offer of assistance to General Manager Duggan: "The UMWA is ready and willing to provide town officials with the names of 500 good men and honest citizens to act as special police to protect coal company property!"

From all accounts, Duggan did not appreciate the offer, but witnesses noted that a considerable number of PWA converts joined UMWA strikers on the picket line after McLachlan's approach, which had been accompanied by an offer to guarantee the safety of the very men who were continuing to work during the strike. The county council had accepted Duggan's list of so-called trusted men to be sworn in from the ranks of PWA men as special constables, McLachlan reasoned, so why should they not accept an optional list of UMWA men for the same task?

As tensions mounted and the mood of the crowd grew uglier, the special police were forced back to the gates of the colliery. General Manager Duggan, fearful for the safety of his constables, now decided to play his winning hand. He now called on his new special sheriff, James Campbell, to read the Riot Act in order to protect company property and "loyal" workers.

This was the moment for which Campbell had been rehearsing for weeks. Using a wagon as his platform, and surrounded by company and special police, he now proceeded to read the Riot Act in a loud, ringing voice designed to strike terror into the hearts and minds of even the most militant worker:

Our Sovereign Lord and King charges and commands all persons here assembled, to disperse and peaceably depart to their habitations or to their lawful business. Upon the pain of being found guilty of an offence on conviction, you shall be liable to imprisonment for life!

Without delay, McLachlan and MacDougall dismissed their pickets and called on the crowd to disperse immediately. Once the Riot Act had been read, every person assembled outside the gate of No. 2 colliery could be arrested, forcibly detained at His Majesty's pleasure, and then sentenced to long terms of penal servitude on charges of sedition and inciting mutiny.

The trouble was by no means confined to the No. 2 mine. Although the towns of Caledonia and Reserve Mines reported that all was quiet, No. 3 mine in Glace Bay underwent a siege similar to that at No. 2. PWA men arriving for their early-morning shift were faced by an angry mob of strikers who attempted to block all entrances to the colliery and prevent its being worked. When the situation threatened to get out of hand, the special police drew their revolvers and seemed about to fire into the crowd. Fortunately, UMWA leaders at the scene managed to persuade their striking members that a massacre would surely result unless they vacated the scene immediately. PWA men were then allowed to pass through the picket lines unmolested, but not without running a gauntlet of verbal abuse. Many a man hung his head in shame. Some were persuaded to turn back, others joined striking miners on the picket line.

And finally, as evening approached, thousands of striking miners left the gates of each colliery to return to their families in the tent towns. The coal company won the first round with the assistance of its special sheriff, but there would be other days and other opportunities for the striking United Mine Workers of America to persuade PWA men to join them in their struggle against the Nova Scotia coal producers. For nine long hours McLachlan and his men had effectively blocked the gates of the more important collieries owned by the Dominion Coal Company. Fortunately, the day had ended without serious injury or death, but this was merely the opening day of the struggle. Whether miners could maintain an even temper was anybody's guess. To see other miners' families drawing credit at the company store and filling their bellies while their own families starved could easily lead some workers to violence in the future.

In fact, the second day of the strike did spawn a new outbreak of violence. The Halifax *Morning Chronicle* reported that:

Striking miners stormed the gates of No. 6 colliery, burned some of the property of Dominion Coal Company and fired some shots into buildings throughout the plant. The fence around the mine was almost completely demolished. The small force of company police managed to prevent the strikers from damaging vital machinery but they were hard pressed.... An informer had reported that the strikers were planning a concerted attack on this colliery during the evening and a special train was used to bring eight county constables to the scene to assist company police and specials. When the train appeared, the strikers attempted to drag the police onto the tracks but with drawn revolvers they forced the infuriated strikers back and then ordered the engineer to run the engine through the mob several times to make them disperse.... As soon as it became dark, the crowd went wild. One of the gates was torn from its hinges and much of the guard-fence broken down. A fusilade of shots was fired at electric lights and insulators and while the shooting was going on, stones, sticks or any handy missiles were thrown at the men working inside the fence.... As soon as morning dawned, the crowd dispersed so that it was impossible to identify any of the rioters. Tonight, a company of infantry will probably be stationed with a machine gun at No. 6 which is the most isolated of all the mines in the area.

The next day, July 8, Duggan wrote a formal letter of protest to Mayor Douglas of Glace Bay, regarding his inability to keep order during the strike:

Serious disorders have occurred at all collieries within the town's limits.... Evidently the town is not able to afford adequate protection and we now call upon you to make a formal requisition for active Militia as provided under the statutes.... Mr MacDonald and Mr McCawley, Justices of the Peace, have expressed their willingness to join with you in making this requisition. [Municipal Records, town of Glace Bay, 1909]

The two justices of the peace referred to in Duggan's letter of protest were, of course, employees of the Dominion Coal Company, specially appointed by Warden LeVatte and the Cape Breton County Council at Duggan's request.

The mayor replied immediately, informing Duggan and the Dominion Coal Company that a meeting of the local Police Committee had been held to consider the matter and a decision made to recommend the appointment of twenty special constables to assist the regular force in keeping order during the labour dispute.

The Dominion Coal Company, totally dissatisfied with the offer of only twenty special police constables, made immediate application to the Cape Breton County Council for militia troops to be sent into the troubled areas to keep order. County Warden LeVatte hastened to contact County Court Judge Finlayson for the necessary authority, and within a matter of hours, Judge Finlayson had forwarded an application for military protection to the federal government in Ottawa.

The following day, all leave was cancelled for the armed forces stationed in Halifax and five hundred troops of the Royal Artillery and Royal Canadian Regiment, under the command of General Drury, were loaded into a special train to be ferried across the Strait of Canso to quell rebellious miners in the Sydney coalfield. To demonstrate that they would not be acting as mere policemen in the dispute, all men were paraded in full battle order, complete with machine gun detachments, horses, and artillery.

This was the third time troops had been dispatched to Cape Breton Island since the first labour union had been formed in Springhill in 1879.

When informed of the requisition of troops, the mayor of Glace Bay sent telegrams of protest to the Department of Militia, the Secretary of State, and the general officer commanding the forces at Halifax, demanding their immediate withdrawal. The mayor was perfectly justified in his protest. Under the Militia Act, the responsibility for requesting troops rested with the civil authorities when they considered that control of a riotous situation was beyond the powers or capabilities of the local police. In truth, the Dominion Coal Company had called in the troops against the wishes of the civil authorities by using the willing offices of their political friends in Ottawa, Halifax, and in Cape Breton. Judge Finlayson as a county court judge had willingly complied with their request knowing full well that the responsibility was that of the town authorities, who would now be expected to pay a very substantial bill for billeting and maintaining five hundred soldiers and their horses.

Mayor Douglas' protest to Ottawa could have been upheld if John Moffatt, grand secretary of the Provincial Workmen's Association and pro tem special constable, had not decided to substantiate the request for troops made by Judge Finlayson. In an unprecedented action, Moffatt sent a telegram to the Minister of Militia in Ottawa, requesting that troops be sent forthwith to Cape Breton:

> The U.M.W. who are on strike here and who have indulged in a series of riots are forwarding you a petition, asking that the request for militia be withdrawn. On behalf of the P.W.A. representing about one-half of the workers in the collieries, we ask your protection for our families, our homes and our services. In our opinion the withdrawal of the militia would seriously imperil these and would result in bloodshed and the loss of property. The various lodges of our association have passed a resolution showing the appreciation of the military. [Public Archives, Ottawa]

A long and rambling resolution attached to the end of the telegram claimed that the offer by the UMWA to provide a force of special constables to protect life and property was a farce, as the UMWA was fighting the PWA as ardently as it was fighting the Dominion Coal Company.

The telegram, signed by Moffatt and the secretaries of thirteen PWA lodges throughout Cape Breton and the mainland of Nova Scotia, generated a great deal of ill-will and animosity throughout the coal mining districts of Nova Scotia. If anything, the telegram only served to harden the resolve of the UMWA men who determined to stay out on strike until the battle had been won and their union given full recognition. A hatred had now been generated against the PWA that would be difficult to heal even after all the troubles had been resolved and the details forgotten.

The troops under the command of General Drury arrived

in Glace Bay during the afternoon of July 8, and were immediately divided into detachments to be sent to the various collieries throughout the Sydney coalfield. Sentries with fixed bayonets guarded the approaches to each mine. At No. 2 and No. 6 mines, where most of the trouble had erupted, machine guns were set up. The Riot Act having been read, the situation was now left in the hands of the military. To all intents and purposes, martial law now prevailed throughout the Cape Breton coalfields.

Resembling beleaguered towns, each colliery was surrounded by high fences topped with barbed wire and guarded by soldiers marching back and forth with rifles and fixed bayonets. Inside the fences, hundreds of strikebreakers, hastily recruited from all corners of the globe, were housed in wooden shacks, safe from the wrath of striking miners. Many PWA miners who also took advantage of this protected accommodation were isolated from their families for the duration of the strike. Strings of powerful electric floodlamps were mounted on top of the fences while scores of company and special police prowled from hut to hut, armed with revolvers and long nightsticks or pick handles to repel any attempt by striking miners to breach the defences and attack the strikebreakers.

But the arrival of hundreds of armed troops into the Sydney coalfield served only to exacerbate an already tense situation. Striking miners viewed the military intervention and the declaration of martial law as intimidation and a brazen attempt to beat them into submission. Their anger was not directed against the soldiers, who were only following orders; it was directed instead against their elected politicians, who had prostituted their sacred office as the people's representatives by lending their support to the coal barons at the expense of workers forced to live in abject poverty in a feudal system of company towns where no man was his own master.

McLachlan and MacDougall quickly changed tactics. From now on, the strike must be conducted peacefully; striking miners must not show any resistance or animosity towards the troops. No excuse must be provided for the coal companies to pressure the military commander for support in the intimidation of striking miners.

It was during these opening days of the strike that McLachlan began to be recognized as the true leader of Cape Breton miners. District President Dan MacDougall and the members of his executive recognized his worth and were content to accept his judgement and advice on all matters pertaining to the district's struggle for recognition with the coal companies of Nova Scotia. As the power behind the scenes, McLachlan had been taught his craft by such worthy labour pioneers as Keir Hardie and Alexander McDonald, leaders of British miners' unions and the first labour men to break tradition and enter the British House of Commons as representatives of the workingman.

With the arrival of troops and the cessation of violence on the picket lines, the coal companies began to breathe easier. If they could continue to operate their mines using PWA men and imported strikebreakers, they would be able to maintain a fair proportion of their previous output and the strike would be broken. Company agents searched everywhere for recruits. At Springhill, on the mainland of Nova Scotia, it was reported in the Halifax *Herald* that the Cumberland Railway and Coal Company had imported a large number of strikebreakers from the province of Quebec with the services of the Reliance Labour Exchange in Montreal. Cost was not considered an important factor—breaking the strike and outlawing the militant UMWA was.

Not all imported workers proved to be willing tools of the Nova Scotia coal companies. When miners were recruited overseas by company agents promising bribes, inflated wages, and other incentives, they were not informed of their true role—that of strikebreaking. Six Belgian miners shipped to Cape Breton at company expense were charged with breach of contract when they refused to work at the Springhill mine after learning their role.

The coal companies had not hesitated to bring in troops to break the strike, and armed might was not the only tactic they employed; the law and the courts were another. Dubious legal angles were often used to advantage, especially after striking miners were arrested and arraigned before judges whose appointments had been confirmed by the provincial government in Halifax after being recommended by the coal companies.

From the opening day of the strike, District 26 had arranged for at least one member of the executive to take charge of the picket line at each colliery. At Inverness, David Neilson, a district organizer for the UMWA, was arrested on the complaint of the Cumberland Railway and Coal Company and charged with "supporting a strike contrary to the Industrial Disputes Investigation Act of 1907," which required thirty days' notice be given before a strike could be declared. He was tried and convicted in short order in spite of many protests from organized labour and other concerned groups, and incarcerated in Dorchester Penitentiary.

Day after day, as long as the strike lasted, there were numerous arrests for trivial offences, mainly loitering. The reading of the Riot Act was being strictly interpreted, preventing even small numbers of men from gathering, but with thousands of unemployed men wandering through the streets, it was almost impossible for them not to get together. Outside the union hall or at Senator's Corner in Glace Bay, groups of men sought news and exchanged views on the strike. Wherever they gathered, so did the spies and informers, ever ready to carry tales and information back to the coal company police.

Scores of men were arrested and jailed on trumped-up charges. The arrests were made by the new special police constables who were PWA men "loyal" to the company before the strike.

A reign of terror was instituted against strikers and their families. Evictions from company-owned houses continued at a great pace. Hundreds of families were forced from their homes and their few sticks of furniture dumped in the backyard or on the street at the mercy of the elements. The emergency Bell tents were rapidly filled with striking families but thousands of others were forced to seek shelter with friends or relatives. In many cases where a miner had opened his doors to homeless families, he too was evicted as a warning to others.

Even men buying their homes and paying mortgages were threatened with eviction. Maurice MacDonald of Glace Bay described such an incident:

> During the 1909 strike I had scarlet fever and this young doctor came to our house to give me treatment. Many, many small children were suffering from scarlet fever, diphtheria, cholera, or polio during the strike.

Many more were dying of pneumonia or tuberculosis through living in wet, drafty tents after they had been evicted. It was several days after the doctor had been to see me and I was lying on the cot in the living room when I heard the sound of gunfire and I looked through the window and saw this poor miner who had been paying his mortgage on a house he was buying and the company that owned the mortgage was threatening to foreclose if he didn't go back to work. It wasn't a company house but the coal company had put the pressure on the mortgage company to foreclose because he was a striker.... It just showed the limits they were prepared to go to break the strike.... So he was being escorted to work by one of the Pinkerton detectives employed by the company, and one of the U.M.W.A. pickets tried to argue him out of going to work and the detective shot the picket so they could get past. His name was Sandy "Cape North" MacDonald. He wasn't killed but he was an epileptic for the rest of his life.

At New Aberdeen, a suburb of the town of Glace Bay, where the huge No. 2 mine was located, wholesale evictions began. After the disturbance on the opening day of the strike, the Dominion Coal Company seemed to take a perverse delight in evicting every UMWA man and his family from the company houses. Over 90 percent of the houses erected around the No. 2 mine were company-owned. In the event of a strike, the company thus had a big stick to wield in its campaign against the strikers. When faced with sudden eviction and the loss of the only homes they had ever known, striking miners were severely tested. Those with families had to make a heart-rending choice. If they decided under duress to return to work, they would be protecting their loved ones but at a price no man wanted to pay. For the rest of their lives, they would be despised and ostracized by their fellows—lepers shunned throughout the community. Even their families would be ostracized. Mrs Alice Buchanan of New Waterford witnessed one of the evictions in the area at this time:

I remember this poor woman in 1909 who was evicted with this wee baby, and this miner, who was a good man, took her into his own home for shelter, and then he was fired as a result of his kindness. It was down in No. 2, at New Aberdeen.... My father, who was a miner, used to say that the child that wasn't born when the strike was on would curse their fathers for working during the strike as scabs. They went through hell afterwards for working. This strike put a split through the town—brother against brother, father against son, school kid against school kid.... I remember a child that died of scarlet fever during the strike and there was an argument with the town officials as to who was going to bury the dear little soul—there was no money. People didn't even have ten cents!

Protests were made that evictions without proper notice were illegal. The coal company's response was to legalize the evictions using magistrates sympathetic to their cause. Archie McIntyre, one of Glace Bay's oldest and most respected residents and a retired miner with over fifty years' service, spoke bitterly about some of the magistrates who unhesitatingly carried out their master's bidding during the strike and other subsequent strikes.

Did you ever hear the expression "Magistrate by day and coal company official by night"? That's a fact. The coal company appointed the magistrates and many of the town's officials and councillors. They had this thing where a man had to own property or pay municipal taxes of so many dollars before you even got a vote. The coal company made very sure that their miners never got enough money to pay that much tax so we never got a vote. When it came to an election or the appointing of magistrates or officials, the ordinary miner had no say in the matter, but the coal company made very sure that all their paid officials and businessmen, whose livelihood depended on the operation of the coal mining industry, got out to vote.

To carry out the magistrates' eviction orders, the company used the services of bailiffs and company police. Every day throughout the strike, hundreds of out-of-work miners and their families locked their doors and waited for the fearful and thunderous knock heralding the bailiff and his bully-boys. To fight was useless. The coal company was backed by the law of the land.

Pat Nicholson, a reporter for the Glace Bay *Standard*, a newspaper that gave its unqualified support to striking miners, witnessed many of the evictions:

The bailiffs and the company police went into the homes, removed the furniture, dishes, food and clothing and piled them on the sidewalks before locking the doors behind them.... Miners and their families were left on the streets. Father Jim Fraser, pastor of St. John's Church in the Parish of New Aberdeen, took pity on them and filled the convent, the Catholic schools, the rectory and most of the church with poor, destitute miners' families. But another priest...travelled all the way to Antigonish on the Nova Scotia mainland to see Bishop Cameron and tell him that the coal company was not only fighting the U.M.W.A., it was fighting the Catholic Church due to the actions of Father Jim Fraser. That same evening, Father Jim received word from Bishop Cameron that he must leave the New Aberdeen Parish at once! He was given a new Parish in Antigonish County under the watchful eye of the Bishop and far from the strike scene. The strikers and their families were ordered to leave church property forthwith.

It was shocking but true. Even the churches had taken sides in the strike. While a few ministers and priests had taken their Christian role seriously and tried to provide shelter and sustenance for the destitute and homeless, many others openly expressed support for the coal companies during the strike. The checkoff system had guaranteed a steady weekly income for the various parishes out of miners' meagre pay envelopes in addition to deductions for doctor, company store, coal, and rent. But now that a strike had been called, this lucrative income had ceased for the churches.

During the first week of the strike, the evictions continued at a steady pace, accompanied by indignities and outright contempt for even the most basic human rights. Mrs Jean Robinson, oldest daughter of J.B. McLachlan, related an incident of this nature, which she witnessed as a young girl during the strike.

I was shocked to see this poor miner's wife carried out of her house—totally naked. The lady had been surprised in the midst of her toilet. It was terrible and heartbreaking to see. Around her, clutching at the police bullies with their tiny hands, her brood of small children wailed and sobbed as their few sticks of furniture were dumped on the sidewalk. Doors were locked behind them and the security of the family home was gone—forever!

One week after the strike was called, international board

member Harry Bousefield arrived from union headquarters in Indianapolis to inform striking miners of District 26 that the constitution of the United Mine Workers of America did not allow for strike benefits to be paid during the first thirty days of a strike. He emphasized that the international union gave relief only on the assumption that the men were out on strike for their own good and should therefore be content to suffer in the cause! After the thirty-day period, each man would receive $3.00 a week for himself, $1.50 for his wife, and 75 cents for each dependent child. It wasn't a lot, but it was better than nothing. In addition to cash payments, the international union would pay doctor bills, rents and fuel costs for those not yet evicted, and court costs for arrested miners.

McLachlan told the Duncan Royal Commission in 1925 that hundreds of miners were arrested during the 1909 strike on trumped-up charges of loitering, picketing, etc., and that the strike was very costly to the district and to the international headquarters of the union with over five hundred thousand dollars spent on strike benefits of one kind or another.

Credit at the company stores had been immediately cut off for striking miners and their families on the first day of the strike, and many hundreds of families would undoubtedly have starved to death without union support. Nevertheless, it was a time for belt-tightening, a time when men and women forced themselves to adjust to their new, wageless existence and swallow their pride and independence for the sake of their offspring; they determined to win regardless of cost.

The tradition of working-class solidarity, built at enormous cost and sacrifice during the Industrial Revolution, helped to keep striking miners steadfast and determined even as they sheltered from the keen Atlantic winds sweeping the island. The strike had commenced early in July, but if it continued through the cold Canadian winter, many small children would surely sicken and die—victims of a variety of ailments that their frail bodies would be unable to resist in their undernourished condition. The children and the old suffered most as they shivered under the scant protection of the canvas roofs and walls of their temporary homes. The outlook for striking miners and their families, especially those evicted from their company homes, could hardly be described as promising.

In contrast, John Moffatt, grand secretary of the PWA, said in answer to a query from the Sydney *Post*:

> The outlook is exceedingly bright, and we are hopeful of having the mines fully manned in the near future. No. 2 colliery is working today, and we have sufficient force on hand to keep this, the principal mine of Dominion Coal Company, going indefinitely. Caledonia, Dominion No. 3, Reserve and Bridgeport are all working with increased staffs.

It was difficult to equate this new, ebullient John Moffatt with the popular image of a union chief fighting for poorly paid workers against a despotic and all-powerful coal company. When he spoke of the future looking exceedingly bright while hundreds of men, women, and children shivered under canvas, he sounded more like a corporate executive. And did his statement "*we* have sufficient force on hand to keep this, the principal mine, going indefinitely" refer to the new special police, the company police, battalions of soldiers, or his own PWA men, who were continuing to work during the strike?

In many cases, soldiers were ordered to escort PWA miners to their place of work, even though such odious duties were not included in their orders—their duty was plain—it was to guard coal company property from vandalism and to prevent riots. Much against their will they had taken over escort duties from the civil authorities. The Sydney *Post* reported that:

> Many instances were to be noted about town early this morning of individual miners going to work under military escort, and one case was noted where one miner had a military escort of no less than fifteen khaki-clad Tommies.... One striker named McIntyre who was ordered by a soldier to "move on," and refusing to do so, was prodded in the rear with the usual bit of cold steel. The man thought for a moment he was being transported to the realms above, but has since concluded that with proper care and nursing, the wound will heal sufficiently to allow him to sit down to dinner!

In theory at least, soldiers were forbidden to open fire on unruly strikers without proper authorization or "unless distinctly required to do so by the magistrates in charge of militia." This safeguard against indiscriminate shooting of striking workmen was most commendable except that the magistrates placed in charge of the military by the County Council of Cape Breton were all coal company officials or individuals chosen by the company who would follow directions from their masters without question. In fact, the coal company controlled the actions of the militia even to the point where an order to fire could result in the death of striking workmen.

Mayor Douglas and the town council of Glace Bay had been greatly upset by the "high-handed" action of Warden LeVatte and his Cape Breton County Council in acceding to the Dominion Coal Company's request for the appointment of 625 special constables recruited from the ranks of PWA men and officials employed by the company. At a meeting the Glace Bay council passed a resolution appointing its own force of "special" policemen to keep order during the strike.

Glace Bay swarmed with special policemen, each sporting a brand-new badge, gun, and nightstick. The PWA specials were busy arresting anyone they considered to be loitering on the streets, while the town-appointed specials were kept equally busy arresting their rival PWA specials on charges of masquerading as policemen. It was a scene reminiscent of Max Sennett and the Keystone Cops, but the humorous situation was soon to change.

One of the reasons for the relative calm during the first weeks of strike was the ban that had been placed on all liquor outlets and bars. From the outset, town authorities had threatened severe penalties for anyone convicted of selling intoxicating liquor of any description. With thousands of men roaming the streets, there could easily have been a blood bath if they had been allowed to imbibe freely, but as the strike continued, this problem resolved itself. There was barely enough money for miners to feed their families, even with the help of the international union. Bootlegging thrived throughout the countryside, but a careful watch on all roads leading into the coal towns discouraged any attempt to bring in illicit liquor.

The Sydney *Post*, ever biased in favour of the coal companies, insisted all was now quiet in Glace Bay due to the presence of the troops. But with typical Cape Breton humour, striking miners held a different view. When asked by a reporter, "How do you account for the quiet and good order that now seems to prevail?" a so-called "impartial observer" replied, "Oh, that's easy. All the good guys are out on strike and the toughs are working!"

The coal companies and the PWA reported that the output of coal was most gratifying, but one Sydney newspaper reported the arrival of the steamer *Fritzoe* with a cargo of coal from Germany to be used in Dominion's steel mills; coal that would normally have been supplied by mines owned by the company if production figures had not been drastically reduced during the strike.

But the strike was hurting United Mine Workers of America as well as the company. McLachlan and the district leaders of the union watched the passage of time with mounting concern. The financial burden on the international union was becoming intolerable while the plight of evicted miners and their families posed a special problem—a problem that would increase greatly as the weather deteriorated. Thin canvas Bell tents would provide virtually no shelter during the winter months when the cold Arctic winds moved down from Labrador.

It was now the end of July and no settlement of the strike was in sight. It was a time for reassessment; a time to adopt new strategies to force a quick settlement of the strike. It was a time for some form of shock treatment—a show of strength to dispel the myth spread by the coal companies that striking miners were about to admit defeat and crawl back to the pits, hat in hand, begging for their old jobs. Shrewdly, McLachlan reasoned that a show of strength could play a dual role by persuading PWA men to change sides and join striking UMWA men on the picket lines. And in truth, many PWA men had begun to waver in that direction.

The district executive in Glace Bay decided that any show of strength should be made in the nearby town of Dominion—a PWA stronghold where the mines were almost fully manned during the strike. Plans were drawn up for a giant parade to be held on Saturday afternoon, July 31, 1909. Over three thousand striking UMWA miners would march from Glace Bay, through the suburb of Bridgeport, and on to Dominion before gathering for a great meeting on the beach at Lingan. The call went out to every district local throughout Cape Breton asking striking miners to join the parade in a peaceful demonstration of strength through unity.

Glace Bay Town Council, when informed of the parade, hurriedly passed a by-law forbidding any such action. Ostensibly, the by-law was introduced to prevent possible bloodshed and violence, but more likely, it had been introduced to prevent a show of strength by District 26. A considerable number of the Glace Bay town councillors were in the employ of the Dominion Coal Company, so in effect, the by-law could be viewed as an additional edict from the Dominion Coal Company's office.

The parade formed up at the athletic grounds in Glace Bay, but before marching out, the thousands of marchers were warned by McLachlan and other union leaders to behave in a gentlemanly manner, to respect law and order, and refuse to engage in controversy. After the speeches, the great parade of men marched up Commercial Street to Senator's Corner before turning onto Chapel Hill and out to Bridgeport and Dominion. Over three thousand strikers marched in the parade. Union Jacks and banners waved from one end to the other, giving a carefree, gala appearance heightened by the music of five separate bands. MacDougall, McLachlan, and the other leaders of the United Mine Workers of America marched at the head of the parade, which seemed to stretch interminably over the horizon.

The sidewalks were crowded with spectators, most of whom were cheering lustily for the striking miners. Everything went smoothly until the parade began to pass over Cadegan's Brook, which passes over the borderline separating the towns of Glace Bay and Dominion. Immediately on the other side of the bridge lay the Roman Catholic Church of Immaculate Conception. At the head of the parade, McLachlan and the other leaders were shocked to note that a machine gun had been mounted on the steps of the church. As the parade neared, an army officer stood with arm upraised, waiting to give the order to fire.

Mrs Alice Buchanan of New Waterford was a witness to the dramatic confrontation:

It was a very hot day when the parade arrived at Cadegan's Brook during the 1909 strike. The union wanted to show how many men were supporting the strike. They had five bands and hundreds of flags and banners—even some red ones. In front of the parade, many dignitaries marched with McLachlan, MacDougall, and union organizers. There was nothing which could be described as violent or troublemaking, it was a happy, carefree parade and the music was military marches and lively airs. They had marched all the way from Glace Bay but when they crossed Cadegan's Brook, they were forced to stop. The soldiers had a machine gun mounted on the church steps of Immaculate Conception and it was pointed right down the road to face the parade. The priest, Father Charlie MacDonald, had given the soldiers permission to use the church as a machine gun nest. I saw the parade turn back then; the strike leaders were sensible men and didn't want a killing, but for a minute, it was touch and go. It was a dreadful thing!

Even to this day, old miners remember the incident with great bitterness. It was bad enough for the soldiers to threaten to mow down peaceful marchers—fellow Canadians—but to use the steps of a holy edifice to site a weapon of destruction was, in their opinion, a monstrous sacrilege—a stain on the House of God! Vividly, the incident had demonstrated that the coal companies were not above using any dirty tactic to break the strike, even to the extent of desecrating the church.

Father MacDonald was bitterly criticized for permitting his church to be used in such manner, but he claimed he had been away at the time and had not been aware of anyone giving permission to the soldiers. Few believed his denial.

The Montreal *Gazette* reported favourably on the actions of the UMWA leaders, who averted a possible massacre:

Very sensibly, MacDougall and his senior officers halted the parade before the order to fire could be given. Without the slightest demonstration, the order was given to "right wheel" and the huge parade began its march back to Glace Bay without gaining its objective. On arrival, the men were assembled in a field at the rear of the town hall to hear speeches by Messrs. MacDougall, Bousefield and McLachlan. Protests were made regarding the fact that a body of peaceful citizens, assembled for a lawful purpose, had been held up on the King's Highway and threatened by Maxim machine guns and rifles at the instance of Dominion Coal Company. The proceedings closed with the singing of "God Save the King" and the crowd dispersed to their homes.

The brute show of strength had forced UMWA officials to cancel the planned demonstration in Dominion, but they had gained a great deal of favourable publicity by adopting a passive role and obeying the orders of the military. Suddenly, the general public began to take a sympathetic interest in the Cape Breton coal strike after they had been bombarded with company and news media propaganda for months. The striking UMWA miners, who had been painted "Red" and revolutionary by the provincial government and a monopolized coal industry, were now being labelled the "good guys," while the troops and special police were regarded as bullies and oppressors of liberty. If striking UMWA miners could continue in their fight until the federal government was forced to intervene through pressure from organized labour, they would win the recognition they sought and return to work on their own terms.

The coal companies were just as anxious to end the strike, but on their terms. It was a time when company officials took off their gloves and fought striking miners with every dirty trick in the book. If strong-arm tactics had failed to persuade UMWA men to surrender, then the fight would be carried to miners' families.

During the month of August, evictions continued at a great rate. Sick or dying, young or old, it made no difference to the coal companies. Bailiffs and their henchmen scoured the Sydney coalfield from end to end in a mad witch-hunt. The Sydney *Post* reported in its August 22 issue that nine more evictions had taken place at Dominion No. 2. In one of the evictions, a sick child was dying of cholera.

On Saturday evening we met Mr Nicholson of the UMWA who is attending to the evicted tenants and asked him if there was any truth in the story of the sick child? "Yes," he said, "that was Wray's child, the family was to be removed on Friday, but the Sheriff did not disturb them that day, but when I went back this morning, the house had been cleaned out.

I do not blame the Sheriff, he has been white and square in the execution of his duties. But there is one thing I don't like and that is, there is always a gang of the company's police hanging around and butting into the business. No, the Sheriff is human, but the other men—well, you know what they are like."

With work denied them, and their families evicted from company houses, many men decided to seek work in other occupations. The UMWA encouraged this type of temporary migration. Only a limited number of men were required for picket duty and it was better that most of the strikers be gainfully employed elsewhere so that they could send money back to their families in Nova Scotia. Unfortunately, the coal company's influence had spread far and wide. Within the province of Nova Scotia, striking coal miners found it impossible to obtain any other job. To employ a striking UMWA man was to incur the wrath of the all-powerful coal companies.

With doors closed in Nova Scotia, many out-of-work miners hitched rides or rode the rails to places as far away as Quebec or Ontario. Archie McIntyre told of his uncle, Johnny McIntyre, and six of his friends, who had worked in the Caledonia Mine previous to the strike:

They were young fellers in the 1909 strike and they decided they'd leave for greener fields because there was no money to be had...and eventually they landed in a place called La Terre in Quebec and then they decided to head for Montreal, but they had been around for about five weeks without work and their money had run out and they were having a language problem so they were feeling pretty desperate. And then one morning they were approached by a gentleman who was well dressed and wore a fedora hat and a bow tie, and he said, "Good morning, gentlemen, are you looking for work? You are? Well, you look just the type we are looking for. Do you know of a place called Cape Breton?" And my uncle and his friends said, "No, where about is it?" and the gentleman said, "Well, it's at the far end of Nova Scotia and there is a big mining company in a place called Glace Bay, and they are looking for fellows to mine coal."

"Coal mining!" my uncle exclaimed. "You can get killed at that job, can't you?" He replied, "No, no, of course not. They are well paid for the job too." They asked, "Well, how are we going to get there?"

"Don't worry about that, we'll take care of that little detail," the well-dressed stranger replied, and he was as good as his word. You see, the boys had cottoned on at once to the fact that he was an agent for the Dominion Coal Company recruiting scab labour for the Glace Bay coal mines. So they played dumb. They were wanting to get home to Glace Bay, so why not let the coal company pay for their passage? The agent took them to a bar where they had a few drinks, and being Cape Bretoners, they probably had a few extra too. And then they had a big meal to top it off. Well, at the end of this beautiful day, with the boys having difficulty in keeping a straight face, the stranger said, "Your clothes don't look in too good shape my friends, perhaps I had better buy you some good coveralls to wear before you go to work." Now this was really too much for the boys, but he insisted on buying them coveralls and new boots and then the stranger left them with the parting words, "Now, boys, you be here at six forty-five in the morning and I'll drive you to the station to catch a train to Glace Bay." And so it happened the next day. On the train, they made a point of avoiding all the other recruits, who all seemed to have a hangdog expression, but the railway coach was warm and they had full bellies and at last they were on their way home to Glace Bay at the expense of the bountiful Dominion Coal Company. It was wonderful!

Well, when they got off the train at Sydney, the coal company wasted no time and they drove the boys right into Glace Bay and through the gates of their old pit—Caledonia of all places! They had all been born right under the smokestack. And when the mine officials came out to inspect the new recruits, they just exploded when they saw the boys. They threw them out of the stockade and they went home laughing till their bellies ached.

The joke was on the coal company but the story was changed somewhat when it was published in the August 21 issue of the Sydney *Post*, which had begun to sound like the official organ of the Dominion Coal Company: "According to a company spokesman, the 'prodigal sons' of Cape Breton had been brought back to Glace Bay at company expense because they had been found in a starving condition in Quebec."

Hundreds of men recruited by company agents in Quebec were

rushed into Cape Breton to fill the places of striking miners. No sooner had a family been evicted from their company house, than it was reoccupied with scab labour. As an incentive, the hastily recruited workers were allowed to live rent free with all the amenities such as coal, light, and water added as an additional bonus.

Within the stockades surrounding each colliery under siege, hundreds of other imported workers lived in overcrowded, squalid conditions in long wooden huts, each housing fifty inmates. Down the centre aisle of each hut, rough wooden tables and chairs completed the furnishings while wet and steaming lines of laundered clothes hung in festoons from one end of the hut to the other. To while away the time, the men played cards and gambled their wages at all hours of the day and night. Boredom was the chief enemy; not for them a walk in the country or along the Atlantic shores. They were forbidden to leave the safety of the stockade and the protection of company police and patrolling soldiers. To set foot outside the fence was to invite a severe beating or worse.

Under the circumstances, it was inevitable that living conditions should sink to a slumlike squalor far removed from the comfort and familiarity of their own homes. Sanitary facilities were extremely crude or nonexistent so it was not surprising when the dreaded typhoid fever broke out among the strikebreakers.

Dan MacDougall, president of District 26 of the UMWA, ever ready to criticize the strikebreaking Dominion Coal Company, arranged for a paid advertisement to be placed in Montreal newspapers, urging Quebec workmen not to be enticed by the promise of good jobs with Dominion. He claimed that contrary to the bright picture painted by the company when advertising for strikebreakers, workmen shipped to Cape Breton were being improperly housed under deplorable conditions.

The Dominion Coal Company reacted swiftly to MacDougall's criticism. Using political patronage as a weapon, the company persuaded Quebec judicial authorities to issue warrants for the arrest of MacDougall and the two international representatives of the union, Patterson and Bousefield, who had remained on the strike scene. The charge preferred against all three men was that of criminal libel. The charge and the warrants were issued in the province of Quebec, but were not enforceable in the province of Nova Scotia. The Dominion Coal Company soon overcame this little technicality by calling on their tame Judge Finlayson—the same judge who had arranged for the militia to be called in during the strike—to execute the Quebec warrant in Cape Breton.

On Sunday evening, September 12, 1909, the home of Dan MacDougall was surrounded by armed men. He was arrested and rushed aboard a train bound for Montreal, where he was remanded to jail to await trial without benefit of counsel or communication with the outside world.

Back in Cape Breton, MacDougall's wife and children were distraught with anxiety. McLachlan was quickly informed of his disappearance, but his whereabouts were not revealed and foul play was suspected. Maurice MacDonald of Glace Bay related how the arrest took place. It was more of a kidnapping than an arrest.

> Dan and his family had just returned to their home after attending Sunday evening service at the Presbyterian church in Glace Bay. They had just sat down to a meal when there was a knock at the door. Mrs MacDougall went to the door and a group of men said they wanted to speak to Dan, so she went back and told him. The rest of the family resumed eating and he didn't come back. She went to the door, but he had disappeared. The family was almost out of their mind.... Dan MacDougall was a very outstanding citizen. He enlisted during the First World War and became a major, and then later, he was the postmaster of Glace Bay for many years.

With MacDougall safely removed from the strike scene, the coal companies were convinced the strike would end quickly. For several days, thousands of striking miners scoured every nook and cranny throughout the Sydney coalfield. Enquiries were made as far away as Halifax, the provincial capital, but officialdom denied any knowledge of his whereabouts.

When MacDougall finally emerged from his cell to be formally charged in a Montreal courtroom, his family were shocked and horrified to learn he faced criminal charges laid by the Dominion Coal Company. The news of his arrest and kidnapping to another province hundreds of miles away was received back in Cape Breton with anger and a cry for revenge. Without the sobering hand of McLachlan, there would undoubtedly have been bloodshed and violence. But with the absence of Dan MacDougall, McLachlan began to emerge as the true leader of the Cape Breton miners.

The trial of Dan MacDougall commenced early in October 1909, and from the start, it became obvious it was merely a formality, a ritual to be observed prior to sentencing him to a good, healthy term in the penitentiary where he could no longer influence the course of events in the strife-torn Nova Scotia coalfields. Almost every potential witness for the defence was immediately arrested after giving evidence, and charged with complicity in the "crime" except international union organizers Bousefield and Patterson, who had been attending a session of the international board of the union meeting in Indianapolis at the time of the trial. Since the so-called crime was of a nonextraditable nature, they could not be forced to return to Montreal to surrender to the authorities. But the warrants issued for them served the companies' purpose in that they compelled both organizers to remain in the United States—at least for the duration of the strike.

The coal companies made a fatal miscalculation when they concentrated their malice on President MacDougall and left McLachlan free. As secretary-treasurer of the union, McLachlan was called as a witness and grilled in the witness box continually for several days. At the insistence of the crown counsel, the judge forced McLachlan to produce minutes of all UMWA district meetings, correspondence, financial statements, and a great many other items that were totally irrelevant to the case.

McLachlan fumed. It was becoming increasingly obvious that the crown and the Dominion Coal Company were using delay tactics, dragging the trial out as long as possible. The longer the trial continued, the longer UMWA leaders were being kept from the strike scene, and without responsible leadership, the companies could quite feasibly force the striking miners back to work without gaining a single point.

With McLachlan's anger came inspiration. If the law could force District 26 to produce its confidential books and financial statements after being charged with a criminal offence, would not the same rules apply if the coal companies were charged with a criminal offence? With a mischievous grin and Machiavellian cunning, McLachlan acted at once. He returned to Glace Bay at the earliest opportunity to burn the midnight oil in the union offices preparing his case. Then he travelled to Halifax, the provincial capital, to lay a number of charges against the coal companies of Nova Scotia, alleging that together they had conspired to limit coal production and fix prices between 1900 and 1909.

The preliminary hearing was set for October 19, 1909, and warrants were issued to ensure the appearance of a number of coal company executives to answer charges. President Ross, General Manager G.H. Duggan, and Chief Sales Agent Dick were ordered to appear for the Dominion Coal Company while General Manager Cowans was ordered to appear for the Cumberland Railway and Coal Company. Nine years of correspondence from both companies was impounded by the prosecution and the case was celebrated as the *Cowans-Dick* case.

Headlines in the newspapers revealed McLachlan's inspiration, which had come to him in the Montreal court: "McLachlan Turns Tables on Coal Operators at Halifax." The wily old fighter had indeed turned the tables. In a desperate attempt to placate the District 26 executive before it could press the case against it, the Dominion Coal Company arranged for the immediate release of Dan MacDougall and within two days he was back in Glace Bay ready to continue the fight.

His return on October 14, 1909, was marked by triumphal processions in every mining community in Nova Scotia. At Springhill and Sydney Mines, his train was met by huge rallies, but it was at the Dominion Coal Company's No. 4 mine that the real demonstration took place. It was reported that a vast crowd of well-wishers awaited his arrival from Sydney. As he stepped from his car, he was hoisted onto the shoulders of stalwart miners amid deafening cheers and carried to a carriage to be seated alongside McLachlan, the man responsible for his release. Behind them, a brass band struck up a lively march and thousands of miners formed a procession stretching the whole length of Main Street to the offices of the Dominion Coal Company, where General

Manager Duggan and his officials sat behind closed blinds.

The strike continued, but Messrs. Ross and Duggan found to their chagrin and dismay they were to be forced to appear in the felons' dock in Halifax Police Court to answer charges levelled against them by McLachlan. The disgrace proved to be too much for them to bear and shortly after, in November 1909, both gentlemen announced their early retirement from the Dominion Coal Company after Ross had sold $5 million of Dominion Coal Company common stock to a syndicate of Dominion Iron and Steel Company interests headed by James H. Plummer of Toronto. The suggestion had been made that a consolidated company would be better able to resist the intrusion of international trade unionism in Nova Scotia. In return for the proposed merger of the two companies, President Plummer pledged to continue the fight to resist the entry of the United Mine Workers of America and lock out striking members of that organization until they were ready to capitulate on the company's terms.

When General Manager Duggan resigned, he was presented with a gift from the officers of the Provincial Workmen's Association, who had continued to work during the strike. At the ceremony, Duggan congratulated Moffatt and his officers for their loyalty in refusing to join the strike and for the splendid manner in which they had stood behind the company throughout the trouble.

Moffatt replied, "Your affability and condescension were always matters of current comment."

Shortly after Ross and Duggan had announced their retirement, McLachlan withdrew the charges against them; they had served their purpose—President Dan MacDougall had been released from jail to continue the fight for recognition of the UMWA in Nova Scotia.

It was not reported whether Ross and Duggan ever regretted their decision to surrender control of the Dominion Coal Company, but any delusions striking miners may have had that the new president would be more tolerant than his predecessor were soon to be dispelled. Plummer knew he held all the cards. It was only a question of time. Where discrimination, evictions, and firings had not succeeded in bringing striking miners to their knees, hunger, cold, and disease would. Huddled together for warmth, thousands of poor souls lived under the scant protection of canvas as they prepared for the forthcoming ordeal of the long Canadian winter.

The strike dragged on, and as November faded into early December, the weather changed for the worse. The first winter blizzards swept the island as temperatures plummeted to zero and snow and sleet buried the tent towns occupied by hundreds of evicted families.

The first to sicken and die were the children.

The pitiful lack of even the most primitive form of sewage disposal led inevitably to outbreaks of highly contagious disease. The tent colonies proved to be fertile breeding grounds for all forms of bacteria. Cholera swept from one end of Glace Bay to the other. Tens, and then scores of little children died throughout December 1909. In their weakened condition, without proper nutrition and shelter, the very young offered little resistance to virus or disease.

Maurice MacDonald of Glace Bay recalled that the standard treatment for cholera, especially for babies, was lime water. “It was all they had. Many died. It was terrible. Every day, you’d see tiny white coffins being carried away to be buried with their mothers and brothers and sisters weeping as the little ones were lowered into the ground.”

The cholera was followed by scarlet fever and diphtheria. The Glace Bay area was hard hit once again. The doctors did their best but the multitude of cases became a nightmare. Parents had to cope as best they could. Most miners had large families, and the lack of hospital isolation facilities added to overcrowding, greatly increasing the chance of infection. Mrs Margaret MacDonald was one of the distraught, overworked wives and mothers whose children contracted the dread diphtheria.

My daughter Katherine had a very sore throat this day and when I looked inside her mouth she had yellow puss in her throat. Dr McKoyn gave me some pills and told me to keep her throat swabbed.... With diphtheria they had a very high temperature and were dying for water. They usually strangled. I had six kids but I had to try to keep her away from the rest.... In our family, we had twelve cases of scarlet fever as well as the diphtheria. We had had some bread pudding and I blame that. We had six sick kids in the house and everybody broke out in a rash. I wanted Father to keep at his work so I dragged a bed from upstairs and kept them all huddled in one room—sick.... Every day, I'd open up all the doors and windows to get rid of the germs and I'd make them put their heads under the blankets while 1 did so. It was in December.

Mrs MacDonald's belief that the bread pudding had been the culprit was very close to the truth. Consecutive outbreaks of scarlet fever in the area led to an investigation some years later. The milk used in the pudding and distributed in Glace Bay was found to be contaminated.

Dr Kendall of Glace Bay testified before the Duncan Royal Commission in 1925 that there had been no milk inspections or tests prior to 1920. "Anyone could sell milk in Cape Breton so long as it was white!"

Cholera, typhoid, scarlet fever, diphtheria, smallpox, tuberculosis, influenza, and pneumonia—all took their toll during the long, terrible winter of 1909–10. Scarcely a household was left untouched.

Accompanying the sickness and bereavements came physical and verbal abuse. With the strike now entering its seventh month, the new president of Dominion Coal Company, J.H. Plummer, began to step up the pressure. Early in January 1910, using the political clout of the provincial government and its law enforcement agencies, picketing was outlawed at every coal mine affected by the strike, even though it had been lawful to picket for many years. Harry Bousefield, international representative for the UMWA, was arrested and charged with inciting others to stop work. The case was heard in the Superior Court of Nova Scotia in April 1910, and judgement found for the Dominion Coal Company.

Daily now, every UMWA leader was subjected to a barrage of abuse. The Dominion Coal Company spies, under the command of an ex-British army intelligence officer, Captain D.A. Noble, reported every move and every conversation made by union leaders. Company goons hid around every corner, waiting to waylay

UMWA men foolish enough to walk the streets alone. Mrs Jean Robinson, oldest daughter of Jim McLachlan, told how her father collected the union money to pay striking miners each week.

Poppa used to walk all the way to Port Morien from Glace Bay in the wintertime to collect the money. We were all worried because he used to walk alone through the woods and across the sandbar on Big Glace Lake. One night, someone bashed him on the head with a brick, but his bowler hat saved him. That was when we persuaded him to carry a gun for protection. I don't know if he ever learned to fire it, but at least it was something.

There were assaults and there were murders—cold-blooded murders of union organizers and sympathizers. H.J. McCann, later appointed general manager of the Dominion Coal Company, was placed in overall charge of Captain Noble's special police, company police, Thiele and Pinkerton detectives, and a small army of informers, spies, and infiltrators during the strike. Questioned before the Duncan Royal Commission in 1925, regarding a number of murders committed during the 1909 strike, he admitted having heard of the murders but denied coal company complicity. Evidence given to the commission revealed that several UMWA men had been found drowned in Glace Bay; another man named Passerino had been shot and killed in New Waterford; the publisher of a small newspaper in Sydney, the *Vindicator*, had been found with his throat cut in the Windsor Hotel in Sydney (he had written critical articles deploring the conduct of the coal company during the strikes), while one poor man who disappeared mysteriously was believed to have been dismembered and burned in the furnace at the Sterling maintenance yard owned by Dominion Coal Company.

Evidence given by Jim McLachlan to the Duncan Royal Commission told of harassment during the strike.

I couldn't walk down any street in Glace Bay without being followed by a company policeman, and I could not hold a meeting without a policeman attending. I had a French miner come here to speak to our French miners.... Probably fifty miners showed up for the meeting and at least thirty company policemen. I had hired the hall and paid for it and it was mine. I attempted to get them out, great hulking men, but they wouldn't look at me.... They sat with their heads bowed over and refused to leave. I appealed to the town police but they wouldn't interfere. The French miners were terrified they'd lose their jobs by attending the meeting and so they left.... That is why the company police had forced their way in—for the purpose of intimidating French speaking miners.

It was a time to end the strike and end the suffering. Early in 1910, T.L. Lewis, international president of the United Mine Workers of America, wrote formally to J.H. Plummer, the new president of the Dominion Coal Company, requesting a meeting to discuss recognition of the UMWA and ending the crippling strike. Plummer replied on February 8, 1910. His letter, which was arrogant and rude, contained such phrases as:

An interview with the representatives of your association is unnecessary, and in addition might be misunderstood and regarded as recognition of the United Mine Workers of America, which is against our policy.... I can only suggest that when a line of action has been adopted which is found to be mistaken, the really honourable way out is to admit the mistake and start afresh. [Records,UMWA, District 26]

Plummer could afford to be arrogant. Prior to receiving T.L. Lewis' request for a meeting to end the strike, he had completed the arrangements for the merger of his Dominion Iron and Steel Company and his newly acquired Dominion Coal Company. The new consortium would be formally named Dominion Steel Corporation. The merger of steel and coal interests in Cape Breton had now created a monopoly and a united front against organized labour in the province of Nova Scotia.

The press had started its own campaign to end the strike. By the end of February 1910, everyone knew that the strike was lost. McLachlan and MacDougall bitterly resisted any suggestion that the strike be ended, but secretly even these stalwarts recognized the futility of continuing with the struggle. The only question remaining was how to return to work with dignity, without loss of face, and with an assurance there would be no discrimination against UMWA miners.

As if to amplify the knowledge that the strike was over, the troops started to withdraw from Cape Breton. Even the electrified fences were removed from the collieries, leaving PWA men and imported strikebreakers free to come and go.

As the fight entered its final round, Plummer arranged for full-page articles to be inserted in all the local newspapers. Appealing to striking miners to return to work now that Duggan and Ross had left the scene, the articles were cleverly worded to suggest that because Dominion Coal Company was controlled by new management, they were sure to get a new deal.

And then finally, even the District 26 executive council of the United Mine Workers of America was forced to admit defeat. A special meeting of the executive held on April 28, 1910, officially ended the strike and members were ordered to return to work as soon as possible.

The news was received throughout Cape Breton with a profound sense of relief, and then, slowly at first, striking miners began to drift back to the mines. By the end of April, men were returning in the hundreds. For ten long months, they had defied the coal companies, company-appointed magistrates, the courts, company and special police, and the armed forces of the crown. But eventually it had been hunger, privation, and sickness that had beaten them.

They returned to work beaten but proud!

4

World War One and Union Amalgamation

One of the principal reasons for ending the strike was the Dominion Coal Company's solemn assurance through the news media that there would be no discrimination practised against UMWA men returning to work. The company had published a number of incentives to persuade striking miners to return to work, and at first sight, they appeared generous. All former employees involved in the strike would be taken back as soon as possible and without discrimination. They would be given work similar to what they had been doing before the strike, and allowed to return with their families to the company houses they had been forced to vacate. As a final sweetener, the company promised to receive a committee of employees to discuss any grievances that might arise after their return.

But the final act of treachery and deceit in the drama was about to begin. Once the strike was over, the Dominion Coal Company initiated a campaign of revenge against all men reported by company spies to have taken more than a token part in the strike. Hundreds of miners who reported for work in response to the newspaper and union appeals found themselves permanently blacklisted. For months after the strike had ended, trainloads of Cape Breton coal miners left the island never to return. Penniless immigrants and transient strikebreakers replaced them.

All members of the District 26 executive board had been blacklisted back in 1908 before the strike had started. For them there was no future—at least as far as a regular job and a living wage were concerned. The strike had ended, but the persecution and discrimination continued unabated. Those fortunate enough to be allowed to return to the mine after the strike were again given wet, low seams three feet or less in height, where their daily wage, calculated on tonnage mined, was greatly reduced. PWA miners and imported strikebreakers were given the more productive seams, five or more feet in height with a corresponding increase in wages.

In many cases, men returning to work after the strike found their company houses occupied by strikebreakers, forcing them to seek alternate accommodations with friends or relatives. The continued discrimination bred discontent and hatred, providing new, fertile grounds for revolution and future strikes; but many felt the UMWA had died an unnatural death in the province of Nova Scotia and would never return. The coal companies would have been happy if that had been truly the case, but District 26 was still active behind the scenes with a large number of men continuing to pay dues and owe allegiance to the UMWA even though the coal companies automatically removed PWA dues from their pay envelopes each week.

McLachlan and his men had lost the strike and been forced to capitulate on the coal company's terms, but they were by no means defeated. With stoic determination they suffered in silence, gathered their strength, and waited for the next time.

Mrs Kate McLachlan, with her four small children, had arrived in Cape Breton in the summer of 1902 to find her husband again involved in union activities. With deep insight and woman's intuition, she fully realized that union organization for the betterment of his fellow workers would always remain a deep, integral part of his life.

Like many others, McLachlan had been evicted from his company house. After they were evicted, McLachlan moved his family to the nearby town of Glace Bay to take possession of a house owned by his friend Dan MacDougall, who had retired after his blacklisting. The rent was minimal, for McLachlan's only source of income was now the honorarium received from the union for his work as secretary-treasurer for the district. Like the rest of his colleagues in the executive, McLachlan found himself in dire circumstances. Blacklisted throughout the entire Nova Scotia coal mining industry, he realized he must find work of some kind to keep his family from starvation. The family had increased to nine children and he was now forty-one years of age. Work he must, but it would not be in a coal mine.

In 1911, with a generous loan of two hundred dollars provided by rank and file members of the UMWA, McLachlan purchased six acres of virgin land on Steele's Hill overlooking Glace Bay and the stormy Atlantic Ocean. With the help of his family and many well-wishers, a house was built, then a cow byre and milking shed, to transform the holding into a small dairy farm that would support the large McLachlan family. Before her marriage, Mrs Kate McLachlan had belonged to the Greenshield clan. Country living, farming, and market gardening had been bred in her from an early age, and now under her influence and perseverance, Hilltop Farm rapidly took shape. A few cows and horses were purchased plus farm implements to till the virgin ground and Kate achieved her life ambition—a vegetable garden to supplement the family fare.

Their years of travel from one rented home to another were now at an end. Ably assisted by his eldest son, Jim, McLachlan started a milk route delivering milk to miners' families throughout the district. At 5:30, before first light, he could be seen harnessing his favourite mare, Queenie, to the shafts of the milk float before starting his route, and the McLachlan family was now in business—at least in theory. But times were hard, money was scarce, and McLachlan had a big heart. His daughter, Eva Pemberton, recalled the early farm days with a shake of the head and a rueful smile. In an interview, she told this author:

Mother had this little patch of garden and she used to make up baskets of vegetables such as radishes and little white turnips and Poppa and little Jimmy would go around and sell them along with the milk.... The trouble was that they seldom got paid in cash. He had few customers who paid and Poppa was always sorry for people who were poor. Cinnamon, bologna, and rolled oats is what we got paid in. I recall my mother...saying, "If I get another package of spice, I don't know where I'll put it to use."

Milk, vegetables, and money were all given to the poor. Some repaid their debts when times were better but many never did. Jim McLachlan's oldest daughter, Jean Robinson, who still lives in the family home at Steele's Hill, agreed that the milk route was unprofitable due to the generosity of her father but added that his giveaway policy was not confined only to food and money:

I'm telling you he was the funniest man. He had bored coal and stone all his life and he always had this nagging cough and my mother, she was always so careful that he never went out in bad, leaking shoes or without warm clothing. I can hear her just as if it was yesterday saying, "What are you doing with those old shoes on? You'll get your feet soaking." And my Poppa said, "Well, Katie, I'll tell you. This poor fellow, he's getting married, and he came up to me and asked me if I'd give him five dollars so they wouldn't have to walk to church. Well, I stretched it a bit and gave him ten; and the shoes he had on were a disgrace." So my mother said, "So you gave him your good shoes and took his old ones for yourself?" And my Dad said, "Yes, but I was sorry for him because he's just starting out in his married life."

Mother just shook her head and laughed. She was a saint, no two ways about it. She understood his ways and never criticised.

McLachlan's generosity and kindness to fellow miners and their families greatly reduced any profits Mrs Kate McLachlan and her children hoped to raise from Hilltop Farm, but in truth, his interests lay elsewhere. Organization of workers into a strong, militant union remained his primary goal in life. Once farm chores were completed, McLachlan trudged through the fields and woods to attend to union business in Glace Bay, where District 26 of the United Mine Workers of America still maintained an office and continued union business. The problems were many.

Company spies and informers continued to circulate among miners' groups, eavesdropping on all conversations and union meetings and reporting back to their coal company masters. They even managed to infiltrate closed executive meetings of District 26, UMWA, adding their own strident voices to the condemnation of coal companies. Sometimes the infiltration backfired.

Retired miner Dan "Dancer" MacDonald described one such incident, which occurred during a UMWA meeting in Glace Bay in 1911:

In 1911, the UMW of A used to hold little meetings at the local branches in the district—"neighbours dozens" they used to call them. This meeting was held by the Phalen local and they had invited Jim McLachlan to speak to them.... Well, there was this feller, Jack McIntyre, commonly known as "Sprick," who had been employed by the coal company secretly as an informer, and he got hold of a man named Murphy, who was a poor ignorant feller who hadn't even been to school, and another feller named Bryant. They walked to the union meeting together and, on the way, "Sprick" decided to get them drunk so they would do his dirty work, and so he called on a bootlegger, known in Glace Bay as Captain McNeil, and he bought some rum for the two men to drink. "Sprick" was going to wait until McLachlan started to speak and then nudge one of his companions to start trouble and then beat the hell out of him [McLachlan].

Well, it didn't work that way. The secretary of the Phalen local was a man called Beale and, unknown to anyone, he was a Pinkerton detective working undercover for the coal company. He and "Sprick" had never met so they didn't know they were on the same side. Beale got up to speak and he had a quiet polite way of talking, which annoyed Murphy, who was well plastered by this time, and he started to mimic him and use bad language. Beale resented the bad language and told him to shut up and sit down, and of course, this was all that Murphy needed to start a ruckus, so he swaggered up to Beale and before you could say "Boo," Beale had pulled out a gun to defend himself.

Murphy was a great big hulking feller and could easily have beaten him to a pulp. Poor old Bryant, who was a decent feller, jumped in to stop bloodshed, and grabbed the gun, but in the struggle, the gun went off and shot him right between the eyes. And then Beale turned the gun on Murphy and shot him as well.... Beale was eventually charged with both murders but it came out at the trial that he was an undercover man for Dominion Coal Company and the charge was dismissed. The instigator of the whole thing—"Sprick" McIntyre—left town and was never seen again.

Any doubts Nova Scotia miners may have had regarding the

wisdom of replacing the old PWA with the more militant UMWA were soon to be rudely dispelled. After the strike ended, Moffatt and his PWA executive became even more acquiescent in their dealings with the coal companies. Militancy was the farthest thing from their minds.

By 1911, the cost of living had risen almost 23 percent higher than in 1905 when the last contract had been signed, although daily workers had received only a 2 percent increase in wages during the same period. Contract men, the key workers in every mine, received nothing.

The anger and frustration of Nova Scotia miners was indicated by a resolution passed at a mass meeting held in the Dreamland Theatre in Glace Bay, October 30, 1911. The resolution, which was sent to the Minister of Labour in Ottawa, was a protest against a new two-year contract about to be signed by Moffatt (without the consent of the men), effective from December 31, 1911, to December 31, 1913, that would give no increase whatsoever in spite of the spiralling cost of living. Part of the resolution read:

> Whereas this meeting of the employees of Dominion Coal Company believe that the company and John Moffatt and Stephen B. MacNeil have mutual interests and pecuniary advantages to gain by binding the men to wages which are greatly less than those paid to other miners in Canada and altogether inadequate to meet the increasingly high cost of living....

Their protest was ignored. The government did not wish to become involved and the coal company, after forcing striking miners into an ignominious surrender, refused to be concerned with mere protests. Moffatt was firmly in control of the PWA and in full agreement with the coal companies, which maintained that wage increases must wait until the trade price of coal rose. Trade competition had increased—especially from the United States—and to add to their woes, much of the lucrative Quebec market had been lost. But the Dominion Coal Company was still making vast profits for their shareholders in spite of the small recession and could have afforded cost-of-living wage increases without appreciable loss. Their adamant stand on the issue was to be repeated in future years—miners' wages must be governed by profits and markets even though the take-home pay of most of them was far below the poverty level.

How the coal companies must have loved Moffatt, their faithful servant and leader of the Provincial Workmen's Association.

The years from 1911 to 1917 were years of protest, of intimidation, and of labour unrest both in Canada and the United States.

On the Canadian scene there was a change of government; the Conservatives, led by Robert Laird Borden, ousted the Liberals in 1911 to take over the reins of power in Ottawa. The Conservative victory under the austere Prime Minister Borden was to have a profound and far-reaching influence on Canadian labour affairs over the next ten years.

War was declared by Great Britain and her Commonwealth in 1914, and as Canada entered the fray, countless millions of dollars were poured into the manufacture of munitions, weapons, and all the accoutrements of war. Millions of men were used as cannon fodder and coal became king! Almost overnight, Canadian coal mines and their thousands of low-paid miners became vitally important to the war effort. As naval and mercantile vessels steamed in the hundreds into the harbours of Halifax and Sydney to fill their bunkers with coal, and factories all across Canada geared up to full production, government pressure mounted for increased production of coal at all costs. Labour unrest was not to be tolerated. Nothing must stop the flow of coal needed to produce the instruments of war. Strikes were forbidden in vital industries.

Profits increased enormously while miners' wages remained below the poverty level. Coal, which had been sold at the low price of ninety-three cents a ton, was now being shovelled into the bunkers of warships at a new, inflated price of twenty-eight dollars a ton.

The cost of living continued to spiral upwards in Canada with the outbreak of war and bloated profits gathered through the instruments of death and destruction. Between 1905 and 1915, it was estimated the cost of living had increased over 50 percent, yet miners' wages in the province of Nova Scotia had remained virtually unchanged.

It was obvious to all that the Provincial Workmen's Association had become totally ineffectual as a bargaining agent for Nova Scotia miners. If long-overdue wage increases were to be obtained, another, more militant union had to be sought, but where to find such an organization now that the doors had been effectively barred to "foreign" unions?

In spite of McLachlan's untiring efforts, district membership in the United Mine Workers of America had declined gradually since the strike ended in 1910. Loyalty to the "foreign" union remained high, but common sense and practicality persuaded most former members that token membership in an organization without power was not the answer to their urgent problems. Through political pressure, Nova Scotia's coal companies had succeeded in outlawing a foreign union such as the UMWA while actively supporting Moffatt's PWA, which was now denigrated to little more than a company union.

The international reluctantly withdrew the District 26 charter in January 1915, believing it was useless to continue the struggle. The union offices in Glace Bay were closed, the furniture placed in storage, and District 26, UMWA, became merely a hope and a dream for the future.

A new union, the United Mine Workers of Nova Scotia, was formed in 1915. Thousands of miners, disgusted with Moffatt's obsequious dealings with the coal companies, rushed to join, and overnight, the PWA began to founder. After refusing to recognize a "foreign" union such as the United Mine Workers of America because of what was claimed to be foreign ownership and domination, the coal companies were now obliged to recognize the new union with its provincial connotation, which denied any affiliation or contact with foreign international unions.

It was obviously the brainchild of McLachlan.

The leader of the Nova Scotia miners had not been vanquished; behind the scenes he was as active as ever. A fellow Scot, Robert Baxter, was chosen as president of the new union, with a Newfoundlander, Silby Barrett, as vice-president. McLachlan retained his old office of secretary-treasurer.

The following year, 1916, another provincial election was held in Nova Scotia and this time, the Socialist Party's unanimous choice for a candidate was James Bryson McLachlan. But when the votes were counted, McLachlan received only a thousand votes. Nevertheless, as he optimistically pointed out, it was an increase of seven hundred votes for a Socialist candidate in a provincial election, proving that the Socialist Party of Cape Breton was making headway.

Meanwhile, the Dominion Coal Company had become thoroughly alarmed by McLachlan'a vigorous recruiting for the new union. On November 4, 1916, it reopened its contract with the PWA to award an immediate 10-percent wage increase to its members. The small increase was not extended to men who had joined the new union and who were forced to survive on starvation wages as the cost of living rocketed to new heights to match the bloated profits of the company.

The PWA, forced on the defensive by mass desertions to the new union, began to adopt a long overdue militancy in their dealings with the Dominion Coal Company. In a rapid about-face, Moffatt now demanded a 30-percent wage increase for his members, but the company refused even to acknowledge the demand. Instead, they launched a new wave of terror and intimidation. Prominent union members were either suspended for a few days or placed on short time so that their take-home pay was insufficient to feed their families. Other, more subtle forms of coercion were to assign potential troublemakers to non-productive work areas or to disagreeable work.

The familiar program of spying, victimization, and blacklisting was continued. By January 1917, the victimization was stepped up to such an extent that a work stoppage was inevitable. Trouble broke out at the Dominion No. 1 mine when the day shift of miners walked out in protest. Captain Noble and his vicious band of company thugs tried to prevent the walkout, and in the ensuing struggle, several miners were beaten to the ground and hospitalized.

A mass protest meeting was held in the Casino Theatre, Glace Bay, where McLachlan, in a never-to-be-forgotten speech, condemned the Dominion Coal Company for its brutal attack on defenceless miners before calling on both levels of government, provincial and federal, to conduct an investigation into mining conditions in Nova Scotia.

Now forty-eight years of age, McLachlan had lost none of his unique flair and style, which had been evident during the 1909–10 strike. Striding up and down the stage, brown eyes flashing with righteous indignation, McLachlan lashed out at the Dominion Coal Company and its policy of outright discrimination against members of the new United Mine Workers of Nova Scotia. Shaking his fist, he told of many instances of victimization and oppression by the company through the use of hired hoodlums and so-called company police. And as the hundreds of miners roared and cheered his every phrase, it was evident to all that he had once again assumed his rightful place as leader of the Nova Scotia miners.

A resolution condemning the beating of workers without provocation was adopted at the meeting and forwarded to the federal government in Ottawa, but the protest was ignored. The only positive reaction was a slight reduction in the number of company police hired by the Dominion Coal Company. Meanwhile, the victimization continued unabated.

In an effort to settle the wage dispute, both unions, PWA and UMW of Nova Scotia, applied for the services of a Conciliation Board through the Department of Labour in Ottawa. This time, Nova Scotia miners received unexpected support from the federal government, which had previously remained aloof from coal mining disputes in Nova Scotia, claiming they were a matter for the provincial government to resolve. It was now 1917, the third year of the war, and coal had become increasingly important to the war effort. Miners must be kept working at all costs.

Instead of appointing a Conciliation Board, the federal Department of Labour appointed a Royal Commission under the chairmanship of Justice A. Chisholm. Its terms of reference included a complete investigation of the Nova Scotia coal mining industry and a study of the problems arising out of the existence of two different unions representing coal miners. Also included in its terms of reference were the thorny issues of wage increases and cost-of-living clauses to compensate for the spiralling wartime inflation.

The commission's report was released in May 1917. An immediate raise of 12½ percent in wages was recommended and was reluctantly put into effect by the coal companies. The issue of dual unions was resolved by recommending an amalgamation. With the backing of the federal government, leaders of both unions were persuaded that the proposed amalgamation was the only sensible solution—at least for the duration of the war—and in June, delegates from both factions met in Sydney to thrash out a merger.

It was agreed that the new organization, known as the Amalgamated Mine Workers of Nova Scotia, was to remain unaffiliated with any international union—the old bogy of "foreign" unions was still greatly feared by the coal companies—and interim officers were chosen to lay the groundwork and to prepare for an election later in the year. When the vote was counted, Silby Barrett was elected as president, Bob Baxter as vice-president, and J.B. McLachlan as secretary-treasurer. It was significant that neither John Moffatt, grand secretary of the PWA, nor Stephen B. MacNeil, grand master, was chosen for office in the new union. Moffatt announced his retirement from union activities after the names of the new officers were released, although he let it be known he was remaining as a so-called "labour correspondent," working for the Dominion Coal Company in opposition to McLachlan and the new amalgamated union.

Recognition of the new Amalgamated Mine Workers of Nova Scotia was extended immediately by Dominion and the other coal companies operating in Nova Scotia after government pressure was applied. The checkoff system of union dues was to be continued, but now, all such dues were to be forwarded to the headquarters of the new AMW of Nova Scotia.

The coal companies throughout Nova Scotia did not extend recognition to the new union willingly, but at this stage of the war it was quite conceivable that the government would have even considered a cancellation of mining leases to enforce a settlement.

McLachlan was delighted. At long last, the PWA was ousted. It had accomplished a useful function initially, but in recent years, under the stewardship of Moffatt, it had become completely subservient to the coal companies.

The new amalgamated union was to prove its worthiness in a

short space of time. It brought miners from both camps together again and it healed much of the bitterness left over from the 1909–10 strike. In doing so, many advantages were gained for its members. When McLachlan and his trusted lieutenants formed the "Amalgamated," they had intended it only as a short-term, interim measure to eliminate the company-controlled PWA and to lay the groundwork for the reintroduction of the United Mine Workers of America into Nova Scotia. If future events could have been revealed to them, they would no doubt have wished to retain the AMW of Nova Scotia as the coal miners' union. In the years ahead, McLachlan did express regret about not retaining the temporary amalgamated union.

For the present, the new union had brought peace to the troubled coalfields of Nova Scotia—at least for the remainder of the war when coal production was deemed so vital to the nation's war effort.

Events taking place in the United States of America in the spring of 1917 were to have a profound effect on the miners of Nova Scotia. Thomas L. Lewis, international president of the United Mine Workers of America, had been succeeded by John P. White, but when the United States entered the war on the side of the Allies, White was appointed to the War Labor Board for the duration of hostilities. White was then succeeded by Frank J. Hayes, an amiable but ineffectual member of the international board, who was rumoured to be spending more time over a bottle than looking after the affairs of the union. As his vice-president, Hayes selected an "up and coming" member of the union's inner circle, John Llewellyn Lewis, an opportunist reported to be utterly ruthless in his ambitious climb to the top.

John L. Lewis quickly inherited the presidency of the UMWA by assuming all Hayes's duties and responsibilities. Hayes remained as the titular head of the union, but it was Lewis who made all the important decisions without taking the time to sober up his benefactor. Lewis had taken over the reins of power at a critical period in the union's history. The cost of living in the United States had skyrocketed just as in Canada. Profiteers and war manufacturers were making vast profits at the expense of low-paid miners who still worked a twelve-hour day in many districts throughout the United States.

The United Mine Workers of America was the most powerful union in the United States with almost five hundred thousand members, and it was under Lewis' forceful leadership that it began to win its long fight for the eight-hour day and an increase in wages. As in Canada, coal had to be produced at all costs during the war. Federal and state authorities who had previously used all the power and might of their office to quell striking miners and support corrupt coal companies, now backed the union in its demand for better wages and working conditions. With the war, U.S. miners received for the first time in their troubled existence a certain measure of human dignity in addition to the more obvious material benefits. Previously condemned to a serflike existence in the feudal atmosphere of coal towns under the tyrannical dictatorship of local coal barons, U.S. miners now began to regard the United Mine Workers of America as a symbol of hope and security, not merely a collective bargaining unit or a convenient source of strike benefits. The war enabled the union to become strong and to make demands for improved wages and benefits that were quickly settled by the coal companies to keep the peace and avoid catastrophic interruptions to the vital coal supply.

Events that took place after the war ended taxed coal miners' blind faith in the union and its leaders, but rebellions were met with totalitarian rule and the imposition of a dictatorship. John L. Lewis had gained his throne through the fortunate circumstance of war and without being elected through a proper democratic process. Once he had reached the pinnacle of success, he was not about to step down. Opponents of his rule would be eliminated or destroyed by any means, fair or foul, but for the moment, miners belonging to the United Mine Workers of America benefited greatly from his handling of union affairs.

5

The New Waterford Explosion, 1917

The town of New Waterford was born overnight when the directors of the Dominion Coal Company made plans to mine one or more of the rich coal seams in the area. Like Glace Bay and other towns throughout the Sydney coalfield, New Waterford's coal mines were submarine in nature, extending east under the Atlantic Ocean for several miles—some believed all the way to Newfoundland. The town was built on the site of an early settlement—Barrachois Cove—its few inhabitants scratching a meagre living from fishing or working the infertile land.

With a great bustle of activity, workmen imported into the area by the coal company feverishly commenced work on the sinking of slope shafts extending from the shore towards the rich coal seams under the sea—"towards the slope" as miners say. Around the mines, hundreds of simple miners' homes were built to house the multitude of men soon to follow, and a scant six years after the first sod had been turned, the town of New Waterford had come into being in the summer of 1913. The population at the time of incorporation was already in excess of five thousand, the great majority of whom were miners and their families. The town took its name from the Irish county town from which many of the early settlers came. The Irish imprint, which was strong in street and place names, vied with English, Scottish, and Acadian as the chief ingredient of the local population, but within a short space of time, the Irish settlers were rubbing shoulders with newcomers from all parts of Canada, the United States, and from many lands across the sea. Even to this day, the population is a cosmopolitan one where people of Ukrainian, Italian, Jewish, Polish, Greek, Russian, and German origin live in peace and harmony with the descendants of early pioneers of Canadian or New England heritage.

The mayor and his council envisaged a permanent and pleasant community where the people could raise their families in peace and prosperity. The main street was named after the president of the Dominion Coal Company, J.H. Plummer, who had made it all possible.

Unfortunately, the town council did not attach sufficient importance to certain vital facts relating to "their" town, facts that would eventually cloud much of their ambition and hope for the future, for the new town did not really belong to them at all. It was a company town where the company owned everything within its borders: the houses, streets—which, with the exception of the main street, remained unpaved—lighting, water supply, and everything else considered essential to the operation of the town and the well-being of its captive inhabitants. Everything that is, except an adequate sewage treatment and disposal plant, which the company did not consider important in its overall scheme of things. Testimony given by several local doctors to the Duncan Royal Commission of 1925 condemned this lack of sewage treatment as the direct cause of serious epidemics throughout the area and the loss of hundreds of lives—mostly young children. But sewage treatment represented a nonproductive expenditure of precious capital. Coal was the thing to be considered above all else. Coal, mined and brought to the surface as cheaply as possible.

Two slope mines, No. 12 and No. 14, were sunk at New Waterford. (Although the Dominion Coal Company sank a total of twenty-six mines throughout the Sydney coalfield, there was never a No. 13. Miners are hard-working, fearless individuals but they are also notoriously superstitious, due perhaps to the very nature of their occupation, which is fraught with danger and disaster, often unpredictable.) The two mines, driven towards the deep, were to harvest the rich Victoria seam. Only one mile apart, each mine was allotted one and three-quarter miles of sea frontage plus an unspecified submarine area where the seam wove back and forth off the coast of Cape Breton.

When choosing the Barrachois Cove area as a site for their new collieries, the Dominion Coal Company had been influenced by the results of an offshore survey it had conducted throughout the Sydney coalfield. Drillings had confirmed that the richest deposits lay under the ocean floor, with a geological slope extending steeply from the shore to a point many miles out at sea. The company's engineers and surveyors made plans to construct the two collieries as close to the shore as possible to provide for an economical mining operation.

The building of a coal mine is a far more complicated process than most laymen realize. Above ground, only about twenty acres are usually required to contain the many buildings and workshops associated with the mine, but below ground, the workings creep outward like the trunk, branches, and twigs of a large tree. The underground excavations of even a moderate-sized mine can cover an area of from twelve to fourteen square miles, but the workings are not allowed to spread spasmodically as time passes. Every inch of the mine, from top to bottom, is preplanned and designed by a skilled team of engineers, geologists, and surveyors.

Before 1920, there were only four types of coal mining operation in North America: the strip mine, where the topsoil is removed to uncover coal deposits lying close to the surface; the drift mine, where a tunnel is driven horizontally into the side of a hill; the shaft mine, where a vertical shaft is sunk to recover coal that lies at great depth; and the slope mine, where a shaft is driven at an angle to the surface corresponding to the geological slope of the coal seam.

Cape Breton's submarine coal seams, which descend steeply from the shore towards the ocean, are admirably suited to slope mine operation, although the angle of descent of the main shaft, known as the main deep, is often a staggering 30 percent or more from the horizontal.

The main slope shaft for each of the two collieries in New Waterford was sunk close to the shores of the Atlantic Ocean to follow rich coal seams sloping towards the deep and under the ocean. Two other slope shafts, known as air courses or back deeps, were sunk at the same time, one on each side of the main deep.

A huge ventilation fan mounted on one of the back deep shafts forced great volumes of air down through all the workings of the mine, where it was evenly distributed using a variety of devices known as trapper doors, brattices, stoppages, split level dividers, underpasses, overpasses, balance tunnels, and lower balance tunnels. The returned air was allowed to escape into the atmosphere through the other back deep shaft. The ventilation served a dual purpose in that it provided fresh air for miners to breathe deep in the workings of the mine, while removing dangerous noxious and explosive gases that seeped continually into the mine workings from roof and coal face.

Descending into the mine at vertical intervals of one thousand feet, levels or landings were dug at right angles to the slope shafts to provide roadways for mined coal to be hauled in coal boxes for long distances—sometimes as far as two miles—to the main deep, where they were attached to an endless steel rope for haulage to the surface. Other tunnels, known as balance tunnels or lower balance tunnels, were dug parallel to each landing to provide a return path for air circulation, and each landing was then intersected every twelve hundred feet by headway tunnels sloping back uphill to connect with the next landing above and at an angle corresponding to that of the slope shaft, which carried coal to the surface. Back headway tunnels were also dug to provide a return path for air circulation.

Each landing, plus all its auxiliary tunnels and rooms, was divided into two sections—one on each side of the main deep haulageway for easy identification. As the main deep at each New Waterford mine had been sunk in a north-south direction, the divided landings were known as the east or west sections, with each section containing a total of sixty rooms numbered upwards in relation to their distance from the landing. On each side of the headway tunnels, "rooms" were then dug at intervals of fifty feet. Each room, which measured 600 feet by 25 feet, was divided into two equal portions by a cross-cut tunnel. The divided portions of each room were likewise known as the east or west rooms.

Every experienced miner was familiar with all areas of a mine. At the commencement of a shift, once given a specific work assignment—for example, in number one landing east, number one headway, number one room east—a miner could proceed without delay to his place of work, understanding the directions as plainly as a city dweller when directed to Sixth Avenue and Fifty-sixth Street.

Above ground, the bankhead was the largest and most important of the many buildings scattered throughout the compound. Three storeys high, it towered above all the rest. Coal boxes brought to the surface by an underground haulage winch and endless steel rope were pulled to the top floor of the bankhead to be checked and weighed. A boy then disconnected each coal box from the rope before "spragging" it to a halt on the weighing machine, where the amount of coal was weighed and credited to the miners whose tally identified the box and its contents.

Two checkweighmen, one company-appointed and one union-appointed, were responsible for crediting the amount of coal to a miner's weekly wage. The presence of a union-appointed checkweighman was a custom established in Britain in the nineteenth century. Until that time unorganized miners had been forced to accept falsified figures submitted by the company checkweighman, thereby adding greatly to the coal company's profits at the expense of miners. This odious practice was largely eliminated by the use of a union-appointed checkweighman, whose wages were paid by the men. Obviously, the man chosen for this much envied position was a person universally respected by his peers for honesty and integrity.

After weighing, the coal box was pushed onto the tipple, where a mechanical device turned the box upside down to empty its contents onto screens in the room below; it then moved swiftly past an army of small boys who scrambled madly to separate coal from stone and shale. The screens, which moved along with a deafening clanking noise, the dimly lit room and the choking clouds of coal dust combined to paint a terrible, heart-rending picture of toil and suffering. For ten hours each day, six days each week, these little children slaved under intolerable conditions to earn a few pennies a day screening coal. Many were maimed.

From the screening room the coal was poured down through chutes into rail cars to be shipped to distant points in Quebec, the United States, or overseas.

Adjacent to the bankhead was the lamphouse, where the oncoming shift of miners received their safety lamps. Prior to the introduction of the safety lamp, miners used open-flame lights mounted on their caps. Shaped like a small teapot and filled with whale oil, they provided light from a wick protruding from the spout. Many mine disasters had resulted earlier from the use of these open-flame lights. The safety lamp also burned oil, but the wick and flame were surrounded by a protective gauze cylinder of fine wire mesh to prevent the heat of the flame from igniting the explosive gases in the atmosphere. It was this very property that enabled miners and inspectors to use the safety lamp as a detector of the dreaded firedamp gas—a mixture of methane gas and air formed by the decaying action over millions of years of the wood and vegetable matter compressed into coal. By raising the safety lamp to the roof, the presence of gas could be detected by the appearance of a pale blue flame surrounding the wick. After long experience, the amount of gas could be estimated and the work area evacuated without delay. All safety lamps handed to a shift of miners first had to be thoroughly checked by a mine deputy working under the authority of an overman.

Each section of mine was supervised by an overman and his deputy. Before miners were allowed to enter a section of the mine at the commencement of a shift, a deputy—often known as a mine examiner—was responsible for testing for the presence of gas or other adverse conditions. An inspection report was then completed, and signed by the underground manager and overman to acknowledge conditions in that particular section of the mine prior to the commencement of the next shift. Once these officials had read and signed the reports, the decision to send men into a particular section then became their sole responsibility.

Each of the officials, underground managers, overmen, and mine deputies, had been certified by the Department of Mines only after many years of intensive study and experience followed by rigid examinations. From the miners' point of view, there had to be great trust in a mine examiner and his inspections prior to their entry into a particular section of the mine. When a room or roadway had been tested, written instructions were chalked in conspicuous places to direct an oncoming shift to correct adverse conditions such as high levels of gas or poor support of a shifting roof. In many cases, the high levels of gas were due to inadequate ventilation. As the coal face advanced each day, increased ventilation was provided by a number of devices such as split level dividers, stoppages, overpasses and underpasses, and brattices. The latter was a length of sacking tarred heavily on one side and secured with cleats to the top and bottom of the roof-supporting pit props to provide an airtight channel between pit props and ribs (walls) of the mine workings.

The safe operation of a coal mine depended to a great extent on the removal of dangerous gases by forced ventilation, but even under the most favourable conditions, there was never enough air to breathe or to remove obnoxious gases—especially in the lower levels of the mine, thousands of feet beneath the bed of the Atlantic Ocean. In wartime, safety was considered secondary in importance to increased production and profits. Requests for additional brattices to keep pace with increased production and a rapidly advancing coal face were often denied and some mine examiners and underground managers were forced to stifle their consciences in the name of economy and expediency—the two greatest enemies of the coal miner.

In 1917, handpick mining was still practised in Cape Breton coal mines. Few mines were even equipped with pneumatic drills or undercutting machines, which are considered standard equipment in modern mines. Pit ponies and human labour were used for underground haulage with young boys employed as drivers. Long "trips" of coal boxes were pulled by the ponies on narrow-gauge rails for long distances underground before hooking them onto the main deep haulage system to be brought to the surface.

One of the most backbreaking jobs performed by early coal

miners was the pushing of fully loaded boxes of coal from the coal face to the nearest headway, where it could be hitched onto a horse-drawn trip. Each coal box weighed an awesome 2,240 pounds! This punishing and time-consuming labour was totally unsuited to humans, leaving them exhausted and twisted in body, each working day of their lives.

Long before dawn, miners working the day shift left their company houses to report for work at pitheads all across Cape Breton. Miners' wives rose at 4:30 to boil the inevitable porridge and prepare lunch pails. If breakfast was a frugal meal, lunch was little better. In 1917, the third year of the war, miners' wages were still far beneath the poverty level. Many a miner reporting for work at the pithead and many a child attending school had to stave off pangs of hunger with a lard sandwich consisting of two pieces of bread heavily larded and soaked in water to give it bulk! Exhausting though their work was, many miners subsisted on a lard sandwich and a can of water or cold tea before staggering home at the end of a twelve-hour shift. Old miners such as Tom Lamey recalled the early days of handpick mining in New Waterford:

> I was fifty years in the mines, started in 1910. Then it was just handpicks. A miner in those days took three sharp picks on his back. He had a rope and a lunch pail and a tea can hanging from his belt.... I walked two miles to work at five in the morning through the woods and the same in the evening after I left work, even through snow drifts. That's the way it was in those days. If you didn't want to walk, well, you didn't get paid. We were paid by the yard of coal you dug, and in those days there was no limit to the number of hours you worked. I started at a dollar-sixty a day, but a trapper boy only got a dollar for his ten hours.

Boys nine years of age were often forced by family circumstances to leave school to work in the mines in a variety of jobs, but those chosen to be trapper boys, opening and closing ventilation doors to allow horses and trips of coal cars to pass through, had an especially nerve-wracking task. For ten long hours each day or night, they would be left alone in the awful blackness of the mine with only the rats for company and the frightening hiss of escaping gas and the creaking and groaning of roof props the only sounds to break the monotony. Miner Gordon MacGregor, former superintendent of mines in the Glace Bay area, told how the responsibility fell on the shoulders of the oldest boy in a family to be the breadwinner when the father became ill or died:

> The young boys were only nine years of age when they started work in the mines. They were given a rough time. The initiation on their first day would be to take all their clothes off and then the older boys would grease them all over. Poor little guys! I had a cousin, Peter, whose father died when he was only nine. Peter became the breadwinner and had to go into the pit. He was so small. They lived on top of a hill and there was a graveyard in between the pit and his home. He was so young that when he had to leave early in the mornings before it was light, his mother would have to take his hand to lead him through the graveyard. He was brave enough to go down the pit but he wouldn't go through the graveyard alone!

They went to work when it was dark, and they came home when it was dark. Sunday was the only blessed day when they could see the blue sky and feel the healing warmth of the sun. Their ancestors had left their homeland to escape from a life of serfdom, but in Canada, boys of nine were exploited just as badly if not worse.

It was a time when handpick mining was regarded as a science, a craft, a skilled trade where old miners took great pride in their handiwork, where muscle and brawn took the place of machines not yet developed, and where miners were paid only for each ton of coal mined from the coal face, not for the ever-present shale and dirt surrounding it, nor for the hours spent crawling or walking to or from the coal face.

Latter-day miners testify to the skill of the old-time miners whenever they discover an example of their craft in abandoned workings. Straight and true as a die, the ribs of landings and headways appear to have been carved out by sophisticated machinery rather than by painstaking manual labour. They were true craftsmen, proud of their handiwork and skills.

A room was worked by one coal face miner and his "buttie" (mate). As contract miners they were regarded as independent contractors working within the company's framework and under its safety rules and regulations. They were paid by results, not for the number of hours worked, and as contract miners were obliged to purchase their own tools and explosives. They worked without supervision and could return to the surface if and when it suited them, but when rates were low, a twelve- or even a fourteen-hour day was the rule rather than the exception.

Coal mining was accomplished in each room by tumbling the coal face after cutting or digging along the base. In 1917, the undercut had to be done laboriously by hand. One typical old handpick miner, Tius Tutty, told *Cape Breton's Magazine* how he used to dig such an undercut using a pick:

> You'd lay on your side after putting a little soft coal under your shoulder...and you'd get in so far. Course when you had the undercut opening out wider, you'd be on your knees. Then you'd get so far in, you'd have to get down on your side again, underneath the wall of coal, picking away.... You'd go in about five feet I guess, just as far as you could reach in. Then you'd back out, bore and shoot...blow it all down. That was in the rooms. In pillars you had to sprag your coal face. If you were mining what is called "pillar" work, there was a room on both sides of you and the pillar was the coal remaining after the two rooms had been mined. When you were undercutting the pillar, you'd have to sprag it when you were working the undercut.... The sprag was made of wood. You mined on a bench of coal so high. You'd dig a hole in that and put your sprag in and wedge in over it so it wouldn't move while you were underneath.

The operation related in simple terms such as these does little to describe the danger involved in digging an undercut by hand. Lying on one's side and swinging a pick to remove the coal supporting thousands of feet of dirt and rock above the undercut requires a great deal of courage in addition to skill and experience.

The undercut completed satisfactorily, the next step in the operation was to drill holes across the coal face and near the roof to pack with explosive charges. Handpick miners had to drill these holes laboriously by hand, using an auger, and the holes had to be drilled to the same depth as the undercut—no more, no less. Tius Tutty described the drilling and blowing of the coal face:

> You had this little thing called a breast auger for boring the charge

holes.... You'd bore it and then fill it with powder, shoot it yourself. You didn't have to call a shot firer in those days...not when they had the handpick mining. You did it yourself.... You had all loose powder then, not prepared charges like now.

The robbing of pillars in room and pillar work was even more dangerous. As each room was advanced across a coal face twenty-five feet wide, a pillar of coal was left between each pair of rooms to support the roof, but once a room had been worked out, miners had to start "retreating" or robbing the pillars to obtain as much coal as possible before the roof collapsed. Robbing the pillars called for cool nerves and long experience. The more the pillar was robbed, the weaker the roof became. As the roof weakened, it began to "work" as the strata began to shift. Pit props began to groan and splinter as they were forced to take over support of the roof from the weakened pillar, but it became a matter of professional pride among old handpick miners to rob as much coal as possible from the pillar before the roof collapsed. They worked calmly under conditions that would have sent a novice fleeing to the surface in terror; but as they worked, they became attuned to the sounds of the mine as pit props groaned and creaked in their effort to support the roof above their heads. A subtle shift in the noise ratio, or a sudden crack followed by the seeping of finely ground stone from the roof, and they knew it was time to leave! Added to the physical senses of sound and sight, they learned to take heed of a nagging sixth sense urging them to vacate immediately, even though all appeared normal. Duncan Currie of Glace Bay described the robbing experience in room and pillar work as a test of nerves and experience:

An inexperienced man would get the hell out of there as soon as the roof started working and groaning, but the old miner would know exactly when to quit. Timbers would begin to splinter and then fine stone dust would start to trickle down from all the cracks in the roof as tremendous forces ground the stone to powder. That was the time to get out, but before we left, we'd take out the rails and the coal boxes to leave the place just as we had found it.

Experience and skill were one thing, a keenly developed sixth sense was another, but there was always the human factor to be taken into consideration, and there was always the unpredictable element remaining hidden and undetected, ready to strike without warning, to kill, maim, burn, and destroy.

From the outset, No. 12 mine at New Waterford was reported to be extremely wet and gassy—hazardous working conditions where the utmost caution would have to be taken to prevent accidents or explosions or even disaster on a large scale.

Duncan Currie's graphic description of a mine explosion says it all:

> An explosion, fire and gas, is what a miner fears most. There is nothing worse than gas. Once a gas explosion occurs in a mine, a tremendous force is developed which sweeps everything movable from its path. It just sweeps through the whole section or even down to other levels. It's just like a ball of fire. A man can't live after an explosion unless they can get an air line in there. The carbon monoxide is deadly.

The force of the explosion confined within the narrow tunnels of the mine sweeps everything from its path; steel rail lines curl up like spaghetti; men's bodies are torn to shreds; and others die with their lungs burned out as the tremendous fireball roars through the workings.

The explosion that caused the deaths of sixty-five men and boys occurred in the Dominion Coal Company's No. 12 colliery at New Waterford at seven-thirty on the morning of Wednesday, July 25, 1917.

Henry MacKay, who at the time of the explosion was only fourteen years of age, was employed in the No. 12 mine as a horse driver. He told *Cape Breton's Magazine*:

> I was standing on No. 8 landing when the explosion happened.... I had the shafts over my shoulder and then there was a breeze of wind came out of the level.... Oh it was carrying everything before it. Lumps of coal were flying and dust, you couldn't see anything. Pieces of wood flying. It knocked me and the horse down.... But I never thought it was an explosion. I was only a kid. I got up out of there. When I got back up, the overman said—"Listen, boy, there's been an explosion. How about going

back in after those loaders?" There were four. So I took one box in and I got the loaders in the box and we started back. Got out at the landing. They jumped out of the box and took off. I took the shafts off the horse and started to walk. I didn't get far in the dark. From No. 7 landing up to No. 2...the stables were on No. 2, I walked all that way in the dark. Of course I had ahold of the horse's tail.... The rakes were at No. 2 with the rescue Draegermen on. They had canaries in cages and had their masks on, but they wouldn't go down where I had come through the smoke.... When I got up in the fresh air, there were thousands of people around. They had everything fenced off.... I lay down and blacked out. Somebody found me and took me home. I thought there'd be nobody killed, being as I made it, but when they brought my father home at two o'clock in the morning, my mother woke me. Told me my father had been killed. He was blamed for firing the shot that set off the explosion but it wasn't his fault.

The Sydney *Post* of July 26, 1917, proclaimed the disaster the worst in Cape Breton's mining history:

The worst explosion in the history of the Cape Breton coalfields occurred at 7:30 yesterday morning in the No. 12 colliery of the New Waterford district.... The dead include 30 native miners, 22 Newfoundlanders and 10 foreigners. About 270 men were in the mine at the time, and colliery officials express surprise that the loss of life was not greater.... The crowd had grouped themselves, discussing the disaster in low tones, and watching with worried, strained faces the wagons, ambulances and teams as they passed to and fro from the pithead.... The rescue party worked unceasingly and no greater deeds of heroism have been or will ever be written than some that were enacted at New Waterford yesterday.... They came across bodies which were totally dismembered by the force of the explosion. Nearly a dozen were lying quite still, evidently from firedamp. Then came groups of twos and threes and here and there a lonely one. The gruesome scenes at the bottom of the slope shaft cannot be described. They were not brought to the surface until midnight when they were placed in caskets.

Late at night, the company warehouse at the pithead was used as a temporary morgue where the dreadful task of identification and embalming was carried out before relatives were allowed to view the remains of their loved ones. Everywhere white-faced and weeping women huddled in forlorn groups, while throughout the town of New Waterford, drawn window blinds and crepe-hung doors spoke vividly of the disaster.

The following day, a special train left New Waterford carrying the bodies of eighteen miners in hastily constructed coffins. At Sydney, they were loaded aboard the steamer *Kyle* to be taken home to mourning widows and children in Newfoundland. The funerals in New Waterford were described in all their tragic detail by the Sydney *Post* on July 29, 1917.

> At the Catholic church in the morning, a small inkling could be seen of the cosmopolitan nature of the town of New Waterford when the relatives of the dead miners entered the church. First the Italian women with their black mantilla lace; then the Russians with their burning candles; the Belgians with snowy "kerchiefs" and coloured shawls; English, Scottish and Irish, and even the Jewish element was represented in the congregation, all honouring the dead.... A pathetic incident was the burial of the foreigners who had no relatives here at all. All were buried in one grave and around it the people gathered, not curiously, but as if to take away the lonely feeling.

Even before the funeral, ugly rumours began to circulate throughout the mining communities of Cape Breton that Dominion Coal Company had been criminally negligent in its disregard for safety and proper ventilation in the No. 12 mine. Groups of angry men gathered on every street corner in New Waterford and Glace Bay, demanding action to bring those responsible to account for their negligence.

The inquest opened on July 31 with many witnesses giving evidence for and against the company. Deputy mine examiners testified that, in their opinion, the amount of gas in the mine prior to the explosion was not excessive or higher than usual. When called, the ventilation boss for the No. 12 mine stated that the mine was well ventilated and that there had been no skimping of the number of brattices supplied. He refused to believe that air courses had collapsed, forcing men to crawl over the top of them to reach their place of work, in spite of evidence to the contrary.

John Cameron, a machine runner, testified that the ventilation in the mine was so bad on occasion that his lamp gave very poor light and he had had to go home because of the poor air supply. He had asked for brattices and had been refused.

Witness after witness corroborated Cameron's charge that company officials had allowed air courses to collapse and that they had been refused brattices when requested.

Angus MacDonald, the mine manager, testified that he had not been instructed to keep down expenses at the mine, and that to his knowledge, brattices had never been refused to any man. The mine was admittedly a gassy mine, but no more so than other mines.

There was so much testimony given of a conflicting nature that the coroner and jury were anxious to have the provincial government's Deputy Inspector of Mines give evidence, but this gentleman refused to do so. The jury brought in a verdict that placed the blame squarely at the door of the Dominion Coal Company and its officials. They stated that gross irregularity of mining had been largely responsible for the retention of gas, thereby causing the explosion that had resulted in the death of the men, and found the officials guilty. They further castigated the Deputy Inspector of Mines for refusing to testify.

After the inquest, demands were made for a Commission of Enquiry to be set up by the provincial Department of Mines. Public outrage and threats of legal action made by J.B. McLachlan and the newly formed Amalgamated Mine Workers of Nova Scotia forced the provincial government to accede to the demands, and Hiram Donkin, Inspector of Mines, was ordered to make a full investigation of the disaster and submit a report to the Honourable E.H. Armstrong, Commissioner of Public Works and Mines in the province of Nova Scotia. (At a later date, Armstrong became premier of the province.)

Assisting in the investigation were union appointees Silby Barrett, Robert Baxter, Alexander Campbell, and William J. McKay. Independent members of the commission included Thomas J. Brown, general superintendent of the Nova Scotia Steel and Coal Company, and George B. Burchell, general manager of the Bras d'Or Coal Company. Appearing for Dominion Coal Company were Alexander McDonald, district superintendent, and Alfred J. Tonge, General Superintendent of Mines. Mining engineer Norman McKenzie was called to give a technical report, while Neil A. Nicholson, Deputy Inspector of Mines for the district, acted for the government.

Witnesses testified that a searching examination had revealed that the explosion had occurred in a cross cut tunnel partly driven between Rooms 3 and 4 on the east side of Long Balance No. 2 on Landing No. 6. The cross cut was found to be undercut all the way across the coal face to a depth of six feet. Two wall holes were found bored, one near each rib; the holes were well placed with sufficient clearance from wall and roof and of a depth corresponding to the depth of the undercut. The shot on the east rib had been loaded and fired but had not brought down the coal as expected.

Everything appeared normal in regard to the depth of the undercut and the placement of the explosive charges, except that one charge appeared to have misfired. When the shot hole was opened up, it was found that the solid coal at the back of the coal face had been affected by the explosive charge, which had fired backwards into a cleavage or fault that had acted as a pocket for escaping gas. The explosive power had escaped as flame down the unsuspected cleavage and out into the mine to cause a massive gas or dust explosion. In an instant, the searing blast had roared up Long Balance No. 2 and in and out of Landing No. 6, killing and dismembering men and beasts alike.

The investigation into the root cause of the explosion had been most meticulous, but no evidence was offered regarding the shortcomings in the ventilation system and the lack of adequate brattices, which could have contributed to the explosion. The provincially appointed Deputy Inspector of Mines for the New Waterford area, Michael McIntosh, who had declined to give evidence during the inquest, was ordered to appear before the commission. Under oath, he stated he had made his last visit of inspection to No. 12 mine on the day prior to the disaster. He had gone down to No. 1 Balance on Landing No. 1 eight west, but was unable to complete his examination because he had felt sick and had to return to the surface. Inspector McIntosh then went on to make the extraordinary statement that while in the mine, he did not observe any dangerous quantity of gas or find defective ventilation. He did add, however, that he could not say that the mine on that occasion was safe and in a workable condition owing to his not finishing the examination because he was ill.

The commission chairman did not press the point or ask the nature of his illness or if his indisposition had been caused by gas.

The commission's report made recommendations for ensuring better ventilation in future, but it was a bland document that laid no blame for the disaster on company or employees in spite of overwhelming evidence to the contrary.

Several witnesses had told of the lack of brattices to keep up with the advancing coal face and the refusal of officials to supply them when requested. One witness had even told of a collapsed airway where the roof had fallen in weeks before and blocked off the vital air supply. A report had been made but nothing had been done to correct the situation. Cost of production was the main factor. Profits and bloated profiteering during the war were deemed more important than safety.

J.B. McLachlan, secretary-treasurer of the Amalgamated Mine Workers of Nova Scotia, appeared on the final day of the commission's hearings. Grim-faced and tight-lipped, he listened as the majority members worded their final conclusions. It had been a whitewash, just as he had feared it would be. Sixty-five men and boys had perished—most of them family men with large broods of children to support. The provincial government had chosen the commission with care and foresight. With the exception of mining engineer McKenzie and the four union appointees, the members had all been top executives of Cape Breton coal companies or provincial employees.

Immediately following the commission's report, McLachlan, Barrett, and Baxter held a meeting of the union executive to determine their next course of action. The minority report submitted by the union members of the commission differed radically from the published findings. Stating that the Dominion Coal Company had been guilty of culpable and criminal neglect in its safety practices, they demanded action be taken against the company and its senior officials.

Their only recourse now was through the courts. The indictment was very long and technically worded. The company was charged with negligence of duty and disregard of mining laws and regulations, thereby causing the death of sixty-five employees. McLachlan attempted to lay charges of murder against Dominion and its top officials, but was advised by E. MacKay (counsel representing the union) that a corporation could not be charged with murder because there was no way under the laws of the land that such a charge could be laid no matter how justifiable. The company was then charged with causing grievous bodily harm instead of murder. The indictment also charged Alex MacEachern, Dominion superintendent for the New Waterford area, Angus R. MacDonald, manager of No. 12 colliery, and Michael McIntosh, provincial Deputy Inspector of Mines for the New Waterford area.

The case was adjourned until February 1918 when the Supreme Court of Nova Scotia sat in Sydney, but the case was again remanded when the crown attorney, representing the province of Nova Scotia, complained he had not had sufficient time to prepare the case. Three separate times this excuse was offered by the crown to avoid the issue, and then finally the trial was held on October 28, 1918, one year and three months after the disaster. A newly appointed supreme court judge, Justice Mellish, presided.

After hearing all the evidence, most of it damning and proving conclusively that the Dominion Coal Company had shown criminal negligence in its operation of No. 12 mine prior to the disaster, Judge Mellish directed the jury to bring in a verdict of *Not Guilty* against the company, because he did not think there was sufficient evidence to warrant their consideration.

On the same day, Michael McIntosh, the provincial mine inspector for the New Waterford area, who had been charged with manslaughter for having illegally permitted No. 12 colliery to be operated in an improper and negligent manner, was also found *Not Guilty* after the crown counsel had stated he had no evidence to submit.

Angus R. MacDonald and Alex MacEachern were dismissed

in like manner after the crown counsel said he had no evidence to submit.

A monument was erected in New Waterford, through public subscription, to the memory of the sixty-five men and boys killed. The case was closed. Perhaps the monument should have been erected as a symbol of futility. The *cause célèbre* had proved to be just one more instance of Dominion Coal Company's political ties with the provincial government of Nova Scotia. The coal company got off scot-free, but the total rejection and dismissal of the serious charges only served to strengthen miners' resolve in their continuing battle with Dominion Coal Company.

J.S. Woodsworth, M.P. for Winnipeg Centre, and leader of the Labour Party of Canada, made reference to the appointment of Justice Mellish to the Supreme Court of Nova Scotia in a protest to the House of Commons in Ottawa, March 4, 1924:

> Mr Justice Mellish received his appointment in a manner which makes him an outstanding corporationist on the bench. His appointment was made shortly after the criminal trial of the Dominion Coal Company and its officials for causing the New Waterford explosion on July 25th, 1917.... The then Mr Mellish was a member of the firm of "McInnis, Mellish, Fulton and Kenny" of Halifax, Nova Scotia. This firm was the chief solicitors for Dominion Coal Company and Mr Mellish appeared in court on all their actions.... The office of McInnis and Mellish was preparing the case for the companies involved. Shortly before the trial, Mr Mellish received his appointment as Judge of the Supreme Court of Nova Scotia. His first case was the New Waterford explosion case in Sydney, the defence of which had been prepared for the company and its officials. Mr Hector McInnis, senior partner in the law firm, being chief counsel for the defence during the trial in Sydney.

Prior to his address, Mr Woodsworth had emphasized that he was not for one moment accusing the said judge of wilfully prostituting his office, but that a man who had for many years been financially interested in certain concerns might find it very, very hard to dissociate himself from points of view that he would almost inevitably have acquired.

Woodsworth could have extended his criticism to the crown

attorney, W.F. (Billy) Carroll, who had not attempted to press criminal charges against the Dominion Coal Company in spite of overwhelming evidence proving guilt. (Carroll had been employed as a lawyer for the Dominion Coal Company during the 1909 strike and had been instrumental in obtaining writs for the eviction of striking miners' families from their company homes.)

McLachlan left the courtroom a sadder and wiser man. After the pitiful charade he had witnessed, he now realized the full extent of the company's influence on the courts and laws of the land. The distortion of justice had reinforced his belief that union activity had to be accompanied by political representation if workers' just grievances were to be heard and corrected. He determined to enter the political arena as a labour candidate in any future provincial or federal election.

The final word in the New Waterford disaster should come not from the judge, but from McLachlan. His daughter Eva Pemberton, then aged twelve, arrived home from school the day following the disaster to find her father in distress:

> We didn't know Poppa had been one of the volunteers who had entered the mine after the explosion in a rescue attempt. He had lost a relative whose name is still on the monument at New Waterford. He brought his body out of the mine and then returned home. He was all red in the face and gasping for breath after the gas, and his clothes smelled just awful. I asked him what the smell was, and I recall he just looked at me so sorrowfully and said, "That smell, Eva, is Death for Profits!"

6

Labour Battles and Postwar Depression

The year 1917 brought a great deal of labour unrest and turbulence. The number of strikes increased dramatically in spite of the war and the terrible sacrifices made by hundreds of thousands of young Canadian men. Vast fortunes were being made by unscrupulous employers who saw the war as a God-given opportunity to make bloated profits at the expense of poorly paid workers. The government of Canada saw the strikes as treason, but was forced to accede to workers' demands to prevent any disastrous interruption of vital war supplies.

In Canada, the Independent Labour Party, an early socialist party, was launched with the support of the powerful Trades and Labour Congress, which controlled almost every trade union in Canada. McLachlan's fervent belief in political representation for workers had been taken up by others since the disastrous coal strike in 1909. The blatant manipulation of provincial and federal governments by the Nova Scotia coal companies during the strike had undoubtedly influenced the TLC delegates in their decision to add support to a workers' party.

With the news of the new Federal Labour Party, McLachlan hastened to form a provincial wing in Nova Scotia, and shortly after, when the Independent Labour Party of Nova Scotia was formed, two candidates were chosen to contest ridings in Cape Breton in a federal election to be held later the same year. But when votes were counted, both Federal Labour candidates had been soundly beaten. The reigning Conservative Party under Prime

Minister Robert Laird Borden triumphed at the polls and the war dragged on interminably.

In the United States, a revolutionary syndicalist association known as the Industrial Workers of the World was making great strides in its crusade to organize the millions of unskilled workers—the despised migratory and transient workers, the labouring classes—previously ignored by the craft-conscious American Federation of Labor. The IWW clashed with the American Federation of Labor and its irascible president, Samuel Gompers, longtime foe of socialism and left-wing unionists. With the enthusiastic support of the giant United Mine Workers of America, Gompers and the AFL hastened to introduce rules forbidding what was termed "dual unionism" by any union or district of a union affiliated with the American Federation of Labor.

With the entry of the United States into the war in 1917, a further clash was inevitable between the IWW and government. For years the IWW had preached that a struggle between classes was inevitable and that workers' only hope of salvation lay in revolution and the overthrow of capitalist-controlled government and capitalism. With the call-up of millions of young Americans to fight a war overseas, the IWW now began to preach pacifism and to urge workers to resist any form of military service.

Accusations of sedition and treason against the IWW were suddenly reinforced by the news in October 1917 of a bloody revolution in far-off Russia and the overthrow of the monarchy. With more power now in the hands of the Russian working classes, the news generated great alarm both in Canada and the United States. Fearing a socialist uprising of a similar nature, both countries rushed to introduce severe repressive measures against working-class movements and socialist organizations, just as the British government had done after the French and American revolutions during the eighteenth century.

Overnight, the Industrial Workers of the World was outlawed in a number of states, and many of its leaders thrown into jail on trumped-up charges of sedition and pacifism.

On April 26, 1918, workers' discontent in Canada was further inflamed by the visit of Samuel Gompers to Ottawa, where he was welcomed by a joint session of both Houses of Parliament. Later, at a banquet attended by Conservative government leaders and industrialists, Canadian union members were treated to the spectacle of the president of the American Federation of Labor, the man sworn to uphold workers' struggles for better working conditions, openly fraternizing with some of the more notorious exploiters of cheap labour in Canada—the same people who had in the past expressed bitter anti-union sentiments while employing militia troops and private police to beat their workers into submission.

The press described the affair as "unique." The workers described it in a less complimentary manner and, by 1919, began seriously to consider secession from the international unions to link up with the new, radical One Big Union, which was formed that year in Western Canada, where it was accepted with open arms.

In October 1918, Prime Minister Borden's Conservative government made haste to ban all organizations considered radical-socialist. Overnight, hundreds of innocent people were rounded up and thrown into military stockades or jails where all were suspect and none allowed the democratic right of consultation with a lawyer or informed of the nature of the charges preferred against them. With the news of a bloody Russian Revolution fresh in the minds of the populace, the "Red Scare" easily convinced the man on the street that socialist and labour pioneers were dangerous Soviets, Bolsheviks, and worse.

The wartime measure banning socialist organizations was to have severe repercussions in Canada for many years after, especially during labour disputes, when unscrupulous employers resorted to the old familiar cry of "Red" or "Bolshevik" to persuade governments and the people that a strike had been fomented by radical union leaders of leftist persuasion.

The Armistice was signed on November 11, 1918, and the war was ended, and with the return of millions of servicemen who had served overseas, a new power emerged. They returned to Canada to be discharged from the Armed Forces and take up life as they had left it. Instead, they found they had returned to a land that was in the grip of unemployment and insecurity. With the end of the war, thousands of industries were discontinued overnight.

Many others shut down to retool for peacetime production. Daily the ex-servicemen grew more dissatisfied with their lot. They remembered not only the hell and suffering of war, the stinking mud of the trenches and the constant presence of death; they remembered the negligence of a wartime administration that had issued rifles that failed to fire, shells that failed to explode, and boots that rotted on their feet. Now that they had returned, they saw manufacturers and industrialists who had grown rich and fat at their expense; profiteers who had looked forward to the start of the war and regretted its end. They had been welcomed back to a "land fit for heroes to return to" only to find themselves rejected by an unfeeling bureaucracy and a capitalist-controlled government. Their prewar jobs were filled by foreigners and war dodgers while their families were reduced to a poverty-stricken existence in the midst of plenty.

With mass unemployment and little hope of finding a job, returned veterans felt their sacrifice had been in vain, and that profiteers who had made millions during the war were the real enemies of the people. Fearing insurrection in a land beset with mounting unemployment and rumours of a Bolshevik uprising, the popular press rushed to the defence of capitalism and free enterprise. The Halifax *Morning Chronicle* of January 5, 1919, published a cartoon of a sinister bewhiskered figure handing out Bolshevik propaganda leaflets to gaunt, hungry ex-soldiers. Headlines shrieked of Red atrocities in Russia and of radical communist leaders in Britain and the United States.

Novelist John Dos Passos once said that after 1917, some people caught socialism as others caught influenza. The spread of the socialist "virus" in North America after the Armistice had been announced in 1918 was seen as the cause of major strikes in places all over North America, but contrary to popular belief, the spread of socialism was not totally due to the example set by Red Russia; it was caused by massive unemployment and hunger and then escalated by vicious repressive measures by the Canadian and U.S. governments.

Many ex-servicemen returned to the coal mines to continue the only occupation they knew. If they had had any false illusions regarding their "triumphant return," they were soon shattered by the pettish complaints such as expressed by the president of the Dominion Coal Company, who stated that "as a result of their army experience, many of my miners have grown to like working in the sunlight and do not take kindly to their old tasks, which is a great hardship on us!" Unfortunately, the record does not show ex-servicemen's reactions to the complaint. No doubt they would have pointed out that "working in the sunlight" in the hell and muck of Flanders was very little different from working in Dominion's coal mines.

In semi-retirement, McLachlan watched and waited for the next turn of events. The Amalgamated Mine Workers of Nova Scotia had served its purpose during the war. It had averted a strike between the two opposing factions—the PWA and the United Mine Workers of Nova Scotia. Considerable gains had been made in miners' wages, but little progress had been made toward levelling wages paid by different coal companies operating in the province, or in obtaining the long-sought eight-hour day, which coal miners in the United States and Alberta had secured years before.

Early in 1919, delegates representing the Amalgamated Mine Workers of Nova Scotia met in Sydney to prepare new contract demands. The first item on the agenda was a motion to dissolve the Amalgamated and to request the United Mine Workers of America to grant a new charter to District 26 in Nova Scotia. Acting International President John L. Lewis was more than willing to grant the request after his union's defeat and ignominious withdrawal from Nova Scotia in 1915. But the credit was due to McLachlan, who had cannily left the door open for the reentry of the UMWA by the introduction of the United Mine Workers of Nova Scotia in 1915, followed by a forced amalgamation with the PWA.

After the conference at Sydney, coal companies throughout the province were asked to meet with a union wage committee to discuss proposals for wage increases and other matters, but each company refused to recognize the UMWA as the official bargaining unit for Nova Scotia miners without a prior agreement guaranteeing that wage parity would never be demanded with U.S. miners belonging to the same union. In addition, they demanded complete autonomy for District 26 from the international headquarters of the United Mine Workers of America to prevent Nova Scotia miners from striking in sympathy with U.S. miners. Demands for wage increases and a levelling of wages from colliery to colliery were rejected with the excuse that economic conditions would not allow any increase in the cost of production. Surprisingly, the long-sought eight-hour day was granted, and recognition was finally won for United Mine Workers of America to represent Nova Scotia miners after international president John L. Lewis had assured the coal companies that District 26 would be granted full autonomy as requested.

The cost of living had increased almost 70 percent since the 1905 contract had been signed by Moffatt and the PWA, but miners' wages had been increased only an average of 35 percent. The wage increases, which had failed to adjust miners' wages in proportion to the inflationary spiral, had not been granted freely by the Dominion Coal Company and its competitors. Only the exigencies of war had forced the federal government to back miners' demands; but now the war was over, and wage increases would have to be fought for tooth and nail.

In the first District 26 election of officers held shortly after the coal companies had agreed to recognize the UMWA, Robert Baxter, a well-known and respected Glace Bay miner and town councillor and former president of the United Mine Workers of Nova Scotia, was elected president, with David Ryan vice-president, Silby Barrett international board representative, and James Bryson McLachlan secretary-treasurer. It was a curious mixture of right and left. Baxter was one of the two unsuccessful labour candidates in the 1917 federal election, but he could not be described as a rabid socialist by any means; neither was Silby Barrett, who had a morbid fear of extreme left-wing socialists advocating strike action as the only means of settling labour disputes. On the other side of the scale, McLachlan and Ryan were ardent socialists who had been converted to their beliefs as a result of the suffering and privation miners and their families were forced to endure during the 1909–10 strike.

The political differences within the District 26 executive were soon to cause a split that would be exploited to the full by the Dominion Coal Company. Meanwhile, events taking place in Winnipeg, Manitoba, were about to involve workers in Cape Breton, thousands of miles to the east.

The Winnipeg General Strike was declared in May 1919, after workers belonging to the Metal Trades Council had been refused a wage increase and union recognition. On May 15, the workers went on strike, followed shortly after by workers in many other industries. Metal trade and railway shops closed, construction came to a halt, and streetcars stopped running. The strike spread quickly to include firemen, policemen, and postal and telephone workers and the city ground to a halt. Behind the scenes, the One Big Union was at work. Its call for unity—"All for one and one for all"—threatened to bring the whole country to a halt in a nationwide general strike unless the demands of the Winnipeg workers were met and threats of ultimatums and firings were cancelled.

The reaction by the federal government, led by Prime Minister Borden, was vicious and extreme. Legislation introduced in a great hurry in the House of Commons in Ottawa amended the Immigration Act to allow for the deportation of British subjects not born in Canada (many of whom were leaders in the strike). Within twenty minutes, the amendment passed three readings without debate. It was then granted approval by the Senate and given royal assent in less than an hour. An all-time record!

Immediately following this choice piece of legislation, an amendment was added to the Criminal Code of Canada to "clarify" the section relating to sedition. Section 98 was passed in an emergency debate, making it a crime (punishable by jail terms of up to twenty years) to belong to any association whose purpose was to bring about governmental, industrial, or economic change by force or to advocate or defend the use of force for such purpose. If it could even be shown that a person had attended meetings of such an association or spoken publicly in its support or distributed its literature, "It shall be presumed in the absence of proof to the contrary, that he is a member of such unlawful association."

During the early hours of June 17, 1919, the principal strike leaders were dragged from their beds in Winnipeg and thrown into jail. Support for the jailed strike leaders was immediate. All across Canada, labour and union leaders pledged support. In Nova Scotia on June 19, J.B. McLachlan, secretary-treasurer of District 26, wired the Prime Minister in Ottawa: "We pledge ourselves to do all we can to bring about a general strike all over Canada."

But the Conservative government, headed by Borden, was determined to break the strike, which was regarded as insurrection against the government. By a single stroke of the pen, laws had been passed to deny the right of free speech and the right of collective bargaining between employee and employer.

With the indiscriminate use of Section 98 of the Criminal Code of Canada, anything not deemed in the best interests of an employer during a labour dispute was termed "seditious libel," justifying harsh penalties and the suppression of free speech. It was a pattern to be repeated many times in the years ahead—especially in the island of Cape Breton on Canada's eastern seaboard.

In Alberta, coal miners belonging to District 18, United Mine Workers of America, had also joined the ranks of the One Big Union in spite of dire warnings from John L. Lewis that their action would provide grounds for expulsion. The warning may have been sounded by Lewis, but behind the scenes, the iron hand of Gompers, president of the American Federation of Labor, had dictated the rigid stipulation against "dual unionism."

Lewis' fear and detestation of militant socialism after the Russian Revolution in 1917 had provided the excuse to cancel the charters of any UMWA district opposing his authoritarian rule and replace elected officers with a provisional board of officers of his own choosing. The provisional officers would then impose the international executive's will on the local membership—even against their wishes. Rebellious districts would have their charters permanently withdrawn if they refused to toe the line.

The militant officers of District 18 in Alberta were now replaced with Lewis appointees. Provisional district take-overs were soon to become a frequent occurrence in the UMWA.

With the coal companies' rejection of Nova Scotia coal miners' wage demands, District 26 was forced to apply to the federal Department of Labour for the services of a Conciliation Board to resolve the dispute without further delay, and in November 1919, the government announced it had acceded to the request. A Conciliation Board set up under the chairmanship of Dr Clarence MacKinnon was authorized to hear evidence from the Dominion Coal Company and District 26. Another Board was set up to hear complaints from miners employed by Nova Scotia Steel and Coal Company, who were being paid wages even lower than those paid to fellow union members working for Dominion.

The MacKinnon Board sat for months, heard scores of witnesses, and examined mountainous piles of company financial statements, all purporting to show a depressed coal market, falling sales, and a complete inability to pay higher wages to miners belonging to District 26 of the United Mine Workers of America. No mention was made of the bloated profits made by Nova Scotia coal companies during the war, or the grossly inflated dividends paid to stockholders even after the war had ended. McLachlan demanded the right to examine the Dominion Coal Company's books to judge whether the financial statements were true, but the company strongly objected, piously maintaining that such records were sacrosanct and an open inspection would allow competitors an unfair advantage. The MacKinnon Board concurred with the company and retired to write its recommendations.

The year 1919 was one of depression. With the end of the war, many companies had found the transition to peacetime production a traumatic experience. Bloated with excess profits gained from the production of war materials, a number of the more unscrupulous companies found it expedient to close the doors of their factories for months at a time to convert their production to other products and to seek new markets. Little thought or concern was spared for the plight of millions of workers thrown onto the streets to starve while the retooling was taking place.

The Cape Breton steel industry was hard hit. The Dominion Iron and Steel Company closed its Northside steel mills and overnight the town of Sydney Mines became a depressed area of misery and despair, with three out of every four workers thrown out of work and left without any means to obtain sustenance for themselves and their families. Within a short space of time, hunger and malnutrition stalked the streets of Sydney Mines. Hundreds of poor families were reduced to a level of starvation without any hope of relief.

Answering the public outcry against such inhumane treatment, Superintendent Brown of the Dominion Iron and Steel Company stated that the company was unaware of any suffering among workers who had lost their jobs as a result of the shutdown. He piously asserted he did not know of a single case of want or privation among his ex-employees, but if any evidence was presented to him to the contrary, the company would take immediate steps to provide assistance.

Brown's "kind" offer was taken up by a committee of citizens headed by Forman Waye, superintendent of machine shops in the company, who told him of hundreds of starving people suffering untold hardships as a result of the layoffs. The plea was ignored. At a later press conference, Brown repeated his statement—that he didn't know of a single case of actual want, but that if such a need existed his company would not hesitate to provide assistance.

Immediately following Brown's offer of assistance, orders were issued by his office for starving families to be forcefully evicted from company houses for nonpayment of rent. Many of those evicted were ex-servicemen who had recently returned to the "land of the free." Forman Waye was dismissed from his post and blacklisted for his defence of unemployed and starving workers.

District 26, UMWA, now decided to add its support to unemployed steelworkers, even though they were not members of the union. On July 22, 1919, McLachlan organized a mass protest meeting in the town of Sydney Mines. Thousands of hungry, desperate people gathered to hear McLachlan, Silby Barrett, and a Winnipeg strike leader, Fred Tipping, appeal for money, food, and clothing to relieve the suffering that had by now reached chronic proportions. The meeting was orderly and well conducted, but the company-controlled press reported it as "one more instance of Bolshevik agitation aided and abetted by seditious rebels from the west!" Barrett and McLachlan were branded in the Sydney *Post* as "wild revolutionaries who wilfully pervert the truth."

McLachlan and Barrett could not let these scurrilous untruths pass unchallenged. The following day, they composed a rebuttal of the Red bogy charge:

> The best material for the making of a discontented man is a hungry man. Give Canadian labour a decent chance to live and it has no more use for this Red revolutionary idea than anyone else has. Nova Scotia labour is sound, but unless some speedy relief is forthcoming, the conditions existing today in the industrial districts of Cape Breton are going to lead to...who can say what they may lead to? The people of Cape Breton are peace loving, hard working people. Give them work and a fair show, and you will not hear a murmur from them. But some of them are being asked to do an impossible thing. They are being asked to live on nothing!

Miners' voluntary contributions were gathered to assist the needy in Sydney Mines. Telegrams were sent by McLachlan and the district executive to Prime Minister Borden in Ottawa, but shamefully they were ignored. After the Russian Revolution and the Winnipeg General Strike, which he believed had been inspired by Red subversives, Borden had classified all labour groups as dangerous Soviets intent only on overthrowing the lawful government of Canada. Pleas for urgent assistance were regarded in much the same light as funds to feed a revolutionary movement. Immediately following the Russian Revolution in 1917, the Royal Northwest Mounted Police had been instructed to compile secret dossiers on hundreds of known radicals and more militant labour leaders. McLachlan's name was included.

The suffering continued in the town of Sydney Mines all through the winter of 1919. It was not until the spring of 1920 that Dominion Iron and Steel Company resumed production, and even then, it was at greatly reduced capacity. Thousands of steelworkers returned to the steel mills in Sydney Mines, but the reduced hourly wages did little to alleviate suffering. Forman Waye and a large number of other dedicated workers who had made public appeals to the company to help the unemployed and their families during the shutdown were never reemployed by the Dominion Iron and Steel Company.

In January 1920, the MacKinnon Conciliation Board published

its recommendations. Cape Breton coal miners were to be awarded a general wage increase of 10 percent to compensate for the greatly increased cost of living, but the union request for a levelling up of wages from colliery to colliery was refused.

The new contract, including the 10 percent wage increase, was to run for a period of one full year, but an important clause, which had been inserted into the contract at the insistence of the wily McLachlan, stated: "Should there be any change in the cost of living or any disturbance in economic conditions...the wage schedule would be opened for revision at the instance of either party to the agreement and at the end of each four month period."

McLachlan had insisted on this vital clause because the cost of living was continuing to rise in the postwar period. Already, it was 15 percent higher than in 1919. This open-ended clause was to be the cause of future disputes between coal company and union. Dominion had no intention of observing the all-important clause, which had been signed in good faith by the union and the members of the Conciliation Board.

McLachlan and the other members of the District 26 executive returned to Glace Bay to face thousands of hostile miners. McLachlan and President Baxter bore the brunt of the criticism, with international board representative Silby Barrett siding with dissident groups of miners in a surprise about-face against the district executive he had helped establish.

The MacKinnon Award was not overgenerous, and it had not taken into account the greatly increased cost of living since 1919, but under the circumstances, with the depressed state of the economy, it was probably the best possible contract that could have been obtained for Nova Scotia miners.

The Dominion Coal Company's refusal to open its books for inspection had been the key factor in keeping the award to a minimum. A more forceful Conciliation Board chairman would have insisted on the company producing its books for inspection before reaching a decision, but books can be duplicated and figures falsified to show low profit margins and a depressed market. These truisms were all too apparent to McLachlan, but for the moment he was forced to accept the decision. Most important, he had obtained the all-important assurance that cost-of-living increases would be made over the life of the present contract.

The next day, McLachlan called a mass meeting in a Glace Bay theatre. Striding onto the stage to face over eight hundred hostile miners, he gave a masterful performance. Old miners like Billy Pittman still chuckle proudly when recalling McLachlan's stage performance:

I've never heard a better speaker than J.B. McLachlan. He'd get up there on the stage, or even standing on a soap box on the sandbar at Lingan, and as soon as he opened his mouth he had his audience in the palm of his hand. Brown eyes flashing and his big red moustache bristling with anger as he pounded the table before him, he could sway any audience. As he warmed up, he'd doff his coat to roll up his shirt-sleeves and then, striding up and down the stage waving his fists in all directions, his melodious Scottish burr becoming more and more pronounced as time went by, his audience became spellbound. First he'd lower his voice to a mere whisper, then he'd roar defiance at the coal company in a voice that threatened to lift the roof tiles! Lastly, he'd take out his false teeth and pop them in his pocket without missing a single word. That's when his men loved him. He was one of them. A miner, a brother, and a true friend.

Patiently, point by point, McLachlan explained the new contract to the miners' meeting. The contract was only for a four-month period, he emphasized; it could be opened up at the end of every quarter, if the men so desired. The Halifax *Herald* of February 2, 1920, reported that at this point half a dozen men arose and cried, "Throw him out," but they were shouted down by the majority of miners present:

"I have always said that you men should get your increases according to the increased cost of living, and this contract says we can open negotiations with the Dominion Coal Company if there is a change in economic conditions.... If we have slipped up we have the right to go back to the Dominion Coal Company to get a re-adjustment."

The Halifax *Herald* reported the meeting ended with rousing cheers for McLachlan, who had scored a big personal victory. But on the same front page, a large cartoon titled "Gratitude!" depicted a Caesar-like McLachlan lying mortally wounded on a bier surrounded by weeping miners. To one side a Roman senator, complete with flowing toga and sandals (and miner's cap), held a bulging sack labelled "MacKinnon Award"; not surprisingly, the senator was labelled "Marcus Antonius Baxterus"—a Roman *nom de plume* for Robert Baxter, president of District 26. In the foreground, another senator, more sinister in appearance, who stood with arms folded over a dripping dagger, was labelled *Silbius Brutus Barrettus.*

The cartoon referred to a reporter's description of the betrayal of McLachlan by his friend and long-time colleague, Silby Barrett. The reporter suggested the criticism of McLachlan was "the unkindest cut of all, since Brutus (Silby Barrett) and his gang let daylight trickle through Caesar's imperial slats."

McLachlan confided later that Silby Barrett's condemnation was totally unexpected and certainly unwarranted. Miners showed their continued confidence in Baxter and McLachlan and their opposition to Barrett when elections for district officers were held later the same year. Baxter and McLachlan were reelected, but Barrett was soundly beaten by "Red" Dan Livingstone. The appointment of Livingstone was not viewed with any great satisfaction at international headquarters of the UMWA in Indianapolis. Lewis hated and distrusted left-wingers such as McLachlan and Livingstone. When the time was opportune, he would intervene in District 26 affairs and replace the elected officers with a provisional executive of his own choice—men with rightist views.

Lewis and the international executive of the union had supported Gompers and the American Federation of Labor in their condemnation of the IWW and the One Big Union. Without hesitation they had joined in the popular witch-hunt for socialists during and after the war, even to the point where names of union leaders suspected of leftist tendencies had been supplied to the authorities. Now, with the defeat of Barrett and the reelection of McLachlan and Baxter in the District 26 elections, Lewis saw growing opposition to his fawning policies of cooperation with Gompers and conservative governments. Any doubts regarding the left-wing tendencies of the District 26 executive in Nova Scotia were dissolved when McLachlan urged delegates attending the

April 1920 district convention to send a substantial sum of money to pay for defence costs for jailed Winnipeg strike leaders, and to demand their release on bail prior to the trial.

An appeal by the Winnipeg Defence Committee for a nationwide demonstration of support for the jailed leaders was answered by a one-day strike on May 1, 1920, when McLachlan ordered every coal miner in Nova Scotia to stop work in the first political strike in the history of the Canadian coal mining industry. The work stoppage did not endear McLachlan to the Nova Scotia coal companies, and it did nothing to increase his popularity with Lewis and the international board of the union. The work stoppage, which was considered illegal while the men were working under contract, left them open to possible court action.

Communists in Canada had been outlawed with Borden's introduction of Section 98 of the Criminal Code, but the new Labour Party continued to gain in popularity. In Nova Scotia, McLachlan and the Independent Labour Party determined to oppose the reigning provincial government of Premier Murray in the forthcoming election. Meanwhile, farmers in Cape Breton had decided to organize a party to represent their own interests, and returned soldiers belonging to the Great War Veterans' Association of Glace Bay had also determined to be represented in a new provincial government. Finally, all three groups were persuaded to combine and field candidates on a Farmer-Labour-Soldier slate with each group pledging allegiance to the Independent Labour Party of Nova Scotia.

The election was held on July 27, 1920. Liberal newspapers labelled the new labour candidates as Farmer-Labour-Bolshevik-Atheist and gave dire warnings that a vote cast for labour was tantamount to near treason and could lead only to a Red revolution in Canada with Russian Bolsheviks in control.

The propaganda could not have been very convincing, for when the votes were counted, Murray's Liberal government had been returned to the provincial legislature but with a reduced majority, while the new Farmer-Labour-Soldier Party triumphed with eleven candidates elected, including blacklisted Forman Waye and Dan Willie Morrison, a coal miner from Glace Bay.

The lessons taught McLachlan by Scottish miners' leader Keir Hardie had been passed along to the workers of Nova Scotia. Without political representation, workers' requests for better working conditions were futile. Now they had a voice in the provincial legislature of Nova Scotia, and the future seemed bright with hope. But new influences were beginning to make themselves felt on the political scene—influences of international scope and magnitude involving many millions of dollars that would nullify any advances in living standards and working conditions for the miners and steelworkers of Nova Scotia.

7

Besco and the Montreal Agreement

Roy Mitchell Wolvin was invited to be president of the Dominion Iron and Steel Company in March 1920. A former transportation expert from Duluth, Minnesota, Wolvin was also the president of the Montreal Transportation Company, a director of Canada Interlake Lines, Ltd., and a partner in Canada Steamship Lines—companies involved in lake shipping and the carrying of cargoes of iron ore, coke, and coal for the manufacture of steel.

With such a background, it was hardly surprising that Wolvin readily grasped the huge, almost untapped potential of a total amalgamation of all steel, coal, and shipping interests in the province of Nova Scotia. Huge deposits of iron ore at Wabana, Newfoundland, vast submarine coalfields in Cape Breton, and steel and iron mills at Sydney and Sydney Mines—the Dominion Iron and Steel Company had the only plate mill in Canada—were all close to modern loading piers where oceangoing ships could load cargoes for easy and cheap transportation to the world's markets.

Apart from the obvious mineral advantages enjoyed by the company, Wolvin was struck by its strategic position "halfway between two continents where Canada could be supplied, Europe taken care of, and the British steel industry rejuvenated. Ultimately, iron ore and coal could be shipped into Pittsburgh itself!"

If the equally prosperous Nova Scotia Steel and Coal Company could be persuaded to join a vast consortium of companies visualized by Wolvin, the amalgamation would be complete and the coal and steel industries of Nova Scotia would be monopolized to gather vast profits at little cost.

Inspired by his vision, Wolvin began to purchase large numbers of the Dominion Iron and Steel Company shares to gain a minor controlling interest in that company before making an approach to its competitor—the Nova Scotia Steel and Coal Company. His financial wheeling and dealing had not gone unnoticed in the business community. Shortly after he had become president of Dominion Iron and Steel Company, Wolvin was approached by a British syndicate that had been acquiring shares for the same purpose. The syndicate represented powerful financial interests in Britain—English and Scottish iron masters, coal operators, railway companies, and at least two London financiers.

Wolvin's ascendence to the presidency of Dominion Iron and Steel Company had not been totally due to the large number of company shares he had purchased. At the end of the war, shipping was at a premium after the great merchant fleets of the world had been decimated by four years of submarine warfare. With the chronic shortage of merchant vessels, transportation of steel and coal had reached the critical stage. Wolvin with his shipping interests could replace the weak link in the chain.

In Halifax, Wolvin had recently entered into a partnership with J.W. Norcross, president of Canada Steamship Lines—a company that had gained notoriety for issuing watered stock. With lucrative orders for the building of four ships, Wolvin and Norcross now launched a holding company, Halifax Shipyards, Limited, to allow them to enter the exclusive shipbuilding fraternity, and plans for a future amalgamation of coal, steel, and shipping interests in the province of Nova Scotia were complete.

Shortly after Wolvin had become president of Dominion Iron and Steel Company, J.W. Norcross was invited to join the board of directors as a special representative for the syndicate and the operation commenced. On March 15, 1920, the promoters of the amalgamation scheme applied to the federal government in Ottawa for letters patent incorporating the vast new consortium to be known as British Empire Steel Corporation, Limited, with an authorized capital of one hundred thousand dollars. But on

May 13, before the government could give its approval to the new incorporation, the promoters applied for supplementary letters increasing the authorized capital to five hundred thousand dollars. The unprecedented move alarmed the business community, which lost no time in calling the federal government's attention to this most questionable practice. The government reacted with a promise of a thorough investigation of the new company and its financial assets.

The setback did not deter Wolvin and his syndicate in the least. There were other means of securing a charter. Fourteen companies representing the greater part of the coal and steel industries of Nova Scotia had been merged into the new British Empire Steel Corporation, or Besco as it became known. The financial interests controlling the fourteen companies had a very substantial influence on the provincial government of Nova Scotia. The cheque for incorporation fees had already been mailed to the federal government in Ottawa along with the application for increased capital, when the premier of Nova Scotia, George H. Murray, wired President Wolvin, in his Montreal headquarters, reminding him that provincial charters, not federal, had been the usual practice for businesses operating within the province of Nova Scotia. The notification ended with a polite request for Besco to be incorporated in the provincial capital of Halifax.

The request came at a very convenient time. Besco withdrew its application and cheque from Ottawa and, on May 22, secured its charter from the legislature of Nova Scotia. The total issue of stocks was listed as $63 million common stock and $19 million preferred stock, making a grand total of $82 million.

The inflated stock issue prompted charges of watered stock resulting from the inclusion of liquid assets that appeared to be entirely derived from the addition of relative items from the balance sheets of the Dominion and Nova Scotia companies, plus the surplus created by writing up the value of the estimated mineral deposits of both companies. A further disturbing factor was the proposed distribution of the various securities of Besco among the constituent companies. Charges were made that the amount allocated to the minor companies was greatly out of proportion to their standing and importance compared with that of the principal companies included in the merger. The Montreal *Star* claimed that "a lot of lame ducks were to be brought into the merger and the paying companies were to pay for the lame ducks."

After the merger, the *Star* continued, the allotted issues were increased and transmuted. The common stock became $24 million and the preferred stock $77 million. By a minor miracle, the "fishes" had been turned into "loaves" and the "loaves" into "fishes." They had also multiplied exceedingly to feed the hungry mouths and pockets of a voracious financial consortium.

The principal companies in the merger—Nova Scotia Steel and Coal Company, Dominion Iron and Steel Company, Dominion Coal Company, Eastern Car Company, and Halifax Shipyards—were given the cream of the crop, the valuable cumulative first preference shares. The British group was also given fifty thousand shares of preferred stock, while Wolvin and the directors of the fourteen companies merged into Besco were given the remainder. No new capital was introduced into the new consortium, which was condemned by the financial community for its top-heavy capitalization and watered stock.

Charges were levelled that a change in the character of securities and the increase in capital stock issued would cause a future demand from directors and stockholders for a substantial increase in the earnings of the companies to pay interest on the huge block of stock; dividends that could be derived only from increased output or profit from the coal mines owned by the company; increased output that could be obtained only through increased efficiency of operation or through an increase in the price of coal.

After 1919, markets for Nova Scotia coal dropped drastically. An increase in the price of coal was therefore impossible. Due to over-capitalization during the merger, money was not available for additional mechanization to improve efficiency and boost output from the company's mines. History was repeating itself. Costs could be reduced only through wage reduction. Miners' wages were to be slashed continuously to maintain profits and pay lucrative dividends to shareholders.

J.B. McLachlan, testifying before the Duncan Royal Com-

Catherine (Kate) and James Bryson McLachlan, 1924,
after J.B.'s release from prison

Caledonia Company Store and Company Houses

A cartoon of J.B. McLachlan in the Halifax *Herald*; right: John L. Lewis, president of United Mine Workers of America

Top centre: J.E. McLurg, vice-president of Besco; above: Roy M. Wolvin, president of Besco, 1920–25

Below: Soldier behind barbed wire, colliery behind, in the 1909 Strike

Newspaper photo of children during the 1925 Strike

Coal miners in *The Company Store*

Archie McIntyre

Gordon MacGregor

Billy Pittman

Dan "Dancer" MacDonald

Monument to the New Waterford Explosion (1917); right: grave of William Davis, killed at the battle of Waterford Lake, 1925 Strike

Left: A bootleg mine during the 1925 Strike; below: soldiers camped inside the Sydney steel plant— 1923 Strike

The United Mine Workers District 26 Executive of 1909. Front row, left to right: J.B. Moss, vice-president; Dan MacDougall, president; J.D. MacLennan, organizer. Back row, left, J.B. McLachlan, secretary-treasurer, Charles Bond, Murray Graham, Ernest Bond. Below: monument to J.B. McLachlan in Glace Bay, NS.

J.B. McLachlan (left) sails for Russia in 1931, a trip paid for by miners and steelworkers of Nova Scotia.

The grave of Catherine and J.B. McLachlan.

mission in 1925, described the watered stock most succinctly when he said:

Besco included $19,000,000 of water: wine for the company and tragedy for the workers of Cape Breton.... When they had applied for corporate powers in Ottawa, Besco had been asked some awkward questions which they couldn't or wouldn't answer, so they left to secure corporate powers in Halifax from the provincial government. They were writing in millions of dollars of watered stock and prepared to take it out of the miners' wages. They would not give as good a wage as paid elsewhere to other miners. They would starve them!

By some very doubtful juggling between common and preferred stocks, fourteen companies, some very large and others weak and barely holding their own, had been combined into the largest industrial corporation in Canada. The dividends paid on watered stock would eventually reach millions of dollars annually. To pay dividends to stockholders in Canada and Britain, costs would have to be reduced drastically in the coal and steel industries of Nova Scotia. Wages would be the prime target.

Wage negotiations by District 26, United Mine Workers of America, were about to enter into a new dark phase. Any past grievances against Dominion and other Nova Scotia coal companies would pale into insignificance when compared to Besco's ruthlessness in its dealings with Nova Scotia miners. Men, women, and children would be starved, beaten, and shot to allow international financiers to receive bloated dividends on their watered stock. Roy Wolvin was to become the most hated employer in the long, bitter history of Nova Scotia labour and his utter indifference and callous attitude to the pleas of workers and their families would earn him the doubtful sobriquet of "Roy the Wolf," and his amalgamated consortium of companies the equally bad name of "Beastly Besco."

In April 1920, Jim McLachlan served notice on Besco that the union was seeking a revision of its existing contract with the company in accordance with the clause allowing for a reopening of the contract every four months if the cost of living increased. The cost of living had spiralled upward since the MacKinnon award, but Wolvin's only response to the union's request for a meeting was to send evasive letters. And then, when it became apparent that the company had no intention of honouring the agreement, militant factions within the union began to demand action—in the form of a strike if need be.

At this point, the federal government intervened to prevent a direct confrontation between Besco and its miners. A Royal Commission was appointed under the chairmanship of E.M. Quirk of the Department of Labour, and in September 1920, to the pleasant surprise of the miners, the commission recommended that the wage demands of the men be met in full. To keep pace with American and Alberta miners, McLachlan and his executive had asked for a one dollar a day increase for daily workers and certain increases for contract men on a tonnage basis.

All wage demands were met, but the increases were to be conditional on an increase in output per man-day.

The increases were also subject to existing rights under the contract. McLachlan had not failed to draw the commission's attention to the company's shortcomings in the matter of the cost-of-living revision, and had urged the award be made retroactive from May 1, 1920, when the company had first been contacted for a revision. The commission promptly agreed and the claim was allowed, to give a cost-of-living increase to be added to the new raise in wages.

To avoid future disputes and the risk of crippling strikes, the commission recommended that an Adjustment Board be set up to hear evidence from company and union. The findings of such a board would be binding on both parties.

While the commission report was an unpleasant surprise for the coal companies, clauses relating to increased output and compulsory arbitration made it far from acceptable to the union. On the advice of McLachlan, the whole award was rejected. A pithead vote called for a strike if better terms could not be arranged.

At this point, the federal Department of Labour again intervened to call both parties in the dispute to a conference in

Montreal. A settlement was finally reached on November 8, 1920. The agreement provided for a daily increase of fifty-five cents for daily workers and an extra ten cents a ton for contract workers. The union executives, with the exception of McLachlan, recommended acceptance by their miners even though the rates offered were less than those offered previously, because the company demand for increased output had been dropped.

McLachlan recommended that the company offer be refused, but a pithead vote by the men ignored his advice and the new rates went into effect as of November 1, 1920. It was a one-year agreement lasting until November 1921. The agreement, which was known as the First Montreal Agreement, gave Cape Breton coal miners the highest rate of pay they were to receive for the next twenty-one years. After 1921, the struggle would not be geared to keeping pace with the rising cost of living, it would be to *retain* the rates set by the 1920 contract. A great part of C.B. Wade's *History of District 26, UMWA*, from the end of 1921 to the fall of 1925, is the story of a series of battles to restore the 1920 level of wages.

The agreement was not welcomed by all and sundry. Many miners believed they had been shortchanged by their union executive. First they had been offered a dollar-a-day increase, which had been rejected; then they had been offered half that amount, and most of their union executive officers had recommended acceptance. Dominion Coal Company did its best to encourage this false misunderstanding, knowing that it would create resentment and distrust among miners towards their elected officers.

Before a huge meeting of angry miners, Jim McLachlan tried to explain the terms of the Montreal Agreement and his belief that it was the best possible contract that could have been obtained under the circumstances. McLachlan's daughter, Mrs Eva Pemberton, who was present at the meeting, described his rough reception:

I remember coming home late one night, just after he had returned with the new contract in November 1920; he was walking around our little farm with his hands stuck in his trouser pockets, deep in thought. I asked him why he was up so late, and he said, "Eva, if you want to clear your brain, get out under the stars and close to the good earth, that is when you see life very clearly." It wasn't a good contract he brought back, but it was the best anyone could have got. I was only fifteen at the time, but I accompanied Poppa when he faced the miners on Lingan beach to explain the new contract. His first words were, "I ask no quarter; this is the best I could do for you." And then they began to pelt him with eggs and tomatoes. I asked him in tears why he bothered to try and help them. I was so furious. "Oh," he laughed, "that was just a few of the men who had got some false courage from the bottle!"... And by the way, he was the only one of the District executives to show up to face the miners. I went to all his meetings just to hear him speak. He was such a great speaker and his whole life was dedicated to improving the workers' lot.

But if District 26 miners were unhappy with the terms of the Montreal Agreement, the new president of Besco was even more so. Wolvin deeply resented the government pressure that forced the agreement. Giving evidence before the Duncan Commission in 1925, Wolvin said:

In November 1920 I had my first experience in labour negotiations on a large scale. It resulted in what is known as the "Montreal" agreement.... I thought it was a great mistake for the company and for the men. They were forcing a big wage and that before the end of the year it would be found that these wages were on too high a scale for our business.... I was influenced very much during these negotiations by government pressure from Halifax and Ottawa.... The Minister of Railways and the president of the Canadian National Railways made it very clear to me that under no circumstances must I permit the stoppage of coal production.... I stated to the Assistant Deputy Minister of Labour that I would not agree unless he made it a government request. Which he did. I have always felt it was a mistake and I have never considered the Montreal agreement was a proper basis for comparison of future wage scales.

The future wage scales Wolvin had in mind were a mere fraction of the rates set in 1920. Determined to force a reduction in wages in future contracts between Besco and District 26, the work week was reduced drastically. In some mines, men were lucky to obtain two full days' work per week. Many others were laid off in an effort to reduce the work force, and in a short space of time, thousands of poor miners' families throughout Cape Breton were suffering from hunger and want.

McLachlan's warning was about to come true. In 1919, he and Silby Barrett had warned that if the government did not provide immediate relief to ease suffering and want in Cape Breton, the people would be forced to turn to the panacea of communism for help.

Faced with a period of depression during 1921, Besco closed down its shipyards and steel mills. Burdened as it was with an outrageously inflated capitalization of its company, Besco saw only one way to retain its current bloated profits—smash the miners' union, which under the strong hand of McLachlan was now twelve thousand strong, and make the increased profits from coal production pay dividends on its watered stock to subsidize the many "lame duck" companies within the Besco merger.

As a preliminary to destroying the union and reducing miners' incomes to the starvation level, an intensive newspaper campaign was now launched to plead that the high price of Nova Scotia coal was making it impossible for Besco to sell it on the world market, where coal mined in the United States and other countries was available at a much reduced cost.

The stories were greatly exaggerated but it wasn't hard to convince many workers and their families that such was the case, especially after they had been reduced to working a two- or three-day week and their weekly income lowered to a mere pittance.

Besco's next step in its campaign to destroy the union and slash miners' wages was the signing of a contract to deliver millions of tons of iron ore from its mines at Wabana, Newfoundland, to its competitor, Hugo Stinnes Steel Company, in Germany, to be manufactured into steel using cheap German labour. Then with twenty-five hundred steelworkers walking the streets of Sydney and Sydney Mines, and twelve thousand coal miners working for less than half time, Wolvin made plans for his *coup de grâce*.

The War Measures Act, followed by the equally iniquitous Section 98 of the Criminal Code of Canada, had launched a hysterical witch-hunt against suspected Reds and leftists of all description. But the witch-hunt had tended only to drive the militant leaders of the communist movement in Canada underground. Overnight, every labour leader suspected of communist leanings became a hunted criminal liable to prison terms of up to twenty years. But with the lean postwar years and mass unemployment and suffering, belief in the communist doctrine and philosophy continued to flourish in Canada in spite of oppressive laws and overzealous security forces.

The Communist Party of Canada was formed in June 1921, when twenty-two delegates from central Canada met secretly in a lonely farmhouse in Guelph, Ontario. The establishment of the CPC, and its close affiliation with the Red International of Labour Union movement (RILU) was to have a very significant effect on future labour disputes in Nova Scotia, especially those involving steel and coal workers. J.B. McLachlan and "Red" Dan Livingstone were to become ardent disciples of the Communist Party after its formation in Canada. But their stated allegiance to communist ideology was to lead to persecution not only from the law but also from the international headquarters of the United Mine Workers of America. President John L. Lewis was continuing a ruthless policy of expelling district executives suspected of socialist tendencies, and replacing them with provisional district officers selected from toadying favourites at international headquarters in Indianapolis.

In the state of Kansas, the elected officers of District 14, United Mine Workers of America, were deposed by Lewis and replaced by a provisional district executive headed by Van A. Bittner, an associate of Lewis. District president Alexander Howat and his vice-president had been temporarily jailed for defying a choice piece of anti-union legislation, the Industrial Court of Kansas, introduced by Governor Henry J. Allen as an arbitrary means of settling labour disputes. Seizing upon the pretext of an alleged violation of the union agreement, the Kansas coal operators appealed directly to John L. Lewis, who responded by ordering Howat and his miners to surrender unconditionally. Howat defied Lewis' order and was immediately expelled from the union.

In Nova Scotia, Canada, the Kansas take-over by Lewis appointees was soon to be repeated.

The lessons learned at bitter cost during the federal election of 1920 would never be forgotten by McLachlan and other labour leaders in Cape Breton. With every newspaper owned and operated by interests closely allied or sympathetic to the coal and steel industries of the province, the voters had been subjected to a repeated barrage of propaganda, warning against labour candidates and their alleged "Red" leanings. To drum up popular support for the labour cause, McLachlan knew he had to appeal to the workers of Cape Breton through the medium of a newspaper.

Remembering Keir Hardie's impassioned writings in the British newspaper *Labour Leader*, McLachlan determined to follow suit and produce a labour newspaper written for workingmen by workingmen to counteract the vicious anti-labour propaganda being published by the popular press—especially during labour disputes or elections. But the task of financing and managing even a modest printing plant seemed insurmountable until he was introduced through labour circles to Douglas Neil Brodie.

Born in Halifax, Nova Scotia, of Scottish and Irish parents, D.N. Brodie had been forced to abandon his education at age fourteen when his father died. To support the family, he was apprenticed to a print shop to learn his trade as a printer, but moved with his family in 1900 to Glace Bay. Putting his printing experience to work, he borrowed the money to equip a small printing shop, using scrap machinery and a great deal of hard work. Most of Brodie's business was found in the printing of handbills and notices of forthcoming events, until early in 1921 when he was approached by McLachlan with an offer to purchase the printing plant and engage him as the publisher of a new labour newspaper. Brodie, whose sympathies had always lain with the labour movement and the emancipation of the working classes, readily agreed.

Brodie entered into the new venture with a great deal of enthusiasm and energy and, within a short space of time, the first issue of the *Maritime Labour Herald* was being sold on the streets of Glace Bay and throughout the surrounding communities. Impassioned editorials and comments by McLachlan, Brodie, and other stalwarts of the labour and union movements were read and reread as they passed from hand to hand until every word had been memorized and quoted in workshops, workingmen's clubs and meeting places, over dinner tables, and even in the offices of the Dominion Coal Company, where the new venture was regarded with righteous indignation.

The *Maritime Labour Herald* was launched with voluntary subscriptions from miners, steelworkers, and working-class people everywhere. Its majority shares and voting control were vested in trade union organizations, but the choice of staff was left to Brodie. When it was decided to engage a full-time editor, Brodie contacted a young Quebec lawyer, William Cotton. It was a fortunate choice. A lawyer by profession and a socialist by conscience, Cotton had been reared in Cowansville in the province of Quebec. A brilliant student (he had been a MacDonald scholar in 1901), he had set up practice in 1904, but abandoned law four years later to follow a career in journalism after purchasing the Cowansville *Observer*. In the same year, 1908, he had been chosen as the Liberal candidate for the town of Brome, but was unsuccessful in his bid for a political career. The experience prompted him to launch yet another newspaper—the *Cotton Weekly*, a periodical devoted to the cause of socialism.

With Cotton at the helm, the *Maritime Labour Herald* became even more bitter in its condemnation of the Dominion Coal Company and its master—British Empire Steel Corporation. The new demagogue, Wolvin, was left to McLachlan's vituperative pen. "Roy the Wolf"—as the old rebel nicknamed him—was allotted a special column each week, as McLachlan wrote about the many social and economic issues facing miners and steelworkers in Cape Breton. Wage negotiations, layoffs and shorter work weeks, complaints of company houses in bad state of repair, malnutrition and suffering of miners' families due to inadequate wages—all were covered in detail, much to the discomfort of Besco and the provincial government.

The October 14, 1921, issue of the *Maritime Labour Herald* showed the bill of fare at the Russell Theatre: Harold Lloyd was starring in *Among Those Present*; at the Savoy, Charlie Chaplin starred in *Police*, while the Strand featured a good old cowboy silent movie with Buck Jones starring in *Straight from the Shoulder*.

Groceries from Miles and Company, Glace Bay, were advertised, with sugar selling at 10 pounds for 90 cents, a 90-pound bag of potatoes for $1.50 and a 100-pound bag of flour for $4.75. For the extravagant, a one-pound tin of New York coffee was advertised at the ridiculously high price of 50 cents, while another 25 cents would purchase 5 bars of laundry soap or 6 pounds of Goldust Cornmeal.

The price of groceries may have appeared low, but compared to miners' wages in 1921, it was beyond the reach of most families, especially when miners were working short time with only two or three days' wages earned at the end of a week. Everywhere, the unmistakable signs of hunger and want were beginning to show. The editorial in the same issue of the *Herald* told of famine in Russia with thousands of people starving to death. The news sent shivers down the spine, but most felt the news from far-off Russia had little relation to their existence in Cape Breton.

In October 1921, the federal government announced there would be a general election on December 6, 1921, and the *Maritime Labour Herald* was proud to report that two labour candidates, J.B. McLachlan and E.C. Doyle, were the unanimous choice of the Farmer-Labour convention held in Sydney, Nova Scotia: "the result of the most harmonious and enthusiastic convention ever held in Cape Breton. The Farmer-Labour Party has picked a winning ticket."

At long last, Jim McLachlan had been chosen to represent Cape Breton's workers in a parliamentary election. Just as his mentor Keir Hardie had broken through the rigid barrier of class distinction and prejudice to represent the workingmen of Great Britain in the Mother of Parliaments, McLachlan had been judged by his peers and entered as a labour candidate in the forthcoming federal election.

The future seemed bright for the workers of Cape Breton, but the Dominion Coal Company and its master, Besco, were about to enter their own candidate against McLachlan, and the fight was to be a most uneven affair, where lies, deceit, and outright chicanery would replace Marquis of Queensberry rules—at least for the election.

Wolvin's first step in the election campaign was an announcement on October 26, 1921, to all miners employed by the Dominion Coal Company. Unless miners were prepared to accept a wage cut in the near future, Wolvin warned, the company would be forced to close down a number of mines throughout the Sydney coalfield. The Glace Bay *Gazette*, the medium through which the coal and steel companies spread their propaganda, devoted a full and impressive seventy-six inches of space to quote Wolvin's statement in full. Facts and statistics, presented in great and complicated profusion, showed or purported to show, that U.S. coal was being produced cheaper per man-hour than Nova Scotia coal, and that, therefore, miners employed by the Dominion Coal Company should be willing to accept a lower wage to allow the company to compete in U.S. markets.

Writing in the *Maritime Labour Herald*, J.B. McLachlan dismissed the figures contemptuously as just another instance of coal company hypocrisy. Warming to his theme, McLachlan pointed out that different costs were involved in the mining of coal from the Sydney coalfield, and that if comparable costs had been based on a miner's daily wage instead of tonnage produced, a truer picture would have been revealed—especially if the cost sheets of the Dominion Coal Company's operation were open for public viewing as the union had many times requested.

In the United States, McLachlan continued, miners were paid $7.50 for a day's work, and as each man was reported to have produced an average of 3.78 tons of coal each day, the actual cost of mining a ton of coal was $1.98. In Nova Scotia, coal miners were paid only $3.90 for a day's work, and as each man was credited with producing 1.78 tons of coal each day, the cost of coal produced in Nova Scotia was $2.19—a cost slightly higher than in the United States.

But to cover the difference, which was due to geological and production difficulties rather than muscle power, the Canadian coal industry was protected by a government tariff of 53 cents a ton, or 32 cents more than the reported difference in cost between U.S. and Nova Scotia coal.

In a masterful argument, McLachlan then proceeded to prove conclusively that not only was Nova Scotia coal being mined more cheaply than U.S. coal, but that Dominion Coal Company could easily afford an additional wage increase of 10 percent in a new contract. McLachlan insisted a 10-percent increase in wages would amount only to an added 22 cents for each ton of coal mined and still leave an additional 10-percent protection against cheaper U.S. coal. Wolvin had greatly distorted the tonnage of coal-per-miner figures. With a great deal of justification, McLachlan pointed out that most of Dominion's coal mines were old and inefficient, difficult and costly to work, and that the very nature of Cape Breton's submarine coal mines, with their long haulage ways under miles of ocean floor, added additional costs to production—costs that U.S. coal producers did not have to contend with.

In the same issue of the *Maritime Labour Herald*, it was announced that Sydney steelworkers employed by the Dominion Iron and Steel Company and its master, Besco, had had their meagre wages reduced another 10 percent—the third cut in as many months. Without the protection afforded by a militant union such as the UMWA, steelworkers were completely at the mercy of Wolvin and his cutthroat policies of wage slashing to increase profits.

Wolvin now began to step up the pace. The infamous spy and informer program, used with such devastating effect during the 1909 strike, continued. Firings and blacklistings increased at an alarming rate—usually against miners and steelworkers taking any active part in the union or being indiscreet enough to voice anti-company sentiment within the hearing of company spies or informers.

And then the mines began to close and thousands of miners were thrown onto the street to starve.

Wolvin answered the public outcry with the bland assertion that the mines that had been shut down were uneconomical in their operation, making the price of Nova Scotia coal noncompetitive with U.S. coal. By a strange coincidence, most of the mines closed were hotbeds of unionism, many of the more militant miners belonging to District 26 being employed in them.

When the time was ripe, it would not be difficult to persuade Cape Breton miners they should be willing to take large wage cuts in order to put bread on the table. Any job, even at reduced wages and hours of work, was better than being unemployed and starving.

It was in this atmosphere of uncertainty and oppression, that Bob Baxter, president of District 26, and Dan Livingstone, vice-president, opened negotiations with Besco for a new contract to take effect after the Montreal Agreement expired in November 1921. While the contract talks were continuing in Halifax, McLachlan remained in Glace Bay, preparing his campaign for the forthcoming general election, and had, therefore, little to do with negotiations.

Towards the end of October, rumours began to circulate throughout Cape Breton of the forthcoming cut in wages that Besco was proposing to put into effect after the present contract expired. As this proposal had not even been made to President Baxter at this stage of the negotiations, it must have been deliberately leaked by the provincial Liberal Party to discredit the union and the Labour Party in the forthcoming federal election. The "dirty tricks brigade" made a beeline for McLachlan, a labour candidate and driving force behind the UMWA District 26. It began with a whispering campaign—a sly dig in the ribs and a "Guess what?" method of spreading false rumour and lies, using paid informers and company spies. McLachlan was rumoured to be the villain of the piece who had agreed to a huge wage slash of 50 to 60 percent!

The slander became more positive when Billy Carroll, the Liberal candidate, addressed campaign meetings at St. Peters and Arichat in Cape Breton. According to the *Maritime Labour Herald*, with righteous indignation the "good" Carroll told his audiences. that "all of the candidates running in the forthcoming election were Christians of some sort, either Catholic or Protestant, excepting this man McLachlan who did not believe in God."

Jim McLachlan replied to this slander through the medium of his *Maritime Labour Herald*. In a letter to W.F. Carroll, dated November 4, 1921, McLachlan lambasted Carroll:

Now Billy, when you told the people that about me, you were a liar and a dirty character assassin.... Did you tell the good people of St. Peters how much money you made in the winter of 1909–10 when you were working for the Dominion Coal Company when they required lawyers to do the dirty work of evicting the wives and children of striking miners?... Did you tell how Father Fraser had to give the basement of his church for a very large number of families? Did you tell the people of St. Peters about the Liberal government annexing the house of the Prince of Peace into a temple of the God of War? Did you tell about the machine guns placed on the church steps at the request of your Liberal friends to shoot down miners if they dared to walk past the church?

This was McLachlan at his best: his outraged sense of honesty manifesting itself through a pen dripping with scorn and ridicule. In declaring Carroll to be a liar, he was daring him to sue, knowing full well that the lawyer, Carroll, would not contemplate any such action because his accusation against McLachlan had been a blatant lie. "You did not tell them any of these things which are going to knock the 'L' out of Carroll on December 6th. You kept these things quiet and made a complete ass out of yourself as well as a stupid liar by telling them 'this man McLachlan does not believe in God!'"

McLachlan's opponent had made a fatal mistake in declaring him to be an atheist and worse. McLachlan's article, which slashed and chopped Carroll unmercifully, would have forced many a man to fade from sight after delivering a humble apology, but not Carroll. If anything, the article only served to intensify his program of character assassination as he dreamed up lies of even greater infamy to be laid at McLachlan's door.

Unfortunately, Carroll's greatest allies in the character assassination of Jim McLachlan were the ministers and priests of Cape Breton who continued to wave Union Jacks from the pulpit as they condemned this "godless man" who had openly embraced the communist doctrine. "They would all be murdered in their beds by this Bolshevik monster who respected neither God nor State," they thundered. Their words fell on fertile ground. The Highland Scots, with their strict Catholic or Calvinist upbringing, were greatly under the influence of the so-called "men of God." If the minister said McLachlan was an atheist, then it must be so.

In actual fact, J.B. McLachlan was a devout man who believed in God and in Christianity. If he had embraced the socialist doctrine, it was because he had lost all faith in the two political parties of the age—Liberal and Conservative, neither of which had championed the workingman in his fight for decent working conditions and wages.

Eva Pemberton, daughter of Jim McLachlan, spoke bitterly of the accusations hurled at her father at this time:

> Anybody who had the guts to stand up and be counted in those days was labelled Bolshevik and godless. My father read his Bible every night before he went to sleep. I remember one morning when I awoke at about four-thirty in the morning—I couldn't sleep, and my father was a great one for getting up early. I looked through the window and my father was striding down the road to look at Momma's vegetable patch, so I got up and ran down to join him and he shushed me with a finger on his lips as he stood stock still and pointed to the veg patch. He said, "Eva, just stand still and I'll show you something that you'll probably never see in your life again." And there was this family of deer in a band of fog. The father and mother deer were standing watch while the little fawns were munching Momma's prized vegetables and Poppa wouldn't interfere. This was the night before they had splashed great big headlines all over the Glace Bay *Gazette* that he was an atheist and didn't believe in God, and he said to me, "Eva, when you see things like that, you have to be awful stupid not to believe in God." And another time when we were coming through the hay, I found a tiny blue flower and Poppa said,"Don't pick it, Eva, it'll just die right away. These are the things that make you know there is a hereafter and there is a God."
>
> I was only nine or ten years old but I've never forgotten it.

Jim McLachlan never swore or used swear words in his life. Even in his slashing counterattack on Carroll, it is noticeable that he did not use the word "hell." The letter "L" was used in its place.

A strict teetotaller, his early Calvinistic upbringing, added to his natural abhorrence of drunkenness, had led him into a life of abstinence. Strange characteristics for a man who was being accused of plotting to murder innocent people in their beds in a forthcoming Bolshevik uprising!

With the election only two weeks away, the Liberals now lost all restraint and let fly with both barrels at the labour opponent—J.B. McLachlan. At a crowded meeting in New Aberdeen on November 23, 1921, Carroll claimed McLachlan had been guilty of making a secret deal with Besco, betraying the miners of Nova Scotia by agreeing to a huge wage cut of 33⅓ percent. Through their official mouthpiece, the Glace Bay *Gazette*, the Liberals reported that: "Mr Carroll charged McLachlan with consenting to accept the 33⅓ percent reduction which the operators proposed to enforce, provided that the company would postpone negotiations until after the election, and Mr McLachlan almost went down on his knees begging them to do so."

This blatant lie triggered another blast from McLachlan in his *Maritime Labour Herald*. It was one thing to call a man an atheist—he could laugh at that because it was so absurd. But when he had been falsely accused of selling his beloved miners down the river, it was time for strong action!

> A couple of weeks ago I had occasion to publicly call Carroll a liar. If he is correctly reported on November 23rd, then I wish to say again he is lying.... When he said I consented to accept ANY reduction he LIED.... When he said I asked the operators to postpone negotiations he LIED. The whole statement is a lie from beginning to end. There was not one thing occurred at the meeting of the coal companies and the miners' representatives while I was present that could even be remotely construed as a discussion of the wage-rate at all.

Again, Carroll did not take up the challenge. He had been called a liar and a character assassin in a published statement by McLachlan. As a lawyer, he was fully aware of the legal course of action to follow, but the good Billy had no intention of facing McLachlan in a court of law where the tables could easily be turned to McLachlan's advantage. Instead, he continued to press the charge that McLachlan had made a secret agreement with the coal companies for a massive wage reduction and, in doing so, had betrayed the men who trusted him.

Liberal organizers moved into Cape Breton for the final stages of the campaign to drum up last-minute support for their candidate—Billy Carroll. Drinks were liberally supplied to out-of-work miners and steelworkers as the reigning Conservative government in Ottawa was blamed for the slump in the coal mining and steel industries of Nova Scotia. "Vote for a Liberal government—throw out the capitalists in Ottawa, and a new era of prosperity will dawn in Cape Breton." This was the message repeated over and over again by the Liberal dirty tricks brigade in the final days of the campaign. The fact that the Liberals controlling the provincial government of Nova Scotia had made no effort to persuade the coal companies to cease their shut-down program was not mentioned.

It now only remained for the *coup de grâce* to be delivered to McLachlan and the fight was over. Liberal Party organizers gathered in Cape Breton to plan their final strategy and give a knockout blow to the labour opposition. It has often been said that a lie oft' repeated will become "truth"—especially if some form of "proof" is produced to substantiate the false accusation.

Through devious means, using paid informers from the ranks of labour, McLachlan's supporters were persuaded to issue an open challenge to Carroll to produce proof of his charge against McLachlan at a joint meeting at the Lyceum Theatre in Sydney on the Monday night before the election. Eager to exonerate McLachlan from the false charges laid against him, Labour Party organizers readily agreed to the terms suggested by the Liberals. It was to be a public forum. Carroll was to speak for the first thirty minutes—without interruption; McLachlan would speak for another thirty minutes, and then Carroll would be given an additional ten minutes to reply.

Oh, what lambs they were, these Labour Party organizers. By allowing Carroll to speak for the last ten minutes of the debate, they had been neatly manoeuvred into an untenable position. No doubt they believed Carroll's final speech would be followed by an open discussion and questions from the floor, but the honest workingmen forming the Labour Party campaign committee were no match for the scoundrels who were even then setting up the trap. It was an uneven fight—no holds barred; lies, deceit, chicanery, and now, forgery was to be added to their list of crimes.

On December 5, 1921, the debate was held in the Lyceum Theatre in Sydney. Hundreds of miners and steelworkers packed the hall to capacity. They trekked to Sydney to hear their champion slaughter the Goliath of the Liberal Party, who had dared suggest their candidate had connived with coal companies to lower their wages. It was the night before the election and the meeting could be crucial to either candidate.

Carroll opened the debate and to everyone's surprise, his opening speech made no mention of the alleged sellout of miners to Besco. Instead he spoke in generalities. McLachlan explained the negotiations between union and company that were being conducted at that moment in Halifax. Not until agreement had been reached could any information be released. Certainly, the union contract must not become the subject of political debate at this stage of negotiations, McLachlan emphasized, but the membership could be assured that the executive was holding out for a good contract with an increase in the standard of living for Nova Scotia miners. Those were the facts and anybody who suggested otherwise was a liar!

Jim McLachlan returned to his seat amid cheers and thunderous applause from his many supporters in the audience. Then his opponent, Carroll, stood up to have the last say. Now the trap was sprung. With a flourish, Carroll suddenly produced a sheet of paper from his pocket. Waving it before his shocked audience, he alleged it was a letter written by David Ryan, former vice-president of District 26, to Donald "The Boo" Mclsaac of New Aberdeen, reporting he had overheard McLachlan selling out the miners of Nova Scotia. The letter had been typewritten—even the signature had been typed—and to complicate matters further, Donald "The Boo" Mclsaac was known to be unable to read or write.

After reading the letter to the audience, Carroll, accompanied by Donald "The Boo" Mclsaac and the Liberal Party organizers, left the theatre by a rear exit. The band struck up a lively air, which effectively drowned out McLachlan's protest that the letter was a forgery and that the whole affair had been elaborately staged to discredit him on the eve of the election.

The audience streamed from the hall to be met by a special edition of the Sydney *Record*, which had been printed hours before the public meeting. Glaring headlines read: "Carroll produces conclusive proof against McLachlan!" The newspaper was not for sale—it was given free. The alleged letter from David Ryan was published in full below the headline:

Thorburn, N.S.
October 12th, 1921

Mr Donald McIsaac,
New Aberdeen, C.B.

Dear Friend,

Your letter of October 6th about the statements of Michael Ryan has given me some worry. I intended making a public statement about J.B. McLaughlin [misspelled] and his underhand methods. He is in league with Coal Company officials. He has agreed to get the U.M.W. to accept a cut of thirty-three and a third percent after the company had made a cut of somewhere about forty-five or fifty-five. I overheard the talk between Mr McLaughlin, Mr McCann and McDougall the engineer, and I know what I am saying. Any person who was there as a delegate will remember the secret way the deal was put through. I hope to be in Cape Breton soon.

Yours truly,
David Ryan

How had Carroll obtained the letter? That was later explained in the Sydney *Record*. McIsaac had been motivated by a sense of civic responsibility in bringing the letter to the attention of the Liberal candidate, Mr Carroll!

The following day, December 6, 1921, the general election was held and the people of Cape Breton cast their votes. When the results were announced, Carroll and his running mate were elected to the House of Commons and McLachlan and Doyle were narrowly defeated. The reigning Conservative government in Ottawa had been defeated and a Liberal government elected in its place. But for the first time in the history of Canadian politics, a Labour Member of Parliament, J.S. Woodsworth of Winnipeg General Strike fame, had been elected to the House of Commons. Woodsworth was accompanied by his friend William Irvine, who had also been elected on an Independent Labour ticket.

After taking his seat in the House of Commons, William Irvine rose to inform the speaker there was a new political group represented in the House: "Mr Woodsworth is the leader of our group and I am the group!"

The "group" should have been further strengthened through the election of another old stalwart of the Labour Party, J.B. McLachlan, but he had been deprived of his seat in the House of Commons by means of a despicable trick. Typically, McLachlan did not cry over spilt milk. Philosophically, he accepted his defeat even though his opponent had used lies and deceit to destroy his reputation and gather workers' votes. In the *Maritime Labour Herald*, December 9, 1921, he wrote:

> The election is over. The duty of the hour is to rally the workers and prepare for the next test of strength, whether it be over wages, working conditions or an election. We must work, work until it shall become impossible to split the ranks of labour.

8

Wage Cuts, Slowdown and Strike: 1922

On December 19, 1921, Roy Wolvin ordered the Dominion Coal Company to post notices at each of its Cape Breton collieries to announce immediate wage cuts of 33⅓ percent, effective as of January 1, 1922, and to abolish all local union contracts forthwith.

The huge wage cut shocked and distressed Cape Breton's miners, who began to suspect collusion between their District 26 officers and the British Empire Steel Corporation. The magic figure of 33⅓ percent seemed to provide conclusive evidence that Carroll's accusation against McLachlan was true. The false accusation, coupled with the publication of the Donald "The Boo" letter, had done much to discredit some members of the executive. By announcing the 33⅓ percent wage cut shortly after the federal election, Wolvin had cunningly placed a rubber stamp of authenticity on the slander. The miners' leaders began to move to the right and the left. McLachlan and "Red" Dan Livingstone led the leftist faction while Silby Barrett and Bob Baxter led the more conservative right.

Billy Carroll's "Red" smear campaign had borne fruit; Cape Bretoners were beginning to search under their beds every night for Bolshevik murderers and rogues.

When the District 26 election was held the same month, Robert Baxter deposed Dan Livingstone as president; W.P. Delaney, another rightist, was elected vice-president; and Silby Barrett regained his old position as international board member. McLachlan was reelected as secretary-treasurer, but only by a narrow margin.

Wolvin returned to Montreal to spend Christmas with his family. His sumptuous Christmas fare could hardly be compared with that of a Cape Breton miner or steelworker. Breast of turkey against "potato and point." With typical Cape Breton humour, Ben Boone explained that miners made light of the cruel fact that they could no longer afford to buy meat for their daily sustenance. When a minuscule portion of meat was uncovered among the inevitable potato hash that comprised almost every evening meal, they would "point" at the precious speck as proof that their meal, often shared by eight or more children, was not totally devoid of meat!

With the wage slash, McLachlan made immediate application for a Conciliation Board under the terms of the Industrial Disputes Investigation Act and then applied for a court injunction restraining Besco from carrying out the wage slash until the Conciliation Board had convened. In his court appearance before Mr Justice Russell in Halifax, McLachlan argued that the IDI Act was designed to prevent disputes arising from any intended change in working conditions or wages until the case had been heard by a Conciliation Board and recommendations made to alleviate the problem. Judge Russell agreed with McLachlan's forceful argument and issued an injunction to prevent Besco from cutting miners' wages on December 30—two days hence.

Jubilation throughout the Nova Scotia coalfields was short-lived however. Besco filed its own appeal against the injunction and the case was heard by Justice Mellish, the same learned judge who had dismissed the charges against the Dominion Coal Company after the New Waterford explosion in 1917, and whose firm had been engaged as solicitors for Dominion. Judge Mellish quickly discovered a loophole in the law and reversed the lower court's decision. When Judge Russell had granted the request for an injunction against Besco, he had done so in the belief that the wording of the Industrial Disputes Investigation Act was quite clear—that neither party in the dispute, union or company, could change the conditions of employment with respect to wages or hours until the Conciliation Board had considered all the evidence and presented its findings. Judge Mellish, however, differed with this strict interpretation of the law. The learned judge argued that the wording and intent of the act did not apply in this particular case, because District 26 miners did not have a contract with the company—*it had expired in November 1921!*

Immediately the injunction was suspended by Judge Mellish, a grateful British Empire Steel Corporation applied its wage cut, and every miner's wage was slashed by 33⅓ percent. The decision left the district executive dumbfounded and then righteously indignant. There had been many scores of Conciliation Boards appointed after the expiry of a contract—in fact, it was the recognized method of complying with the law—to apply for a Conciliation Board after the *present* contract had expired and the union and the company had failed to come to terms on a new contract.

The notification of the wage slash was received with sorrow and despair throughout the coal mining communities of Nova Scotia. Already they had been brought to the brink of starvation by the coal companies' policy of reducing the work week from six days to three or less. Under the new schedule proposed by Wolvin, day labourers in the mines would receive only $2.44 per day! As McLachlan pointed out in his *Maritime Labour Herald*, with the men working only an average 290 days in the year, their total annual income—providing the mines did not close down for part of the year—would now be only $707.60.

To focus public attention on the plight of his Nova Scotia miners, McLachlan used the medium of his *Maritime Labour Herald* to list household and personal expenses that the average miner with a family of five had to pay over one whole year. Under the title "How Can They Live?" he made a very convincing argument against Besco's wage cut. After deducting expenses for family clothing and footwear of $125, rent for the company house, $100, coal, light, sanitation, water, and taxes, $120.50, checkoff dues for doctor, hospital, church, trade union, and insurance, $136.40, only the paltry sum of $225.70 remained out of an annual wage of $707.60 to purchase food for the family.

By dividing the remaining $225.70 by the number of days in the year, McLachlan was able to show that only 62 cents remained each day to feed the five persons in the household, and that if the princely sum of 62 cents was divided five ways, each person in the family was left with twelve and four-tenths cents for each day's meals. *With a minimum of three meals a day, this left only four and one-tenth cents for each person's meal!*

This was the amount of money that "Roy the Wolf" Wolvin insisted was more than sufficient to provide food for a Nova Scotia miner and his family after the huge wage slash had been enforced. For men working deep in the bowels of the earth, labouring like beasts of the field, good and plentiful food was essential; yet, as the meagre diet began to take its toll, many miners gave up their own slender rations to feed their children.

In the *Maritime Labour Herald* of January 12, 1922, McLachlan made a comparison between the allowance for each prisoner in His Majesty's prisons in Canada with wages earned by his Nova Scotia miners. Quoting the 1920 estimates, he was able to show it had cost the province of Ontario the sum of $1.94 per day to feed, clothe, and provide heating for five prisoners for a total of $708.10 per year which was 50 cents more than the wages paid to a day labourer in the Nova Scotia mines under the proposed new wage scale enforced by Wolvin.

With the massive wage cut, the communities of Cape Breton began to suffer acute malnutrition. Conditions among the many thousands of unemployed and their families became unendurable and the danger of riots more pronounced as anger against the Dominion Coal Company mounted. Children began to stay home from school as the pangs of hunger and weakness of limbs forced them to stay in bed to preserve what little strength remained. It was midwinter and the cold Atlantic gales swept down from Cape North to cut through threadbare garments and chill bony limbs.

Cries were made for the provincial government to provide some measure of relief before it was too late. Newspapers reported that relief money had been provided in Montreal after demonstrations and street parades had been held to protest growing unemployment. In Ontario, steps had already been taken by the provincial government to cooperate with the worst-hit towns to provide food and clothing to the poor, but in the province of

Nova Scotia, nothing was done. Wolvin determined to starve his mining communities into submission and the provincial government headed by Premier Murray, ever mindful of the precious royalties from coal mining, closed eyes and ears to the cries of suffering and pleas for help, as they fawned on Roy Wolvin, president of the British Empire Steel Corporation.

Threats began to surface from some of the more militant sections of mining communities. If the government would not provide relief, food riots would result. Company stores would be raided and the poor would take what food they required. The trouble was brought to a head after the Dominion Coal Company closed its No. 9 mine and laid off its miners indefinitely. The company justified its action by claiming the shutdown was necessary "due to a lack of shipping," although its No. 2 mine, which was joined underground with No. 9, and shared the same boiler house, powerhouse and mining shaft, was allowed to remain open. As a further punitive measure, miners laid off at the No. 9 mine were refused credit at the company store.

It may have been coincidence, but many of the more militant miners in District 26 had been employed at the No. 9 mine. It was believed the mine had been closed and credit cut off at the company store to punish and silence company critics.

With many young mouths to feed after credit had been cut off, laid-off miners now became desperate. Many determined to flout the laws of the land and a corrupt judicial system that had allowed the company to ignore a court injunction and impose huge wage slashes.

The *Maritime Labour Herald* reported that the raiding of the company stores began when "Big" Frank McIntyre, a miner from Glace Bay, tried to obtain food supplies for his hungry family of nine children; the oldest was a boy of fourteen with an injured spine who would never be able to work. McIntyre's wife was ill in hospital, and the family had fallen heavily in debt because of expenses involved in the treatment of her illness. After being locked out of No. 9 mine, and with nothing in the larder to feed his children, he was forced to swallow his pride and beg the store manager to extend credit to obtain food. When refused in no uncertain terms, he told the manager to step aside and helped himself to supplies of butter, sugar, and flour. No thief, he asked the manager to weigh the food taken so that he could repay him at a later date, but the manager refused. The company had promised credit and credit had been refused, so other miners followed McIntyre's example, taking only what was urgently needed.

The following week, Frank McIntyre and twelve other miners were arrested and taken to Sydney in chains to be tried for the heinous crime of stealing food from the company store to feed their hungry children. They were tried and convicted in rapid succession, before being jailed for periods of from two to three years. With their father in jail and an ailing mother in hospital, the Mclntyre children were left destitute.

Prior to the trial, coal company officials had cried for vengeance against "criminals" daring to steal from a "benevolent" employer. The Sydney *Record* and the Sydney *Post* had printed the anguished demand for justice made by the coal company officials, but neglected to inform their readers that the men who had stolen the food had done so only to feed their children.

The harsh sentences handed out to starving miners brought McLachlan out of his corner with both fists flying. In a ringing editorial in the *Maritime Labour Herald* of February 3, 1922, he flayed a judicial system that allowed financiers and millionaire swindlers to go free while filling the penitentiaries with workers whose only crime was poverty and hunger. Under the heading "One Law for Wealth and Another for Poverty," judges were singled out for special attention:

> A judge is not appointed for his knowledge of the law, nor for his righteousness nor his character. A judge is a capitalist politician who is put upon the bench because he has faithfully served the capitalists as a politician and will continue to serve them as a judge.... Politics in Canada are notoriously corrupt.... The average Member of Parliament is a crook and judgeships are not given to backbenchers.

This was pretty strong stuff even for a labour newspaper. In one fell swoop, McLachlan had declared war not only on the capitalist class, on which he blamed Nova Scotia's labour problems, but also on politicians, the judicial system, and the courts, which he declared were covert allies of the corrupt stock market swindlers who had launched the British Empire Steel Corporation on watered stock and liquid assets.

By exposing the rotten system, McLachlan knew he was placing his head squarely on the execution block.

The Conciliation Board, under the chairmanship of U.E. Gillen, now published its long-awaited report. It was a great disappointment to Nova Scotia miners. It recommended that the wage increase obtained in November 1920, known as the Montreal Agreement, be rescinded and wages reduced to the level prevailing before the agreement had been signed. In addition, all rates were to be reduced a further 20 percent across the board. This amounted to an overall reduction of 30 percent compared to the company's posted wage cut of 33⅓ percent.

The Board had finalized its recommendations after hearing lengthy briefs from company representatives regarding the state of trade and profit and loss statements that were mostly verbal in nature and did not constitute proof of the true financial standing of the corporation.

Mayor James Ling of New Waterford, the workers' representative to the Conciliation Board, submitted a minority report against the wage cut, with the argument that the company had not provided a single shred of evidence to prove the need for such a cut. In spite of union protests, the Board had not ordered the company to open its books for inspection.

This familiar pattern continued in the years ahead. At times, even false figures were submitted to substantiate company claims that they could not afford to increase wages and retain their present markets. Mayor Ling advised the Board in his minority report that the proposed wage cuts would condemn thousands of men, women, and children to live in a state of semi-starvation. Only "copies" of different pages of Besco's financial report for the fiscal year ending March 21, 1921, were submitted to the Board for their inspection, but Mayor Ling pointed out that even the copies showed net profits of $9,663,548 for the fiscal year. With such vast profits the company could well have afforded a raise in pay rather than a reduction, but much of this profit was to be used to pay dividends on watered stock, which had launched the British Empire Steel Corporation in 1919.

Besco immediately put the new rates into effect and paid the retroactive difference between their 33⅓ percent wage slash and the 30 percent recommended by the Conciliation Board. But as expected, the Conciliation Board's recommendations were overwhelmingly rejected by Cape Breton miners, who had been working without a contract since November 1921 when the Montreal Agreement had expired.

District 26 delegates met in Truro, Nova Scotia, to decide on the next course of action. A delegation of union officers, including McLachlan, was sent to Montreal to meet with Wolvin and his Besco management, but when an agreement in principle was finally reached on March 1, 1922, Nova Scotia miners were shocked and angered to learn that the new contract proposals agreed to by their District 26 executive provided for basically the same wage reduction recommended by the Gillen Board of Conciliation.

Again, the District 26 officers had shown they split into two different factions: the right, headed by President Bob Baxter and Silby Barrett; and the left, headed by the rebel, McLachlan. The new contract had not been agreed to by all members of the union executive board. McLachlan had been vehemently opposed to any reduction in wages but most of the other union officers had reluctantly accepted the premise that the state of the depression, added to a slump in the coal mining industry, made such reductions inevitable and necessary.

In reaching this reluctant decision, they had been influenced by John P. White, ex-international president of the UMWA, who was present at the meeting with Besco in Montreal as a special representative of John L. Lewis. After the great sellout, as it was termed by Nova Scotia miners, many of the District 26 delegates claimed they had been influenced in their decision to accept Besco's punitive terms by warnings issued by Lewis that District 26 could expect little or no assistance from the international treasury in the event of a strike. Every district of the union in the United States was making plans for a fight in April "therefore we feel that in the best interests of all concerned, the company offer should be accepted."

In reaching their unpopular decision to accept Besco's huge wage slash, the rightist elements controlling District 26 had not taken into account the wily experience of J.B. McLachlan. Knowing full well that a strike, if unsupported by the international body of the union and its treasury, would undoubtedly result in great suffering for Nova Scotia miners and their families (as it had during the 1909–10 strike), McLachlan decided on different tactics. Remembering the "Wee Darg" (the small day's work) slowdown strike called by Alexander McDonald, the great Scottish miners' leader, McLachlan persuaded the District 26 executive to introduce a "strike on the job" to reduce coal output by at least the same percentage that miners' wages had been reduced.

The vote to call such a strike was by no means unanimous and produced an even greater split in the executive, with Baxter, Barrett, and other rightist members opposing it, and McLachlan, Livingstone, and the leftists vigorously supporting it. The rank and file membership of District 26 wholeheartedly supported McLachlan in his rejection of the proposed wage slash, which he had repudiated after returning from Montreal. A pithead vote had condemned Baxter and the rightist members of the executive for recommending acceptance of the wage cut. The difference of opinion between the leftist and rightist factions within the District 26 executive widened into a serious breach until it became obvious to even the most ill-informed union member that a battle was about to begin.

On March 17, 1922, James Bryson McLachlan declared war against Besco when he issued his famous manifesto. Calling on every miner in the province of Nova Scotia to fight the oppressive policies of the huge international corporation that had brought so much misery into their lives, his clarion call to arms was reminiscent of the ancient battle call for freedom prior to the storming of the Bastille. From the McLachlan Family records:

Brothers! War is on—a class war.

During the past week, three children died at Dominion No. 4; children under one year of age whose parents were unable to provide them with milk.... The children of Cape Breton are naked and shoeless, yet because they have failed to attend school, the parents are threatened with prosecution.... John Doucette's five children are shoeless and covered with rags. He saw them slowly starve and in desperation "stole" a small bag of flour to feed them. For that "crime" he is now serving two years in jail.... There is only one way to fight this corporation and that is to cut production to the point where they cannot any longer earn profits.... You are fighting for a living for your wife and family, the stock gamblers are fighting for profits on watered stock.... Up men and in your organized thousands attack them.

Action not words count now!

After such a stirring call to arms, was it any wonder the miners of Nova Scotia rallied to McLachlan's banner? When asked to describe "striking on the job," McLachlan said, "You men work with coats on.... We will see that the price of coal goes up. They are snatching the babies' milk, you snatch the dividends—strike on the job."

To reinforce his manifesto, McLachlan sent a letter of explanation to every Member of Parliament. If there was going to be a debate on the Nova Scotia slowdown strike, then they would be provided with the truth. The letter was pure McLachlan, hiding no facts, exposing the rottenness of Besco and financial wheeling and dealing that had been responsible for the present tragic situation. Phrases such as "Do you know that the British Empire Steel Corporation is paying such a low wage to its workmen that thousands are not receiving enough to live on?... Do you know that hundreds of parents are unable to provide for their children, and that children are actually dying because they are undernourished?" were combined with accusations of complicity by ministers of the Nova Scotia and federal governments in the act of incorporation of Besco using watered stock. "To pay dividends on this watered stock and idle junk, miners' wages have been cut approximately 32 percent. This wage reduction affects twelve thousand men." The letter ended with a heart-rending appeal for justice:

Whether you take action or not, ten thousand mine workers in Nova Scotia who have no money, nothing but their naked hands to defend themselves and their hungry families with, shall use every means that can occur in the hearts of desperate men to resist this invasion of their homes and living by a corporation which was born in legislative corruption, and which is making this raid on the homes and lives of the people in order to pay dividends on junk and watered stock.

The "Wee Darg"—the slowdown in production ordered by Jim McLachlan—was put into effect immediately. Men reported to work, but worked with their coats on rather than stripped to the waist as was the usual practice, while drivers and haulage men worked at a slower pace collecting filled coal boxes or delivering empties. Almost immediately, the slowdown began to show in a greatly reduced output of mined coal.

Although daily workers received their normal rate of pay, coal face workers, paid at contract rates, were the ones to lose financially. It was greatly to their credit that the slowdown continued without faltering, but McLachlan knew that his men trusted him implicitly.

The slowdown policy, which made headlines across Canada, was widely hailed in labour circles but condemned by business generally. James Murdock, the Minister of Labour in Ottawa, wired McLachlan to criticize the work slowdown and to appeal for a return to an honest day's work by the Cape Breton miners.

McLachlan hastened to reply to what he considered to be unjust criticism. In a letter dispatched March 20, 1922, he flayed the Minister of Labour for his hypocritical condemnation of the slowdown strike. Reiterating that he had ordered District 26 miners to cut down production to a point where all profits for Besco would vanish, McLachlan declared:

This tactic is a means of retaliation for a highly unjust encroachment on the wages of Besco's workmen.... There is nothing dishonest about it.... I have preached this with the blessing of my friends and amid the curses of my enemies. I have preached it to tens, hundreds and thousands. I have done it on land and on sea, in miners' halls and in churches, on the hillsides of Nova Scotia and on her busy streets—and Mr Minister, what are you going to do about it?... We shall continue to fight the imposition of this iniquitous wage reduction, if we have to rock the ramshackle institution known as the British Empire Steel Corporation from its rotten sills to its bending and shaking rafters.

The exchange of telegrams and letters continued—each more heated than the last, but Murdock was no match for the fiery McLachlan. A second Murdock telegram to McLachlan on March 21, was even more pompous than its predecessor:

> In my judgement it is un-British, un-Canadian and cowardly to be pretending to be working for a wage rate in effect while declaring to the world that only partial grudging service will be given.... Two wrongs do not make a right, the red blooded Canadian citizens will not, in my judgement, follow your advice in the pretence of loyalty, staying on the job for the purpose of penalizing the employer.

By the end of March 1922, the suffering throughout Cape Breton's mining communities had reached disastrous proportions. The mayors of Glace Bay, New Waterford, Dominion, and Springhill led a delegation to Ottawa to present the Cape Breton miners' case to the government and to plead for a Royal Commission to investigate all matters pertaining to the coal mining industry of Nova Scotia. The new Prime Minister, William Lyon Mackenzie King, who had previously been the Minister of Labour, was believed to hold views sympathetic to workers in the present dispute, but the delegation returned to Nova Scotia with its hopes dashed to the ground. Mackenzie King received the mayoral delegation in his office and listened politely to their pleas for federal intervention but refused to intervene.

A letter from that erstwhile gentleman followed the next day. Not only had he refused to intervene to save the children, he had also refused the request for a Royal Commission of investigation. From the Mackenzie King papers, Ottawa: "I beg to inform you that the government has had this matter under consideration and is of the opinion that the situation is not one which in the public interest, can be satisfactorily dealt with under the existing circumstances by a Royal Commission."

On March 30, 1922, William Irvine, Labour Member of Parliament for Calgary East, moved an adjournment in the House of Commons for a debate to discuss the urgent situation in Nova

Scotia. After describing the events that had led up to the present impasse, Mr Irvine informed the House that conditions in Nova Scotia "almost rival those reports which have come to us from the famine districts of the Volga after the Russian Revolution." Passionately, he pleaded the cause of the Nova Scotia miners. They had appealed to the provincial government for an enquiry but without success. They had then sent a deputation of mayors from the hardest-hit mining communities to tell the Prime Minister of children undernourished and suffering, of a large increase in the death rate, and of parents given summonses for being unable to send their children to school because they were unable to provide them with shoes and clothes or proper nourishment.

But the government of Mackenzie King had refused to intervene or to appoint a Royal Commission to investigate the whole matter.

Irvine went on to say: "If it is necessary to pay dividends on watered stock to the amount of $19,000,000, it can only be done by reducing the wages of the producers [miners] and I understand that is exactly what is taking place."

Other speakers followed Irvine to add their plea for the government to investigate and effect a settlement as soon as possible. And then, the Liberal member for Cape Breton South, W.F. Carroll, rose to his feet to add his own contribution to the debate; the same Billy Carroll who had been engaged as a lawyer for the company that was being accused of starving Cape Breton coal miners into submission; the same Billy Carroll who had been elected after accusations of fraud, deceit, and forgery during the 1921 election. With the proper note of solemnity, the honourable member now told the House he was deeply interested in the success of the coal mining industry in his province, but equally interested in the welfare of miners and workers generally:

A finer body of men does not exist in the Dominion of Canada, although it is true they did not treat me very well during the last campaign.... I want to point out that Dominion Coal Company did increase miners' wages beyond that recommended by the members of the conciliation board, although the increase was small it is true (3⅓ percent).... The provincial Minister of Mines has said that if the miners would go back to work and not loaf on the job, he would appoint a Royal Commission to investigate the situation, but I am sorry to say his recommendations were turned down.

Was it any wonder the offer of a provincial investigation had been refused? The miners of Nova Scotia believed they had been betrayed countless times in the past by their provincial government. They also believed it would be foolish to place their blind trust in the same people who had encouraged the incorporation of Besco using watered stock.

Changing direction, the worthy Mr Carroll now made a direct plea to Nova Scotia miners to ignore their rebel leader and seek provincial arbitration to resolve their differences with the coal company. If they were not satisfied with the findings of the arbitration board, Carroll promised they could always appeal to the Supreme Court of Nova Scotia, consisting of seven judges "who have always been, and I believe yet are, eminently fair men."

At this point, Carroll was interrupted by Irvine, who asked if it were not true that certain members of the Nova Scotia government were major shareholders in the Dominion Coal Company? But Carroll, feigning ignorance, continued:

I am deeply concerned from the personal standpoint, because if the trouble continues...it will mean that the provincial government will not be able to carry out its legitimate business because it will lose its royalties amounting to millions of dollars which are normally paid by the Dominion Coal Company.

And there, of course, was the real reason why Billy Carroll was deeply concerned about the dispute. His own Liberal Party back in Nova Scotia was hurting due to the loss of royalties. The same provincial government that had ignored the plight of thousands of starving women and children and had refused to intervene in the strike was now openly begging miners to apply for an arbitration board to settle the dispute—on the company's terms.

Carroll was followed by the Honourable James Murdock, Minister of Labour, who again asserted that "red-blooded" Canadians would never strike on the job. "Labour has to be fair and decent." Murdock did not mention that Besco had not played "fair and decent" by suddenly announcing a huge wage slash of 33⅓ percent, but he did admit under pressure that a wage of three dollars a day or less was not sufficient to feed and clothe a family.

Murdock went on to expose a public scandal that had occurred during the reign of the previous government—Conservative—before its defeat in December 1921:

> Personally I regard it as a misfortune indeed that the British Empire Steel Corporation could not have utilized a portion of the $3,000,000 paid to them out of the Demobilization Fund on November 25th, 1921, to give a little more consideration to the workers of Nova Scotia. But they have not done so. It has been suggested by the members of this House, that the $3,000,000 went to pay dividends on watered stock.

Returned soldiers starving with their families in Nova Scotia must have wept when they heard this gem. The Demobilization Fund had been set up to assist men to return to civilian life and find them jobs. In some instances, it could be used to subsidize an employer to offer jobs to ex-servicemen, but in Nova Scotia, the money had been used to feed the owners of watered stock while returned soldiers roamed the streets—hungry and desperate for work.

Murdock completed his speech and sat down amidst a chorus of hisses and boos from the opposition benches, but not before he had admitted that McLachlan's replies to his long-winded telegrams of protest had been sent "Collect" and that the Ministry of Labour had been forced to pay the sum of $18.50 for them. The canny Scot had had the last laugh!

Following the spirited debate in the House of Commons on the Nova Scotia labour dispute, Prime Minister Mackenzie King hurriedly arranged for the Gillen Board of Conciliation to reconvene, but after being castigated by miners' leaders and municipal authorities in the coal mining towns of Cape Breton for his pro-company recommendations, Gillen was not anxious to reexamine his findings. Under pressure, however, he agreed to do so.

In the *Maritime Labour Herald* of April 18, 1922, McLachlan bitterly condemned the Gillen Board for ignoring the plight of miners and their families during the strike. Never once had the members of the Board visited Cape Breton to see conditions at firsthand, McLachlan charged; if they had, they would undoubtedly have been influenced in their findings. Instead the Board had chosen to sift through the evidence from afar. If the union agreed to abide by the findings of the reconstituted Gillen Board, McLachlan warned, the cost sheets of coal companies would have to be studied to determine their true profit and loss. And while the members of the Board were about it, he suggested, they had better examine the cost sheets of miners, which were reckoned not in dollars, but in hungry, shoeless, coatless women and children, and in order to do that "*Gillen would be forced to tour the mining communities of Cape Breton even if he, McLachlan, had to buy him a pair of hip boots to wade through the muck!*"

The Gillen Board made only a token appearance and then resigned without submitting a report. Within a matter of days, Mackenzie King announced that yet another Board had been set up, and that it would be headed by Dr D'Arcy Scott.

The Scott Board of Conciliation started work early in May 1922, and, contrary to the actions of the Gillen Board, began to visit every mining community in Nova Scotia, taking statements from miners and their wives, businessmen, clergy, and community leaders. This course of action was exactly what the deputation of Cape Breton mayors had requested when they had made their fruitless visit to Ottawa to plead for Mackenzie King's intervention in March. But firsthand evidence of suffering and want seemed to have little effect on the members of the Board.

The Scott Board issued its report on May 25, 1922. Basically it was much the same as its predecessor, the Gillen Report. It recommended a small increase of fifteen cents a day in the basic rate of pay, but as the basic rate had already been slashed 33⅓ percent below the 1921 rate, the small increase still left miners' wages far beneath the poverty level.

The Scott Board had been greatly influenced in its findings by the argument put forth by Wolvin when he claimed the state of the mining industry would not allow an increase at this time.

The report was rejected almost unanimously by District 26

miners on the recommendation of McLachlan. Later that same month, May 1922, the rejection proved justified and Besco's claims that wage cuts were the only viable means of cutting production costs to allow the company to remain competitive were proven false when the company's first annual report was published, showing that a very healthy profit of $4,400,000 had been earned between April and December 1921.

The union rejection of the Scott Conciliation Board Report was followed by a call to arms. Stronger measures would now be necessary if miners were to secure a living wage from Besco.

The climate was ripe for communist recruitment. For over twenty years, Nova Scotia coal and steel workers had fought to obtain decent wages and working conditions. Only during the war, when an almost hysterical demand for coal had prompted provincial and federal governments to force coal companies to raise miners' wages to keep pace with the spiralling cost of living, had they received any consideration. And now, in one fell swoop, all their wage gains were to be taken away and their take-home pay savagely reduced.

With the outlawing of the Communists in Canada through the introduction of Section 98 of the Criminal Code in 1919, Communist Party leaders were forced to go underground or face lengthy prison sentences. In limbo, it was decided to form a dual organization. The Workers' Party of Canada would operate publicly as a front for the parent body, the Communist Party of Canada. Under its innocuous title, the WPC would function as a socialist workers' party similar to the Labour Party of Canada, but orientated and controlled by the Communist Party of Canada, owing allegiance to the Soviet Union.

The Workers' Party of Canada now moved to Cape Breton to add support to striking miners and to gain much needed recruits. Led by "Moscow" Jack MacDonald, general-secretary of the Party, noted communists Tim Buck, Malcolm Bruce, Tom Bell, Sam Scarlett, Annie Buller, and Rebecca Buhay spoke at every miners' meeting, on street corners, in meeting halls, or on the sandbanks at Lingan.

Everywhere they spread the gospel of communism: "Workers

of the World, Unite, you've nothing to lose but your chains."

The first recruits were McLachlan and fellow union leader, Dan Livingstone.

Immediately after joining the Communist Party of Canada, or to be correct, the Workers' Party of Canada, McLachlan wrote a fiery rejection of the recent Scott Award in his *Maritime Labour Herald*.

> The Scott Conciliation Board's award takes the place of the cross dipped in blood as the signal for war. The fight is not against another clan. The fight is directed against as bold a band of cut-throat robbers as ever disgraced a country. So the miners gather to the fight, with weapons the profit gluttons little dream of.

McLachlan's manifesto of March 17 had called his miners to arms. Now in this June 9 edition of the *Herald*, he gave notice that from now on, the "Wee Darg" would be followed by "all-out" war, a full-blooded strike that would shut down every pit in Nova Scotia with twelve thousand miners heeding the call.

With the rejection of the so-called award, demands were made for a convention of District 26 delegates representing every miners' local of the union throughout Nova Scotia. On June 20, 1922, they gathered at Truro to plan the next move in the dispute. After condemning the Scott Award, the delegates severely censured the members of their district executive who had recommended acceptance of the wage reduction in Montreal and who had consistently opposed McLachlan's slowdown or "strike on the job." The right-wing faction of the executive, President Baxter, Vice-president Delaney, and international board representative Silby Barrett, resigned after the vote of censure had been coupled with doubts concerning their ability to lead District 26 miners during the present crisis. Elections for a new district executive were then set for August 15, 1922, but the left-wing faction led by McLachlan and "Red" Dan Livingstone was left firmly in control until the date of the elections.

The resignations were the turning point in the affairs of District 26. From then on, hundreds of miners, disillusioned with a democratic system of government that seemed to favour the interests of big business over the rights of ordinary workingmen, began to listen avidly to the disciples of communist doctrine as they moved through the Cape Breton coalfields preaching their message of hope for the downtrodden working class.

Years later, many Cape Breton coal miners insisted they had merely been "Cape Breton communists"—not the Moscow variety, which demanded the overthrow of the state as well as the capitalist system. Indeed, there may have been more than a grain of truth in this simple statement; prior to the troubles, most miners had voted staunchly Liberal or Conservative with only a very few voting for labour candidates, but after suffering so long in successive strikes and lockouts, they had lost all faith in a parliamentary system that ignored their sorry plight while authorizing and supporting suppressive measures against them.

In May 1922, Cape Breton miners were visited by members of the ultra-radical Friends of Russia Association, who painted a glowing picture of the overthrow of capitalism in Russia and the take-over by workers. Wide-eyed, they had listened to stories of a "just society," which had been developed from a social experiment and revolution. But at the same time they were told of the tragedy of Russia—of millions of peasants facing certain death from starvation after drought and crop failures. An emotional appeal was made for funds to alleviate the suffering, and the workers of Nova Scotia responded even though their own cupboards were bare. In their present plight, they felt a kinship with working-class brethren in Russia—thousands of miles distant.

District 26 miners voted to appeal directly to Prime Minister Mackenzie King in Ottawa for a loan of $10 million to aid the Russian famine relief program, and then, on the advice of McLachlan and Livingstone, made application for membership in the Red International of Labour Unions (RILU) based in Moscow. In making the decision to join the communist-controlled RILU, they had been greatly influenced by Tim Buck, member of the Central Committee of the Communist Party of Canada. In a very persuasive argument, Buck had emphasized that membership in the RILU provided support from worldwide trade union movements dedicated to world labour unity. Swayed by Buck's argument,

District 26 miners agreed to seek joint action with fellow miners from District 18 in western Canada on the application to join the RILU and to send a delegate to its second convention in Moscow later in the year.

With a full strike now in the offing, District 26 made an emotional appeal to security forces to remain neutral if and when miners decided to strike.

> Over the heads of government we appeal to all soldiers and minor law officers to join with us in our attempt to secure for our class and the working class of Canada, a living and free access to all means of life in this country. To all soldiers and law officers we appeal, when you are ordered to shoot the workers, don't do it.

The appeal to law officers not to shoot obviously referred to the tragic Winnipeg General Strike in 1919 when the North West Mounted Police fired indiscriminately into a crowd of innocent bystanders, killing and wounding men, women, and children. To date, the military had maintained a neutral attitude whenever they had been ordered into Nova Scotia to keep order during strikes, but with children starving to death in the midst of plenty, the district executive was concerned that violence would erupt on the picket lines and that soldiers and police would return the violence. If there had been any doubt that Nova Scotia miners still believed in a democratic system of government with duly elected representatives, then the final portion of the union's policy document irrevocably dispelled the doubts. Workers' bitter dissatisfaction with a capitalist-controlled industry that had forced them to beg for charity in the midst of great industrial wealth was reflected when the delegates declared: "We proclaim openly to the world that we are out for the complete overthrow of the capitalist system and state, peaceably if we may, forcibly if we must, and we call on all workers, soldiers and minor law officers in Canada to join us in liberating labour."

This was not just another protest—it was a call for the overthrow of the state, a call for a revolution by force if necessary. Unfortunately, the call for a "cross dipped in blood as the signal for war," the statement that Nova Scotia miners were out for nothing less than "the complete overthrow of the capitalist system and state...forcibly if we must," lent a great deal of substance to the old cliches of "Red," "Bolshevik," and "Revolutionary." Any future requests for troops or strong, forceful action against striking Nova Scotia miners would undoubtedly be received with a great deal of sympathy in spite of tactful government acknowledgement that Besco's miners were not receiving a living wage. By declaring openly to the world that miners in Nova Scotia were now affiliated with the communist international through the medium of the Red International Labour Union, the miners of Cape Breton and Nova Scotia hoped to embarrass the government and force an early settlement of the slowdown strike before people began to die from malnutrition. Their hopes in this regard were not fulfilled; instead, the Dominion Coal Company began to build defences against an all-out strike. Vast stockpiles of coal were shipped from Glace Bay, Sydney, and Louisbourg to Montreal and New England. Just as in the 1909 strike, barbed-wire fences were erected around each colliery and the mining towns of Cape Breton began to assume a martial air, with extra guards stationed at each mine as company officials prepared for the worst.

The month of July 1922 passed slowly, with sickness and malnutrition taking an ever-increasing toll of the young and the old. And as the weeks passed, the mounting bitterness and militancy grew to the point where many union leaders feared they would be unable to control their men if trouble broke out. Tight-lipped and angry, Nova Scotia miners continued their slowdown in production and waited patiently for the signal for an all-out strike. Miners and their families were being hurt by the slowdown strike, but so was the company. Production figures for mined coal showed an alarming decrease during the months of June and July 1922. Profit margins were being cut to the bone and majority shareholders were beginning to sound the alarm.

It was generally believed the strike would be called during the District 26 election of officers to be held on August 15. Besco's spies relayed the information back to Wolvin, who reacted with a request for militia troops to protect coal company property and miners ignoring the strike call. The request was not made directly, but through a firm of solicitors in Sydney, Crowe, Ross, McVicar and MacNeil, which had long been retained as legal counsel for Besco.

The somewhat devious request for militia troops was followed closely by another letter, dated August 5, 1922, from the so-called "Labour Correspondent" in Glace Bay, John Moffatt, to F.A. Acland, Deputy Minister of Labour in Ottawa. Marked "Personal and Confidential," the letter reported that in anticipation of a strike, the Dominion Coal Company had placed fences around the large powerhouse at No. 2 colliery in Glace Bay, and that the stockpiles of coal (upwards of one hundred thousand tons) were being frantically shipped out before the strike:

> And here the trouble may begin. Again, because of the violent language of some of the leaders towards the employers, it may be difficult to get firemen, pumpmen or others to stay on the job if the stocks of coal are fired. Property must be protected. I am of the opinion the leaders will be unable to control their followers.

Poor old Moffatt, ex-grand secretary of the Provincial Workmen's Association, had never forgiven McLachlan for his ouster back in 1917. Since his PWA had been forced to disband, it had been reported that John Moffatt had been well looked after by Dominion Coal Company—he was now returning the favour.

In Ottawa, the request for troops and Moffatt's gloomy predictions regarding a possible riot situation and damage to company property precipitated a crisis.

The mayor of Glace Bay, Dan Willie Morrison, had already rejected Besco's request for the requisition of troops, firmly reiterating that the situation was extremely peaceful and law-abiding and that the entry of troops would only serve to inflame the situation. Such action, he emphasized, would be extremely ill-advised and totally unnecessary as the town police were fully capable of handling any possible disorder arising out of a strike.

And there the request for militia troops should have rested, but Besco still had an ace up its sleeve. Just as the Dominion Coal Company had in the 1909 strike, Besco now called on its favourite judge to fill out the necessary requisition, and on August 15, 1922,

Judge Duncan Finlayson of the County Court of Cape Breton made an official request for troops to be sent into Cape Breton, after stating that trouble was likely to erupt and that the civil authorities would not be able to prevent violence.

In spite of civil protest and assurance that the situation was peaceful and showed no signs of escalating violence, the coal company had once again succeeded in requisitioning troops to take over civil authority.

Two days before the threatened strike was due to take place, Wolvin made a conciliatory offer to the union, but it was too little and too late. The new rates offered would have boosted miners' wages only by an average of 10 percent, leaving them 23 percent below the 1920 Montreal Agreement.

At midnight, Monday, August 14, 1922, twelve thousand Cape Breton miners left the pits. The strike was on!

John Moffatt wired the Deputy Minister of Labour in Ottawa:

> All collieries on strike and all men out including pumpmen, firemen and others in charge of property and machinery. Company officials trying to keep up steam but miners interfered this morning at Number Two colliery. Union executive told company this morning they had lost control of the men and were helpless. Situation very critical.

Moffatt's pecuniary interests in the Dominion Coal Company were in danger.

With the widespread suffering throughout the Sydney coalfield, McLachlan and the District 26 executive made an unprecedented decision to withdraw the vital maintenance men from the pits to force an early settlement. With the huge pumps idle and water and gas creeping through the mine workings towards the shafts, each mine would soon become unworkable. If the strike lasted long enough, roof supports would collapse and the mines would have to be permanently closed.

The withdrawal of maintenance men was an extreme measure, frowned upon by government, company, and the international headquarters of the United Mine Workers of America. The decision had not been made lightly. McLachlan and his colleagues were well aware of the dire consequences of their action, but after years of frustration, persecution, and oppression under a feudal system functioning with the wilful assistance of provincial and federal governments, they were in no mood to consider financial losses the companies could possibly suffer.

The following day, August 15, the first contingent of troops, two hundred and fifty strong, arrived in the Sydney coalfield where they were immediately dispatched to the vital power station at No. 2 mine in Glace Bay. Moffatt again wired Acland in Ottawa: "Soldiers arrived today to protect Number Two power station and to keep the mines from being flooded, but officer would not assume responsibility in face of massed miners and men sent back to Sydney. Mines filling up and lights out tonight. Situation most critical."

Posterity has not seen fit to record the identity of the officer in question, but he must have been a person of uncommon wisdom. To force a showdown with thousands of enraged miners would have been extremely foolish.

McLachlan and the District 26 executive were determined to conduct a peaceful strike without violence of any description. With the whole-hearted support of Dan Willie Morrison, mayor of Glace Bay, all liquor outlets, including the many "blind pigs" and bootleg distilleries, were closed up tight, and their owners cautioned not to sell or provide liquor to striking miners or any other person for the duration of the strike. To reinforce the order, pickets of striking mineworkers set up roadblocks on roads leading into the coal towns of Cape Breton to search vehicles for illicit booze.

Other UMWA patrols were assigned to assist town police in keeping the peace on the streets, and at colliery gates where soldiers stood guard with fixed bayonets behind the protection of barbed wire and machine gun nests. Every night, searchlights swept the area surrounding each colliery, but the situation remained peaceful and no untoward incidents marred the uneasy truce between military and striking miners.

The Great War Veterans' Association (forerunner of the Royal Canadian Legion), Cape Breton branch, passed a resolution condemning the action of the government in sending in militia and requested it be withdrawn immediately. The resolution, which was forwarded to both federal and provincial governments, insisted that good order had been maintained in Cape Breton since the strike had started and that all returned veterans belonging to the association were prepared to assist local authorities in preserving law and order.

The GWVA resolution protesting the use of armed troops was reiterated by Mayor Morrison of Glace Bay. The Halifax *Herald* of Wednesday, August 16, 1922, reported that Mayor Morrison, a returned veteran himself, and an elected member of the provincial legislature of Nova Scotia, had forwarded a dispatch to Prime Minister Mackenzie King to protest his action:

> I have been today twice requested to sign a requisition for troops, and I have refused because I do not feel there is any need for troops here. Everything is as quiet as the grave. There is absolutely no disorder, much less violence. To bring armed men into the district under these circumstances is in my opinion, unfortunate, ill-advised and totally unnecessary. Today I had the Chief of Police make a careful investigation of the situation and he has reported to me there is not the slightest necessity for outside interference.

The Dominion Coal Company, through its former union chief, John Moffatt, did not agree. In a further dispatch to the Deputy Minister of Labour, Moffatt hastened to report that the situation was rapidly growing more serious. Water and gas were filling the idle mines. No. 10 colliery pumps had been abandoned to allow the mine to flood, while mines No. 6, 11, 21, and 22 could be expected to hold out only until noon of August 17.

Moffatt must have been most persuasive. The same day, the Minister of Militia in Ottawa reported he had received a request from the officer commanding District No. 6 in Nova Scotia for an additional five hundred troops to be sent to Cape Breton. With this new influx, a force of over one thousand soldiers of the permanent force were now to be used to keep order even though the situation remained calm and the mayor of Glace Bay reported that not a single arrest had taken place since the walkout began on August 15. In the year 1922, Canada's total defence force was estimated to be only five thousand strong, thus one fifth of the total armed forces of Canada were now being used to keep order in the idle coalfields of Cape Breton.

The Sydney *Post* of August 19 carried black headlines to report: "Thousands of Striking Miners Halt Troop Train by Placing Rail on Track at Wallace Crossing."

The outsize headline made the affair appear far more serious than it actually was. McLachlan ordered striking miners to stop and search all vehicles entering Cape Breton's coal towns for scab workers imported by Besco and also for illicit liquor, which could lead to violence during the strike. Orders were orders and a vehicle was a vehicle, whether it be a car, bus or train—it made no difference to Cape Breton miners. On the evening of August 18, 1922, a troop train carrying two hundred and fifty men of the Royal 22nd Regiment from Quebec was halted outside Sydney by several hundred striking miners blocking the track.

With admirable sang-froid, strike leaders boarded the train to inform the officer in charge they wished to search for scabs, and thinking it a diplomatic means of handling a dangerous situation, the officer had complied with the request. The miners took their time and went leisurely through the train, inspecting soldiers' paybooks and searching under the seats for scabs and liquor.

The situation must have been hilarious! The inspection of battle-trained soldiers by straight-faced miners behaving with the utmost decorum and politeness certainly confused the issue. The military had been briefed that Cape Breton miners were a bunch of desperados who would not hesitate to resort to violence to achieve their ends. To add to the confusion, several of the miners boarding the train were veteran soldiers who had fought in the war and had served overseas with the very men who were now being ordered to quell them. To the embarrassment of senior officers, hands were being wrung and backs slapped as old acquaintances were renewed up and down the aisles.

As Glace Bay became inundated with soldiers, McLachlan sent a telegram to Tom Moore, president of the Trades and Labour Congress of Canada, which was meeting in Montreal:

> Strike has been on here since August fifteenth and not one arrest has been made to date. The federal and provincial governments are pouring in

soldiers and provincial police. Will Congress pass resolution protesting against this importation? Strike is one hundred percent effective and can only be broken by military force and the actions of the government leave us no other alternative than to believe soldiers are being sent here for this purpose.

President Moore replied to McLachlan's telegram by firing off his own telegram of protest to the Prime Minister. Pointing out that the mayors of various Cape Breton mining towns had refuted the necessity for military assistance and that there had been no acts of violence to justify the presence of soldiers, Moore demanded in the name of the Trades and Labour Congress that they be removed at once as they were obviously being used to intimidate striking coal miners.

Prime Minister Mackenzie King had dismissed the protests of Cape Breton's mayors, but as a shrewd politician he had no wish to antagonize the powerful Trades and Labour Congress, representing organized labour from every province in Canada. Replying to Moore's telegram of protest, King made some pretence of ignorance regarding the shipping of militia troops to Cape Breton. No troops had been sent other than those requisitioned by the local authorities to aid civil police, he insisted. *Local requisitioning of militia troops was in strict compliance with the provisions of the law which Parliament in its wisdom thought it proper and advisable to enact*, King piously concluded.

The plea of ignorance did not fool President Moore for one minute, but the protest had its effect. Secretly King determined to withdraw the troops at the first opportune moment. The decision was not shared by the military commander of District 6 in Halifax, Nova Scotia. Solemnly he warned Brigadier General Andrew McNaughton, General Staff in Ottawa, that the situation was soon to become much worse; there was a serious shortage of food in New Waterford and Glace Bay, and disturbances could be expected shortly. New Waterford had been without light and fresh water for some days and miners and their families were being warned against the danger of paratyphoid by doctors in the area.

The military commander could have mentioned that the serious shortage of food was due to the closing of the company stores to starving miners and their families, even though many tons of food were stored within. Likewise, the electricity and water supplies had been cut off by the same coal company as a repressive measure to force an end to the strike. The outbreak of the virulent paratyphoid was due to the drinking of impure water from ponds throughout the area after the coal company had shut off the supply of fresh water. To control a possibly dangerous situation and damage to property, the military commander proposed that Royal Canadian Mounted Police be sent to Cape Breton from the west of Canada, and that "British battleships in the neighbourhood of Newfoundland be despatched to Glace Bay and given the authority to land marines in support of the Canadian troops if the necessity arises."

The telegram ended with the cryptic message that all was well and trouble free in the strike area!

Anxious to bring an end to the strike, Prime Minister King now arranged for the Attorney General, the Honourable D.D. McKenzie, to go to Nova Scotia as his special adviser during the state of emergency. On August 20, after conferring with McLachlan and the District 26 executive, the Attorney General met with provincial premier George H. Murray and the general officer commanding the military district. The same day, a meeting was arranged between the union and British Empire Steel Corporation—overlords of the Dominion Coal Company involved in the dispute. On one side of the table, J.B. McLachlan and "Red" Dan Livingstone were seated—on the other, President Roy M. Wolvin of Besco. Premier Murray acted as chairman.

It was a time to trade. Wolvin had been forced to the meeting by government pressure and out of fear for his Cape Breton coal mines, which were steadily filling with water. Premier Murray was equally concerned for his royalties, which were being endangered—perhaps permanently.

McLachlan and Livingstone knew they had won. In no uncertain manner they stated their terms: the union would instruct the vital maintenance men to return forthwith to the mines provided the troops were withdrawn immediately. To add muscle to their demand for troop withdrawal, the Trades and Labour Congress of Canada requested their president, Tom Moore, to send another telegram of protest to Prime Minister Mackenzie King. The second telegram was worded in much stronger language to leave King in no doubt as to the feelings of the TLC in the matter.

Poor Mackenzie King. He was being squeezed between the "devil and the deep blue sea." As a Liberal Prime Minister, he had always insisted he was sympathetic to workingmen's rights and fair dealing between employer and employee. On the other hand, big business, adequately represented in Parliament, was demanding that coal company property be protected by troops even though there had been no evidence of disorder during the strike.

On August 23, the Prime Minister wired Tom Moore, acknowledging receipt of the TLC telegram and promising to communicate with Nova Scotia authorities immediately with a reminder that his government wanted troops withdrawn as speedily as possible. The Prime Minister's message "expressed appreciation for the prompt, courteous and sympathetic attitude therein expressed," was read to the Trades and Labour Congress convention.

And then, suddenly, it was announced the strike was over!

The settlement could not be considered a great victory for the Cape Breton miners, who were forced to accept a wage cut lowering their wages 18 percent below the 1920 Montreal Agreement. But on the positive side, the coal company had been forced to modify its original wage cut. Miners had refused to accept the premise that their meagre wages should be decreased whenever the selling price of coal was reduced, or when the state of the market and the financial standing of the British Empire Steel Corporation made it impossible to pay wages above the poverty level. They had challenged and beaten a huge monopoly through a very successful slowdown strike followed by a 100 percent walkout, with all miners leaving the pits including maintenance men. Most important, they had found their strength lay in unity.

Nova Scotia miners returned to work unhappy with the wage settlement but it is doubtful if they could have obtained better terms by staying out. A world slump had forced wages down everywhere. When McLachlan was asked why he had eventually agreed to a wage decrease that was smaller than that originally applied by the coal company, he replied, "Well, I felt we had gone the limit of our strength and there was nothing more to be gained by prolonging the strike." He could well have been right. With vivid memories of the 1909–10 strike still fresh in the minds of District 26 miners and the prospect of a long-drawn-out battle with little chance of receiving strike benefits from the international board, they could eventually have been starved back to work, just as in 1910.

"Red" Dan Livingstone, now president of District 26, would have liked to continue the strike, but was forced to admit to the Duncan Commssion that "The wage settlement was accepted by miners under the muzzles of rifles, machine guns and gleaming bayonets with further threats of invasion with troops and warships standing by. Miners were facing hunger, and with the federal and provincial governments lined up with Besco, the men were forced to accept the proposals."

Livingstone spoke the truth, but in April 1923, J.B. McLachlan told the communist newspaper *The Worker* that the 1922 strike had served its purpose—it had emancipated the miners of Nova Scotia:

> Only a few short years ago, the miners of Nova Scotia were on their knees, afraid of the bosses while they kicked them in their contempt. The miners were reasonable then; today they are off their knees and stand erect and organized, drilling and disciplining themselves for the day when they shall be in the saddle.

Now, more than ever before, McLachlan came to be recognized as the real power and strength behind the union. He had defied the government and the corporation and won. As a true radical, he had laughed when told of dark threats being made against him, but people in powerful positions of authority were making plans to still his voice.

When Besco's books were finally examined by the Duncan Royal Commission in 1925, it was found that Wolvin's plea of a "poor state of the market and low profits" was untrue. All through the so-called hard times of 1921 and 1922, the corporation had made enormous profits—especially from its coal mining operations, which were used to prop up its tottering steelworks and watered stock. The Duncan Commission condemned Besco for its dubious policies of 1922, declaring: "The operators were not justified in insisting on a large reduction in wages in 1922, even in spite of the change which they estimated had come over the market and future prospects by the end of 1921."

But Roy Wolvin had the last word when he reviewed business in 1922 at the Annual General Meeting of Besco stockholders held in Montreal on March 21, 1923.

With every desire to be fair, just and liberal in all our dealings with employees, the coal company officials have been hampered by incessant plotting on the part of outside agitators who have concentrated their efforts on Cape Breton. These agitators have impaired the efficiency which might otherwise have been reasonably expected, and all this was eventually reflected in the earnings of the corporation.

The statement must have made McLachlan rejoice.

9

Steelworkers, Miners and Troops: 1923

Mass support for the Nova Scotia miners during the 1922 strike had forced the federal government to press for an early settlement of the dispute between British Empire Steel Corporation and District 26 of the United Mine Workers of America. Working men and women across Canada had applied pressure through the Trades and Labour Congress and their Members of Parliament in Ottawa to end the strike and force the company to greatly reduce the huge wage slash that had been the root cause of the labour discontent and subsequent strike.

Some of the staunchest supporters had been the steelworkers employed by the Dominion Iron and Steel Company in Sydney, Cape Breton. On August 19, 1922, thousands of sympathetic steelworkers had organized a giant parade through the streets of Glace Bay. According to the press, the parade stretched for many blocks, displaying colourful banners bearing the provocative slogans "God Speed the Striking Miners!" and "A Living Wage or Revolution!" After the parade, thousands of assembled steelworkers and miners were addressed by Arthur McLellan, secretary of the steelworkers' union, who accused the aging premier of Nova Scotia, George H. Murray, of using Winnipeg General Strike tactics to break the coal miners' strike. Amid rousing cheers, the steelworkers were reported to have pledged support for striking miners before trekking home to Sydney, fifteen miles away.

In less than a year, the situation was reversed, with steelworkers on strike and coal miners acting as their staunchest supporters.

At the turn of the century, the same financial interests owning the Dominion Coal Company had formed the Dominion Iron and Steel Company. With the launching of the vast complex known as Besco, both companies had been taken over by Wolvin and the consortium of financiers forming an amalgamation of most of the coal, steel, and shipping interests in Cape Breton.

If the statement was true that miners' wages had been reduced to pay dividends on watered stock, then the same charge could surely be levelled by steelworkers employed by the same corporation.

The communist newspaper *The Worker* described working conditions in the Sydney steel plant as a "Hideous Hell of Low Paid Toil where rows of long chimneys raised their ugly heads to the sky to belch forth clouds of black smoke and choking sulphur."

And hell it certainly was to the slaves forced to toil day and night in the black, ugly foundries where steel was produced at a cost far below that of other steel complexes in Pittsburgh or Bethlehem, Pennsylvania. For eleven hours a day, seven days a week, they toiled. Not even Sunday was set aside as a day of rest. In the Sydney steel mills, the teachings of Christianity appeared to have fallen on barren soil. The chimneys belching forth choking clouds of sulphurous gases gave evidence of worship of another diety —dividends to be paid to stockholders and speculators, hundreds and even thousands of miles from Sydney—entrepreneurs who knew nothing and cared nothing about the hellish working conditions that made their dividends so lucrative.

For three hundred and sixty-five days each year, a vast army of workmen slaved continuously without holidays or vacations of any kind to break the monotony or to give tired and prematurely aged bones a chance to rest like workers in other industries. Retired steelworker Dan MacKay recalled it was a common saying then that the steelworker going home, especially in the winter time, never saw his family until the following spring. When he left for work, they were in bed and when he came home at the end of a long shift, they were still in bed.

We were slaving under conditions that were hard in this day and age to believe. You were at the whim and wish of your boss. He could send you home if he didn't like the colour of your hair, if he didn't like the church you attended, or the way you voted on election day.... We didn't have a union so the bosses could do as they liked. This was why the men decided something had to be done and the union was organized and slowly worked up to a strike.

Steelworkers were not given any holidays. The company decreed that, every second week, day-shift workers were to change over to the night shift; this meant they were forced to stay after finishing a full eleven-hour day shift and work right through the thirteen-hour night shift to complete a staggering twenty-four hours of relentless toil. From seven o'clock on Sunday morning, they were made to work until seven o'clock the following morning. Covered with dirt and sweat, exhausted in mind and body, they staggered home to sleep like the dead for a few short hours before returning to work for the new weekly shift. In many cases, men had to work for as long as thirty-six hours at a stretch, under conditions that beggared description.

No other section of the working class was so grossly exploited as the steelworkers of North America, who were forced to produce an output two or three times greater than that of English or German steelworkers for wages many times less.

The pitiful wages paid steelworkers for their long hours of toil explained the fat dividends given by Besco to its shareholders. Unskilled labourers were paid the magnificent sum of thirty cents an hour while skilled machinists were paid fifty-eight cents an hour. Out of thirty-eight hundred men employed at Dominion's steel mills in Sydney, over 65 percent were paid at the lower rate.

Inevitably, with family incomes amounting to practically nothing, grocery bills at the company stores mounted to astronomical figures to put workers and their families hopelessly in debt to the company. And with the poverty and lack of nourishing food, sickness and epidemics took their toll.

Canon F.G. Scott, who had taken an active role in the Winnipeg General Strike, travelled extensively throughout the steel and coal communities of Cape Breton to see conditions at first-hand. On his return to Toronto, he wrote a scathing denunciation of the companies that had caused the tragic living and working conditions in Sydney, Glace Bay, and all the surrounding areas under the domination of Besco. Citing the low wages, long hours, squalor, oppression, general poverty and wretchedness, he called for an immediate government investigation to remedy the situation and to introduce emergency measures to save many of the sick and needy before it was too late—the children suffered the most.

Except for a brief period after the turn of the century when the Sydney steelworkers had been represented by the PWA, they had remained unorganized until 1917 when an international union, the Amalgamated Association of Iron, Steel and Tin Workers of America, tried to represent them. But after a large number of workers signed union cards, Dominion Iron and Steel Company refused to recognize the union as a bargaining agent and instituted the usual terror tactics to discourage efforts to organize the remainder. Mass blacklistings, intimidation, and evictions from company-owned houses were introduced using a strong force of company police under the command of the infamous Captain Noble, who had played such a notorious part in the 1909 coal strikes. Under Noble's direction, a more efficient spy system was organized to carry tales and information back to company officials ever watchful of union organizers and their followers, who were labelled agitators and troublemakers.

In a move calculated to check Amalgamated's bid to represent Sydney steelworkers, Dominion Iron and Steel Company announced the formation of a company union—the Joint Employer-Employee Council—to listen to workers' grievances and discuss them "in a civilized, dignified manner without labour unrest."

In retaliation, the Amalgamated then demanded a vote be taken among Dominion's steelworkers to determine if they wished to be represented by the new company union or by the Amalgamated. When the results were tallied, the great majority of steelworkers had voted in favour of the Amalgamated Association of Iron, Steel and Tin Workers of America.

After the vote, the Amalgamated union asked Besco in January 1923 to apply for a Conciliation Board under the terms of the Industrial Disputes Investigation Act, to determine wage demands, hours of work, and recognition of the union for dues checkoff and bargaining rights. But the company refused to have anything to do with a Conciliation Board or to recognize the Amalgamated, in spite of the vote they had promised to abide by. Roy Wolvin, president of Besco and overlord of Dominion Iron and Steel Company, made the position crystal clear when he released a press statement to the effect that "the policy of the Dominion Iron and Steel Company is to maintain the open shop.... The check-off system is wrong in principle and will not be tolerated or accepted by this company."

Wolvin had good reason for opposing the entry of an international union and for supporting an "open shop." With his many thousands of steelworkers unorganized, wages could be continually slashed to provide a convenient means of increasing profits and dividends for Besco stockholders.

With lists of workers supplied by company spies, a mass witch-hunt began. Hundreds of men whose only "crime" had been that of attending a union meeting, or daring to voice opposition to savage working conditions, were fired at a moment's notice. It was the same form of intimidation used so effectively and so cruelly against coal miners employed by the same Besco consortium that owned both companies.

In February 1923, a large number of steelworkers downed tools and walked out of the steel plant on strike. By the second day, it was a 100-percent strike, with maintenance men joining those already on the picket line, and in spite of strenuous efforts by supervisory personnel or "faithful" employees, as the company termed them, the huge Sydney steel mills ground to a halt.

Forman Waye, ex-superintendent of machine shops with the same company, who had been elected secretary of the new Amalgamated union after his blacklisting in 1919, was summoned to a meeting with the manager, Mr Bischoff, four days after the walkout began. After greeting Waye like a long-lost friend, Bischoff begged him to end the strike. In return, he offered to give full union recognition to the Amalgamated and to sit down with union representatives to discuss terms for a contract that would include improved working conditions and wages once the men had returned to work. On behalf of the union, Waye agreed, but once the men had returned to work, every solemn promise was broken.

Instead, notices posted in the plant informed workers there would be no wage increase and no change in the hours of work.

The strike had been in vain; steelworkers had gained nothing by the walkout. As Forman Waye described subsequent events: "Needless to say, once we had got the men back to work, management forgot their promises and began figuratively to hang the workers separately."

In retaliation, the Amalgamated redoubled its recruitment drive and introduced silent days when union men were forbidden to speak to non-union men. As tensions mounted, it became obvious that it was only a matter of time before another strike would be called, and this time, it was hoped the great majority of workers would heed the call.

But behind the scenes, management was busy organizing its own forces. If there was going to be a fight, then the company was determined to enter the ring with every possible weapon at its disposal, including political influence. After a series of telegrams had been exchanged between Wolvin and the provincial government in Halifax, Premier Ernest Howard Armstrong, who had succeeded Premier Murray in January 1923, announced that the provincial police force was to be greatly expanded to "counteract the growing threat of Bolshevism." And on March 28, 1923, a large force of special provincial police was dispatched to Sydney at the request of the local Board of Trade and "other concerned citizens" believed to represent Besco interests. The special police had been recruited from the Halifax and Montreal waterfronts, where most of them were known alcoholics and thugs. Without formal training in policework, they were dressed in uniforms and equipped with pistols and clubs to quell recalcitrant strikers; the clubs were weighted pick handles or thick iron bars known as "persuaders" or "peacemakers."

The force arrived in Sydney on a troop train headed by the same type of heavily armed gondola car used against striking Cape Breton miners. In command was Colonel Eric MacDonald, destined to be linked with a period of terror and intimidation through the use of brutality and outright sadism against innocent victims.

In Sydney, Colonel MacDonald was ably assisted by the ruthless Captain Noble and his force of company police. They used paid informers instructed to infiltrate the ranks of unionized steelworkers. Giving evidence at a later date to the Duncan Royal Commission, Colonel MacDonald bragged, "I had people phone me to tell of meetings that were being held in such and such a place, whether they were communistic meetings etc. More than one caller was a clergyman."

Since the unsuccessful strike in February, many of the ringleaders, and even those suspected of taking more than a token part in the strike, had been blacklisted and forced to leave the province in search of work. Their vacant jobs were filled with imported scab labour from Newfoundland, Montreal, and Halifax. A special force of four hundred "faithful" employees was supplied with heavy iron bars to protect company property in the event of a strike, but the protection of property was secondary to intimidation. Violence against employees joining the union was actively encouraged.

The mass importation of provincial police was followed by an influx of communists from the Toronto headquarters of the Workers' Party of Canada. Tom Bell, a noted communist from western Canada, was invited to join the editorial board of the *Maritime Labour Herald* to write bitter denunciations of Besco and its president, Roy Wolvin, the "wolf" who was bleeding the hearts out of workers and their families to feed watered stock. Communist leaders Tim Buck, "Moscow" Jack MacDonald, and Malcolm Bruce all joined in the fight.

The appearance of noted communists in Cape Breton attracted the attention of Premier Armstrong of Nova Scotia. Like his predecessor, Armstrong had boasted he was going to destroy the "Bolshevik" menace threatening the forces of law and order in his province, and, immediately after assuming the office of premier, appointed Joseph Aloysius O'Hearn attorney general of Nova Scotia. If anything, O'Hearn was even more determined to rid the province of what he called the evils of socialism or communism—they were all one evil as far as he was concerned. "I am determined to lock horns with men of this nature," was his favourite theme, and the good citizens listened avidly to the fiery dialogue and began to believe sincerely that they were indeed threatened by a secret underground Red menace seeking to undermine the very foundations of their law-abiding society.

Few steelworkers or miners had been eligible to cast a vote for or against O'Hearn during the provincial election. Most lived in the miserable hovels described as company houses and were not considered property owners—a necessary qualification for the franchise. A great many others were denigrated as "ignorant foreigners" whose politics were suspect—at least to the comfortable middle class, which constituted the establishment and chose suitable candidates for political office.

Fears of a communist take-over seemed to be confirmed when Malcolm Bruce, the outspoken, left-wing editor of the communist mouthpiece *The Worker*, was reported to have made a particularly vitriolic speech in Glace Bay on Sunday, May 1, 1923. He was quoted in the Sydney *Record* as saying, "I hope to see the day when the Union Jack will be dragged in the mud and the Red flag will be flying in Canada as the standard of freedom for the workers."

When informed of Bruce's alleged sedition, Attorney General O'Hearn ordered his immediate arrest, but the bird had flown. Believing Bruce had returned to Toronto, O'Hearn ordered the chief of police in Sydney to wire the authorities in Toronto requesting that Bruce be detained until a police officer from Sydney arrived with the necessary warrant for his arrest.

In actual fact, Bruce had returned to Toronto to campaign as a communist candidate in the municipal elections there, and had not flown the coop to escape arrest as O'Hearn alleged. The Sydney *Record* demanded that Bruce be brought back to Cape Breton in chains to face trial for "the most extreme and most vituperative revolutionary speech yet heard in Cape Breton." But then, the *Record* could not be regarded as a neutral observer. In 1922, Billy Cotton, the caustic editor of the *Maritime Labour Herald*, had written: "Every time you buy the Sydney *Post* or the *Record*, you spend five cents to be chloroformed!"

Malcolm Bruce went into hiding in Toronto, while back in Nova Scotia the industrial towns were subjected to a series of raids in a massive manhunt conducted by detachments of provincial police armed with every imaginable weapon, but lacking the proper search warrants.

On Monday evening, May 14, 1923, the UMWA headquarters in Glace Bay was raided by a large force of thirty mounted police. The Sydney *Post* reported that the raid was carried out with so much secrecy that it took the UMWA officials completely by surprise.

The raiding force left Sydney under cover of darkness, troopers on horseback, Colonel MacDonald and his officers in automobiles. They reached the town of Glace Bay by little frequented roads and lane-ways to descend like the wrath of God on the union building before an alarm could be given and incriminating evidence destroyed. A quick search revealed a quantity of what was alleged to be literature of a communistic nature, while in a closet, a large red banner was found. Triumphantly the police held up the flag which they claimed was the identical flag which had been waved by "Red" anarchists in the recent May Day parade, and which had caused such a sensation.

From the UMWA headquarters, the raiding party moved on to the boardinghouse where Dan Livingstone, president of District 26, Alex M. Stewart, international board member, and Tom Bell, the communist business manager of the *Maritime Labour Herald*, resided. These gentlemen were dragged roughly from their beds while their rooms were searched. Again, the searchers reported they had found only a small quantity of suspicious literature.

The bully-boys then rode over to Steele's Hill to raid the McLachlan home. After throwing a cordon of heavily armed provincial police around the house, MacDonald hammered on the front door, commanding the occupants: "Open in the name of the law!" Mrs Eva Pemberton, daughter of J.B. McLachlan, recalled the frightening incident, which was still fresh in her mind after more than half a century:

It was late at night after we had thrown a birthday party for my sister Esther's little daughter. Papa was wearing a red straw hat belonging to my sister Esther when this thunderous knock came on the front door. Papa was very brave. They could have blown us all to kingdom come. There was a gun at each window and we were completely surrounded by goons dressed as policemen. Papa walked to the door, pipe in his mouth, and a little amused smile on his face. He made them wait until he had read every word of the search warrant. They were supposedly looking for Malcolm Bruce the communist.

McLachlan's family will always remember the terror and the humour of the invasion of privacy. Colonel MacDonald and his special provincial police forced an entry into their home using a search warrant issued by a magistrate under the control of Besco. The search warrant allowed them to search McLachlan's home for the communist Malcolm Bruce, but it did not entitle them to search for documents or literature. In fact, they did rummage through McLachlan's library, and even removed certain books that would one day be used to incriminate him in a court of law. Mrs Jean Robinson, daughter of McLachlan, said:

> They told us not to interfere and then started throwing the books out of my father's desk. They confiscated a little red booklet which was the constitution of the United Mine Workers of America. I'm sure the ignorant fools couldn't read, because they said it was evidence of communistic doctrine because it was red!
>
> Then they took the lamp off the table and started upstairs to search the bedrooms.... There were five girls sleeping upstairs. My father said, "Where do you think you're going with that lamp?" and this lout said, "I'm going to search upstairs." So my father took the lamp away from him and told him he'd go ahead of him saying, "I wouldn't trust one of you with my little girls."...
>
> When they came down they went to leave by the front door so, cheeky like, I said, "You missed the incubator!" This was a little box we kept baby chickens in to keep warm, so the silly fools came back and looked inside the incubator for Malcolm Bruce. He wasn't that small!

And so ended the first raid. It wasn't to be the last. Jim McLachlan was a marked man. He had defied the coal and steel companies, federal and provincial governments, and even his own international union headquarters in the never-ending struggle to uplift the coal miners and steelworkers of Nova Scotia. If legal means could not be found to restrain him, then illegal means would be used. False witnesses, lies, innuendoes, and outright perjury were all weapons to be used against him in the years ahead.

The Sydney *Post* reported the raids the following day with the news that crown prosecutor Malcolm Patterson of Sydney was now examining the seized literature to determine whether or not it came under the heading of seditious and communistic propaganda. "Charges of propagating seditious matter will probably be placed against some or all of the persons raided."

Malcolm Bruce returned to Sydney on May 27, 1923, to surrender to the police. He appeared before Magistrate A.B. MacGillivray and was then released on fifteen hundred dollars bail. The Halifax *Herald* reported that five hundred dollars of the bail money had been put up by one James Bryson McLachlan, secretary-treasurer of the UMWA District 26.

The crown stated at the preliminary hearing that it had found a number of witnesses who claimed they had heard the alleged seditious words. The same newspaper reported that UMWA officials were busy collecting affidavits from two hundred or more persons who swore they had been present at the meeting. Every one of these witnesses, including Alex S. McIntyre, vice-president of District 26, stated he was prepared to swear in court that Bruce did not make the statement attributed to him. The case was heard by Magistrate MacGillivray at the Glace Bay Town Hall on June 6, 1923, and after hearing all the evidence, for and against, the good magistrate, who had always had a reputation for square dealing, dismissed the case against Bruce and he was immediately freed. Significant was the magistrate's charge that many of the witnesses for the prosecution were obviously lying; there was no evidence that Malcolm Bruce had uttered the seditious words which had led to his manhunt and his subsequent arrest.

Following his defeat at the hands of the leftists, Silby Barrett was appointed Special Organizer for District 26. The appointment, which carried no authority, was made by John L. Lewis without consultation with the district executive. Declaring Barrett to be nothing more than a paid spy for the Lewis faction in the United States, McLachlan and his colleagues ignored his presence and refused to allow him to attend executive meetings or to be informed of any business conducted by the district.

As a front-line observer, Barrett had been instrumental in persuading Lewis to order District 26 to withdraw its application to join the Red International of Labour Unions. To keep the peace, President Livingstone had complied with the autocratic demand even though the executive considered the application to be none of Lewis' business. The withdrawal of vital maintenance men from the mines during the 1922 strike and the May Day celebration parade in Glace Bay, when miners had displayed a huge red banner as a token of their affiliation with the RILU, had convinced Lewis that the leftist faction in control of District 26 were dangerous communists and worse. Determined to gather evidence of communist infiltration into the district, Lewis appointed a special commission of five members of the international board to carry out a thorough investigation.

On May 27, 1923, Silby Barrett informed the press that an American UMWA commission had arrived in Glace Bay to investigate the affairs of District 26. All favourites of John L. Lewis, their names had a familiar ring. When questioned, Barrett admitted that the international investigation corresponded very closely to that taken the previous year when Kansas district president Alexander Howat and his executive had been summarily ousted from office for flouting the authority of John L. Lewis.

The Halifax *Herald* quoted Barrett: "The members of the commission are all fine men with long experience and good common sense who have been through many a bitter struggle in the organization.... The membership of District 26 can feel assured that the verdict rendered by these men will be in the best interests of the U.M.W. organization and the working class as a whole."

The newspaper cartoon of February 2, 1920, had depicted a Caesar-like McLachlan lying mortally wounded at the hands of his friend Silbius Brutus Barrettus, and now, three years later, the betrayal was taking place. John L. Lewis was determined to rid the district executive of every suspected communist, including Livingstone and McLachlan, but the communist witch-hunt was really an excuse to eliminate all opposition to his own autocratic regime, which was facing rebellion from many districts at this time.

The commission sent by Lewis to investigate District 26 affairs was only the beginning. Plans were being drawn up to take over the district and replace it with one of Lewis' infamous provisional district executives, which would follow the bidding of international headquarters without hesitation, even though its decisions and agreements with the coal companies might not be in the best interests of Nova Scotia miners.

Meanwhile, the contentious issue of cost-of-living increases to be added to miners' meagre wages continued. Livingstone and McLachlan were insisting that the 1922 contract, which had been forced on Nova Scotia miners at the point of a bayonet, be reopened for negotiation. Claiming that the Dominion Coal Company had already violated the contract by discharging prominent union men from its mines at Florence, Cape Breton, McLachlan demanded a meeting with company officials in an effort to have the victimized men reemployed and to seek a cost-of-living increase for District 26 miners.

Besco and the Dominion Coal Company refuted all such claims, quoting the "sacredness" of the existing contract, which it had already contravened on a number of occasions. The refusal to meet with the union to discuss the firing of union men and a reopening of the contract was regarded as a direct challenge by the District 26 executive and resulted in a strike that tied up every coal mine in the Sydney Mines area and paralyzed all shipping of coal from the Dominion Coal Company's piers at North Sydney.

Striking miners were addressed by McLachlan at a mass meeting held in Sydney Mines on June 13. Threatening to extend the strike to every coal mine owned by the Dominion Coal Company and Besco, McLachlan advised striking miners to hold fast and be of good cheer. They were going to win this fight, he assured them.

McLachlan was speaking the truth. The strike was settled on the union's terms, twenty-four hours later. Besco announced the strike had been the result of a "regrettable misunderstanding" and that the miners who had been fired at Florence Mines had been the result of necessary reorganization due to the company having an unusual number of coal face workers on their books.

Officials promised to reemploy the fired men, even if it meant a transfer to other mines owned by the company. At the same time, requests for a reopening of the contract to allow for a cost-of-living addition were refused.

The union had won this round in its continuous battle with Besco and the Dominion Coal Company, but plans were already afoot to force McLachlan and Livingstone out of office. Wolvin had lost face when he was forced to back down before the union's show of strength, and for this unforgivable sin, Wolvin and his officials now regarded the canny old Scot as an implacable enemy to be rendered powerless at the earliest opportunity.

The UMWA fact-finding commission returned to Indianapolis to report to John L. Lewis. On June 19, 1923, a telegram from international headquarters was received by District 26 in Glace Bay. Lewis ordered an immediate election, claiming that the impromptu election held to depose President Baxter and international board member Silby Barrett had been illegal. President Dan Livingstone replied that the district elections would be held on August 21: "Previous to receiving your telegram, the District convention had changed the constitution making the third Tuesday in August the date of the elections. This obviates the necessity of a special election as suggested in your wire." It was a small but important victory. In no uncertain manner, the district had told the autocratic Lewis to keep his nose out of the affairs of District 26. They acknowledged the overall direction from the international headquarters in Indianapolis but insisted on retaining their own autonomy as a Canadian district of the international union.

The following day, a declaration from Lewis and the international executive board warned District 26 against giving what was termed "aid and comfort" to the promoters of a breakaway faction of the union, the Progressive International Committee of the UMWA, which had been formed by officers of many districts of the union deposed by Lewis.

"The international executive board views with great concern," Lewis wrote, "the activities of certain sinister individuals who are obviously attempting to create discord and confusion within the UMWA." Lewis continued in a rambling, semi-hysterical chant to blame the One Big Union, the Industrial Workers of the World, and the Red International of Labour Unions for much of the discord in the ranks of the union. All of these radical organizations Lewis classed as "dual unions," which had been set up first to control, and then destroy the UMWA. Claiming that William Z. Foster, one of the leaders of the communist IWW, Alexander Howat, deposed president of the Kansas district of the UMWA, and James Bryson McLachlan, secretary-treasurer of the Nova Scotia District 26, were the leaders of a band of self-styled industrial crusaders who had classified themselves under the high sounding title of The Progressive International Committee of the U.M.W.A., Lewis angrily lashed out at those he claimed were seeking to depose him as president. Lumping the new committee with all organizations suspected of communist leanings, he declared open war on all "Moscowism" and threatened dire consequences for any UMWA member supporting Howat and his rebel movement.

Lewis' paranoia regarding opposition to his autocratic regime was due to a sense of insecurity. He had never been elected to the presidency of the UMWA; he had entered through the back door in time of war when the reigning president had been chosen to head the Federal Fuel Board in the United States. Once seated on the throne, however, Lewis determined to remain there and ruthlessly eliminate all who dared question his leadership.

McLachlan, Howat, and the other radicals were just as determined to unseat Lewis and elect a new president through a democratic vote cast by delegates representing every district of the union. But such an election would have been disastrous for Lewis and many of his fellow executives on the international board at this time in the union's turbulent history. Beetle-browed, angry at the new militants who threatened his throne, Lewis determined to wipe out the opposition by fair means or foul.

Events now began to follow a familiar pattern. A top union official, Van Bittner, was sent by Lewis to Nova Scotia to whip the rebellious faction into submission and cement a shameful alliance between the international headquarters of UMWA and British Empire Steel Corporation. Van Bittner was the same head office axe-man who had been sent to Kansas to form a provisional district executive after district President Alexander Howat and Vice-president Dorchy had been jailed for defying the "Industrial Court of Kansas" that forbade strikes.

Alexander Howat, who had been specially invited by Jim McLachlan to address several miners' meetings, was on the same train that bore Van Bittner into Canada. When the train crossed the border at McAdam Junction in New Brunswick, Howat was arrested and turned back by the Department of Justice. (The Minister of Justice, Lomer Gouin, was a director in nine of the most powerful corporations in Canada; his investments included a financial interest in Besco.) Van Bittner, on the other hand, was received with honours and endorsed by Besco, the government, and officialdom.

In spite of his welcome crossing the border, Van Bittner found the ranks of District 26 closed solidly against him. Lewis again wired Dan Livingstone, president of District 26, to demand that new elections be held forthwith and that all those who had supported the district's recent application to join the Red International of Labour Unions be ruled out. The district convention was being held at this time and Lewis' telegram was read to the assembled delegates, who responded with an angry telegram to Lewis that read in part:

> This convention declares that it will firmly stand by the principle that in District 26 we shall defend freedom of thought, whether expressed by tongue or pen, and cannot consent to enact special rules to bar any member running in elections in this District because of their beliefs, and this convention is amazed at your request to violate the ideals upon which our great union has been built. Telegram adopted by convention by unanimous standing vote.
>
> Dan Livingstone, president.

The district convention then decided to call for a referendum on the question of striking for restoration of the 1920 wage scale. The company had repeatedly refused to discuss the subject, maintaining that its coal contracts were based on the existing scale and that revision was impossible. The men were unconvinced. Trade conditions had greatly improved since the 1922 contract had been rammed down their throats at the point of a bayonet. Wolvin wired John L. Lewis at international headquarters to protest this threatened abrogation of the existing contract. In turn, Lewis wired the district to insist the agreement be kept until its expiry.

McLachlan echoed the defiance of Nova Scotia miners against Lewis' autocratic edict when he wrote in his *Maritime Labour Herald*: "Miners of Nova Scotia will refuse to allow Lewis to order them what to think; they will elect whoever they please to District office, and will fight to the bitter end to prevent Lewis from smashing the ranks of the District organization."

On July 3, the strike vote was taken. By a narrow margin the men voted to strike, but this time events taking place in nearby Sydney gave the miners' strike vote only academic interest.

In the Sydney steel plant, the firings and blacklistings had been stepped up. Scab labour was being imported wholesale as beatings and intimidation became the order of the day. It was the same pattern that had been followed by the Dominion Coal Company and British Empire Steel Corporation against its employees during previous strikes.

With the suffering reaching epidemic proportions, the Amalgamated union moderated its demands and announced it would drop all requests for wage increases provided the company recognized the union as the steelworkers' official bargaining unit and arranged for an automatic checkoff for union dues. But Dominion Iron and Steel Company refused even to discuss the matter, and at three in the morning on June 28, 1923, the night shift downed tools and quietly left the steel mills and picketed each gate. They were joined by the day shift when they reported for work at seven, and almost immediately, violence erupted. The Sydney *Post* reported that a large crowd of striking steelworkers stormed the No. 4 gate at the steel plant, overpowered company police, and rushed through the coke ovens:

With a medley of loud hurrahs, the mob rushed No. 1 boiler house and attempted to drive out the maintenance men who were keeping the furnaces going. Their object was apparently to frighten men who had failed to heed the strike call. As far as the *Post* could learn at a late hour, the strikers were unsuccessful and were driven off by company police and loyal men.

Emerson Campbell, vice-president of the Amalgamated Steel Workers Association during the strike, scoffed at the *Post*'s account of the incident, stating it was ridiculous to say the men wanted to shut down the boilers and force maintenance men out of the plant. Once the boilers had been extinguished, the blast furnaces would have been shut down and it would have been at least two months before they could have been restarted. Campbell told the author: "After all, the plant was their bread and butter. What in hell were they going to do if the plant had been destroyed? They had to work there when it was all over; we had over 2,800 men on strike and that's a hell of a lot of mouths to feed."

As the mob outside the No. 4 gate became more unruly, city police, under the command of Chief McCormick, rushed to assist company police holding the gates. The strikers were ejected but when the crowd refused to disperse, a police magistrate, W.A.G. Hill, was called to the scene to read the Riot Act. This unfortunate gentleman managed to read only the first sentence before collapsing. He was carried into the nearby gatehouse, where he was examined by a physician who pronounced him not seriously ill. The press reported that magistrate Hill had been struck by a brick thrown by one of the strikers, but later it was determined that this was not the case—he had collapsed because of illness; he had been in failing health for some time prior to the strike.

Whether the story of the brick-throwing assault was true or not, it provided the necessary excuse for the British Empire Steel Corporation to request the civil authorities to requisition troops to assist town and company police during the disorder as prescribed in the Militia Act. The requisition was hurriedly signed by the same Judge Finlayson who had willingly complied with the Dominion Coal Company's request for military assistance during the coal strikes of 1909 and 1922, and a force of two hundred soldiers was immediately dispatched from garrison headquarters in Halifax. At the same time, orders were sent to London, Ontario, for a company of the Royal Canadian Regiment to hold themselves in readiness to proceed to the strike scene in Sydney.

The special force of provincial police under the command of Colonel MacDonald had by now reached a strength of over one thousand, but their appearance did nothing to reassure the civilian populace. Emerson Campbell gave a graphic description of these so-called upholders of the law who had been specially recruited by the provincial government in Halifax to terrorize striking workmen and their families.

The special provincial police came down from Halifax. They were drunk all the time. They had 15 horses when they left Halifax. They loaded them into a railway boxcar and when they got to Sydney, the poor things were all dead—smothered. Then they got some of the coal horses to take their place. But all the time they were here, they were drunk; I guess you had to be a drunk to get the job. They had batons about three feet long, made right here in the steel plant. Strapped on their wrists just like a wristwatch and they were swinging them pretty hard.

And then on Saturday, June 30, troops arrived aboard a special armoured train headed by the familiar gondola bristling with machine guns and protected by walls of sandbags. With military efficiency, the troops were dispatched to various strategic points around the steel plant; searchlights were set up to bathe the gates in light, and machine gun nests were built and manned outside every gate to lend support to company police. Sentries armed with rifle and bayonet were then posted all along the factory boundaries.

The same day, a pitched battle erupted between striking steelworkers and imported scab labour. Many strikers were injured, some seriously, as the bully-boys from Halifax rode into the mob swinging their three-foot clubs and slashing with whips. The following day, Sunday, July 1, Colonel MacDonald decided on a show of strength to teach striking steelworkers a bitter lesson.

The "lesson" shocked and dismayed Canadians in every walk of life.

McLachlan, who had been keeping a watchful eye on the Sydney strike, had been invited to speak to striking steelworkers at their union hall in Sydney. The meeting over, he left the hall to stroll down Victoria Road in the Sydney district known as "Whitney Pier." It was a quiet, peaceful Sunday evening with families thronging the sidewalks, blissfully unaware of the horror about to erupt all around them. Many of these innocent citizens had been worshipping in a church situated at the end of Victoria Road. Suddenly a mounted squadron of provincial special police, under the command of Colonel MacDonald, charged down the road at full gallop, sweeping everything before it; men, women, and children, babies in arms, old people tottering on their canes, lovers strolling arm in arm, all were swept aside in a mad, hateful terrorization of the civilian populace. Morris MacDonald of Glace Bay told how a little dog was shot by one of these drunken beasts while its young master, a small boy of ten, fled for his life. Fences were knocked down and windows wantonly smashed as the mounted thugs in police uniform entered houses to beat up the occupants or chase them upstairs. Doane Curtis, a retired steelworker, recalled the beatings with great clarity even after so many years:

They made a raid on the city warehouse where they stored the stuff to cheer, and then they rode up to the city hall where MacDonald told them he was going to put on a "show" that evening, and that the strikers were to be deliberately aggravated.... They galloped down to Whitney Pier, past No. 4 gate and down Victoria Road with their gallant, drunken army. With three foot clubs they went up and down the sidewalks hitting people. Some of them were coming from church. They even hit a man who had just been released from hospital and was crippled with his wife leading him along the street. Then they went to the Atlantic Hotel and hit the proprietor who was sitting on the veranda—he was an invalid too—they jammed him up against the side of the building and then hit his brother-in-law over the head. The marks of horses' hoofs are still on that veranda today.

Many people were driven into the subway and beaten unmercifully, but the Sydney chief of police gave a different version in an interview with the Sydney *Post*:

This stuff is all bunk! I know these people personally and saw many of them heckling the police and throwing stones after the troops. Now they have got what they were itching for.... Perhaps it was unfortunate that the charge should have taken place just at the time church was coming out, but I don't think many people got mixed up in the raid.

"Unfortunate" was hardly the word to use. Mrs Bernie Gallaway, a Sydney resident who witnessed the dreadful savagery, said:

> Those thugs were swinging those billies hitting the people. A beautiful Sunday evening after Church and crowds of people walking, as we were doing.... They drove their horses right in the front door of the hotel, right to the foot of the stairs, chasing people. My father-in-law was standing at the door—an elderly man, and they split his head open.... My mother was at the front window looking out and one of them put a gun up to her head and told her to get inside.

The Halifax *Chronicle*, ever sympathetic to Besco and Dominion, had a different version:

> At 8.45 p.m., a small body of provincial police moved out on foot and requested the crowd to disperse as the Riot Act had been read.... The belligerent section of the crowd yelled "Rats," "Scabs" and other names and proceeded to resist the advance of the police. At this moment, the mounted squad of provincial police under Colonel E.W. MacDonald appeared suddenly at the city end of Victoria Road and charged the mob, using their batons freely. The crowd ran into the nearby subway.... Some of them resisted and engaged in hand to hand fights with the dismounted police. During this charge, many innocent bystanders received blows from the police because in the confined space it was impossible of course to tell who were strikers and who were spectators.

After the dreadful episode, Victoria Road resembled a battlefield. Ripped clothing, discarded handbags, bowler hats, and ladies' veils were pitifully scattered from one end of the road to the other. What had started out as a quiet, peaceful Sunday evening stroll had turned into a night of terror—a terrible experience that would remain with many of its victims until the day they died.

The wounded and the battered lay on the sidewalk. Ambulances began to appear and severe cases, those with fractured limbs or skulls, were rushed to city hospital. Weeping women tended to scores of wounded men lying where they had been struck down by cowardly, drunken thugs masquerading in the uniforms of provincial police. The young boy who had fled the scene returned to cradle his wounded dog as he wept unashamedly.

From a doorway, Jim McLachlan witnessed the terrible scene from beginning to end.

News of the Sydney beatings filtered back to Glace Bay and all the surrounding mining towns within a matter of hours. With feelings running high, McLachlan consulted with district president Dan Livingstone and the union executive before calling a mass meeting the following day in the Alexandra Ice Rink in Glace Bay. With tears in his eyes, McLachlan told a packed audience what he had witnessed the previous evening in Sydney. Angry miners then passed a resolution to down tools at midnight the following day, July 3, 1923, unless provincial police and federal troops were withdrawn from Sydney. The ultimatum was sent by McLachlan to the federal Minister of Labour in Ottawa and to Premier Armstrong in Halifax.

In Sydney, an emergency meeting of the city police commission was held after hundreds of complaints from outraged citizens had been received. In support of the charges of brutality, a number of men and women, many of them with bandaged heads and limbs, appeared before the commission to tell their stories. Colonel MacDonald, who was present at the enquiry, was questioned regarding his actions, but told the commission that "he had had his instructions from Halifax and was not at liberty to make them public."

Did the colonel mean that he had been instructed by Premier Armstrong or the new Attorney General of the province, Mr O'Hearn, to carry out the reign of terror against the civilian population on the fateful Sunday evening? Or was the colonel using a subterfuge to mask his own violent actions?

Whatever the truth was, the provincial government had no hesitation in lying about the incident to protect government leaders. On Tuesday, July 3, 1923, the Glace Bay *Gazette* published a large paid advertisement on the front page, notifying District 26 miners that "The Provincial Police had not injured women and children." The editor did not disclose who had paid for the advertisement, but it was obvious to all that the provincial government was running scared and desperately trying to avoid a mass shutdown of Nova Scotia's coal mines, as Jim McLachlan had threatened. Royalties from coal were still a vital necessity to the provincial treasury in Halifax.

On July 6, 1923, McLachlan issued an official letter from his Glace Bay union headquarters to all miners' locals within District 26, UMWA. The same letter was published in the *Maritime Labour Herald*:

This office has been informed that all the New Waterford, Sydney Mines and Glace Bay sub-districts are out on strike this morning as a protest against the importation of provincial police and federal troops into Sydney to intimidate the steelworkers into continuing work at 30 cents per hour.

On Sunday evening last, these provincial police, in the most brutal manner, rode down the people of Whitney Pier, who were on the street. Most of them were coming from church. Neither age, sex nor physical disabilities were proof against these brutes. One old woman over 70 years of age was beaten insensible and may die. A boy nine years of age was trampled under the horses' feet and had his breastbone crushed in. One woman, beaten over the head with a police club, gave premature birth to a child. The child is dead and the woman's life is despaired of. Men and women were beaten up inside their own homes. Against these brutes the miners are on strike. The government of Nova Scotia is the guilty and responsible party for this crime. No miner can remain at work while this government turns Sydney into a jungle: to do so, is to sink your manhood and allow Armstrong and his miserable bunch of grafting politicians to trample your last shred of freedom in the sand. Call a meeting of your local at once and decide to spread the fight against Armstrong to every mine in Nova Scotia. Act at once—tomorrow may be too late.

It would be argued that by calling his men out on strike, McLachlan had broken the contract between Besco and District 26—a contract that had been forced down their throats by armed might—the same armed might that was being used to intimidate the Sydney steelworkers.

The Sydney *Post*, a long-time foe of miners' and steelworkers' unions, commented on McLachlan's letter:

Many of the men who foolishly obeyed the call to strike in sympathy with the Sydney steelworkers, are beginning to realize their emotions were played upon by the circulation of false statements regarding the actions of the provincial police in Sydney. It has not been proved that any of the incidents recorded above actually took place.... A tremendous revulsion of feeling may be expected when the miners find how low their best and manliest sentiments have been appealed to by a series of falsehoods and recital of incidents of which no record can be found, of which no actual witness of the crimes outlined can be produced.

Already, the great betrayal was being spawned in the boardrooms of the British Empire Steel Corporation. If the chief troublemaker, James Bryson McLachlan, was to be removed, he had to be discredited, then shown up as a liar indulging in falsehoods and fantasies. Everything that had happened in Sydney on that terrible Sunday evening was now discounted as a lie—an infamous blackmail against the "beneficent" British Empire Steel Corporation, which had brought great prosperity to the island of Cape Breton. Those who condemned McLachlan did not specify who were the recipients of this "great prosperity"—striking steelworkers certainly were not, neither were the coal miners employed by the same corporation.

The same "ingrates"—the coal miners of District 26—were even then preparing for a total strike, a 100-percent shutdown of every mine throughout the province of Nova Scotia. A 100-percent strike meant that even the boys who looked after the welfare of the pit horses would be called out.

The coal company was notified it would be allowed reasonable time to lead the pit horses from the deeps before all miners were withdrawn. The quarrel was with the British Empire Steel Corporation not with dumb beasts of labour slaving under the same feudal system. It was to be a total strike with all the vital maintenance men and pump men withdrawn from the pits. The popular press wailed that the union planned to leave the pits drown, but in truth it would be weeks before any serious flooding took place as a result of the shutdown, and this strike had to be settled quickly if the Cape Breton coal miners were to help striking Sydney steelworkers.

A last-minute meeting between the district executive and the provincial secretary, Honourable Dan A. Cameron, failed to resolve the issue and avert a strike. Cameron was reported to have urged the union executive to order their men to stay on the job until an investigation of police brutality had been carried out by provincial authorities, but when asked by Jim McLachlan for an assurance that a return to work meant that the force of special provincial police would be withdrawn immediately and unconditionally, Cameron refused.

To add to the controversy, the Halifax *Herald* now reported that provincial government authorities had announced plans for a further recruitment of provincial police in Halifax for strike duty in Cape Breton: "Inspector La Nauze of the R.C.M.P. has been appointed recruiting officer and this morning in the Halifax dockyard he will receive applications for the force.... Preference will be given to men who have had experience with horses."

Experience with horses seemed to be the only criterion necessary for the donning of a provincial police uniform. Many old-timers still living in Cape Breton believe other necessary qualifications must have included a fondness for the bottle and lower-than-average intelligence.

On his return to Halifax, Provincial Secretary Cameron held a press conference to lay the blame for the impasse squarely on McLachlan's shoulders. He stated that during one of his verbal clashes with McLachlan, he had heard him make the damaging statement, "*for all he cared, the property of the Dominion Coal Company could go to hell!*" When the issue eventually came to trial, McLachlan insisted the statement had been taken out of context and that what he had actually said was: "When you put the property of the Dominion Coal Company on one scale and the wives and children of workers earning thirty cents an hour on the other, then I say—the property of Dominion Coal Company can go to hell!" [*King* v. *McLachlan*]

McLachlan's statement, true or untrue, was construed as damaging evidence of a destructive, fiery nature and would be used as evidence against him. He had been accused of plotting to destroy the enormously valuable coal resources of the province of Nova Scotia leased under a monopoly to the Dominion Coal Company and its overlord, Besco. He had been labelled a communist, a dangerous anarchist, and a Soviet agent intent on bringing about by violent means the overthrow of the government and the capitalist system, and now, with his alleged statement that the coal company's property could go to hell for all he cared, the many falsehoods appeared to have more than a grain of truth.

The federal Minister of Labour, Honourable James Murdock, who had accused McLachlan and his Cape Breton coal miners of being cowardly and un-British during the slowdown strike in 1922, now issued a statement from Ottawa: "Cape Breton coalminers would be contravening the Industrial Disputes Investigation Act by striking in sympathy with the Sydney steelworkers," he claimed. McLachlan retorted that the IDI act provided only for disputes arising out of differences concerning wage scales or hours and conditions of labour. The present situation was, in his opinion, outside the scope of the act; the miners had stopped work in order to enforce the removal of provincial police and militia units from the district and therefore the IDI act had no bearing whatsoever on such action.

All previous miners' contracts with the coal company had provided against a stoppage of work, but this clause had been expressly and purposely eliminated from the present contract. On the other hand, McLachlan continued, the company had repeatedly and persistently violated the contract in the matter of wages. As to the presence of soldiers in the district, his comment in the *Maritime Labour Herald* was that "bayonets might be good for pitching hay, but they were useless for bailing drowned mines."

At midnight, Tuesday, July 3, 1923, ten thousand Nova Scotia coal miners downed tools and quietly left the pits in support of striking Sydney steelworkers and to force withdrawal of provincial police and federal troops.

The Halifax *Herald* announced that a Cape Breton coal and steel tie-up was now complete. Additional forces of militia troops were requisitioned but the situation remained calm. It was reported that another mass meeting at the Alexandra Ice Rink had been addressed by many speakers, in addition to J.B. McLachlan, President Dan Livingstone, Vice-president Alex S. McIntyre, and Mayor Morrison of Glace Bay, who was himself an old miner, returned soldier, and very popular figure. Morrison was hoisted onto the stage to make a speech, but all he said was "Go to it, boys, I'm with you to the finish."

Within hours of the declaration of the coal miners' sympathy strike, a letter of protest was sent by A.S. McNeil, superintendent of the Dominion Coal Company, to Dan Livingstone, president of District 26, UMWA. In no uncertain terms, McNeil demanded that the contract between his company and District 26, which was not due to expire until the following year, be carried out in its entirety and that miners be ordered back to work immediately. The letter ended with an ominous threat to notify the international headquarters of the UMWA of the contract abrogation and to demand immediate compliance.

Livingstone, in reply, refused to order his men back to work until such time as the military and provincial police were withdrawn from Sydney. With the refusal, the road was open for Wolvin to request assistance from his new ally John L. Lewis, international president of the United Mine Workers of America.

When McLachlan was questioned regarding the attitude of the international executive during the present strike, he stated that the international body had never given the Nova Scotia miners its moral support in the past, and therefore he did not expect it would extend any support, financial or moral, in the present situation. The Nova Scotia miners would be entirely dependent on their own resources.

Already the battle lines were being drawn between the company, the international body of the UMWA, and Nova Scotia District 26. Long afterwards, scholars must have questioned if Jim McLachlan was already preparing for the great betrayal by Lewis, Barrett, and the international executive. His statements to the press seem to indicate a precognition of the shameful events soon to follow.

Eva Pemberton, daughter of McLachlan, reiterated that her father was an extremely religious man although he despised ministers of all the various denominations who had aligned themselves with the coal and steel companies against the workers of Nova Scotia. Daily he read his Bible and could quote lengthy passages entirely from memory. A verse in his *Bible*, *St. John* 13:21, describing the Last Supper, was underlined at this time by Jim McLachlan. It read "Verily, verily, I say unto you, that one of you shall betray me." To which Judas was he referring? John L. Lewis or his old friend Silby Barrett, former international board member who was now openly beseeching Lewis to depose the district executive and install a provisional executive in its place?

At the strike scene, the situation continued to remain calm but Sydney was now ringed by steel bayonets and searchlights—virtually under martial law. On July 5, one week after the steel strike had commenced, the Halifax *Herald* reported that the Royal Naval cruiser H.M.S. *Wisteria* was anchored off the Royal Cape Breton Yacht Club; the guns were trained fore and aft in the rest position but the strikers were left in no doubt as to the real reason for the ship's presence at the strike scene. To mask the implied threat of force, it was reported that the ship's Royal Marine Band would daily play gay tunes for the hundreds of appreciative listeners lining the shores. At the same time, it was announced that a unit of a "Flying Force" had arrived at the strike scene and that a Major Shearer had left the eastern passage in a seaplane headed for Sydney. The aircraft was to be used in reconnaissance and observation work for the military force recently arrived.

In Toronto it was announced that various details of regular troops, including units of cavalry, infantry, and auxiliary units, gathered together from Niagara Camp, London Barracks, Manitoba, and other points in Canada, had entrained for Sydney, under the command of Captain G. Heresford, to add to the military force already assembled at the strike scene. At Kingston, Ontario, one hundred and fifty members of the Royal Artillery were also ordered to leave immediately for Sydney.

Proudly, it was announced from Ottawa that with the latest troop movements, all branches of the military were now represented at the strike scene. Infantry, artillery, cavalry, Air Force, Army Service Corps, and the Navy would all be used to control the "rabble" causing the trouble in Sydney. On the same day, the press reported that Defence Headquarters in Ottawa had denied that the formidable presence of H.M.S. *Wisteria* was in any way connected with the strike. The huge warship was merely paying a courtesy visit to Sydney.

In Montreal, the Canadian Trades and Labour Council forwarded a strongly worded resolution to Prime Minister Mackenzie King, the Minister of Labour, and to the Minister of Militia, condemning the use of military force in the present dispute in Nova Scotia.

In Glace Bay, it was reported that a serious fire had broken out in the huge coal banking station at No. 2 colliery, owned by the Dominion Coal Company. Denying accusations of sabotage, striking miners accused the coal company of committing arson to gain public sympathy. The coal company then accused the Glace Bay Fire Department of refusing to fight the fire to show its sympathy for striking miners. The Glace Bay fire chief vigorously denied the charge, claiming his men had not been asked for assistance in fighting the fire, which was on coal company property.

At the same time, it was announced that the Dominion Coal Company's fleet of Black Diamond colliers had been diverted from Nova Scotia ports to New Hampshire in the United States to pick up cargoes of American coal to maintain its contracts with markets in the province of Quebec.

And then suddenly, Dan Livingstone and Jim McLachlan were arrested. The arrests were made late at night after several carloads of heavily armed police had surrounded the union building in Glace Bay. Just as they had in the Malcolm Bruce affair, the quasi-military convoy left Sydney after dark and under great secrecy, using little-known lanes and byways to travel to Glace Bay to arrest and abduct the miners' leaders without fuss and with the least possible publicity. Their precautions may have been justified. Advance publicity could quite possibly have caused an armed insurrection at this stage.

As a concession, McLachlan was allowed to collect his overcoat from his home at Hilltop Farm. Two of his daughters, Eva and Jean, were sitting around the kitchen fire with their mother, Kate, when Jim opened the door and walked in. Eva described it:

He came over to Mother and put his arm around her as he said, "Kate, where is my overcoat?" and she looked so shocked, she said scoldingly, "And where on earth are you going to at this time of the night?" and he said, "Kate, I'm going to jail and I want no tears." My poor mother went white as a sheet as she said, "Oh, Jimmy, I've been listening to them telling you to drive a hard bargain for years, and one day, they'll drive me into my grave." And that was the one and only time I remember her protesting anything that he did in his union activities. She loved him so much. He kissed us and then left and went to jail, and she was heartbroken.

From Glace Bay, McLachlan and Livingstone were driven at high speed to Sydney. Undetected, an old Ford Model "A," driven by a one-legged veteran of the war, shadowed the armed convoy. Malcolm Link, like thousands of other disabled veterans, had returned from overseas to find it impossible to obtain work in the "Land fit for heroes to return to" and as a consequence, had become an ardent convert to socialism and a great believer in working-class emancipation. Befriended by the McLachlan family, he worshipped the ground they walked on. In his eyes, Jim McLachlan would always be a great man and he was making sure that an "unfortunate accident" did not occur on the way to Sydney. During the 1909 strike, a number of union officials had met with mysterious fatal accidents or had disappeared.

The accident, when it did occur, was an anti-climax. The car carrying McLachlan to Sydney developed engine trouble and had to be pushed to the top of a rise to allow it to coast downhill to restart the engine. The "prisoner," McLachlan, being the kind of man he was, assisted his captors in pushing the heavy vehicle uphill!

Once the prisoners had been lodged in the Sydney jail, the Attorney General sent word that the necessary warrants were on their way from Halifax and that a police inspector would bring both prisoners back for trial in that city. They were to be charged with contravening Section 136 of the Criminal Code of Canada in that "Messrs. Livingstone and McLachlan wilfully and knowingly published a false tale, which had a tendency to cause injury and mischief to public interest, to wit: the provincial government and the provincial police."

Now the due and solemn process of law was being turned into a mockery. The evidence presented by the crown when a warrant for the arrests had been applied for was the letter circulated by McLachlan to all miners' locals within the district describing the infamous charge of the provincial police down Victoria Road on Sunday evening, July 1, 1923. Hundreds of people had witnessed the same terrible incidents that McLachlan had described in his letter. Scores of reputable witnesses had reiterated McLachlan's statement of the events as they had occurred, yet the provincial government, seeking evidence, factual or otherwise, to remove the miners' leaders from circulation, had charged McLachlan and Livingstone with circulating false tales. At the trial, the crown, represented by provincial Attorney General O'Hearn, would admit that the events described by McLachlan were true, but nevertheless "*the telling of them constituted a criminal act because it had been told with the intent of causing embarrassment and trouble to the provincial government and disrupting its authority.*"

Two days later, Livingstone and McLachlan were hurriedly shipped out of Sydney and driven across the island to the Strait of Canso which separates Cape Breton from the mainland of Nova Scotia. There they were transferred under intense security to a train bound for Halifax, provincial seat of government. On arrival, they were lodged in the filthy, vermin-ridden county jail to await the due course of justice represented by the Premier and the Attorney General of the province, both of whom had expressed bitter anti-union prejudice while assuring Wolvin and the British Empire Steel Corporation of their continued protection and determination to suppress strikes and demonstrations against armed intervention.

Their cell, which was shared by three Spanish stowaways, five drunks, and innumerable uninvited guests—bed bugs, lice, and cockroaches—measured a minuscule ten by ten feet. Toilet facilities, which were extremely crude, unhygienic, and open to view, emitted a powerful, choking stench that turned the stomach and invited constipation. Their "bed" proved to be merely a bedspring minus mattress, with many of its springs ruptured and pointing in every direction. According to his daughter Eva Pemberton, Jim described his first night in the notorious Halifax jail with typical McLachlan humour:

After several unsuccessful attempts at sleep with the bedsprings digging into our backsides and bed bugs and lice having a midnight feast, we abandoned any attempt or pretence of sleep and walked continuously instead around the cell—the bugs did likewise. Every hour we hoped we would eventually tire out the vermin on our long-distance marathon, but it soon became obvious it wasn't a marathon, it was merely a relay race; as one team of vermin tired out, another took its place.

The never-ending ravages of blood-seeking vermin; the stench of filthy toilets and long-unwashed bodies; the cobwebbed ceilings and dirty, graffiti-covered walls; the smoke-filled, dimly lit atmosphere; all added their own squalid contribution to a scene reminiscent of a dungeon out of the Middle Ages. To add to the physical and mental torture, a drunken chorus of singing, cursing, and weeping men made any thought of sleep, or even rest, an utter impossibility.

Breakfast, which was served at 8 A.M—to those who could afford to pay—consisted of something that tasted like very weak tea, a slab of stale bread, and a bowl of unsweetened porridge, into which cockroaches fell with reckless abandon from the cobwebbed ceiling. Jail guards took great pains to see that the two union leaders were not provided with any of the so-called comforts that were available to other prisoners, at a price. Orders from on high had specified that McLachlan and Livingstone were to be accorded "special" treatment and made to suffer for their crimes, which were rumoured to be so infamous they would probably be hanged or jailed for life.

On the morning following their imprisonment, a formal application was made for bail by Colonel G.S. Harrington, the lawyer retained for their defence by the officers of District 26, but to nobody's surprise, the application was summarily dismissed after strong objections were raised by the Attorney General. Colonel Harrington then applied to a supreme court judge for a writ of *habeas corpus*, claiming that his clients had been wrongfully arrested and detained. Justice Chisholm granted the application for the writ to enable Colonel Harrington to again apply for bail. This application was also vigorously opposed by Attorney General O'Hearn. At this stage of labour unrest, it was deemed important that both men remain out of circulation—at least until such time as miners and steelworkers employed by the British Empire Steel Corporation could be forced back to work. The Attorney General claimed that the release of the prisoners would allow them to return to Cape Breton to further incite striking coal and steelworkers. In point of fact, the reverse was true. The arrests had had the opposite effect in Glace Bay and Sydney, where the news was received with a sense of shock, anger, and great bitterness, followed by a unified determination to carry on the strike no matter what the consequences.

When the learned judge of the Supreme Court of Nova Scotia intimated an application for bail would be considered under a writ of *habeas corpus*, O'Hearn played his last hand. He requested the matter of bail for the two defendants be referred to the next sitting of the supreme court *in banco*, knowing full well that at least two weeks would be required for the learned judges to meet to consider the request—two weeks' delay that were vital to Besco at this time.

After receiving Wolvin's request for intervention in the present coal strike, John L. Lewis wired District 26 Vice-president Alex S. McIntyre, in Glace Bay, to order an immediate end to the sympathy strike and a return to work forthwith. McIntyre was acting president of District 26 in the absence of Livingstone.

Lewis then replied to Wolvin's telegram, assuring him that he had already taken appropriate steps to force District 26 miners to return to work. According to the District 26 records, the message ended with the obsequious phrase "will be glad to receive early advice from you indicating full compliance."

The betrayal was now complete. Men, women, and children had been beaten to a pulp by special provincial police and paid mercenaries employed as scab strikebreakers, but the international president of the UMWA had expressed his full support for Wolvin, ruthless president of the British Empire Steel Corporation, and his strikebreaking tactics.

But McIntyre refused to be browbeaten by the international president of the union. After delaying for three days, McIntyre finally replied to Lewis' terse dictate in a long telegram that echoed McLachlan's sentiments:

The membership here has unanimously pledged itself not to return to work until the troops are removed and our officers released. For any District officer to advocate a return to work, would be quite useless in the face of the men's determination to stay out on strike. We have repeatedly guaranteed immediate resumption of work if these conditions are met. This struggle is supported by the trade unions of Canada and is a political struggle of Canadian workers against an evil force from which we have suffered for years. Our international union must understand its jurisdiction does not give it the authority to prohibit workers in Canada from waging a political struggle against the use of armed forces to smash our labour movement.

With this last telegram, the gauntlet had been thrown to the ground. The message could not have been clearer: Keep your nose out of Canadian labour affairs that have a political connotation. To add support to Nova Scotia miners, it was announced on July 9 that District 13 miners from western Canada had gone on strike as a protest against the use of troops in Cape Breton.

Alex McIntyre had spoken the truth. His feelings were reciprocated by almost every miner throughout the province. Hughie Dan MacLean, one of the leading spirits in the strike movement, told the Canadian Press that men in his New Waterford district who had voted against a strike to regain the 1920 rates of pay could easily have been induced to return to work prior to the arrests but had now passed a unanimous resolution to stand fast until McLachlan and Livingstone were cleared of the charges levelled against them.

The jailing of the district union leaders had cemented the ranks of striking miners more closely than ever before. In Glace Bay, five thousand miners assembled in the Alexandra Ice Rink, passed a similar resolution to continue the strike while their leaders remained in custody. It was reported by the Canadian Press that every miner in the audience raised his right hand in a unanimous show of solidarity amid a great burst of cheering. Railway workers were requested not to carry additional troops into the troubled area, and provincial police and the provincial government were severely denounced. John L. Lewis was censured by each of the speakers and it was reported that every mention of his name brought hoots of derision from the five thousand miners in the audience.

In Calgary and Winnipeg, representatives of labour organizations met to take sympathetic action in support of Nova Scotia steelworkers and coal miners, while in Brantford, Ontario, the Labour Member of Parliament, M.M. McBride, forwarded a telegram to the federal Minister of Labour, the Honourable James Murdock: "If you think it advisable, will undertake to do my best to see that Ontario supports you in any legitimate effort to see that justice is done in the Nova Scotia dispute."

This then was the message from the Canadian Labour Party and from organized labour to the federal government of Canada. They would support any *legitimate* means to solve the Cape Breton dispute through negotiation and honest effort—not through the use of armed might, bullying, and intimidation. The eyes of Canadian labour were on the Cape Breton strikers and the illegal confinement of McLachlan and Livingstone.

Anxious to convince Canadian labour leaders of his willingness to intercede in the dispute if requested by the government of Nova Scotia, Murdock did not hesitate to lay much of the blame on Besco and Premier Armstrong. With Canadian labour aroused to fever pitch, he determined to tread warily. But Murdock's apparent concern over the arrest of miners' leaders did little to convince organized labour of his sincerity in the matter. Workingmen remembered this was the same man who had pompously accused McLachlan and his Cape Breton miners of being un-British and un-Canadian during the 1922 slowdown strike.

On July 8, additional charges were laid against McLachlan and Livingstone when they were arraigned in court before a Halifax magistrate. Now, the crown charged, both men had been guilty of a seditious libel concerning the government of Nova Scotia. They were remanded until the following Thursday, the date set for the preliminary hearings. Noted barristers J.A. Walker and Colonel G.S. Harrington were retained for the defence while Andrew Cluney, K.C., represented the crown.

The new charges were of an extremely serious nature. If

found guilty of seditious libel, McLachlan and Livingstone faced a possible jail term of twenty years, the harsh penalty having been introduced by Prime Minister Borden as an emergency measure during the Winnipeg General Strike of 1919.

From a simple statement of fact, an eyewitness account of the cruel events that had occurred in Sydney on that fateful Sunday evening, the two union leaders were now to be tried for publishing a seditious libel.

History was repeating itself. In 1835, eighty-eight years prior to the McLachlan and Livingstone arrests, another newspaper publisher, Joseph Howe, had faced similar charges in the same city of Halifax for publishing an open letter of criticism in his newspaper, *The Nova Scotian*. He had been indicted on the charge of "wickedly, maliciously and seditiously contriving, devising and intending to stir up and excite discontent and sedition among His Majesty's subjects." The jury acquitted him, to win a great victory for the freedom of the press, but now with the arrest of McLachlan and Livingstone, the same battle was being fought all over again. They had arranged for a true account to be published in their newspaper, the *Maritime Labour Herald*, and the provincial government had reacted by throwing both men in jail on the same charge of seditious libel.

On July 20, 1923, the Supreme Court of Nova Scotia met to consider the application for bail for McLachlan and Livingstone on a writ of *habeas corpus*. In spite of strenuous objections from the crown, Justices Russell, Mellish, Rogers, and Chisholm reached a unanimous judgement in favour of the accused; bail was granted. Both men were released on surety to await trial at a later date.

For twelve days and nights they had been incarcerated in a cold cell without blankets or even a pillow to ease their suffering. Only on the last day of their ordeal had they been allowed a visit by a kindly Salvation Army worker, who had been appalled by the primitive jail conditions and by the cruel treatment accorded both union leaders. The good samaritan had prevailed on prison authorities to provide a mattress and blanket to ease their suffering before release. True, the mattress was stained with urine and smelled like a midden, but after sleeping on bare springs for almost two weeks, both men felt they had slept on fleecy white clouds on the last night of their stay.

The privations and physical maltreatment they had suffered caused both men to suffer a temporary loss of speech in addition to emotional and mental fatigue, but these were only the visible signs of their ordeal. The brief incarceration had wrought even greater damage to their health. In the filthy, overcrowded jail, with their body resistance weakened by lack of food and sleep, they had been prime targets for the feared pulmonary tuberculosis which had been transmitted to them from a cell mate. Highly contagious, the deadly tubercle bacillus was even then multiplying and coursing through the veins of both union leaders. For some time yet, the disease would lie dormant—its virulent bacillus ever multiplying as it attacked lungs already weakened by long exposure to the occupational hazards of coal mining.

They returned home in triumph. Any hope the Nova Scotia government may have had of ending the ruinous coal and steel strikes by charging the two union leaders with the heinous crime of seditious libel was dispelled very rapidly. The triumphant cavalcade of cars bearing Mclachlan and Livingstone back to the District 26 headquarters in Glace Bay made provincial authorities and Wolvin realize they had badly misjudged the character of the Cape Breton people. Far from being intimidated by the jailing of their leaders, they had determined to fight the injustice to the bitter end regardless of cost.

In far-off Ottawa and Toronto, lies and propaganda spread by Besco and the provincial government of Nova Scotia had convinced the great mass of Canadian people that "those damned Cape Breton Bolsheviks were only out to stir up trouble and overthrow the government and the private enterprise system."

Shortly before the release of the miners' leaders, an honest reporter visited Sydney and Glace Bay to investigate the situation and write a true and accurate account of the conditions leading up to the strike of the Sydney steelworkers. A.D. Merkel, Maritime Superintendent of the Canadian Press, was sent to Cape Breton on instructions from the general manager of the prestigious news agency to seek information and write a report that would be "scrupulously fair to both company and men." His four-column article, which appeared in all Canadian newspapers on July 13, 1923, did just that. When he had received the assignment, Merkel confessed he had had preconceived, definite views as to the root cause of the trouble—views that he admitted had been based on biased newspaper reports flooding daily out of Cape Breton:

I have now returned with these views either extremely modified or completely reversed. My most striking impression is the vehemence with which miners believe that every man's hand is against them. One mentions the newspapers, "To hell with the newspapers" or the Minister of Labour—"To hell with the Minister of Labour" or their own international leader—"To hell with Lewis." The deep underlying reason for this state of mind, I found to be the *persistent spreading, day in and day out, of false tales to the discomfort of the men.*

Merkel dismissed coal company charges that the huge coal dump at No. 2 colliery in Glace Bay was in imminent danger of total destruction through arson—"Investigation showed there to be no danger whatsoever." Company propaganda regarding the possibility of mines filling with water and being permanently ruined was also dismissed contemptuously—"Investigation showed they are not filling rapidly." Condemning the coal companies and the press for publishing false stories about the strike, Merkel wrote: "Five thousand miners hear their leaders speak, and the next day they find that words have been put into the mouths of those same leaders which the men know were never uttered."

McLachlan was interviewed by Merkel to explain his alleged remark "the property of the Dominion Coal Company can go to hell." McLachlan told how his remark had been deliberately taken out of context. Persistent to the end, Merkel then interviewed Colonel Eric MacDonald, Commissioner of Provincial Police, who had accused McLachlan of making the inflammatory remark to Provincial Secretary Cameron.

At first adamant that McLachlan had indeed made the statement about Dominion, he retreated in utter dismay when Merkel proved that the stenographer—employed by MacDonald—was inexperienced and could easily have misquoted McLachlan.

After their release on bail, McLachlan and Livingstone had spared no effort to seek public support for Cape Breton's beleaguered workers. When it was announced that the Governor-General of Canada, Lord Byng of Vimy, was travelling to Pictou on the mainland of Nova Scotia to participate in the celebrations for the one hundred and fiftieth anniversary of the arrival of the *Hector*, first Scottish immigrant ship, Livingstone, McLachlan, and Mayor Dan Willie Morrison of Glace Bay also attended.

Weary of the refusal by provincial and federal governments to listen to the Cape Breton workers' many grievances, McLachlan and his fellow union leaders had determined to take the bull by the horns and make a direct if unorthodox appeal to the Governor-General. Lord Byng listened sympathetically to McLachlan's plea for intervention before leaving with a promise to visit Sydney and Glace Bay to see the conditions at firsthand.

It was reported later that provincial authorities at the scene were deeply shocked to see workers' leaders "buttonholing" the highest authority in the Dominion of Canada. The concerns must have been passed along to the federal government in Ottawa, for Prime Minister Mackenzie King wired Lord Byng, reminding him that his "royal" position forbade any involvement in political or labour matters—that was a job for professional politicians!

With mounting public concern across Canada, it was more than possible that all charges against McLachlan and Livingstone would have been dismissed and the troops and provincial police withdrawn from the Cape Breton strike scene, but then, suddenly, John L. Lewis made his long-awaited move. The officers of District 26, UMWA, were notified that their charter had been lifted as of that date and that all elected officers were deposed from office.

According to the records of the UMWA, District 26, in communicating his autocratic action to the union's deposed president Dan Livingstone, Lewis bitterly condemned him for "inciting, encouraging and conducting" the sympathy strike:

> Not only did this strike interfere with the production of coal in mines working under agreement with the U.M.W., but it resulted in the withdrawal of pumpmen, enginemen and other vital maintenance men with the resulting jeopardy to property interests.... On July 6th, after the

situation had been officially drawn to my attention by the formal protest of British Empire Steel Corporation Limited, I wired you for an explanation, but although you admitted bringing 10,000 men out on strike, you attempted to justify your action by specious arguments.

Here was the international president of the great United Mine Workers of America allying himself with the British Empire Steel Corporation, one of the most ruthless enterprises ever launched on the North American continent. Not only was he openly backing the corporation against the workers, he was protesting the abrogation of a so-called contract that had been forced down Cape Breton miners' throats at the point of a bayonet after they and their families had suffered the torments of starvation and illness in the midst of plenty. A contract that had been broken time and time again by the same corporation when they had blacklisted union leaders and openly practised discrimination by forcing many miners to work in areas where working conditions were deplorable and nonproductive.

1 have in mind you are a self proclaimed revolutionary. I am aware of the constant intrigue between yourself and your evil genius McLachlan and your revolutionary masters in Moscow. You enunciate sentiments with the cold ferocity of a five year old defying its mother.... You are a believer in revolution by force. No doubt the present strike in Nova Scotia corresponds with your idea of a revolution against the British government.... Your deliberate breach of the existing contract is indefensible and morally reprehensible and cannot be condoned by the United Mine Workers of America.

By virtue of the authority vested in me by the constitution, I hereby advise that the charter of District 26 stands revoked, effective this date and you are automatically deprived of your office as president thereof. Alexander McIntyre, vice president and J.B. McLachlan, secretary treasurer, likewise have their offices vacated and all members of the executive board are automatically removed from office.... I am today creating a provisional district to function under the direct authority and control of the international union. International Representative Silby Barrett of Glace Bay has been designated as provisional president with sweeping authority to function in compliance with the laws of the international union.... You will turn over to Silby Barrett all monies, official records and documents belonging to the District and vacate union premises forthwith.

The act of treachery was now complete. Ostracized by the great mass of the Canadian public, verbally abused by the daily press, condemned and vilified by municipal, provincial, and federal governments, beaten and trodden into the mud by special provincial police and soldiers, they had received the final stab in the back—the *coup de grâce*—by their own union.

From all over Canada, protests over the outrageous take-over poured in. Coal miners belonging to District 18 in western Canada struck in support of the District 26 miners. Lewis immediately ordered them back to work and, to save the union from disruption, western miners complied but with the greatest reluctance. The *Financial Post*, official organ of Canadian capital, stated on July 20, 1923, "Lewis has demanded that Nova Scotia miners return to work. His demands have been rejected and so he has set out to wreck the union and set up a provisional union." The influential Montreal *Gazette* wrote: "Lewis has asked for the cooperation of the British Empire Steel Corporation and that cooperation, president Wolvin has readily promised."

Openly now, Lewis was cooperating with the hated Besco to smash local autonomy and force out the militants. It was a blatant act of treason against the labour movement, but the precedent had been set a number of times prior to the take-over of District 26. Jim McLachlan and Dan Livingstone had joined the ranks of UMWA martyrs, such as Alexander Howat, Dorchy, Myerscough, and a host of other worthy union leaders who had dared challenge Lewis' autocratic rule and double-dealing.

How the directors of British Empire Steel Corporation must have loved Lewis at this time. President Wolvin stopped just short of sending an affectionate love letter to Lewis' offer to cooperate: "Telegram received and appreciated. To assist you to restore normal conditions at the earliest, I have requested the representatives of our company and the managers of our collieries to cooperate with Silby Barrett as provisional president."

The take-over occurred just after McLachlan had arranged

for appcals to be sent out for financial assistance for the miners of Nova Scotia. Every organized labour body in Montreal, Toronto, and throughout the Dominion of Canada received the text of the appeal, which admitted the district treasury was empty and that miners and their families had been refused credit at the company stores and were suffering from hunger and malnutrition. From the McLachlan family records:

> The miners of Nova Scotia are on strike as a protest against the use of armed force in industrial disputes. The steelworkers employed by the British Empire Steel Corporation made a demand for a twenty percent increase in their wage rates, which means an increase from 30 cents per hour to 38½ cents. When they finally came out on strike after a year's negotiations, Federal and Provincial governments rushed in armed troops; the miners are on strike protesting against the brutal methods used by these government troops in their interference in industrial disputes. Can your organization give us financial help to carry on the struggle? We have sworn to carry on to the last ditch.

When the news of Lewis' treachery was conveyed to McLachlan, he immediately retaliated with a message of defiance that was wired to every local of the UMWA throughout the province of Nova Scotia.

> District executive board meets Thursday (July 19th) to take into consideration Lewis' telegram revoking district charter. Don't allow Lewis or his so-called representatives to divide our ranks. Urge that men stand by present attitude towards provincial police until their duly-elected representatives have come to a decision.

Brave words from McLachlan, but the opposition was also mustering support. In Ottawa, Tom Moore, president of the Trades and Labour Congress and worthy disciple of his American counterpart Samuel Gompers, now launched a scathing attack on McLachlan and the militant District 26 officers deposed by Lewis. "The miners of Nova Scotia," he pompously announced, "would do well to remain loyal to their international union by giving their full support to the new provisional president Silby Barrett." Calling the strike ill-advised and valueless, there is a document in the Trades and Labour Congress records wherein Moore blasts McLachlan, who he said was only seeking publicity and power: "After appealing foolishly for $10,000,000 to be sent to Soviet Russia in 1922, he then turned for support from Moscow and since then has conducted a continuous campaign for communism through the 'Workers' Party' and the 'Trade Union Educational League.'"

If Moore thought to persuade Nova Scotia miners to desert McLachlan and support Lewis and Barrett, his efforts were in vain. The same evening, a mass meeting of miners in Glace Bay unanimously rejected Lewis' call for a return to work and recognition of a provisional executive headed by Silby Barrett, the man they had voted out of office in favour of the more militant Stewart. Roaring defiance, the miners passed a resolution condemning Lewis for his authoritarian action in cancelling the district charter and replacing the officers with Lewis-appointed puppets. The principal speaker was Jim McLachlan, who accused Lewis of lining up with the British Empire Steel Corporation and the provincial and federal governments to smash the miners' union of Nova Scotia. Reviewing the events that had led to the sympathy strike by the district's coal miners, McLachlan revealed that Besco's net profits for the past fiscal year had amounted to the enormous figure of $7,673,201, although it had pleaded it could not afford to pay a few more miserable cents each hour to steelworkers who were being paid the starvation wage of thirty cents an hour.

Those who are against you, the Ernest Howard Armstrongs, the John L. Lewis, and the Silby Barretts, can disrupt your organization if you allow them to, but the rank and file of Canada are with you. You are winning every day. Stand solidly together men, and no power on earth can ever defeat you. [*Maritime Labour Herald*, July 20, 1923]

The following day, McLachlan and Livingstone organized a huge parade of thousands of striking miners that stretched for miles. On all sides, support was growing for the deposed executive while hatred and contempt for Lewis and Barrett mounted daily.

The arrival of the Governor-General in Sydney gave striking miners and steelworkers an opportunity to present their grievances and to beg for his intervention. The Dominion miners' local of

District 26 forwarded a petition to Lord Byng that stated:

The mineworker has found the hand of all men arrayed against him. The Press, the Pulpit, Board of Trade, municipal, Provincial and Federal governments, the Banks, all have gone out of their way to misrepresent us, to brow-beat us, to smite us. The power and influence of the Church and State have been employed to starve us. Like Ishmael we defy them all. The spirit of the mineworkers in this community is as unquenchable as the spirit of the troops your Excellency led to victory. [McLachlan family records]

Lord Byng toured the steel plant and saw conditions for himself. He afterwards confessed to Prime Minister Mackenzie King that he couldn't help but notice "that so little was done for the steelworkers.... Moreover, although the strike is considered to be almost over, the men are not returning with feelings of having been treated fairly but that they have been starved into surrender, and that they will come out again when their prospects are brighter."

Prime Minister Mackenzie King, who had become more than a little tired of the British Empire Steel Corporation and its continued demands for armed forces to quell and intimidate its workers, agreed:

The British Empire Steel Corporation is very far behind the times in its labour policies, if indeed the Corporation has any worthy of the name. The condition of chronic unrest over a period of many years is sufficient evidence. No work is harder or more unpleasant in some of its aspects than that of steelworkers and soft coal miners and I agree, that too great consideration cannot be shown in those matters which make for the humanizing of all phases of employment. [Mackenzie King papers]

In spite of these remarks by the Governor-General and the Prime Minister, the witch-hunt continued unabated in Sydney. O'Hearn's anti-Bolshevik, anti-union activities spread far and wide. "Red" Jack MacDonald of the Workers' Party of Canada was arrested on Saturday, July 21, and charged with seditious utterances after addressing groups of striking steelworkers in Sydney. The "seditious utterances" had been a condemnation of Besco and its anti-union policies. On July 26, six members of the Phalen local of the UMWA were arrested on various trumped-up charges such as "interfering with traffic on the railway" or "molesting workers" when showing up for picket duty. Over several weeks, hundreds of striking workmen were arrested on trivial charges before striking miners and steelworkers formed a protective association, the Nova Scotia Workers' Defence Committee, to defend those arrested.

The witch-hunt continued. To have a foreign-sounding name, especially a Russian, Polish, or Ukrainian name, was an open invitation to arrest and deportation. One of the most infamous and pathetic cases was that of a man whose name was Kolonko. The Sydney *Post* reported that since Kolonko could not speak English he was solemnly warned by Mr Justice MacKenzie through an interpreter, that he had to observe the laws of the country and as long as he did so, he would enjoy the freedom that the country afforded under law. Poor Kolonko could not even understand why he had been arrested and imprisoned, but nevertheless, he was sentenced to a two-year jail term in Dorchester Penitentiary for being "masked by night and riotous conduct." Today, the report reads like a drunken, Halloween spree, but in truth, Kolonko had been snatched off the street by special provincial police, beaten severely, and then thrown into a cell to repent.

The steel strike was almost over. Hunger and desperation were accomplishing what beatings and intimidation had failed to do. With the aid of special provincial police, company police, hundreds of soldiers armed to the teeth, and a judicial system heavily weighted in favour of the British Empire Steel Corporation, striking steelworkers had been beaten before the strike started. Despairingly, they knew that a return to work under Besco's terms meant wholesale firings and blacklistings and a return to working conditions and wages that could only be described as medieval.

Back in Glace Bay, striking coal miners were being exposed to a massive propaganda campaign from the Liberal press and their newly appointed provisional district executive. Silby Barrett and ex-president Baxter were holding a number of miners' meetings to show "popular" support for a return to work as ordered by John L. Lewis. No matter that every miner attending such meetings was an avowed supporter of Barrett's and the rightist wing of miners' leaders, the press reported each meeting with blazing headlines that declared "Sanity Must Prevail" and "Stampede Back to the Pits on All Sides." From all points in the United States, Lewis began to send in his favourite union leaders and other prominent people to exhort Cape Breton miners to support provisional president Barrett and return to work. But the great mass of coal miners stood solidly behind Livingstone and McLachlan, the men who had martyred themselves for their cause, which they knew was just and right. Like the steelworkers in Sydney, it was but a question of time. The district treasury was bare and even if it hadn't been, its assets had now been frozen by Lewis.

When appeals and coercion failed to win miners' support, Lewis resorted to the courts. The Nova Scotia supreme court readily granted an injunction that prevented the "elected" officers of District 26—McLachlan, Livingstone, McIntyre, and the executive board members—from acting in any official union capacity while authorizing Silby Barrett and the new provisional executive to take over the union offices in Glace Bay.

To enforce the injunction, a solicitor, Neil R. MacArthur, engaged by Lewis and the international board, entered the union offices to take formal possession. Two burly police officers accompanied him to provide the necessary moral and physical backup. Once the district records and financial accounts had been handed over, Silby Barrett formally installed himself in the president's chair to issue his first official directive to the ten thousand striking coal miners in his district. They were ordered to report for work before July 28, 1923, or face the consequences.

And so the miners began to return to the pits. At first, there had been tremendous opposition to Barrett's order. Every miners' local of the union held meetings where vigorous protests against the order were expressed. A slashing editorial in the *Maritime Labour Herald* written by McLachlan after Barrett had donned his false crown rallied all striking miners to the cause and told them to defy Lewis and his take-over:

Lewis has lined up with the corporation and provincial and federal governments against the miners.... He has appointed a so-called provisional president, a man who was rejected by the membership of this District at the last election. This man, incapable of conducting the District for the benefit of the membership, has been given full authority to do as he pleases.... Do not allow anyone to drive you out of your local.... Stand as a body and fight against disruption.

In the same issue, an appeal was published for donations for the defence of miners' leaders in their forthcoming trial. It had been estimated that at least thirty thousand dollars would be required in lawyers' fees, etc. Both McLachlan and Livingstone were penniless and the district treasury had been taken over by Barrett and his provisional executive. The funds remaining in the depleted treasury were to be the source of another controversy at a later date, but McLachlan made sure that all union account books were up to date and correct before turning them over to Barrett.

With the District 26 coal miners forced back to work, Sydney steelworkers were left to fight alone. On Saturday, July 21, 1923, the same day that Lewis had taken over District 26 union headquarters in Glace Bay, striking steelworkers organized a last mass meeting at Whitney Pier, Sydney, to determine their future course of action. Roaring defiance, they refused to accede to Besco's demands and return to work without gaining any advantages from their walkout. It was too good an opportunity for provincial police to miss. The meeting was dispersed with another mounted charge. Clubs and even sabres were used to smash men to the ground. The Sydney *Post* of July 23 claimed that the provincial police had only retaliated after they had been subjected to a barrage of verbal abuse: "After laying about them with clubs, they were joined by a cavalry patrol which bared sabres and swept the crowd in all directions. No resistance was offered by the strikers and in scurrying away, one of them received a sword thrust through the shoulder. Many of them were knocked unconscious."

The renewed violence, instead of acting as a catalyst to convince striking steelworkers to return to work, had the opposite effect—they now resolved to continue the fight against Besco and its brutal bully-boys no matter what the cost. But hunger and deprivation are stern masters as Cape Breton coal miners had discovered so often in their fight with the same ruthless employer. Roy Wolvin and the British Empire Steel Corporation now decided to adopt other, more cruel tactics to force the men back to work. If the men couldn't be persuaded, then the women and children, innocent victims of the strike, would be used as weapons. Just as they had during the infamous 1909 coal strike, the company now began to evict workers' families from their company-owned homes.

It was one thing to serve on a picket line during a strike, but quite another to see one's loved ones turfed out of the only home they'd ever known—to see their few sticks of furniture heaped on the sidewalk and to realize they must sleep under the stars or, if they were lucky, in a barn or cow shed not directly owned by the company. Hundreds of poor families were made homeless overnight as eviction squads toured working-class districts, complete with bailiff and sheriff's eviction notice.

The steel strike lasted until August 2, when the strike committee called a meeting to announce that their funds were exhausted and that a vote must be taken to decide whether to continue with the strike or capitulate. When the votes were counted, the strike was over, but if returning steelworkers thought the company was prepared to forget past grievances and start afresh, they were mistaken. Hundreds were permanently blacklisted and forced to leave Cape Breton forever. The British Empire Steel Corporation held a monopoly of all steel mills and coal mines throughout the province of Nova Scotia. To be blacklisted at the Sydney steel mills meant a blacklisting at every one of the company's operations throughout the province. For months after the strike ended, the long sad exodus continued. Hundreds of poor families moved to western Canada or to the United States, far from the baleful influence of British Empire Steel Corporation and its czar—Roy Wolvin.

The blacklistings were not confined to steelworkers. Coal miners obeying provisional president Barrett's directive to return to the pits were subjected to similar mass blacklistings and firings. All ex-members of the district executives were told they would never again be allowed to work in any coal mine owned by the British Empire Steel Corporation or its many affiliates. Hundreds of other miners were informed they would not be reemployed because of their activities as union men during the strike. At No. 5 colliery in Glace Bay, the manager volunteered the information that the men who had been refused work were considered "agitators" who had violated the contract between the UMWA and the corporation, and had "broken the constitution of the United Mine Workers of America." Here was a corporation with a previously bad labour record attempting to preserve the constitution of a labour union by blacklisting. At first sight, the action appeared ludicrous, but then it was realized that the blacklistings and discrimination against certain miners had been instigated by John L. Lewis, international president of their union, who had made a sweetheart agreement with their arch enemy, Roy Wolvin, president of Besco. By driving the true union men from the district, Lewis hoped to make provisional president Barrett's task easier.

Barrett had been installed as Lewis' provisional president of District 26, but he would never command either the respect or allegiance of Nova Scotia coal miners. With the blacklistings came a demand for a new union to replace the United Mine Workers of America, which was now regarded by most members as nothing more than a company union. They remembered Wolvin's comments to the news media when asked for his reaction to the news that Lewis had replaced the district executive with a provisional executive of his choice. He had replied in but two words: "Naturally, pleased!"

The editorial page of the *Maritime Labour Herald* of August 11, 1923, reflected the wisdom and the great maturity of James Bryson McLachlan during this unsettled time. Although he had every reason to detest Lewis for the stab in the back he had experienced during and after his arrest, he cautioned his miners against withdrawing from the union in protest:

> We are fully aware of the burning indignation that seethes among the miners of this district over the disgraceful action of Lewis in deposing the district officers and withdrawing the district charter after ordering the men back to work.... In committing this dastardly crime against the miners of Nova Scotia, he lined up with the corporation. He defeated

the miners strike when the corporation had been licked to a standstill in spite of the troops and provincial police brought into the district. Workers will never forgive Lewis and those who aided him in his crime. We sympathize but oppose any attempt by miners to withdraw from the U.M.W.A. and establish another, rival union. Such a move would not help the miners of Nova Scotia, it would only increase the confusion and play into the hands of the corporation.

The coal and steel strikes were over, but the victory, if it could be described as a victory for Lewis and Wolvin, would be short-lived. It was but a Pyrrhic victory with John L. Lewis and the international board of the UMWA discredited. Cape Breton miners had obeyed the call to return to work, but in truth, they had obeyed McLachlan's call, not that of Lewis or his provisional district president, Silby Barrett. They had returned to work in the mines and they would continue to pay their union dues through the automatic checkoff system, but their allegiance could not be bought or borrowed—that belonged to Jim McLachlan, their deposed leader, who was about to be martyred for his part in supporting the oppressed steelworkers of Nova Scotia.

10

The Trial of J.B. McLachlan

On Monday, August 16, 1923, the preliminary hearing against McLachlan and Livingstone was held in Halifax magistrates' court. Colonel Harrington, one of the lawyers engaged for the defence, immediately applied for a change of venue from Halifax to Sydney, where the seditious act was alleged to have taken place. Apart from the difficulty in bringing defence witnesses from Sydney, Harrington expressed concern that a trial held in Halifax could be prejudicial to his clients, as citizens selected for the jury would have no knowledge of miners or steelworkers or of local labour problems in Cape Breton.

As expected, the crown attorney opposed the application for a change of venue. He had received instructions from Attorney General O'Hearn prior to the hearing. After Malcolm Bruce had been acquitted in Sydney, O'Hearn believed that any trial of union leaders in Cape Breton would result in acquittal, with juries heavily loaded in favour of the working class.

> This case involves a plot to overthrow the democratic government of this country by Bolsheviks and subversives, he argued; in Halifax, the case will be heard by ordinary, decent citizens untainted by communistic prejudices. Justice will be served best by holding the trial in Halifax, the seat of provincial government. [*King* v. *McLachlan*]

The magistrate agreed, and the application for a change in venue was dismissed. No defence witnesses were produced but the crown placed several of its most important witnesses on the stand to swear that there had been no undue violence on the part of the provincial police as claimed by McLachlan in his circular letter.

Faced by the impressive barrage of evidence, the examining magistrate decided there was indeed a case for the prosecution and committed the defendants for trial before the Supreme Court of Nova Scotia at its next sitting to be held in October 1923. Bail for both defendants was continued.

Defence costs had been borne initially by District 26, but after Lewis deposed its officers and installed a provisional executive, funds were provided through pithead collections. The newly formed Nova Scotia Workers' Defence Committee estimated that thirty thousand dollars would be required for defence costs for McLachlan, Livingstone, and the many other workers jailed on a variety of charges during the strikes. Appeals for funds through the *Maritime Labour Herald* had netted money from labour organizations all across Canada, but the fund was still woefully short.

To raise funds, McLachlan proposed that he and Forman Waye, secretary of the steelworkers' union, depart on a nationwide speaking tour. They left Cape Breton early in September with a strenuous itinerary that included every major town and city from Nova Scotia to British Columbia. Almost everywhere, they were enthusiastically received by working men and women and labour organizations who were concerned about the suppression of striking workers in Cape Breton and the jailing of union leaders. It was reported they spoke at a meeting of the Toronto Trades Council on September 10. Waye spoke first and, after outlining the dreadful working conditions and wages that had led to the strike in February, told the delegates how the company had declared:

> There would be no discrimination, but men were fired as soon as they took office in the union.... After negotiating for five months the men had been left with no alternative but to strike to force better working conditions. Then it was that the hangers-on and drunks of Halifax were recruited for the Provincial Police, who for sheer brutality, beat all that the Mounties ever did during the Winnipeg General Strike. [McLachlan family records]

Forman Waye was followed by James Simpson, vice-president

of the council, who told the members that ever since he had been sent by a Toronto newspaper to investigate conditions in the Cape Breton strikes, he had wondered at the patience of the workers. Forman Waye told them that he had written to Tom Moore, president of the Trades and Labour Congress, informing him of their proposed trans-Canada speaking tour, but he had received as much sympathy from that gentleman as could be expected from Mussolini. Passionately, Simpson denounced President Moore and other top officials of the Trades and Labour Congress who had refused to interest themselves in the causes of both Cape Breton strikes. "The Congress has lost its soul," he declared. "Our officials cannot continue to play a double game. If this is to continue, the time must come when the workers will organize to depose them."

McLachlan spoke next. He said: "Much has been said of the sanctity of the contract—watch the police clubbing men and women, but don't break the contract."

Scornfully the old master laid the contract on the table in front of him and said he was willing to give ten dollars to Moore, Lewis, or anybody else who could show how the contract had been broken. After describing Colonel Eric MacDonald of the Nova Scotia provincial police as the Larry Semon of the silent screen in real life, McLachlan sat down to rousing cheers and a standing ovation. A hat was passed around the audience and several hundred dollars collected for the defence fund.

Day after day, in towns and cities all across Canada, the scene was repeated as McLachlan and Waye packed union halls, theatres, and public parks preaching the gospel of unionism as they told the story of the Cape Breton steel and coal strikes, which had culminated in the arrest and jailing of strikers and union leaders on charges of seditious libel. And everywhere they appeared, packed audiences of working men and women cheered.

Steadily, money poured into the defence fund as workers pledged support and added their hard-earned pennies at the end of every meeting. Autographed picture postcards of McLachlan sold to well-wishers also contributed to the fund, as did contributions from union organizations, church bazaars, and voluntary donations from men and women in every walk of life.

Crossing the prairies, the two men finally reached the west coast of Canada late in September. The Trades and Labour Congress of Canada was holding its thirty-eighth annual convention in the city of Vancouver when they arrived. Silby Barrett, who was attending as Lewis' delegate for the provisional District 26 of the United Mine Workers of America, tried to persuade his fellow delegates, representing many unions and labour organizations from all across Canada, to bar entry to McLachlan and Waye, but the delegates, who held a profound distrust of Lewis and his brand of provisionalism, voted to recognize both men as official delegates for their particular unions and allow them to speak to the assembly. The Sydney *Post* reported a heated and bitter exchange between Barrett and McLachlan on the advisability of the recent Cape Breton coal strike called by McLachlan in support of the striking steelworkers. Barrett argued it had been ill-advised, while McLachlan insisted the strike had already been won and was on the eve of success when the "arch-traitor," Lewis, had intervened.

The spontaneous acclaim received by both union leaders in Vancouver and a hundred other whistle stops across Canada was not duplicated in Montreal or in any town in the province of Quebec. There had been long declared hostility towards socialists and leftist union organizers attempting to recruit workers in Quebec industries. The priests also had forbidden the predominantly Catholic population from joining unions suspected of being leftist or Red. The Trades and Labour Council in Montreal refused to allow McLachlan and Waye to speak to their delegates.

The two men returned to Cape Breton at the end of September. McLachlan spent a last night at Steele's Hill to be with his family before leaving the next day for Halifax to surrender his bail, which ended on October 2. There he was again incarcerated in the dreadful Halifax County jail to await trial—the date of which had been postponed until October 15. The chief prosecution witness, Colonel Eric MacDonald, was vacationing in Florida and had reported he would not be available until that date. Bail was refused. The ordeal was about to begin.

The *Maritime Labour Herald* at this time printed an interview with Jim McLachlan in the county jail that took place while he was awaiting trial. Reading the article, it is noteworthy that even at this stage, with the sword of Damocles hanging over his head, McLachlan gave little thought to his own suffering and discomfort. Instead, he expressed deep concern for the unfortunate youths placed in such a terrible environment. With deep sincerity, McLachlan told his interviewer:

No man can leave the County jail as good as when he entered. No matter how strong his character. I hold that it is true with the weaker characters and more particularly the young chaps where the results are still more appalling. A term in the County jail has no reformatory effects, its results, on the contrary, are destructive.

The moral deterioration of young people confined behind bars deeply concerned McLachlan:

I have worked in mines in many countries and have consorted with many rough men, but I have never heard anything to equal the conversation of some of the men confined in this jail.... The workers of Nova Scotia will obtain a pretty good estimate of the calibre of these men when it is remembered that it was from such dregs of society as these—thugs, touts and scum, that the Provincial Police recruited the men used to break the Nova Scotia miners' strike.

Strange words of criticism from a man who had been painted as a godless man of violence, a murdering Bolshevik, an uprooter of established forces of law and order and worse. A communist by choice and conviction, he remained a deeply religious man, although he scorned many of the hypocritical ministers of his day.

McLachlan went on to describe the meagre diet, which consisted of bread and tea—the latter served without sugar or milk— for breakfast and supper. For dinner, soup was served every day except the Sabbath when, as a treat, salt herring replaced the soup. Scrupulously fair in his criticism even though his stay in the county jail was a terrible experience, he made it clear he was not criticizing the jail authorities for the atrocious food. "The fault lay with Armstrong's provincial government for curtailing jail expenditure," he claimed, "the same government which had lined up with Besco in defeating the miners last year."

By confining him in the hellish county jail for two weeks prior to his trial, the crown hoped to break McLachlan's spirit, but as J.S. Woodsworth wrote at the time, "McLachlan's attitude to the forthcoming sedition trial is largely indifferent. Persecution will break him and his kind as little as it broke the martyrs." Dan Livingstone had been allowed to return to his home in Westville, Nova Scotia, after his appearance at the preliminary hearing in August. The crown had decided not to pursue charges against him; they had netted the big fish, McLachlan, and they intended making an example of him as the prime instigator of labour unrest in Cape Breton.

The case of *King* v. *McLachlan* opened on October 15, 1923, the Honourable Justice Humphrey Mellish presiding. The prosecution was represented by Attorney General O'Hearn while Colonel Harrington appeared for the defence.

Colonel Harrington again applied for a change of venue, claiming his client would not be able to receive a fair trial in Halifax, but His Lordship, Justice Mellish, dismissed the application after O'Hearn submitted that the motion was inadmissible. "The latitude he [O'Hearn] had allowed the defence in the case of *The Crown* v. *Theakston* would not be extended to J.B. McLachlan who was considered a dangerous subversive." Theakston had been convicted the previous week of stealing thirty-four thousand dollars from the city of Halifax treasury.

The selection of the jury then began. It at once became obvious that Colonel Harrington's concern that a Halifax jury would be prejudiced against his client was well founded. When Grand Juror A.E.V. Cross was challenged for cause, a Mr Hugh Pynn was put on the witness stand to swear that Cross had told him in the presence of others that "this thing must be stopped. McLachlan should be hung or sent up the line." Cross had prefaced his statements by saying, "I am a working man myself, but I am opposed to them trying for higher wages."

Undoubtedly, Justice Mellish should have stepped in at this point and disqualified Cross as a juror, but the selection passed unchallenged. Colonel Harrington should also have strenuously objected, but did not. It was said after the trial, that Harrington had not even been disturbed by the lack of defence witnesses. He had been so confident that the charge of seditious libel would be summarily dismissed, as it had in the Joseph Howe case, that he considered such important matters as jury selection and qualification merely extraneous matters not worthy of serious consideration.

Attorney General O'Hearn admitted in opening the case for the crown, that he did not remember another case in Nova Scotia of a man being tried for seditious libel—he had obviously never heard of Joseph Howe—but he proceeded to state that it was one of the most important cases ever tried in the province, and that "the truth or falsehood of the statements made in the letter attributed to McLachlan, had nothing to do with the question of whether he should be convicted or not." He also pointed out that "*a statement could be seditious under one set of circumstances and not seditious, though worded the same way, under other circumstances.*"

The Attorney General then proceeded to describe incidents that had occurred during the steel strike prior to circulation of the McLachlan letter. He referred to the Truro convention, when delegates from District 26 had voted to apply for membership in the Red International of Labour Unions. Slowly building up a case against McLachlan, he held up a copy of *The Proceedings and Doctrines of the Third International*, which he claimed had been confiscated during Colonel MacDonald's raid on the McLachlan home. An item that he claimed was "seditious literature." Other items confiscated by MacDonald had included a red flag.

From the prisoner's dock, McLachlan said, "*There was no red flag.*" (The "red flag" referred to was a red shawl that Mrs Kate McLachlan had draped over the piano and weighted down with ornaments.) Otherwise he was silent during the trial.

Ignoring the interruption, the Attorney General continued. Books and pamphlets seized at the McLachlan home had included the *Theses and Statutes of the Third International*, a revolutionary book that O'Hearn claimed was proof positive that the prisoner, James Bryson McLachlan, had planned the overthrow of the government and the forces of law and order. The provincial police, according to the Attorney General, had averted insurrection and armed revolution in Sydney during the steel strike only after the local authorities and city police had admitted they were unable to contain the violence.

Addressing the jury, O'Hearn made much of the statement McLachlan had made to the provincial secretary, "The property of Dominion Coal Company can go to Hell!" In righteous indignation, and with an aplomb and acting ability worthy of a great artist, the Attorney General looked every member of the jury straight in the eye as he said, "The property of the Dominion Coal Company is the property of the crown. The company does not own the mines. They belong to you and I." This boldfaced exaggeration was intended to convince the jury that any attempt to destroy or reduce the profits of the Dominion Coal Company or the British Empire Steel Corporation was a blow directed against the government and the people of Nova Scotia and therefore seditious.

Having detailed the charges filed against McLachlan, O'Hearn called his first prosecution witness, Sydney Chief of Police McCormick. Prompted by O'Hearn, McCormick began to describe the Sunday night incident in Sydney when mounted provincial police were alleged to have charged through a crowd of innocent people. "They were perfectly justified in their action," the chief testified, "because that bunch of strikers was nothing but a bunch of 'Reds' who had been causing trouble and abusing the police."

Cross-questioned by defence counsel, McCormick admitted he had been "mistaken" at a previous hearing when he had said there was no church in the vicinity of the subway where the incident took place. And then later, when questioned about the injuries suffered by innocent civilians during the incident, he claimed he wasn't clear on that point. When asked about a specific case, that of John E. Murphy, he muttered, "He's what I consider one of those Reds." Colonel Harrington was quick to seize upon this statement. "Apparently everyone in opposition to you is a Red. Have I gained that distinction yet?" The answer, when it came after a long pause, provoked laughter in the courtroom: "I will shortly."

(Colonel Harrington was a noted Conservative, an ex-mayor of Glace Bay, and a future Premier of Nova Scotia.)

The chief then admitted under cross-examination that he had seen people with their heads bandaged as McLachlan had claimed. He had conducted an investigation, but had not called any witnesses from the ranks of striking steelworkers. "Yes, it was true," he admitted, "that Captain Noble, chief of company police, had known on the Sunday afternoon that Colonel Eric MacDonald would put on a show that evening and drive his mounted provincial police through the crowd to teach the striking steelworkers a lesson."

McCormick, who had not made a favourable impression on the jury, was followed by Sydney Assistant Chief of Police Anthony, who swore there had been no disturbance on the Sunday prior to the occurrence. He agreed that it had been rumoured in Sydney that the provincial police had exceeded their authority in the attack and that it was said that women and children had been injured—some seriously. "Yes," Anthony agreed, "people had appeared at the enquiry with their heads bandaged." The assistant chief would no doubt find he had become *persona non grata* with his chief when he returned to his duties in Sydney, but he had answered defence counsel's questions honestly and without prejudice.

Colonel Eric MacDonald followed with his testimony, but much of his examination was devoted to efforts by defence counsel to obtain definite answers from him. Negative responses such as "I don't remember," "I am uncertain," "I am not quite sure," sprinkled his testimony. When questioned about his alleged statement to his men that "He was going to put on a show" and that when he was told the striking steelworkers would not fight back, he had said, "That's all right, Captain Noble of the Steel Company will provoke them," he paused for a long time, and then finally claimed he couldn't remember whether he had said that or not. Under questioning, he admitted that the warrant he had used to search McLachlan's house only entitled him to look for the communist Malcolm Bruce, who was visiting Cape Breton during the strike.

When questioned regarding the alleged statement made by

McLachlan—"The property of the Dominion Coal Company can go to hell"—he finally admitted, under intense questioning, that he could have been mistaken and that McLachlan had been misquoted.

After MacDonald had been dismissed, the Attorney General took over the prosecution's case by displaying various exhibits including *The Proceedings and Doctrines of the Third International*, which the prosecution had seized in McLachlan's home and in the union offices. When he proposed reading portions of the revolutionary literature to the jury, Colonel Harrington raised strong objections, quoting various legal precedents. Justice Mellish then ordered a recess to study the arguments for and against and ordered the jury to recess until Wednesday morning. McLachlan, who was allowed bail during the recess, booked into a Halifax hotel.

Eva Pemberton, McLachlan's daughter, told of a surprise invitation her father received soon after he arrived at the hotel. Since the trial had commenced, he had become a celebrity, with his case being discussed around every dinner table in Nova Scotia. Everyone it seemed wanted to meet McLachlan, the Cape Breton rebel on trial for the heinous crime of seditious libel. The lieutenant governor of the province was no exception. The Honourable MacCallum Grant magnanimously invited Mr James Bryson McLachlan to dinner at Government House in Halifax.

Jim accepted. After all, he reasoned, it wasn't every day a felon got to share his meal with the king's representative! He was greeted with bluff good humour by his host before being introduced to a number of prominent Halifax citizens and hangers-on, who had been hurriedly gathered together to meet the man of the hour. As Jim recalled later, they sat down to dinner in an atmosphere of royal grandeur, wealth, and opulence. A priceless crystal chandelier cast its warm light over the huge dining table where glittering silver and snow-white linen framed an endless selection of mouth-watering dishes and chilled champagne.

After spending two weeks in the filthy Halifax jail eating bread and "skilly," the scene dazzled the eye and drugged the senses. While the other guests helped themselves to generous portions of roast beef and venison, Jim sat silently before his place setting, making no move to partake of the magnificent feast spread before him. His host, MacCallum Grant, anxious to put his guest at ease in such an unaccustomed setting, asked Jim if he could help him choose the correct eating utensils from the many surrounding his empty plate, but Jim assured him that that was not the problem. "I find it difficult to eat such magnificent food when I think how many poor starving miners and their families this feast would provide for."

The sudden lull in the table conversation was proof positive the verbal barb had struck home!

The case against McLachlan resumed on Wednesday morning, with Justice Mellish announcing he had debated the question of allowing the prosecution to read portions of the revolutionary *Proceedings and Doctrines of the Third International*, taken from McLachlan's home, to the jury. "It could be argued," Justice Mellish said, "that the possession of such a text had nothing to do with the present case—the publishing of a seditious libel—but as the Crown's case rested on proving that the prisoner, McLachlan, had published the libel with the intent of causing civil disobedience, the bench was going to allow the prosecution to introduce the revolutionary material in evidence."

So for the next thirty minutes, the Attorney General did just that. Aloud, he read passage after passage from the text that had been confiscated illegally from McLachlan's house. The jury of butchers, bakers, and tradespeople listened with open mouths as O'Hearn emphasized passages that advocated the overthrow of the capitalist system by force and revolution. When he had finished, he solemnly approached the jury, waving the text above his head, as he said:

> These books contain the communist doctrines of Soviet Russia. I started this prosecution determined to find men of this calibre, and that is why I am here today. Those who commit sedition will find that I will lock horns with them. Just try me and see! This case is one of the most important presented to a jury in years. It is a struggle between the forces of law and order and the strange doctrines of Moscow. The murder case

on the docket is insignificant compared to this case. It is up to you who love our constitution and institutions as much as I do, to do your duty. The strange doctrines of Moscow shall not flourish in Nova Scotia. [*King* v. *McLachlan*]

Colonel Harrington, the lawyer for the defence, followed with an announcement that there would be no witnesses for the defence. The prosecution alleged that McLachlan had published a seditious libel, he told the jury, but while McLachlan may have written the letter, he was only voicing the opinion of thousands of miners he represented in Nova Scotia. If McLachlan was "Red," then the thousands of miners who had elected him must be "Red."

If McLachlan was guilty of sedition by sending this letter to the locals of his union, then why was F.W. Gray of the steel company not also guilty for having it published in the Sydney *Post* and the Halifax *Morning Chronicle*?

Attorney General O'Hearn claimed that McLachlan's pronouncement had been intended to disrupt society, tear out the vitals of government, and bring the crown into disrepute and shame. If this were the case, the crown had become merely a word, a symbol, a mechanism, a refuge, a figure of speech.

It had also been claimed that McLachlan's program from start to finish was intended to upset the present system of law and order and bring Canada under the red folds of the flag of the International, and that his utterances at the Truro convention and his public announcements in other places in Canada proved his intention to be nothing less than the complete overthrow of the capitalist system, by peaceful means if possible, by force if necessary.

On the other hand, Colonel Harrington argued, sedition was not an absolute term. You could not nail that term through and rivet it on the inside. The point of view must be taken into consideration. Sedition was a term capable of more views than one, and any legal mind that undertook to make this word walk on all fours missed the real point in law and ended in a frightful verbal mess. McLachlan's manifesto had never been disproved, and by the same token, had the McLachlan letter regarding the Sunday night beatings ever been disproved? Were any of the steelworkers called to the witness stand? Did the witnesses called by the crown prove that McLachlan's assertions were false?

Warming to his theme, Colonel Harrington then broadened the scope of his dissertation to show that nothing on earth is above criticism.

What is considered sedition in Canada, is called by another name in England, the Mother country.... Beware lest today, we shall be found driving in the thin edge of the wedge that will result in the abolition of the right to think and express one's convictions along the lines of a free people in a free province in a free Canada.

And who gave any special sanctity to the provincial police that they should not be criticized? asked Colonel Harrington.

Criticism is not sedition. Bringing a government under condemnation is not sedition. Expressing one's profound convictions—that is not sedition. Be careful that the word sedition is not warped and twisted into a meaning which excludes everything and everybody that we do not agree with, for that attitude breeds intolerance and class hatred.

Colonel Harrington closed his defence with a passionate plea to free his client, McLachlan: "Until the spirit of tolerance pervades our actions and activities, sedition will always mean the end of free speech, whether by tongue or pen, and the constant fear and dread of that kind of thinking that emancipates the individual and the nation."

The colonel's eloquent and passionate address to the jury was in vain. The jury of tradesmen had made up its mind long before the trial commenced. McLachlan was a self-confessed communist—a "Red"—and as such, he represented everything alien to their own background and upbringing. Tradesmen in Halifax could not be expected to understand the hellish working conditions in a Sydney steel mill or in a Cape Breton coal mine miles under the ocean, nor could they be expected to realize the terrible deprivations suffered by steelworkers and their families on a starvation wage of thirty cents an hour.

If anybody was to blame for the jury's lack of understanding, it was the defence counsel, Colonel Harrington, who had thought it unnecessary to put defence witnesses on the stand. He had based his whole case on the famous Joseph Howe and his acquittal on a similar charge of seditious libel. In doing so, he had failed to appreciate the ugly plot to remove McLachlan from the labour scene using any subterfuge as a weapon. The archaic laws of sedition had proved to be just such a convenient weapon.

Mr Justice Mellish then charged the jury. After informing the members that it was their decision and theirs alone to decide if the McLachlan letter had been seditious in nature and intent, he went on to tell them he had himself felt it could be given a seditious interpretation. McLachlan had ordered his union members to strike in support of the steelworkers in Sydney to force the provincial police to leave that city. "For what reason?" he asked. "If the strikers wanted to redress their grievances by lawful means, why should they object to the presence of police?"

They had objected to the presence of provincial police only after they had been savagely beaten to the ground in an unprovoked attack, but the judge omitted that important fact.

The jury retired at 12:45, but it was only a token retirement; they returned to the courtroom at 2:15 that same afternoon with a unanimous verdict of "Guilty."

The Attorney General had demanded the maximum sentence of twenty years. McLachlan was fifty-four years of age. As a further measure of his vindictiveness, he had recommended that at the end of that time, he should be required to post a large sum of money to guarantee his future good behaviour. He might just as well have demanded a pound of flesh nearest to his heart! Mr Justice Mellish sentenced McLachlan to a term of two years imprisonment on each of three counts, the terms to run concurrently.

McLachlan appealed the conviction and was returned to his cell in the Halifax County jail to await their lordships' pleasure. Bail was refused by Chief Justice Harris of the Nova Scotia Supreme Court pending the appeal, although the law provided that bail could be allowed.

The conviction and the savage sentence sent shock waves

reverberating across Canada and the United States. The Halifax *Citizen* published an editorial on October 19, 1923, that expressed deep concern.

> Whether we or others agree or disagree with the economics or doctrines preached by J.B. McLachlan, everybody must agree that there is not, nor cannot be, any such crime as sedition in a free country or in a country which makes any claim to being free.
>
> Any country which legislates that the preaching or teaching of anything in the press, in the pulpit, upon the platform or otherwise, as criminal, has closed the doors upon freedom and can no longer make any claim to being free.... We claim the right to denounce the government of the province of Nova Scotia if they are so corrupt or fail in their duty to the workers who are the backbone of the country.

Roy Wolvin, president of British Empire Steel Corporation, had the last word. He dispatched a telegram of congratulations to Attorney General O'Hearn after the verdict was announced.

The act of treachery was now completed. Wolvin, Lewis, Barrett, O'Hearn, and Armstrong had all contributed to the "stab in the back" that had finally removed Jim McLachlan from the Cape Breton labour scene.

As a finale, the Glace Bay *Gazette*, a newspaper notorious for its anti-labour stance, especially during the times of strife, now published a bitter denunciation of McLachlan on its front page. The story reported an interview with Louis MacCormick, the new provisional secretary-treasurer of District 26, who claimed that huge deficits had been found in the district treasury after McLachlan had been deposed. The McLachlan family demanded a full retraction of this slander and, some weeks later, a retraction did indeed appear in the same newspaper. The so-called exposé on McLachlan's embezzlement of union funds had been splashed all over the front page. The retraction, which was contained in the social column on the back page, covered but a few lines.

Lewis was using every dirty trick in the book to discredit the old fighter now that he was safely locked in jail.

Dreadful jail conditions began to take their toll on McLachlan's health. When first arrested, he had shared his experience in the filthy cell with his old friend Dan Livingstone, but since surrendering his bail on October 2, he was forced to suffer in silence without even the solace of a companion to lessen the boredom and make light of the degrading and demoralizing aspects of prison life.

As the month of October passed into November, he steadily lost weight and appetite. Racked by a persistent cough, he had difficulty in sleeping on the inhospitable mattress and lay awake each night, burning with fever and troubled by a persistent headache, but true to his stubborn character, he never complained to the prison authorities or requested medical attention. To do so, in his opinion, would have been an abrogation of his responsibilities as a political prisoner unjustly detained for speaking the truth. He may have been right. Any expression of discomfort from McLachlan would have given Roy Wolvin and the Attorney General a great deal of satisfaction.

As often as he was allowed, he wrote to Kate and his children, assuring them he was in good health and spirits and looking forward to a reunion with them in the near future. On November 12, his failing spirits received a boost. His daughter, Kate, gave birth to a son—McLachlan's first grandson! Proudly Kate gave him the same Christian names as his famous grandfather, James Bryson, and Jim, bursting with pride, mailed him a christening present—the only treasure in his possession, a Newfoundland dollar bill.

On December 17, 1923, the Nova Scotia Court of Appeal considered the McLachlan case. Chief Justice Harris, Justices Russell, Ritchie, Chisholm, and MacKenzie heard Colonel Harrington and J.A. Walker speak on behalf of McLachlan, while Attorney General O'Hearn and Mr A.L. MacDonald appeared for the crown.

Colonel Harrington argued that the jury had not been properly impanelled. An affidavit, produced from one George D. Inkpen, stated he was one of the additional panel of standby jurors summoned at the October term of the Supreme Court in Halifax. Juryman Inkpen testified he had been called to serve on the jury when it was discovered one member was missing. But he had not been sworn in like the other members of the jury!

The Supreme Court judges dismissed this portion of the appeal even though the transcript of the trial showed that Attorney General O'Hearn had drawn the trial judge's attention to the matter and that Justice Mellish had said, "There is nothing to do but to go on with the trial as far as I can see; as far as I know, the thing is regular."

Other arguments submitted by defence counsel included the contention that the indictment was defective in that the prisoner had had no seditious intent; the Attorney General had exercised the right of reply even though the defendant had called no witnesses; the trial judge had misdirected the jury in reading to them a section of the Criminal Code that had been repealed before the trial took place; the trial judge improperly received in evidence a book found in the prisoner's home, entitled *Proceedings and Doctrines of the Third [Communist] International of Moscow*; and lastly that the evidence leading to the publication in a Halifax newspaper should be set aside.

Only the latter submission was allowed and the conviction for publishing the seditious libel in Halifax was set aside. As to the publications in Thorburn and Glace Bay newspapers, their lordships said there was ample evidence of guilt and the convictions should be affirmed.

The appeal was dismissed.

With the dismissal of the appeal, a letter was delivered to McLachlan in the county jail. Enclosed was a cheque for the sum of two hundred dollars for wages owed him as secretary-treasurer during the month of July 1923—the month when McLachlan had been arrested. Signed by L. MacCormick, the new provisional secretary-treasurer of District 26 appointed by Lewis, the letter was curt to the point of rudeness.

With a long prison term stretching interminably ahead, the provisional executive was paying off the old fighter with a few crumbs—"blood money" as Jim called it, as he promptly returned the cheque with a message written on the back: "This check issued by traitors who Judas like, pretend to kiss the Nova Scotia miner on the cheek while daily they run a dagger to his heart's core. May be cashed by anyone that can take blood money."

The cheque was accompanied by a short note to Louis MacCormick: "I hereby return your cheque for $200. The men who are betraying daily, the miners of Nova Scotia, could not give me as much as a shoe latch." [McLachlan family records]

Now for the first time since his long and dreadful ordeal had begun, McLachlan openly displayed anger and disgust against Lewis and his puppet provisional executive.

Since his arrest, he had been left to languish in the county jail without any means of support for his family. Money for his defence had been collected through pithead collections and from labour organizations all across Canada after Lewis and Barrett had refused to pay a single dollar from union funds. Now they had the gall to send two hundred miserable dollars in back pay to the man they had been instrumental in sending to jail for his union activities.

It was the kiss of death. It was also the twenty-fifth of December, 1923. *Christmas* in the Halifax County jail!

The Nova Scotia Defence Fund dismissed Colonel Harrington and then instructed J.A. Walker, the very able barrister who had been Harrington's assistant during the trial, to take over the brief. The good colonel had presented his bill for five thousand dollars—a very considerable sum of money in 1923, and many thought the fee excessive. It was generally believed that if Harrington had arranged for defence witnesses to give evidence for McLachlan at the trial, he could quite possibly have won an acquittal, but instead, Harrington had based his whole defence on drawing an analogy between the famous Joseph Howe case, which had ended in acquittal, and the McLachlan case with its communist overtones.

The critics may have been right, but long before the trial the provincial government of Nova Scotia had decided McLachlan was to be removed from the labour scene, preferably for a very long time. It was a decision that had been reached after pressure had been exerted by the British Empire Steel Corporation and by another least expected source, John L. Lewis, president of the United Mine Workers of America.

The fight was not yet over. Walker decided to try one last desperate gamble. He applied through the Supreme Court of Nova Scotia for leave to appeal to the Privy Council on the grounds that evidence presented to the jury from books and documents taken from McLachlan's home should not have been used at the trial.

Again, the Provincial Attorney General vigorously opposed leave to appeal, but this time, the Nova Scotia Supreme Court justices differed with the crown. Chief Justice Harris, Justices Russell, Chisholm, and MacKenzie considered the case carefully before reaching a decision.

It was pointed out that McLachlan could not appeal to the Supreme Court of Canada because there had been no dissenting judgement at his trial. Leave to appeal to the Privy Council could be given only if it could be shown that substantial and grave injustice had been done. Justice Russell now acknowledged he had had grave doubts at the argument of the appeal in December as to the admissibility of the documents found in the house of the accused and the use made of them at the trial, which had been prejudicial to the case of the prisoner, McLachlan.

Chief Justice Harris and the other justices agreed with Russell and the application to appeal directly to the Privy Council was allowed.

McLachlan left the county jail in Halifax to be taken in chains to Dorchester Penitentiary in New Brunswick to begin serving his long sentence pending appeal. His reception by the warden was not indicative of a future free from oppression and prejudice.

Flanked by two burly detectives who had accompanied him from Halifax, McLachlan was paraded before the prison warden, who proceeded to give him a stern lecture on behaving as a model prisoner during his term in the penitentiary. "We have heard a great deal about you, and the trouble you have been causing in Cape Breton. I warn you, we tame lions here." And then, after taking a closer look at the slight, gaunt figure swaying before him, he turned his wrath on the escorting detectives and ordered them to remove the handcuffs from McLachlan's wrists, which were now blue with cold. Whether by design or lack of consideration, McLachlan had been hustled onto the train minus his overcoat. The sub-zero temperatures had brought back the hacking cough he had contracted in the county jail and it was obvious that he was now a sick man.

His stay in the Dorchester Penitentiary was by no means as unpleasant as that in the Halifax County jail however. The food was plain but nourishing. The cells and work areas were spartan in their simplicity but clean and vermin-free. Best of all, McLachlan found to his joy, prisoners were allowed to exercise every day in God's clean air outdoors. During his long stay in the county jail, he had never once been allowed to leave his cell to stretch his legs and to breathe fresh air.

The warden and his jailers were surprised and gratified to note that McLachlan *was* a model prisoner, working with a will and never acknowledging discomfort or complaint regarding jail conditions or his forceful confinement on false charges.

The Halifax communist Joe Wallace interviewed McLachlan in the penitentiary and wrote an article in the *Maritime Labour Herald* entitled "Outcome of the Class War—Some Caustic Comments on the Rewards of Leadership."

Although somewhat lengthy, parts of the article are worth repeating, for they reflect the unquenchable spirit of McLachlan. He may have been behaving as a model prisoner, but he was still carrying on the fight for the Cape Breton workers.

They have a saying in the penitentiary that your friends remember you for a day, your sweetheart for a year, your mother forever. However, my experience hasn't given me any excuse for complaining.... The only difference between jail and a job is that I am separated from my wife and children. Under capitalism, the workers are in jail all the time, and most of them haven't got the security of shelter and food offered in the penitentiary.... You recall what Thoreau said to his friend Ralph Emerson at the time of the agitation against slavery when he had been jailed for protest? "David" said Ralph, "what are you doing in there?" and the reply came back like a shot—"Ralph, what are you doing out there?"... When they tried Joseph Howe for sedition, they erected a monument to him in the shadow of the County jail. When you build mine, build it where I have something worth looking at: place me in the saltmarket in Glasgow where I can watch the workers gather.

McLachlan hadn't lost his sense of humour in spite of his dreadful experiences. His next words confirmed his dedication to the movement for the emancipation of the working classes

You cannot bring peace permanently to the working class under capitalism. To retain the confidence and maintain the interest of the workers, you have to lead them from struggle to struggle. New ideas are born in stables and brought up in jails. Whenever a new cause is struggling its way to recognition, its adherents have to die for it. In the early days of Christianity, many clergymen were dragged to the coliseum—how many of them are in jail today for an ideal?... I look forward to the end of my sentence not as an escape from my servitude, but as an opportunity to dive once more into the struggles of the workers. In the meanwhile, I will enjoy measuring the advance made toward the coming of communism.

McLachlan was put to work repairing boots and shoes, but as he confessed later, he possessed little aptitude for the work and was soon taken off this chore and given a job more in keeping with his training as union secretary-treasurer. He became the trusted bookkeeper for the penitentiary's shoemaking department. Today, such confidential work would be carried out by civilian personnel, but in 1924, jail authorities were only too happy to use the services of a skilled bookkeeper, confidential work or no. Freed from physical labour, he had more time for writing to his family—especially Eva, his eighteen-year-old daughter, who worshipped her radical father as a hero.

Dear Eva,

I never had very much reverence for the institutions of the rich and great, including their jails. One way to wear off the sharp edge these institutions are intended to have on us, is to scoff at them and scorn them, and your letters have helped me do this very thing with this great British institution. How I like to mock it and those who have me here. You see, when they put you in here, you are expected to whine and cry to get out, then they are pleased because their institutions are working. But when they find you mocking it and them, well, that's sedition, and they get awfully sorry about sedition. [McLachlan family records]

Jim McLachlan did not mention the demoralizing effect of penitentiary life in his letters to Kate and the children, but his initial treatment on arrival at the grim fortress in Dorchester had been designed to take away every last vestige of pride and personality. His head was shaved as was his moustache. His beautiful, prized moustache, which he had cultivated for many years, was left on the floor of the prison barber's workshop.

Each day, after the day's labour was finished and he had been returned to the solitude of his cell, he planned future policies after his release from prison. To continue the fight against Roy Wolvin and the British Empire Steel Corporation was his only ambition and objective: his aim—to help his fellow miners in their fight for decent working conditions and wages.

With a stub of pencil he often scribbled verses of revolutionary poetry to sustain his thinking and uplift his spirits during his imprisonment. One such poem, entitled "In the Miners' Row," is worthy of repeating as it reflects the utter determination of Jim McLachlan to do battle with the coal company to alleviate the suffering of his fellow miners:

We all live in Company houses
The Company runs the school.
Dad works for the Company
According to the Company rule.
We all drink Company water,
We all burn Company light,
The Company preacher teaches
What the Company says is right.

But we are little rebels,
With rebel head and heart,
We've rebel hands and rebel feet
And a rebel's fight we'll start
Against the Company preacher,
Against the Company school,

Against the skin game worked on Dad
By the robber Company rule.

And if we're going to battle,
We must first have a plan,
That each pioneer is pledged to,
Then all work hand in hand:
To end all want and hunger,
To banish workers' tears,
To build a workers' world
Is the job of good pioneers.

Daily, letters and telegrams of protest flowed into Prime Minister Mackenzie King's office. "Free McLachlan now!" workers demanded. And the protests mounted until every section of the community was adding its own strident demand for the release of this man who had been unjustly convicted of seditious libel for daring to criticize the government of Nova Scotia for its brutal handling of the Sydney steel strike. Editorials in newspapers of every political following began to demand McLachlan's release and to question the policies of Besco and the Nova Scotia government. In Ottawa, Prime Minister Mackenzie King became increasingly concerned as the protests reached a pinnacle of outrage. He had repeatedly expressed opposition to the policies of Besco and the Nova Scotia government of E.H. Armstrong from the very first day of the steel strike. On several occasions, he had publicly stated he was very much opposed to the use of troops to intimidate striking steelworkers and coal miners, and now, with the whole country up in arms over the incarceration of union leader Jim McLachlan, he was reaching the inescapable conclusion that before long, the federal government would be forced to intervene or the voters would turf out his Liberal Party at the earliest opportunity.

Support from outraged citizens was not only confined to letters and telegrams of protest. Money and gifts flowed into Dorchester Penitentiary addressed to "Fighting Jim McLachlan," and in turn, every cent and every gift was forwarded to his supporters back in Cape Breton to be used to alleviate suffering among the hundreds of miners and steelworkers blacklisted after the strikes.

During McLachlan's forced absence, the Lewis appointed president of District 26, Silby Barrett, had been quick to discover that his new, exalted office under the protection of international president John L. Lewis was not a mere sinecure without worries or responsibilities. With McLachlan removed from the scene, Besco had not softened its anti-labour stance or modified its long-standing policy of introducing successive wage cuts to lower mining costs and to raise profits and dividends on its watered stock.

The 1922 contract forced down miners' throats at the point of a bayonet was due to expire on January 1, 1924. With McLachlan safely locked in jail, and Lewis licking the hand that had starved Nova Scotia miners into submission, Wolvin and his Besco officials had determined to halt new contract negotiations before they could be started. Early in November 1923, Besco had fired the opening shot by announcing there would be no wage increase in any future contract.

The economic conditions at this time were certainly not propitious to union gains. Thousands of miners and steelworkers in Cape Breton were unemployed or only given work for two or three days each week. Appeals to Prime Minister Mackenzie King had recently been made by the District 26 executive, while the Sydney *Post* of December 10, 1923, carried the front-page headline: "Besco Iron Workers at Wabana Must Have Work or Starve This Winter."

Ignoring the demand by Besco that no wage increase be sought in the 1924 contract, the District 26 executive asked for the restoration of the lucrative 1920 Montreal Agreement with its higher wage levels. Besco retaliated with a demand for a 20 percent wage cut! But the wage cut was only to apply to miners in Cape Breton, not to their brothers on the Nova Scotia mainland. Apart from being punitive in nature, the discrimination was intended as a dividing measure, to turn union member against union member, following the old union maxim—"United we stand, divided we fall."

Negotiations finally broke down on January 15, 1924, after the old contract expired, forcing Barrett and his Lewis appointees to call a strike. It was the third coal strike in Nova Scotia in three years. While the great majority of Nova Scotia miners owed allegiance to McLachlan and had no wish to follow the dictates of Barrett, who was believed by many to be a traitor to the cause, they obeyed the union order and left the pits not because of any misplaced loyalty to Barrett, but because they could not accept another large wage cut. Daily wages were already far beneath the poverty level.

Besco reacted to the walkout by cutting off all ancillary services supplied by the company on a pay-as-you-go basis. Credit was again cut off at company stores, while coal, water, and electricity were closed off at the source. Striking miners' families shivered in their miserable company houses while the official temperature in Glace Bay was a bone-chilling ten degrees below zero.

At this point, the provincial government entered the dispute to make arrangements for renewed negotiations to continue in Montreal on February 4, 1924. Under pressure from the provincial government, which controlled its charter, Besco retracted its wage cut and offered a small wage increase in its place. But in return, the company demanded two very controversial clauses be inserted into the new contract. The first prohibited the withdrawal of maintenance men in any future strike against the company. The second clause was of a more personal, vindictive nature aimed at Wolvin's arch enemy, McLachlan. While agreeing to the clause that allowed union dues to be automatically checked off through wage deductions and forwarded to the union's district treasury, Wolvin insisted that union locals be prohibited from using any portion of their union dues to support the publication of the *Maritime Labour Herald*.

The controversial clauses should have been rejected out of hand, but Silby Barrett, provisional president of District 26, agreed to their inclusion in the new contract and ordered union members back to work until arrangements could be made for a pithead vote. Some union locals objected to the unorthodox method of ending a strike before a vote had been taken among the membership, but they were overruled to allow work to be resumed at all Besco's collieries.

It was not until March 6, 1924, one month after the men had returned to work, that a pithead vote was finally taken and the new contract overwhelmingly rejected. This was the first time in the district's history that a contract had been rejected by the membership after recommendation by the executive. Barrett was mortified; Wolvin was enraged.

Later the same day, Wolvin issued a statement to the effect that the new contract and rate of wages would remain in effect as far as Besco was concerned, in spite of the pithead referendum that had rejected it.

The 1924 contract was to remain in force until 1925 even though it was never ratified by the union members.

On Friday, February 29, 1924, the Privy Council in Ottawa ordered the release of James Bryson McLachlan on parole as a "ticket-of-leave-man." The Privy Council, whose members were mainly cabinet ministers appointed to advise the Governor-General, was influenced in its decision by Prime Minister Mackenzie King, who had become increasingly concerned about his personal popularity after massive demonstrations had taken place all across Canada in protest against McLachlan's conviction and harsh sentence.

The expected pardon did not materialize however. To pardon McLachlan would have been an acknowledgement that he had been unjustly convicted and Mackenzie King, a shrewd politician, had no intention of causing embarrassment to the provincial government in Nova Scotia, which was, after all, a Liberal government loyal to the federal Liberal Party, which held office in Ottawa.

In the House of Commons, J.S. Woodsworth, Labour M.P. for Winnipeg Centre, thanked the Prime Minister and his government for their action in freeing McLachlan and six other union men arrested during the 1923 Cape Breton strikes:

Whether or not he [McLachlan] will accept his release on ticket-of-leave, I do not know. His release may be a certain kindness to himself and his family, but it by no means goes far enough, because he still stands as a criminal—for what?... I have here—statutory declarations which were presented to the commission which recently submitted a report on its findings—substantially corroborating the statements which Mr

McLachlan had made and for which he was arrested on a charge of seditious libel.

Woodsworth continued, coldly and methodically, to review the shameful events that had led to McLachlan's arrest. The British Empire Steel Corporation had been refused a federal charter after complaints of watered stock, Woodsworth reminded the House. It had then been offered a provincial charter by the government of Nova Scotia in spite of solemn warnings from the financial sector. The Dominion Coal Company, a subsidiary of Besco, had been charged with making abnormal and excessive profits during the war from government contracts even though heavily subsidized by government grants.

A recent Royal Commission of Investigation had disclosed the "Newfoundland Scandal" whereby Besco had given forty-six thousand dollars to Premier Squires while important negotiations were in progress between the Dominion Iron and Steel Company (another Besco subsidiary) and the province of Newfoundland. The people of Nova Scotia were asking, "Is this the only provincial government involved in Besco's scandals?"

Insisting that McLachlan be given a free pardon with the stigma of a criminal act removed from his record, Woodsworth next informed the House that the judges who had decided McLachlan's case and his unsuccessful appeal had, up to the time of their elevation to the bench, been very closely connected with the coal companies operating in the province of Nova Scotia.

I am not for a moment accusing these judges of wilfully prostituting their office, but I say that men who for many years have been financially interested in certain concerns might find it very, very hard to dissociate themselves from certain points of view which they would almost inevitably have acquired.... I asked when I was in Nova Scotia, concerning the judges of the Nova Scotia Supreme Court, and I was told that the corporation influence was so strong that the court is looked upon by labour as a company department.

Mr Woodsworth was mistaken about one thing in his stirring speech to the members of the House of Commons; McLachlan had not been released from Dorchester Penitentiary in spite of the Privy Council order for his parole.

The warden, who had become convinced of McLachlan's innocence and utter sincerity, brought the glad tidings of his parole, but was astonished when McLachlan insisted on staying in jail for another two days to help train another prisoner as bookkeeper in his place! When questioned later by the Toronto *Daily Star*, April 21, 1924, about his stay in Dorchester Penitentiary, McLachlan puffed silently at his pipe before saying, "Well, the Pen' was like a palace compared to the Halifax jail; the guards were decent fellows. Why, I had a shower bath every Wednesday, clean pyjamas every week and enough to eat."

The interviewer asked him why he had stayed in jail for two extra days after he had been given his freedom. Self-consciously, McLachlan fumbled for words before acknowledging that this had indeed been the case. "Well you see now, I was preparing the cost sheets in the shoe-making department. It sounds funny but I was the only one in there who could write.... The instructor was a pretty decent sort. He was an old fellow and he could hardly see. I wanted to see him all fixed up before I left him, that's all."

On March 4, 1924, just after he had received the news of his release on parole, McLachlan received a letter from his old friend and comrade, Dan Livingstone, ex-president of District 26, assuring him of a real welcome back in Nova Scotia where thousands of miners and steelworkers were taking the day off to greet their hero.

And what a welcome McLachlan received after his release. At Truro a surprise awaited him; Mrs Kate McLachlan stepped aboard the train. She had been brought all the way from Glace Bay to greet her man. As McLachlan told the *Star*: "Kate met me at Truro. She was a regular brick! I have nine children but three are married. They were all decently looked after while I was in prison, the workers saw to that."

The Toronto *Daily Star* reported that in New Glasgow, on the mainland of Nova Scotia, thousands of miners and townspeople from Pictou County had walked seven miles across country to welcome McLachlan at the station. A special train carried hundreds of other miners and their band from Thorburn, Nova Scotia, while at the Academy of Music, a public meeting broke all records for attendance once it was announced McLachlan would speak there.

It was midnight before the train carrying McLachlan drew into the station, but the waiting multitude who had braved the pouring rain and sleet carried him from his rail coach to seat him in a hand-drawn sleigh, which they pulled down the main street of New Glasgow to the local theatre while they sang "All the miners love McLachlan." As he told it later, the hail was stinging his face, but he was happy!

Kate and her children had indeed been looked after, but not through the auspices of the United Mine Workers of America. Pithead collections had raised the money each week to feed her and her children while McLachlan the breadwinner was imprisoned.

The incarceration had taken its toll. Jim McLachlan had aged a great deal since his arrest. His hair was now plentifully sprinkled with silver and new deep lines etched his face, but his spirit was as unquenchable and no word of complaint passed his lips. If anything, his arrest on falsified charges and his suffering in the Halifax County jail had made him more determined than ever in his lifelong battle for fellow workers.

The receptions at Truro and New Glasgow were repeated at every station down the line. At Sydney Mines and Sydney, Dominion and New Aberdeen, thousands of cheering supporters welcomed Jim McLachlan back to Cape Breton. From New Aberdeen, a parade was formed up to lead their hero into Glace Bay in style. The Sydney *Post* reported over eight thousand people led by six bands marched in triumph through Glace Bay. Everywhere, the sidewalks were packed with cheering miners and their families. Not a single miner reported for work at the Dominion Coal Company's collieries and very few schoolchildren obeyed the ringing of the school bell. A cavalcade of automobiles carried McLachlan and Kate, Alex M. Stewart, Alex S. McIntyre, and many other deposed members of the District 26 executive in a huge, winding parade that stretched for miles from one end of Glace Bay to the other. Silby Barrett and his Lewis-appointed provisional district executive were prominent by their absence. So was the Dominion Coal Company, although it was noted with amusement that blinds had been drawn at the company offices as the cavalcade passed in triumph.

McLachlan's premature release from the penitentiary had not pleased the president of the British Empire Steel Corporation, Roy Wolvin. On January 10, 1924, after being informed there was a distinct possibility of McLachlan's being pardoned, he had written to Prime Minister Mackenzie King to argue against such a move. "If McLachlan is put away for a few years, possibly his teachings will be forgotten."

Wolvin's convictions could have been correct; the *Maritime Labour Herald* reported that the meeting, held in the Savoy Theatre after the parade, was unbelievable. From early morning, hundreds of miners had waited in the pouring rain for the arrival of "their Jim." Many of them had been forced to walk miles from the outlying towns into Glace Bay because they had no money for tram or rail fares after being unemployed or blacklisted for long periods.

Right from the start of his homecoming address, McLachlan made it clear that as far as he was concerned there were no strings attached to his release from the penitentiary. He had refused to accept a "pardon" from the federal government because he had done nothing wrong and therefore could not be pardoned. He had nothing to repent, unlike the Armstrong government in Nova Scotia, which was criminal. Lewis had accused him of being anti-American but that was not true; he was not and never had been anti-American—he was anti-capitalist and stood for workers, no matter what their nationality might be.

> When Lewis accuses me of being in favour of the Soviet Republic, I reply that I certainly am. I have never stood with the bosses, I have never been wined and dined by them as Lewis has. I stand alone with the workers of the world on the basis of the class struggle, and I will take that position, cost what it will until I die. [McLachlan family records]

Picking up the contract signed by Barrett and his Lewis appointees that had been voted down by the miners, Jim declared the only thing it reminded him of was the rules and regulations he had found in Dorchester Penitentiary. The proposed contract would have bound the workers to the corporation just as the rules of the penitentiary bound the convicts to their guards. If such shackles were put upon miners, they would be powerless to prevent Besco from squeezing them into abject slavery.

McLachlan returned home to Glace Bay on March 7, 1924, the day following the rejection of the Besco contract offer. He had arrived at a most propitious time. Barrett's reputation had plummeted to zero, allowing McLachlan to take over where he had left off.

The miners of Nova Scotia continued to look to him for true leadership and turned their backs on Lewis and the international headquarters in Indianapolis. Silby Barrett resigned as president of District 26 at the request of John L. Lewis, but the hated provisional district was to remain, with an American—William Houston of Pennsylvania—as a Lewis-appointed president.

On April 24, 1924, Lewis and the international Board of the United Mine Workers of America issued a directive that confirmed Besco's offer and ignored the pithead vote, which had rejected it out of hand. Once again, the international president had worked hand in glove with Roy Wolvin and ignored the wishes of District 26 miners. The acceptance of Besco's contract included the two controversial clauses regarding the nonwithdrawal of maintenance men in the event of a strike, and non-support of the *Maritime Labour Herald*.

Accompanying Lewis' dictates was an order for repayment of international funds used to support District 26 miners during the recent strike. Every one of the relief vouchers issued by Barrett to keep miners and their families from starvation after credit at the company stores had been cut off was now to be repaid through a levy of fifty cents per member per week. Although the strike had been comparatively brief, the total amount owing was $110,000. The demand for repayment came as a great surprise to the district provisional executive and every union member in Nova Scotia. Most of the locals paid up under duress, but the order to repay strike benefits served to cause a great deal of unrest, and to provide an opening for the One Big Union to make inroads into the province at a later date.

If there had been any doubt in the minds of District 26 miners regarding the cosy relationship that now existed between their international president, John L. Lewis, and the hated president of Besco, the corporation's 1923 annual report to its stockholders should have clarified the situation once and for all.

Two strikes were experienced by the Corporation during the summer of 1923; one of short duration amongst the steelworkers and one of longer duration amongst the coalminers, both of which were attended by a certain amount of lawlessness. As a result of the trouble, a Royal Commission was appointed by the Dominion government to enquire into conditions in the steel industry.... The Corporation now expresses the hope that better conditions have now been established and that hereafter, more sympathetic relations will exist between management and the work forces.

Financial results for the year 1923, show higher earnings than in 1922. [*The Canadian Annual Review*, 1923]

The long and endless trek of steelworkers and coal miners forced to leave their beloved Cape Breton isle forever after being blacklisted by this same corporation could have served as an expression of doubt that more sympathetic relations would ever exist between the Besco management and its workers.

11

Standing the Gaff: 1924–25

After his release from Dorchester Penitentiary, McLachlan was asked to take over editorship of the *Maritime Labour Herald*, replacing the noted communist Tom Bell, who had left for the United States after becoming disillusioned with the Communist Party of Canada. Permanently blacklisted in Nova Scotia's coal mining industry, McLachlan was superbly qualified for the post. Week after week, his readers were treated to a continuing barrage of scornful and fearless attacks on Wolvin and the British Empire Steel Corporation. Nickels and dimes donated by thousands of miners and steelworkers helped finance the newspaper to support the only voice raised on their behalf. And the *Maritime Labour Herald* flourished and expanded in spite of threats and demands by Wolvin and Lewis that miners not support it.

In vain did Lewis and Barrett threaten to expel members for that support as McLachlan's editorials continued to pour scorn and ridicule on the provisional district executive and Besco. Urging miners to reject the contract that had been forced on them by Wolvin and Lewis, McLachlan called on them to slow down production. By striking on the job, just as they had during the 1922 strike, they would force Wolvin to accede to their just demands, he told them. In Ottawa, Senator David, an industrialist with more than a passing interest in Besco, communicated with Prime Minister Mackenzie King after reading McLachlan's fiery editorials:

I would like to know if this McLachlan is the same man who was released by the government recently, and if he is the same man, I would like to know if the government intends to allow this dangerous man to continue to express such harmful sentiments, and if the government does not think it proper to send him back to jail, where he should have been kept. [Mackenzie King Papers, 1924]

The senator's demands did not worry McLachlan. In the April 5 issue of the *Herald*, he reported the senator's speech in full: "The senator is of the opinion that Gompers' slogan 'a fair day's work for a fair day's pay' is correct. The only trouble is that the corporation thinks that a fair day's pay is Chinese wages. But then, the senator doesn't care about that, he is a property owner himself, and not a worker."

The threat of a slowdown brought prompt retaliation from the British Empire Steel Corporation. The town of Sydney Mines was hardest hit. "Roy the Wolf" Wolvin had decided to teach his workers another bitter lesson. J.E. McLurg, the newly appointed vice-president, held a news conference to announce the imminent closing of the old Jubilee mine. Only a few key men would be retained, the remaining four hundred and fifty men would be dismissed forthwith. On May 31, 1924, the Sydney Mines town council announced that unless the Jubilee mine was reopened without delay, they would be obliged to ask the provincial government to take over its bonded indebtedness. In a further development, schoolteachers were dismissed, schools were closed, and town officials and employees laid off since all sources of tax revenues had dried up.

The black and heavy hand of Besco settled on the towns of Nova Scotia like a blight and a curse. On June 14, Besco announced that the Princess and Florence mines were also to be closed down. In vain the Sydney Mines town council appealed to the Armstrong provincial government for support. In a last-ditch effort to save the town from bankruptcy, a resolution was sent to Premier Armstrong proposing a town take-over of the coal mines to be closed by Besco. Unemployed miners would work the mines themselves, providing that the government would send in a mining engineer to see that the mines were run properly and safely; his wages would be paid each week by the miners themselves out of their pay packets.

But the Armstrong government seated in Halifax did not even acknowledge the request. Politicians sat supinely by at the request of Wolvin and his industrial giant, Besco, while a whole mining town was being wrecked to satisfy the greed of absent stockholders. To rub salt into the wounds, Besco officials told two hundred and fifty of the unemployed miners they would never be employed again, and that therefore they should get out of town as soon as possible.

By coincidence, the two hundred and fifty men had been the most active in the union.

Roy Wolvin was invited to speak to the merchants of Halifax about the unemployment situation in Cape Breton:

> It is true that my company on the first day of the year proposed a wage reduction, and a few weeks later, was forced to give an increase instead. That change of front on our part, was brought about by the Lewis representatives at the wage conference. They said that mines and communities that were not paying as well as some of the other mines, would have to be wiped out, that in the coal business, the law of the jungle prevailed, that there was no room for sentiment or sympathy, and mines like Princess and Florence would have to be closed down.

McLachlan exploded when he read Wolvin's speech. In an editorial in the *Maritime Labour Herald*, on June 14, 1924, he flayed Lewis as the arch-traitor of Nova Scotia miners. Headlines screamed: "Princess and Florence collieries to be closed down as per Besco and Lewis pact at Montreal."

> Are the miners of Sydney Mines going to stand by and see their fellows driven out? This passing of resolutions and petitioning of your foes in Halifax, is worse than useless. They will only talk to you and divide you, until the idle men are starved out. That is their policy, and that alone. Talk, talk, talk, and nothing is done. One hour's united action is worth more than one month's talk. *Up boys, immediately, and at them! Your living, the living of your wives and children is the only real thing to command your allegiance.*

These were fighting words. But McLachlan's rallying call for action was ignored. On July 6, three weeks after Sydney

Mines had been closed down, Wolvin announced the closing of the Inverness Mine on the other side of Cape Breton Island. Overnight, the town of Inverness went bankrupt. Over thirty-five hundred miners were thrown out on the streets and as coal mining had long been the only industry in the town, it was impossible for them to find alternative work. Headlines in the *Herald* announced that the situation in Inverness was most serious, with hundreds of families in desperate straits. It was reported that many were destitute and depending upon private charity to keep them from starving. Farmers from the surrounding countryside contributed as much farm produce as they could spare to help the most needy cases, but it was far from sufficient. If outside relief could not be provided quickly, it was predicted many would die of starvation.

> Yesterday, one family was discovered in which there were five young children; this family had been subsisting for five days on one meal a day—and that "meal" consisted of a little codfish contributed by some charitable fisherman. It was pitiful to visit some of the miners' homes and listen to little children crying for a drink of milk, while a worn and worried mother tried to pacify them with water.... Besides this dire want of food, no family has any coal to cook by. For some time past, a number of miners have been mining coal to meet this need from outcrops of coal on the surface, but the company's comptroller warned them to desist, informing them such procedure was contrary to the statutes of Nova Scotia.

Families actually starved to death while Lewis and the international board sat back and did nothing to alleviate their suffering. The District 26 provisional president, William Houston, returned to the United States, claiming illness in his immediate family as the reason for his abdication.

Former president Bob Baxter, who had been part of the rightist faction opposing McLachlan in the 1922 slowdown strike, was then appointed acting provisional president in his place, but the news from Sydney at this time overshadowed the appointment.

On July 26, 1924, Wolvin announced that Besco's steel plants were to shut down operations. In one fell swoop, four thousand steelworkers were thrown out of work to walk the streets with the multitude of unemployed coal miners. In a solemn announcement, Wolvin claimed the steel plants were to be closed because the high cost of coal production in Cape Breton would not permit Besco to compete successfully with steel products from France and Belgium. The steel plants would be shut down for a period of ninety days, he warned, and they would reopen only if the company was assured of an uninterrupted supply of cheaper coal. Unable to persuade coal miners to accept lower wages, Wolvin was now using other forms of blackmail. In 1923, miners had left the pits to lend support to the Sydney steelworkers, now they were being asked to take a huge cut in wages as a condition for reopening the steel mills.

Again, McLachlan jumped in with both fists swinging:

> Now that's just too bad that Wolvin cannot compete with Belgium or France.... He might have added he cannot compete with the steel products of India or China and ask the Cape Breton miners to reduce their wages to a point where he could beat out coolie labour. Ninety days from now will put us into October. By that time, the Lewis-Besco flunkies will be discussing a new contract for Nova Scotia miners and a big wage cut will be proposed and in order to intimidate miners into accepting, they will point with a hypocritical finger to the idle and starving steelworkers, and blame the miners for keeping them out of work.... Miners and steelworkers, refuse to starve! Get together and attack! Attack! Never be passive.

There were other ways of enforcing a wage cut. Every miner employed by the Dominion Coal Company received notice of an increase in the rent of his company house. The increase was 100 percent! Refusal to pay the increase meant an automatic eviction. The work week had been reduced and most miners were only working two or three days at the most. The take-home pay after the many deductions was totally insufficient to feed miners' families. They were being starved into submission.

The labour unrest and mounting poverty in Cape Breton provided a fertile area for recruitment by communist organizations. Organizers Ben Legere and Bob Russell for the One Big Union moved in from the west of Canada to stir up rebellion against John

L. Lewis and the UMWA. After the aborted Winnipeg General Strike, the leaders of the OBU had been seeking new territories and converts to their cause, and hungry miners and steelworkers, disillusioned with government, which had ignored their plight, listened avidly to the revolutionaries and their grand scheme whereby all working men and women would belong to the One Big Union which would be the instrument of their salvation.

Disaffection with the United Mine Workers of America and the provisional district executive appointed by Lewis encouraged many miners' locals to seek ties with the One Big Union. Lewis insistence on repayment of strike benefits of $110,000 to the international after the short and inconclusive strike early in the year had added another grievance against the UMWA. As early as May 14, 1924, Louis MacCormick, provisional secretary-treasurer of District 26, UMWA, had threatened to revoke the charter of any union local branch that refused to pay the debt.

While most miners' locals were strongly opposed to the repayment of strike benefits, most backed down in the face of MacCormick's threat. Only two of them refused and their charters were then cancelled, leaving their members without a union.

The *Maritime Labour Herald* of August 9, 1924, contained a scathing article by McLachlan addressed to the leaders of the One Big Union, who, he charged, were causing disruption among miners and steelworkers. But the article did little to discourage its leaders. At a meeting in Sydney, August 13, unemployed steelworkers were addressed by OBU organizer Ben Legere, who strongly urged the steelworkers union to amalgamate with the OBU to gain strength as a bargaining unit. As a result of his urgings, a unit of the OBU was formed in Sydney on August 18, 1924. The steel mills had been closed by Besco for the previous three months and thousands of families were facing starvation.

Legere's success in Sydney encouraged him to extend his recruitment campaign to include miners belonging to District 26 of the United Mine Workers of America. Initially, his efforts were very successful. Thousands of miners had become dissatisfied and disillusioned with their international union and Lewis' Provisional District Executive, which had been forced on them. But on August

23, the recruitment drive was halted when McLachlan wrote an editorial in the *Maritime Labour Herald*. Bitterly condemning the OBU for splitting the miners of District 26 into two factions, he warned against repeating the disastrous experiment of District 18 in western Canada in 1919. Instead of joining the One Big Union, McLachlan advised, Nova Scotia miners should stick to the militants who would turn the UMWA into a real fighting organization.

McLachlan was not alone in his concern regarding the intrusion of the One Big Union. The Communist Party of Canada was becoming increasingly alarmed at Legere's success in Nova Scotia. The communist newspaper *The Worker*, on September 6, 1924, contained a message from Losovsky, general-secretary of the Red International of Labour Unions, to "Moscow" Jack MacDonald, secretary of the Communist Party of Canada, warning against the efforts of "dual unionists" trying to persuade District 26 members to secede from the UMWA.

A similar message was sent from Moscow to McLachlan by the Red International, urging him to take a stand against the splitting policy of the OBU, which could only result in a serious weakening and demoralization of the whole workers' movement in Canada. The message concluded with, "On with the fight against the Lewis gang. Down with disruption and secession. Hail solidarity and unity."

Canadian communists Tim Buck, Malcolm Bruce, and A.T. Hill secretly left Canada to attend the Comintern's Fifth Congress in Moscow. Buck had travelled under his party name of "J. Page," while Bruce adopted the pseudonym "F.J. Masson"; Hill travelled under his own name. Repeatedly, in Moscow, they had been instructed by their communist masters to follow Lenin's directive for "communist rebels to *work inside a reactionary union* to achieve their ultimate goal" (domination of Canadian politics and working-class organization by the Communist Party of Canada). By working from the inside of large international unions, their true purpose—the destruction of the capitalist state—would be masked.

Bruce, Buck, and Hill returned to Canada to spread the gospel and within a matter of weeks, Bruce was dispatched to Nova Scotia to shore up the CPC's organization there after the hurried departure of Tom Bell to the United States. Joining forces, Bruce and McLachlan declared war on the rebel OBU; but Legere and Russell continued to gather converts from the ranks of dissatisfied miners. The OBU *Bulletin* of September 1924 reported a meeting held at Westville on the mainland of Nova Scotia, where "The crowd was plainly in sympathy with the One Big Union and McLachlan and McIntyre were heckled continuously. McLachlan, who was once the idol of these miners, has plainly lost his influence by the weak stand he is now taking."

Legere also made accusations that Bruce had organized gangs to disrupt OBU meetings and that he was in league with John L. Lewis and Besco. The accusations may have been grossly exaggerated but the policy of the Communist Party of Canada, as outlined by Bruce and McLachlan, was for miners to remain within the framework of the UMWA—at least for the time being.

The first definite evidence of a break with the UMWA occurred in mid-September at a meeting of sub-district 5, comprising miners' locals at Stellarton, Westville, and Thorburn in Pictou County, Nova Scotia, when a resolution was passed proposing that they should sever all ties with the UMWA and affiliate with the One Big Union instead.

Lewis and Wolvin hit back immediately. On September 15, 1924, Ben Legere was arrested at the request of Canadian immigration authorities who wished to deport him after it had been reported (by persons unknown) that he had served a prison term in the United States for participating in a strike riot. It was further alleged that he had entered Canada as a tourist but had since illegally taken employment as an organizer with the One Big Union.

Legere claimed in his defence that his work with the OBU was voluntary in nature. He was released on bail until his hearing at a future unspecified date. Miners' locals and other labour groups protested the deportation order. Even the communist Trade Union Educational League, in a complete about-face, urged all workers to fight against the deportation of a labour organizer, on the grounds that the working class, and particularly the radical sections of the working-class movement for emancipation, were being attacked by the establishment.

Their efforts must have been successful for the Department of Immigration and Colonization relented after deciding the evidence did not warrant deportation, and Legere was released from custody.

McLachlan now turned his wrath on John L. Lewis and the international board members who were making plans to betray Nova Scotia miners once again. When Lewis had assisted Wolvin and the Attorney General of Nova Scotia in placing McLachlan behind bars, he had made a serious tactical error and gained an implacable enemy. The *Maritime Labour Herald* published a front-page headline on September 15, 1924, condemning the UMWA supplying striking miners in the United States with pennies while headquarters officials rolled in luxury. Seventy thousand miners were receiving less money in the shape of strike aid than seven of the top officials in the union received in salaries and expenses for a six months' period ending June 1, 1924. During that period, McLachlan revealed, John L. Lewis and his associates were piously telling striking miners that they could not give them more aid, forcing the strike committees to appeal to other labour organizations all over the United States. At the same time, over $1.5 million was lying in the funds of the union.

Here are the names of the seven men who drew the money and the amounts they pulled down while they only gave enough strike money to buy an ice cream cone each week for strikers and their dependants:

John L. Lewis	$7,488.33
Philip Murray	5,053.42
William Green	5,194.02
Ellis Searles	13,197.76
O.L. Garrison	4,153.30
Van A. Bittner	4,076.71
Ed Dobbins	4,066.61
Total	$43,230.15

Now that's not a year's wages that these men were drawing, it was only for six months! In comparison, here are the six districts which carried on the strike during that same period, and the amount of strike benefits paid to their seventy thousand members:

District 15	$1,800.00
" 17	20,000.00
" 18	7,500.00
" 19	5,000.00
" 23	7,500.00
" 26	0000.00
Total	$41,800.00

Lewis read the article, which had been forwarded to him by the Barrett faction in Cape Breton. It was reported he flew into a towering rage and swore an oath to silence McLachlan once and for all.

On September 24, 1924, nine days after the exposé, the *Maritime Labour Herald* building was burned to the ground. The fire had been started late at night. It was no accident. Rumour had it that Lewis had ordered the burning, but more direct evidence pointed to Wolvin and the British Empire Steel Corporation.

If the burning had been intended to muzzle McLachlan and the militant faction within the union, it failed. McLachlan struck back almost immediately. Under his direction, a number of the more prominent leaders or ex-leaders of the union instituted court action to remove the unpopular provisional district executive, which had been installed by Lewis in 1923, and to be allowed to hold free, democratic elections to replace Lewis men with elected miners' representatives. But before the court action could commence, Houston, who had remained in the United States since his ignominious departure from Cape Breton in July, capitulated (after instructions from Lewis) and issued orders for a district convention to take place, September 29, 1924, to allow free election of officers. To save face, Lewis then stipulated that none of the deposed district officers, including his arch-enemy, McLachlan, were to be allowed to hold office ever again at the district or local level.

At the convention, only two names were advanced for nomination to the presidency: Bob Baxter and John W. MacLeod.

Baxter, who had been deposed by Dan Livingstone as president in 1923, was considered a right-wing conservative who would follow the directions of John L. Lewis without question. MacLeod, on the other hand, was known to be a McLachlan supporter and had organized pithead collections to send money to him during his stay in the penitentiary. (MacLeod had also been arrested during the aborted steel strike in 1923, but had been released shortly after.)

When the votes were counted, the new district President, MacLeod, presented McLachlan to the assembled delegates for a standing ovation. The acclaim left Lewis' observers in no doubt as to the sympathies of miners and the direction they would be taking in future.

The district election ousted all of Lewis' provisional appointees. Joe Nearing, an avowed leftist and friend of McLachlan's, was elected vice-president, while Alex J. MacKay replaced Louis MacCormick as secretary-treasurer. The outright rejection of MacCormick must have afforded great satisfaction to McLachlan. The attempt to pay him off with a paltry two-hundred-dollar cheque while he suffered hardships in the Halifax County jail, accompanied by the despicable attempt to destroy his reputation when accused of misusing union funds, had led to MacCormick's own downfall. The smear campaign by Lewis, Barrett, and MacCormick had obviously not succeeded. Cape Breton miners had acclaimed McLachlan as the unofficial leader of their district while Barrett and his cohorts had been ignominiously rejected.

After the election results had been announced, McLachlan spoke for an hour, reviewing the past history of labour negotiations with Nova Scotia coal companies and offering constructive suggestions for the future. "Economic conditions throughout the world were blamed for the depressed state of the industry," he reminded delegates, but pious statements made by company executives blaming market conditions for the lack of work could only be cynically rejected by miners reduced to poverty level. They had been through the process many times before. The shameful contract negotiated by Silby Barrett and his provisional executive was due to expire on January 16, 1925. For over two years, District 26 miners had been forced to work short time as a conditioning for the next round of bargaining with Wolvin and the British Empire Steel Corporation. Three major strikes in 1922, 1923, and 1924 had left the miners in a weakened condition, which had been greatly exacerbated by continued undernourishment and sickness, but fight they must. "If they lost this round," McLachlan warned, "they would be enslaved forever."

Late in November 1924, Besco proposed a wage cut of 20 percent in the new contract about to be negotiated. A wage cut of such magnitude spelled disaster at this time to the coal miners of Nova Scotia. Their take-home pay after deductions was insufficient to maintain a family, so it was not surprising that the proposal met with fierce resistance. McLachlan, while no longer an elected official in the district executive, still controlled the policy and direction of union negotiations. The new district president, John W. MacLeod, and his executive consulted McLachlan at every opportunity. Lewis had banned McLachlan from taking office in the union, but the miners of Nova Scotia still looked up to him and followed his directions implicitly and with great trust. The fierce rejection of the proposed wage cut by the district executive was made only after consulting McLachlan, who had told them to stand fast and refuse to accept anything but a wage *increase*. The company faltered and then proposed a wage cut of 10 percent, but with the slight reduction in the wage cut came a demand for the contract to be extended from January 16, 1925, until November 16, 1926. There was cunning and reason behind the demand for an extension. If the new contract expired in mid-November, miners would be in no position to call a strike with winter approaching. The union was anxious for the contract to end just prior to spring for the same reason.

With the new wage cut, Wolvin added a veiled and ominous threat that this was the last definitive offer from the company, and that if it was not accepted immediately, it would be withdrawn. The union refused and the offer was withdrawn.

Besco then applied for a Conciliation Board to force a settlement without further delay, but the union refused to nominate a representative to the board, claiming that the past history of such Conciliation Boards in the province of Nova Scotia had shown that it was impossible to obtain a fair and impartial hearing. A telegram sent to the federal Minister of Labour reiterated their stand on the issue. The telegram was signed by District 26 president MacLeod, but the wording was definitely McLachlan:

> We do not doubt the sincerity or honesty of purpose of any such board and we mean no discourtesy to it, but we have been through this experience frequently and the procedure is familiar to us. No doubt eventually, we shall be confronted with the batons of provincial police and the bayonets of the Canadian militia as the final reason for us to accept a wage cut. Yet all we ask is for human treatment for our workers and their women and children. Many children can no longer attend school owing to the lack of food and clothing.... Whole families are facing starvation at the present time, yet whoever criticizes this corporation is termed "Red" and we must walk with great circumspection to avoid the jails of our country. We have long since abandoned the effort to obtain a fair hearing before the public and we have become indifferent to public opinion.

It was obvious to all knowledgeable authorities that another major confrontation was shaping up between Cape Breton coal miners and the British Empire Steel Corporation. It was also becoming obvious that this latest dispute would be all encompassing, drastic and brutal—dwarfing any previous strike. Even Premier Armstrong of Nova Scotia had at last appreciated the seriousness of the situation when he requested the federal Minister of Labour to intervene "as the situation was almost hopeless." The only response to Armstrong's panic appeal to the federal government was the appointment of a Conciliation Board—without a miners' appointed representative.

Nova Scotia miners had lost all confidence in the Armstrong government, which they regarded as a mere puppet of the British Empire Steel Corporation—especially after the arrest of their leaders and the kangaroo court that had railroaded them into the penitentiary for union activities. This lack of confidence in the provincial government was rendered more serious by a recent decision by the Privy Council's Judicial Committee, that the Industrial Disputes Investigation Act, popularly known as the Lemieux Act (drafted in 1907 by Mackenzie King when he was Deputy Minister of Labour), violated the provisions of the British

North America Act and was therefore declared *ultra vires* of the federal government. The act, which had forbidden workers to call a strike before a Conciliation Board had declared its findings, had provided a framework for conciliation and the settling of labour disputes (in theory). With the cancellation of the IDI Act, the responsibility for settling the forthcoming strike fell squarely on the provincial government of Nova Scotia.

The union had refused to nominate a representative to the Conciliation Board that was being hastily formed by the Minister of Labour in spite of the recent ruling by the Privy Council. On January 23, 1925, the Board was completed: Colonel W.E. Thompson was nominated by Besco; Dr James W. Robertson represented the Minister of Labour, and the chairman (who had been nominated by the other two members) was J.H. Winfield of Halifax.

The union filed a protest against the "biased majority" sitting on the Board, stating that both Colonel Thompson and J.H. Winfield were mainly interested in companies that were conducting considerable business with Besco. Even the Minister of Labour, the Honourable James Murdock, admitted at a later date that "In his judgement, the men were justified in taking and maintaining their position, for the simple reason that their experience in the past has been that Boards of Conciliation set up to adjudicate the problems between company and workers have never been as definite and searching as they should have been." Which was a polite way of saying that such boards had shown a long history of prejudice in favour of the company and against the workers.

Faced with the union's refusal to participate, the Board was virtually useless, although District 26 President MacLeod did offer to allow the men to continue to work at the old 1924 rates for a period of four months "*provided that the company open its books* to allow a full, fair and impartial examination of all facets of its operations including financing."

As expected, Besco Vice-president McLurg refused to allow such an open-book investigation, stoutly maintaining the company's markets could only remain competitive if the men would accept a wage reduction.

One aspect that was to prove a serious embarrassment to federal and provincial governments was the question of aid to the starving Cape Breton people. After the rejection of the company's final wage offer, President MacLeod had brought Wolvin's attention to the extreme poverty and distress being experienced throughout the Cape Breton coalfields. Families were feeding on a diet of soup boiled up from potato peelings flavoured with dippings from a communal soup bone passed from house to house.

MacLeod could have saved his breath. Wolvin was not interested in hearing of starving miners and their families.

Early in December 1924, after several of Besco's collieries had been working for long periods on short time and miners' families had begun to suffer the effects of prolonged malnutrition, the union and the company had reached what the union considered a verbal agreement by which the company would continue to extend credit at the company stores to miners working short time. In addition to extended credit at company stores, rents were placed in abeyance and domestic supplies of coal for heating and cooking purposes were also supplied on credit. The credit thus obtained was most welcome to men who had been reduced to working two or, at the most, three days each week.

After the old contract had expired on January 16, 1925, negotiations were discontinued, although miners continued to work under the 1924 pay scale. But now, the company began to apply extreme pressure to force their miners to accept a new contract under its own terms, which included another wage slash of 10 percent.

During the months of January and February 1925, three of the more militant miners' locals—Phalen, Caledonia, and Donkin—were singled out for special treatment to reduce opposition to the company's demands. Where other miners' locals might be given work for a maximum of eighteen days in the month, miners belonging to the three selected locals were reduced to only six or seven days' work each month.

It was reported that a union meeting held in Sydney Mines (Local 4535) during the month of February was interrupted by a young, white-faced girl who shyly handed a note to the president to explain the absence of her father, who "regretted he could not attend the meeting because his wife and baby were ill and dying of starvation." The father had not been given any work for the past three months. His was not an isolated case. Hundreds of miners' families were suffering from severe malnutrition and illness even though a strike had not yet been called by the union.

The *Maritime Labour Herald*, in production once again, displayed blazing headlines: "Children Clothed in Sacking Live on Four Cent Meals."

McLachlan bitterly condemned Wolvin, the British Empire Steel Corporation, and Armstrong's provincial government for the appalling conditions in Cape Breton.

One of the largest meetings ever held in Glace Bay took place last Sunday in the Savoy Theatre. The meeting was called by the idle miners of Numbers 2, 4 and 6 collieries for the purpose of exposing the terrible conditions of want and starvation existing at these colliery districts and to protest the action of Besco in keeping these mines idle. Mayor Dan Willie Morrison of Glace Bay took the chair. Many of the Doctors and Clergy of the town took part in the meeting to tell of the terrible conditions found by them during their daily visits to the homes of the workers. The miners have worked less than half time since January, 1923, and since the 15th of November last year, have only been given a total of fifteen days work. One clergyman pointed out that in 1924, families in his district had actually lived on four cent meals. He told of families where the children were clothed in discarded flour bags and where the only bed clothes were old feed bags.

A resolution was passed by the mass meeting demanding the government of Nova Scotia do something immediately to relieve the desperate situation, but as one observer commented afterwards, many of the miners only halfheartedly voted for the resolution because they had lost all faith in the provincial government. On February 24, J.S. Woodsworth, a labor M.P. moved an adjournment of the House of Commons in Ottawa to discuss the distressing situation in Cape Breton. He had received a telegram from famine-ridden Sydney Mines: "Distress very acute at Sydney Mines. Ask immediate relief from government. People destitute. Reply at once."

And predictably, the Liberal government in Ottawa, through

its spokesman, the Honourable James Murdock, Minister of Labour, dismissed the request for an adjournment on the grounds that such matters were a provincial government responsibility, not federal, because the mines in question had been leased to the Dominion Coal Company and its overlord Besco by the provincial government of Nova Scotia. In the same breath, he conceded that Mr Woodsworth was telling the truth about the horrible conditions prevailing in Cape Breton, and not exaggerating in the least.

It was also noteworthy that three Members of Parliament representing Cape Breton remained silent on the issue. One of these worthy gentlemen, Billy Carroll, an ex-coal company lawyer, was the same man who had been elected after spreading malicious and false tales about his worthy opponent—J.B. McLachlan.

The Florence local of the UMWA in Cape Breton forwarded a vote of thanks to Woodsworth, their champion:

> It is gratifying to know that when Besco closed its doors, and M.P.s Kelley, Kyte and Carroll slumber while men, women and children suffer for the bare necessities of life, that we still have men like you who have manhood enough to stand up and demand a square deal for the workers of this country. [Records, District 26, UMWA]

Meanwhile, distress was increasing daily throughout the mining towns of Cape Breton. To add to the problems of starvation, a particularly vicious form of influenza began to sweep through the island. Hundreds and then thousands of poor people were stricken. With the body's natural resistance to disease nullified by prolonged malnutrition and hardship, they were prime targets for any form of illness. Many died. The young and the very old were the first to go.

And then suddenly, on March 2, 1925, all credit at company stores was cut off! Besco, represented by McLurg, the vice-president, stated it felt it inadvisable to extend further credit to miners. The District 26 executive of the union, astonished and incensed at what it termed "a breach of bargain," replied the following day in a strongly worded ultimatum.

> We cannot conceive of such a total absence of administrative ability as would allow you to pursue this course and expect results other than

tumults and disorder. Lacking courage to produce these results by attempting a wage cut, you have taken the circuitous, but equally effective method of producing them by starvation.

Calling on the company to renew normal days of work at collieries 2, 4, and 6 (Phalen, Caledonia, and Donkin) and for credit to be reestablished at company stores, the ultimatum warned of a complete labour stoppage if the demands were not met.

It is senseless for your corporation to anticipate that maintenance men engaged at the collieries, who are members of our union, will continue to function while your corporation slowly starves their brothers into a state of submission. You must realize that your treatment of us constitutes a lockout of our members, which means a lockout of all classifications of labour, and it is easy for anyone to observe the inevitable and almost incalculable loss which may thereby accrue to the coal industry here.... Thus we hesitate to take any steps which may lead to irreparable damage. Failure by your corporation however to correct the situation will produce this result irrespective of what we can or may do.... We ask you therefore to give this matter the most serious consideration possible and to take action within the next twenty-four hours.

Vice-president McLurg replied to the union ultimatum with a very brief message: "The Company has decided it is inadvisable to extend further credit at the company stores, and lack of demand makes it impossible to work collieries 2, 4 and 6 for the proposed minimum of four days a week."

McLurg was now telling the union to do its worst. By even denying the district executive a hearing, he was challenging the union to a duel.

McLachlan now began to call for a 100-percent strike to back up union demands. After the bitter lessons learned in the coal strikes of 1909, 1922, 1923, and 1924, he argued, the long-standing tradition of exempting the vital maintenance men from strike action would have to be discontinued. Without pumpmen, electricians, and steam-boiler engineers and firemen, the mines would slowly fill with floodwater and the electric generators supplying power to the mine machinery and lights would be inoperable. If the strike could not be settled quickly, the mines could be irreparably damaged, and yet McLachlan and the district executive knew that for a strike to succeed, it would have to include a withdrawal of *all* union men. In the past, the company had not hesitated to import foreign strikebreakers by the thousand to break the strikes. Only by rendering the mines inoperable could this practice be stopped and serious contract bargaining resume. It was a desperate gamble, but it was the only remaining weapon.

A correspondent for the influential Halifax *Chronicle*, Stewart McCawley, an ex-magistrate and one-time official of the coal company, wrote a long article warning miners and their families that the proposed 100-percent strike was utter foolishness and would eventually mean:

The tying up of the railway due to lack of coal; no coal for miners' houses, schools or hospital; over 1000 horses down the pits would suffer; there would be no water supply for New Waterford; no light for New Waterford; no work, no food; NO ROYALTIES FOR THE GOVERNMENT; Just Hell!

McLachlan was quick to repudiate this scare tactic. In a bold editorial in the *Maritime Labour Herald*, he urged Nova Scotia miners to ignore McCawley's dire predictions. His scathing editorial, which appeared on the front page opposite a reprint of McCawley's warning, was headed:

LESS THAN A 100% STRIKE MEANS—

If you miners FAIL to call a 100% strike and provide the company with maintenance men for the pumps and long submarine roadways, you have handed over to the company one of your trump cards, and you shall be beaten in your fight. Coal company officials will lie back at their ease while you look after their property. Your children will be forced into the front ranks of the struggle, matching their empty stomachs against the coal company's millions while you play traitor to your families by looking after their properties.

There are over 1000 horses in the pits, it is true, but there are over 10,000 miners' babies under twelve years of age. LESS than a 100% strike means that these horses will be fed while miners' babies starve.

To Hell with the company's horses, make the fight short and sharp for the sake of the babies.

Less than a 100% strike will mean—
No coal for your home,
No food,
No Wages,
Certain Defeat,
Less grub than you get now.
JUST HELL CONTINUED!

In the provincial capital in Halifax, Premier Armstrong held a press conference to express deep concern for the future of a great Nova Scotia industry—coal mining. If the union withdrew its maintenance men and allowed the mines to flood, it could be months or even years before they could be put back into operation again, he complained. While condemning miners' leaders for their irresponsibility, no mention was made at this time of the widespread poverty and suffering that had led to the present impasse with the British Empire Steel Corporation and its ruthless overlords, Wolvin and McLurg.

McLachlan read the newspaper reports reflecting the fears of Premier Armstrong and the provincial government of Nova Scotia and replied with another scathing attack in his newspaper to prove the falsity of the claims. "For the miners to flood a mine by withdrawing their labour is a crime, but for Besco to do the same thing is a virtue." Drawing the attention of the public to the Hub and Jubilee mines in Cape Breton, which Besco had allowed to flood before abandoning them, McLachlan accused Wolvin of destroying one of the best coal seams in Cape Breton because he couldn't get the miners working the mines to accept continuous wage cuts and reduced hours of work.

The union's ultimatum of March 3 had been forwarded to Premier Armstrong in Halifax, who then communicated with Roy Wolvin, president of Besco, expressing "great personal and provincial concern" regarding the overwhelming evidence of acute distress throughout the Cape Breton coalfields. Requesting Wolvin to reopen credit at the company stores, Armstrong, in his strongly worded letter, submitted that the original purpose of company stores was to meet an emergency of the character now existing: "Company expenditures are necessary to keep workmen alive, are not only justifiable, but compulsory.... You are pursuing a course that is disturbing to the public and creating suffering."

If Armstrong had hoped to awaken some feelings of Christian remorse in Wolvin's breast, he was mistaken. The Nova Scotia government had encouraged Wolvin to apply for a charter for Besco after being refused by the federal government. Once launched, the corporation was not about to be influenced or pressured into giving concessions to its workers. Wolvin replied:

> I very much regret any distress in our mining communities, but to be frank, coal must be produced cheaper in Cape Breton.... At the present wage scale, we are financially unable to assist our workmen as we should like.... Under present conditions and the refusal of the men's leaders to accept small wage reductions, what can they expect other than distress conditions? [Armstrong correspondence]

Armstrong read Wolvin's reply to the provincial assembly with the comment that "The action of the president of Besco may be justified, but it is not helpful or encouraging to solve a situation that is distressing, and becoming more so." Hundreds of poor Cape Breton families would have worded Armstrong's feeble protest a little differently. The situation was not only "distressing," it had now reached famine proportions. Without immediate assistance, hundreds more women and children would die in the very near future. It was noticeable also, at this stage, that Armstrong and his provincial government did not propose to send in relief to the distressed areas in the form of money or food or clothes. Such action could presumably have been interpreted as being unfriendly to the British Empire Steel Corporation.

Wolvin's adamant refusal to open the company stores to relieve intense suffering among miners' families could only be construed as a "lockout" as the union had contended all along, and that therefore, any stoppage of work could not be termed a strike but a company lockout.

After consulting with McLachlan, MacLeod and the District

26 executive sent notices to the company and the premier of the province of Nova Scotia informing them that there would be a complete cessation of work at all Besco collieries at eleven on Friday morning, March 6, 1925. The work stoppage would be 100 percent, with all maintenance workers withdrawn except for those men tending the central power plant at New Waterford, which supplied power and water to the homes and hospital in the town of New Waterford in addition to the mines owned by Besco.

All throughout the Nova Scotia coalfields, thousands of miners began to leave the pits as they obeyed their union call, leaving the province's coal mining industry in the throes of a complete shutdown. In defiance, Besco announced that their officials were continuing to operate and maintain the vital water pumps but a number of smaller collieries would be allowed to flood *for economic reasons and not be reopened after the strike.*

The walkout took place in perfect order starting with the removal of horses from the pits. Miners' grievances against the coal company must not be allowed to affect the welfare of dumb beasts of labour—slaves to the system, just as they were.

All "blind pigs" (illicit bootleggers) were closed up tight and pickets placed on all roads leading into mining communities to prevent the influx of alcohol. Following their most commendable practice in previous strikes, the union was going to act as an unofficial temperance enforcement agency. McLachlan and MacLeod were determined to eliminate every possible excuse for troops to be called in to the coalfields during the present strike. Overindulgence of alcohol coupled with privation and suffering could easily have led to a bloodbath.

Vice-president McLurg of Besco, when asked by newspaper reporters if the present impasse could be likened to a game of poker with neither side giving an inch, replied arrogantly, "Game of Poker nothing. We hold the cards. Things are getting better every day they stay out. Let them stay out two months or six—it matters not, eventually they will come crawling to us—THEY CANNOT STAND THE GAFF!" [Canadian Press, A. D. Merkel, 1925]

Asked what he meant by the "gaff," McLurg answered, "privation and hunger."

It was an unfortunate choice of words and an even more unfortunate estimation of the temperament and determination of the Nova Scotia miners. The derogatory term "They cannot stand the Gaff!" became a slogan—a symbol of their determination to hold out whatever the cost. And for the duration of the strike, miners ceased to greet each other with the customary "How you doin'?"; instead they said "How you standin' the Gaff?"

On March 9, Wolvin and McLurg wired Premier Armstrong for troops to protect company property, but for once, Armstrong refused what had become a routine request whenever strikes had been called against coal and steel companies in the province of Nova Scotia.

The Honourable William Chisholm, provincial Minister of Mines, then announced on March 11, that the premier had requested the Great War Veterans' Association in Glace Bay to furnish police protection in case government decided to bring in replacement maintenance men to prevent the mines from flooding.

In a telegram to District 26 President MacLeod, the provincial Minister of Mines pleaded and threatened in the same breath:

> Trust you and your executive will exert your good offices in safeguarding public interests. We would expect the UMWA would provide the necessary men to save from destruction the mines in which they are interested with the province generally. Should the men disappoint us in this respect, then and only then, will it become necessary to take such other measures as will be deemed advisable to protect the public interests. [District 26 records, UMWA]

After sitting back for six months while Cape Breton miners and their families slowly starved to death through the ruthless policies of the British Empire Steel Corporation, the provincial government was now making the preposterous suggestion that miners had a common interest with Besco in preserving the coal mines as a matter of public interest. At a meeting of miners' locals held in Sydney after the telegram had been received, President MacLeod warned that any attempt to bring in substitute maintenance men would probably lead to violence.

The Great War Veterans' Association (many of whom were

miners) rejected the request to provide protection for imported maintenance workers. Old veterans were not about to take part in strikebreaking actions against their own kin.

On March 18, Tom Moore, president of the Trades and Labour Congress of Canada, visited Cape Breton after being invited by the District 26 executive of the UMWA. The following day, he travelled with District 26 president MacLeod to Halifax to confer with Premier Arrnstrong and the Minister of Mines. The provincial government paid no attention to Moore's suggestion that the mines be nationalized and removed from Besco's control, but made a proposal that the men return to work immediately under the 1924 wage scale until a Commission of Enquiry had made its report. In addition, work would be provided at collieries where the men had been laid off or on short time, and company stores would be reopened for credit to miners' families.

The UMWA accepted some of the government's points immediately, but Besco declined even to consider the proposals.

Even Premier Armstrong was now beginning to perceive that management was to blame for the strike and the present impasse, but action not words was required at this point. The suffering was casting a dark shadow over the mining towns of Nova Scotia. If some form of relief could not be provided quickly, hundreds more poor souls were surely going to die of famine. The constitution of the United Mine Workers of America forbade any form of strike pay to be given to a district by the international headquarters until the strike had been in effect for four weeks, the object being to prevent any district from taking a holiday at the expense of the international treasury. But in spite of this ruling, the international executive board had discretionary power to grant such aid within the first four weeks if serious want could be proved.

Even before the strike had been called, McLachlan had been appealing through the *Maritime Labour Herald* for funds to assist needy miners' families. Now, a vigorous campaign was launched for public funds. Local citizens' groups formed relief committees and throughout the length and breadth of Canada, labour organizations, church congregations, and charity groups were sending money to ward off destitution in the Cape Breton coalfields.

Tom Moore, president of the TLC who spoke at labour meetings in Halifax and Moncton, also appealed for relief funds. In addition, he arranged through labour circles for urgently needed relief supplies to be transported free to the famine-ridden areas of Sydney Mines and New Waterford.

The Halifax *Herald* of Tuesday, March 24, 1925, reported that the motion to send relief to starving women and children in the colliery districts had been defeated by government members of the legislature after Premier Armstrong had stated that the reports of distress had been greatly exaggerated, and that the Halifax *Herald* was the only newspaper reporting such destitution. The editor of the *Herald* told his readers that this statement was a lie and to prove it, he reproduced editorials from the Toronto *Globe*, the London *Advertizer*, and the *Christian Science Monitor* in Boston, all of which condemned Wolvin and his British Empire Steel Corporation and the ineffectual government of Nova Scotia.

The editor of the *Globe* in Toronto had obviously given a great deal of careful thought to his editorial, which sought reasons for the strike and the present suffering in the coalfields of Nova Scotia.

Blaming much of the trouble on the lack of a human touch, the editor pointed out that Besco's head office was in Montreal, hundreds of miles away from the problems of Cape Breton coalfields. "No matter how well the company was represented by officials on the spot, the long distance between financial headquarters and the workers was bound to militate against good understanding. *The chimney of the working man's house is fully as important as that of the factory chimney.* Unless workmen and their families are properly fed, clothed and provided with means of intellectual and moral development, the industry is of no value to Canada. The greatest of our natural resources are men, women and children, and the test of civilization is the character of the home."

The *Christian Science Monitor* gave a brief review of the circumstances under which Wolvin had obtained the charter for his British Empire Steel Corporation using watered stock, and then called for an inspection of the company's books to see if he had told the truth regarding Besco's financial situation during the present impasse."Before the workers are required to accept lower wages, a thorough inquiry should be made into the capitalization, financing and management of Besco."

And that, of course, is exactly what McLachlan and MacLeod had been saying ever since the slowdown strike of 1922.

The relief money trickling in from points all across Canada was most welcome but it was still woefully inadequate. Bishop Morrison of Antigonish, Nova Scotia, ordered a special collection to be taken in all Catholic churches in eastern Nova Scotia after travelling throughout the blighted areas to see the desperate conditions for himself. In a pastoral letter written on his return to Antigonish, the good bishop told his flock that there were thousands of men and women, and especially children, in the direst want for the necessities of life. "I have very direct evidence that there is a large number of people who are on the verge of starvation."

In Halifax, the Very Reverend Dean Llwyd, All Saints Cathedral, stated that the appeal on behalf of the women and children of Cape Breton must not be ignored. He urged his congregation and all other congregations throughout the province of Nova Scotia to speed up their contributions before it was too late. His Grace, Archbishop Worrell, the Anglican primate of Nova Scotia, told his congregations that he personally knew of real distress throughout Cape Breton and he therefore joined in the province-wide appeal for relief funds. "I want to press upon you the regrettable fact that a number of our fellow citizens have been reduced to a lamentable state of poverty and distress and the cry for help which has gone throughout the land, appeals to the very heart of every Christian man and woman."

Canon F.G. Scott, well-known champion of the working class, wrote to Prime Minister Mackenzie King asking him to take immediate steps to save the lives of Cape Breton miners and their families and stop the acute suffering there. "An oppressed people is crying for a deliverer today." Prime Minister Mackenzie King replied, "While I share your admiration for the patience of the men, women, and children who have been called upon to endure privation and suffering in the present situation, my government cannot authorize relief...." Vacillating back and forth, King pleaded that the federal government could not provide relief to meet a local situation that was the responsibility of the provincial authorities: "It may shake the ordered constitution of our country.... Such action which would open the door to inroads upon the federal treasury from every quarter of the Dominion and which would only serve to aggravate the present situation in Cape Breton and lead to similar conditions asserting themselves with increasing frequency wherever and whenever industrial troubles arise."

Mackenzie King was more concerned about federal-provincial relations than starving multitudes. Stoutly, he maintained his government could come to the assistance of famine-ridden Cape Breton only at the request of the provincial government in Halifax; but, as King was aware, Premier Armstrong would not make such a request for fear of offending Wolvin and the directors of the British Empire Steel Corporation by appearing to take sides in the present dispute. Meanwhile, thousands of men, women, and children were suffering from starvation.

In the House of Commons in Ottawa, two champions of the working class, Agnes MacPhail and J.S. Woodsworth, were demanding immediate action to save the Cape Breton people. The *Maritime Labour Herald* reported that William Duff, the Liberal member for Lunenburg, Nova Scotia, had lashed out at Agnes MacPhail and other "ill informed persons" in the House, for reporting the so-called suffering in the mining districts of Cape Breton: "I serve notice that the province will brook no outside interference in the Cape Breton miners' strike.... The men of Nova Scotia are big enough to solve 'a serious situation' unaided."

It was reported the burly sea captain's outburst was an attempt to discount reports of suffering in the strike area, but his attack on Agnes MacPhail was mild compared to the vehement attack on Dan Willie Morrison, the Labour mayor of Glace Bay, whom he charged with using the existing situation to ensure his reelection to the Nova Scotia legislature.

Accounts of appalling suffering in Cape Breton were to be taken with a grain of salt, he maintained. It was all very well to say there was near starvation in some districts, but he, Captain Duff, M.P., knew of at least twenty families in the Glace Bay area who had accounts of five thousand dollars in the bank even though they lined up for free issues of soup. Canadians who used the suffering of women and children for political advantage were not worthy of the name, Duff continued; Miss MacPhail toured the district in the company of the Labour mayor of Glace Bay—she should have gone to "responsible" persons instead.

The record does not show who was considered to be "responsible" in this context. But most likely, Captain Duff objected to the mayor of Glace Bay as an impartial observer because of his political beliefs.

Informed by the press of Duff's remarks, the Central Relief Organization in Glace Bay waxed indignant as they challenged him to come to Cape Breton to see things for himself instead of indulging in armchair criticism. Not only was Miss MacPhail's account of the suffering factual, it was understated, the leaders of the relief organization maintained. Day after day they had been in close touch with the actual distress. They had been inside impoverished homes bare of any comforts, seen half-clad children without shoes or stockings or a tattering of underclothes, and doled out relief to thousands of starving people.

Hungry men grow desperate, the association warned, and hungry children only aggravate their desperation. Had no relief been supplied, there would have been food riots and soldiers brought in to quell disorders. "Many independent observers have verified these statements; armchair criticism is small consolation to hungry-eyed and naked children."

An emergency meeting held at the Savoy Theatre by concerned business and community leaders was attended by retail merchants, union officials, and a company official representing coal company stores. Although some of the retail merchants attending the meeting promised to extend a certain amount of credit to those in dire need, the coal company official shocked the meeting with a message from Wolvin, which reiterated the company's stand that miners would be refused credit, no matter what the circumstances! McLachlan, who was present in spite of a lack of invitation, jumped to his feet and demanded to be heard. His daughter Eva told how the chairman pulled out his watch and pompously told her father he would be allowed only five minutes to speak. Ignoring the restriction, Jim McLachlan solemnly warned the meeting that they could expect nothing but trouble if the company stores continued to refuse credit to starving miners. "They will march in the stores, take what they need, and demand that it be charged up to their credit, and woe betide anyone who tries to stop them." [Glace Bay *Gazette*]

From all across Canada came relief funds and bitter criticism of Besco and the provincial and federal governments for ignoring the plight of the Cape Breton people. Arthur Currie, commander of the Canadian Corps in World War I, suggested to the federal government that all ex-servicemen on strike in Cape Breton should be given relief. The bishop of Montreal made a nationwide appeal for the miners' relief fund, while a committee of Canadians living in Boston, Massachusetts, raised four thousand dollars in cash and pledges at a meeting of concerned citizens.

But still the contributions fell short of providing adequate food and clothing for the multitudes. It was estimated that there were over 50,000 men, women, and children in urgent need of assistance in Cape Breton during the month of March 1925.

The Halifax *Herald* bitterly criticized the provincial government for its inaction: "WHY?—Why is there no action from the provincial government on the Cape Breton situation—What is holding the government back? Another day—and still no action to supply relief to thousands of citizens of Cape Breton on the verge of starvation."

Gravely, the editor warned the federal and provincial governments that the people's patience was exhausted and that they were demanding action. Appeals had been coming out of Cape Breton, appeals backed by the most responsible people in the province. Clergymen, physicians, and civic leaders had been signing and issuing appeals for weeks, but as far as the Halifax *Herald* knew, the Nova Scotia Minister of Mines had not yet visited the colliery districts of Cape Breton since his appointment. "There can be no doubt about the situation, it is deplorable—widespread famine conditions exist, but still the government of the province has failed to act."

In the same issue of the Halifax *Herald*, there appeared a solemn warning from Canon Scott to the Nova Scotia government;

addressed to Premier Armstrong, the message was very clear:

The apathy and inaction of your government at the present time are incomprehensible to Canadians. The eyes of the "whole" people are upon you. If death ravages the coal fields now, the blood of the slain will not be lain at the door of Nova Scotia alone, but at that of the Dominion of Canada, and will shake our industrial life to the foundations. If you shrink from accepting the responsibility invite the Federal government in Ottawa to intervene.

Jim McLachlan approached a Russian delegation that was visiting Canada to purchase flour. Reminding them that Nova Scotia miners had contributed to the Russian famine fund some years before, he requested that a carload of flour be sent to the starving miners of Cape Breton as soon as possible. The Russian delegation contacted their miners' association back home, and on March 20, 1925, Comrade Losovsky cabled a generous offer of five thousand dollars on behalf of the Red International of Labour Unions and the All Russian Miners' Union to their comrade James Bryson McLachlan, for miners' relief in Nova Scotia. Unfortunately, the Citizens' Relief Committee in Glace Bay (mostly composed of business and community leaders) rejected the gift on the grounds that "Red" contributions to the fund would tend to discourage other organizations across Canada from joining in the appeal. Their righteous stance was backed by the Anglican archbishop of Halifax, who contacted Prime Minister Mackenzie King in Ottawa to demand the gift be refused. McLachlan had no such reservations; the money had been sent to aid starving miners and their families and that was exactly where it would go. He offered the Russian gift to the District 26 executive and it was gratefully accepted.

On March 28, the president of Besco, Roy M. Wolvin, released a statement to the Canadian Press that claimed that people who contributed to relief funds were intervening in the strike. Urging people not to help striking miners, he piously stated:

In my judgement, the best contribution that can be made to relieve distress in the mining districts, is employment for the miners. The British Empire Steel Corporation has offered such employment and its many mines should now be producing coal and distributing weekly payrolls sufficient to prevent distress and to permit miners to accumulate something towards the part time operations next year.

Roy "the Wolf" Wolvin failed to add that miners' wages prior to the strike had been far beneath the poverty level. Local 4536 of the UMWA at Dominion No. 6 mine published the annual earnings of 142 daily workers when the mine had been worked only for 207 shifts during the entire year. Each man had worked for an average of $3.20 each shift. Taking an average miner's family with six children, the total income over the year had only been $662.40. With deductions of $258 for rent, coal, light, sanitation, and doctor, hospital, etc., each man had been left with net earnings of $404.40 to provide all the necessities of life for a family of eight people for a year. *Or to simplify matters, less than eight dollars each week and less than one dollar per person.*

In the midst of the many protests and appeals for assistance for the starving people of Cape Breton, Senator J.P.B. Casgrain, a director in the British Empire Steel Corporation, met with the Prime Minister to express deep concern for his investment of $163,000 and for the political implications that were, he claimed, intimately linked with the success or failure of Besco.

In Ottawa, it was reported on April 1 that Progressive Conservative and Independent members of Parliament had raised the sum of $550 for the relief of miners' dependants in the Cape Breton districts. No mention was made of contributions by Mackenzie King's Liberal members of Parliament.

The Sydney *Post* reported that Warden LeVatte, Cape Breton County (the same gentleman who had given permission for the Dominion Coal Company to employ 625 special police as strikebreakers during the 1909 strike), said the present situation in the Cape Breton coalfields was "An Act of Providence brought on by the indifference of the people to Christian teaching." The fact that he also held the office of provincial purchasing agent might possibly have influenced his thinking.

Early in April, the provincial government of Nova Scotia was forced to offer some small measure of assistance to the starving multitudes in Cape Breton. The sum of twenty thousand dollars was given to the Nova Scotia Red Cross "for relief of ill health in the mining districts." No mention was made of starvation and extreme privation, which would have proved an embarrassment to the great British Empire Steel Corporation, contributor to the provincial treasury and staunch ally of Armstrong's government.

On April 10, 1925, the combined efforts of the Trades and Labour Congress of Canada and the District 26 executive of the UMWA brought John L. Lewis to the Cape Breton scene to see conditions for himself. McLachlan, bitter foe of Lewis, did not join the district executive in welcoming him to Canada, but by the same token, he did nothing to oppose his welcome. The welfare of his beloved Nova Scotia miners was his sole concern and Lewis held the purse strings.

Shocked by the terrible conditions in Cape Breton, Lewis decided relief from the international headquarters must commence immediately. The sum of five thousand dollars was sent while arrangements were made to forward the sum of ten thousand dollars each week the strike lasted, but even this amount of money was insufficient to feed the starving in the Cape Breton coalfields.

On April 14, Premier Armstrong summoned another conference in Halifax, which was attended by President MacLeod of District 26, John L. Lewis, and J.E. McLurg, vice-president of Besco. Armstrong proposed that the miners resume work at the old 1924 rates of pay until such time as a settlement could be reached. Lewis advised MacLeod to accept Armstrong's terms for temporary settlement but Vice-president McLurg insisted on consulting the president of Besco, Roy M. Wolvin.

The conference was adjourned to await his arrival in Halifax, but any hopes for a settlement were dashed when Wolvin refused to budge from his original position. Miners employed by his company would have to take a 10 percent reduction in wages. In addition, a certain classification of workers would have to be removed from union status and made officials of the company. He was, of course, referring to the vital maintenance men whose withdrawal had been part of the 100-per-cent strike, making the mines totally inoperative even with the help of imported strikebreakers.

Lewis branded these arbitrary terms as "nothing less than economic degradation and declared that, in his opinion, the British Empire Steel Corporation was out to destroy the union." The conference broke up on April 18 with MacLeod stating that Wolvin had been rude, tactless, and truculent.

District president MacLeod told the Duncan Royal Commission at a later date that before the meeting broke up, "Mr Wolvin said he was prepared to leave and do his dirtiest." Forty-eight hours later, the *Maritime Labour Herald* was again burned to the ground. All the evidence pointed to arson. A back door to the plant had been forced. The loss was covered by insurance to a certain extent, but persons unknown had succeeded, at least temporarily, in silencing the voice of the people.

With typical Cape Breton humour, D.N. Brodie, publisher of the *Herald*, described the burning as an "Act of God—under very mysterious circumstances!"

Two days later Armstrong, in a new, desperate tactic to break the deadlock, introduced a provincial Industrial Peace Bill, a reenactment of the federal IDI Act, which had recently been declared illegal by the Privy Council. The new provincial bill was an experiment in compulsory arbitration and was undertaken against the advice of the federal Department of Labour. Because any form of compulsory arbitration was repugnant to the union, the bill (Act) was never enforced. Besco, as expected, expressed hearty support for the bill, certain that any conciliation report would be designed to favour company against worker.

It now became obvious to every union member that it was indeed going to be a long-drawn-out strike. Lewis had called the shots correctly. Besco was more interested in breaking the union than in settling the strike. It had now become a question of staying power. Who would be forced to acknowledge defeat, the union or the corporation? On the one hand, Besco, which had been formed through a merger of fourteen companies, including the Dominion Coal Company, Dominion Iron and Steel Company, Nova Scotia Steel and Coal Company, the Acadia Coal Company, and the Cumberland Railway and Coal Company, had been given coal and land leases by which it controlled almost every coal mine and coal seam in the province of Nova Scotia. In addition, the corporation owned steel plants, car works, iron mines, limestone quarries, dolomite deposits, branch railway lines, steamship lines and even, as some would have insisted, the provincial government.

There had been other strikes in the Nova Scotia coalfields but never before had there been one in which public sentiment was solidly on the side of the workers. One of the more prominent newspapers had declared at the start of the strike, "This is more than a dispute between a corporation and its employees; it affects every home and every business in the province."

The strikers had claimed their strike was really one of resistance to a lockout, as Besco had for many months been preparing to enforce a wage cut and, previous to the strike, had locked out the men from ten of its more important collieries. A condition of semi-starvation, which had existed for almost two years prior to the strike, had become acute. The 10-percent wage cut demanded by the corporation would have had the effect of making the condition of semi-starvation permanent; coal miners' wages in Nova Scotia were the lowest to be found anywhere on the North American continent. The Canadian Department of Labour published figures that showed comparative daily wages between Nova Scotia coal miners and Alberta coal miners:

	Alberta	Nova Scotia
Contract Miners (average)	$8.33	$7.25
Hand Miners	7.02	4.60
Underground Labourers	6.03	3.65

[*Labour Bulletin*, 1925, Department of Labour, Ottawa]

Not only did the figures show that Nova Scotia miners received considerably less than their Alberta counterparts, but that their rate of employment was much less steady. Government figures showed that Nova Scotia miners had been given only an average of 150 days work a year for the three-year period from 1922 to 1925. Since Christmas 1924, even that low figure had not been maintained. At best, Nova Scotia miners had received wages averaging only $550 to $1,100 each year.

OBU organizer Ben Legere wrote an article in the April 1, 1925, issue of *The Nation* entitled "Starving Nova Scotia Miners." Legere reported he had in his possession all the weekly pay envelopes of one Nova Scotia miner dating from February 22, 1924, to October 24, 1924. During the eight-month period, Legere wrote, the man had earned only a total of $344.75. The company had deducted $95.28 for rent of his company-owned house, insurance (in which the company had pecuniary interests), benefit societies, churches, hospitals, doctors, etc., and coal for heating and cooking purposes, leaving him the grand total of $41.18 to buy food and clothing for himself and his large family. In the company's favour was the semi-starved condition which most miners and their families had been reduced to prior to the strike being called. They had been half-employed and hungry for years and the United Mine Workers of America had withheld approval of the strike and strike benefit payments until conditions of near famine existed throughout the length and breadth of the Cape Breton coalfields.

In the union's favour was the realization that the alternative to victory was a life of misery and oppression through an indefinite future. If the men and their families could only hold out, they would win this fight, but in order to win, sufficient food and fuel had to be begged, borrowed, or stolen!

UMWA international headquarters in the United States was now sending the princely sum of ten thousand dollars each week the strike lasted, but this was totally insufficient to feed thirteen thousand striking miners and their dependants, estimated at an additional forty-five thousand. Relief organizations all across Canada were now sending in clothing, food, and money, but the amount was still woefully short.

At McLachlan's suggestion, relief stations were set up in every colliery district, and teams of unemployed men were sent out to scout the countryside for farm produce, groceries, fish, or whatever was available. The wholesalers in Sydney showed their support and sympathy with the strikers by shipping in loads of groceries—*free of charge!* Many merchants in the mining towns also helped by allowing miners to buy on credit, but eventually they were forced to limit their generosity or face bankruptcy.

The Quaker Oats Company of Peterborough, Ontario, in

a good-will gesture, sent in several railway carloads of oats and flour.

Men went out to fish in the ocean and fishermen gave their catch freely to the scouting parties for distribution to the starving population.

A new expression was introduced into Cape Breton dialogue—"carrying the bag"—as once a week, thousands of poor people converged on the relief stations with their grab bags (supplied by the union) for their weekly rations of food. Ben Boone, retired miner from Glace Bay, recalled the grab bags and the meagre rations handed out each week to starving men and women:

> The grab bag, it was a cream-coloured bag which had held oats. I used to go up for the rations and the old feller serving them out would yell "Order for ten!" You'd get a can of turnips and you'd open it in the backyard, the smell was so bad. The bread? We used to make balls out of it and play catch. It was just like India rubber. And one time they brought some fish…you got the first one, and five others were following you! Fish was distributed at St. Mary's Hall. It had been down on the wharf for ages until it became good and ripe. My father ate so much finnan haddie [smoked haddock] during the strike that for at least three years after, my mother was not allowed to buy fish—he was so sickened of it. He ate so much fish, he often said he went up the river to spawn!

Many a boy in Glace Bay and the surrounding districts was dressed in a flour-sack dress; there was no shame in it, everyone was in the same boat; and they all had another thing in common— they were hungry. Few children owned shoes or boots.

Indefatigable, rushing from district to district organizing relief stations and fund raising, Jim McLachlan remained a tower of strength and inspiration to striking miners and their families. When spirits were beginning to flag or when funds were at a low ebb, he was always there to add moral support and to suggest new means of raising money. Unemployment insurance benefits or municipal relief were but a dream of the future. Without work, men starved!

Lack of nourishing food was one thing, fuel was another. Striking miners and their families were still blessed with mild weather, but food had to be cooked, and in the year 1925, the only means of cooking the family fare was on a coal-burning stove. When Wolvin had cut off credit at the company stores, he had also stopped the weekly sale of company coal to miners' houses.

Fortunately, the coal seams in Cape Breton often extended up to the surface, where they could be mined with comparative ease—or should have been. When the provincial government of Nova Scotia had leased its coalfields to private coal companies, they had specified that *all* coal deposits within a specified area were to be considered the exclusive mining rights of one particular company. Anyone "bootlegging" coal, whether it be surface or mined coal, even if it were on a citizen's private property, would be severely dealt with.

With families starving and home fires deprived of coal, striking miners considered the risk of prosecution small compared with the benefits. All over the island, people could be seen digging for the precious black gold. As they dug, they kept a weather eye open for company police and spies who were ever watchful for these bootleg miners. Retired miner Guy Ratchford described the secret mining with great glee: "There's lots of coal beneath here—all kinds of it—even beneath this house. We had our own little mine over there. We used to get a bucket and an old barrel with a rope on it, and we would have our old horse wind it up. About ten or fifteen loads a day."

The coal was sold very cheaply to old people and striking miners, but many who could not even afford to pay pennies for coal could always dig it out of the cliffs where it could clearly be seen as a broad rich seam.

I remember the day a bunch of Newfoundlanders came around here during the 1925 strike and they wanted to know if there was any place they could dig coal, and I said, "Yes, down there in the middle of the stream, lots of it," thinking I was having a joke on them and not wanting to show them where our own hard-earned coal was mined. Well, they went down there laughing and joking as they started shovelling off the earth, and what do you know, there was the coal right there! And I was soaking wet every day and tired out, hauling coal to the surface. I could have kicked myself, the joke had been turned on me!... During the strike, two poor fellers came down here from Sydney to dig coal for their families, but they went in too far and it caved in on them and killed them.

Many families living in Glace Bay who lacked the strength or the facilities to haul coal from outlying coal seams were reduced to crawling up the sides of the slag heaps where thousands of tons of dirt and mine tailings had been dumped. With a bucket and spade they scrabbled for the precious nuggets of coal that had slipped through the screens in the cleaning operation. Hundreds of little children were occupied in this diligent search for coal nuggets. At the end of their long day's labour, they staggered home exhausted, carrying one or two buckets of small coal, sufficient for the family's needs for one more day of the strike.

Food and fuel were necessary for physical well-being and health—alcohol was not. Nevertheless, as many medical authorities would agree, a "wee nip" now and again can often mean the difference between good mental health and poor. Since the strike had been called in March, all booze outlets had been closed up tight to try to prevent violence. Likewise, all "blind pigs" had been shut down, even though prior to the strike, Glace Bay had been liberally supplied with them. Prohibition laws had been passed in 1917, but local police had always regarded illicit drinking places with a benevolent eye. Many old miners could testify that policemen had even been regular customers prior to the strike. Moonshine stills were another matter. It was a favourite Cape Breton occupation. Hundreds of illegal stills had operated throughout the length and breadth of the island although many of them were frequently raided by provincial and Royal Canadian Mounted Police. But deep in the forests they continued to thrive, and many an old-timer will swear that the alcohol produced in these secret stills was far superior to any sold on the market prior to prohibition. The dense woods behind the town of Reserve Mines was noted as the main stamping grounds for the island's moonshiners. Duncan Currie, one of the leaders in the Cape Breton co-op movement and an ex-miner, recalled the halcyon days of the Cape Breton moonshiners with a chuckle:

They were very rough customers—some of them—in those days. There was a family of Murphys who were the most successful of them all. They were the indomitable foes of provincial and Royal Canadian Mounted Police forces, which were always trying to nail them with the goods, but they never succeeded. Some of the moonshiners were just as rough and tough as any Kentucky moonshiner; they carried guns and were prepared to use them. The Murphys were great woodsmen, and were very skilled in the art of natural camouflage. Often, they would build a still behind a waterfall where the smoke and the smell would be undetected. It was a simple operation. They would mix a mash of white sugar and yeast and water into forty-five-gallon drums and warm it so it would bubble. Then the liquid was siphoned into an old clothes washing boiler and boiled. The steam was evaporated through a long copper tube known as a "worm" into another receptacle as booze, 100 percent plus! They ran it through twice to ensure purity with all bad spirits (fusel oil) removed through the process. The stuff was then poured into one-gallon vinegar jugs known as "Hanks" and sold to the bootleggers as pure alcohol. The bootleggers often added burnt sugar to give taste.... There was only once when the Murphy boys were nearly caught. Two Mounties saw them cutting through the bush and left their car to give chase. Well, the boys easily lost them and when the Mounties got back to their car, all hot and tired, they found the tires missing plus the steering wheel!

The fame of the Murphy brothers spread far and wide, even to the extent of radio commercials, although the product advertised was a well-known cough syrup called Masons'. A popular jingle sung on the radio by a barbershop quartet, which went

> Stop that cough,
> Stop that cold
> In the nick of time.
> Don't delay, it doesn't pay,
> Get Masons' 49

was converted by Cape Bretoners, with their impish sense of humour, into "*Get Murphys' 49.*"

Another lucrative source of illegal booze was rum-running—schooners that had sailed from Demerara (British Guiana) with rum and from St. Pierre with whiskey (St. Pierre rum was not considered good rum in Cape Breton, where the inhabitants were connoisseurs of the thick, black spirit). Rum Row, where scores of rumrunners lay outside the three-mile limit off the coast of Cape Breton, provided an income for many an unemployed Cape Breton miner during the 1925 strike. It was a risky business, with grave penalties including jail terms and confiscation of one's boat if caught, but with prohibition gripping both the United States and Canada, the risks were considered worthwhile—especially to men who had been out of work for months. From beaches all around Cape Breton, small rowboats and cutters put out to sea once it was dark. Sometimes they were caught. The arrests were made after they had loaded their boats from the mother ships and were returning to shore with the evidence.

While rum-running provided an income for men willing to risk their freedom, the great majority of unemployed miners were not able to afford the price of a drink during the strike. Many resorted to other, more exotic methods of obtaining a much-needed drink to ease the pain and suffering during the strike. Ben Boone, a great humorist, told of men drinking lemon extract or after-shave lotion, anything containing alcohol, even "Jamaica Ginger."

> We found the old 78 rpm records were the best source of all. The boys used to boil them in water and syphon off the liquid to drink. It tasted God-awful, but it would flatten you! I remember once, I called on an old chum of mine who lived all on his own, and as I opened the door, I was met by this overpowering stink. There was a bucket boiling on the stove and I asked him what the hell he was cooking for supper. And he laughed as he answered, "The Old Wooden Cross!"

Wolvin and McLurg patiently waited for the weather to change. Once the fierce Atlantic gales and sub-zero temperatures had added their contribution to Cape Breton's misery, they believed the strike would be over and miners would be forced to crawl back to the pits, hat in hand, begging to be taken back.

For the strike to succeed, sufficient pressure had to be levied against Besco during the summer months, and the only way that pressure could be applied was through the withdrawal of the vital maintenance men. In spite of the company's efforts using officials to man the pumps and perform the necessary maintenance, each of Besco's pits was slowly filling with water as ventilation fans fell silent and deadly gases made each level a death trap for the unwary. If sufficient time elapsed, the water and gas could permanently ruin each pit and Besco's vast financial gamble would dissolve into useless stock.

The withdrawal of maintenance men during the strike had been bitterly condemned by Lewis and the international union. Wolvin had complained that the withdrawal had contravened the terms of the 1924 contract. A clause, inserted by Wolvin, and agreed to by Silby Barrett, excluded maintenance men from any strike. As the contract had been forced down their throats by Lewis and his provisional district executive, McLachlan, MacLeod, and the present district executive did not recognize the legality of this very controversial clause.

Meanwhile, it seemed quite likely that the strike would last throughout the summer of 1925 before it was settled. With miners and their wives only receiving one dollar each week (children fifty cents) from the international headquarters of UMWA, money had to be raised through dances, theatre performances, boxing matches, etc. Lauchlan D. Currie, a prominent citizen of Cape Breton, set out on an extended tour across Nova Scotia to raise money for the relief committees. Known as the "Silver-tongued Orator," he was in great demand everywhere. Daily, he delivered impassioned speeches pleading the striking miners' cause and begging for contributions to save starving people. At the end of every performance, it was reported he entertained the huge crowds by singing in a fine tenor voice. The same Lauchlan D. Currie was later destined to become Minister of Labour in the provincial government of Nova Scotia and then chief justice of the Supreme Court of Nova Scotia, but during the terrible 1925 strike, his personal contribution was not inconsiderable.

In late April, a story was circulating throughout the mining communities of Nova Scotia that Wolvin had just purchased 60 percent of Besco's second preferred stock at nine dollars a share after being approached by British financiers offering twenty-five dollars a share, with the sale conditional on miners accepting the wage reduction of 10 percent. The rumour added substance to the union's claim that Besco was making vast profits at miners' expense in spite of Wolvin's claims that lower coal costs were necessary for Besco to survive. McLachlan had repeatedly called for an examination of the company's books to check its claim that it couldn't afford to pay a living wage to its miners. When asked if the price of coal would be reduced after miners had accepted a wage reduction, McLurg, vice-president of Besco, had answered, "*We require the money in increased profits for our bondholders and shareholders.*"

In the House of Commons in Ottawa, Prime Minister Mackenzie King was asked to meet with the Miners' National Relief Committee on April 21, 1925, but King refused to assist the Cape Breton miners in any manner. The House then heard a ringing declaration from the Reverend Dr F. McAvoy, a Baptist minister from Glace Bay: "The men will stand tight until they starve, or there is going to be one of the bloodiest fights ever seen. The men will not recede from their position because they cannot afford to."

They were prophetic words. On May Day, 1925, the mayor of Glace Bay, Dan Willie Morrison, led the parade through the streets of the town, carrying the flaming red flag of a socialist republic, while behind him, striking miners carried placards with the slogan "Workers of the World Unite! Down with Capitalism!"

On May 5, Labour member of Parliament J.S. Woodsworth again asked the federal government to intervene in the strike or to send in relief to striking miners and their families. As expected, Prime Minister Mackenzie King refused both requests.

Time was running out. Thousands of men, women, and children were now in the last stages of malnutrition and sickness. Scores of little children had already succumbed, as witnessed by the pathetic daily processions of miners' families carrying tiny white coffins on their shoulders. On May 8, district president MacLeod desperately tried once more to enlist the help of the provincial government in Halifax: "For three months, thousands of men, women and children connected with the mining industry of Nova Scotia, have been on the verge of starvation.... We have ceaselessly appealed to your government for food for them, but not one cent has been voted for relief." [District 26, UMWA]

From the international headquarters of the UMWA came

refusal of an appeal for additional strike benefits. Regretfully, the executive board denied the urgent appeal from Nova Scotia miners, claiming it was already supporting two hundred thousand strikers in the United States.

Early in May 1925, after rumours of strikebreaking tactics by Wolvin, the district executive ordered all miners' locals to mount pickets at each colliery owned by Besco. In spite of a directive ordering pickets to preserve good order and avoid confrontation, three company officials were struck by stones as they attempted to enter one of the mines. In addition, pumps were damaged in several mines to discourage any proposed reopening. One striking miner was arrested and released on one thousand dollars bail after being charged with assaulting P.E. Ogilvie, the chief employment clerk for the company.

The assaults on company officials and the isolated instances of sabotage to mine machinery led to a warning from Premier Armstrong that provincial police or the militia would be sent into Cape Breton to protect company property and personnel unless the union guaranteed they would cease forthwith. Armstrong's threat provoked the executive of District 26 to comment that the scuffles were just what it had predicted would happen if Besco tried to operate the mines using company officials and scab labour. Ogilvie, it claimed, was a "professional scab," and further, it could prove that Besco had added a large number of new men to its payroll—men who had not been employed by the company prior to the strike.

Refusals of assistance from both levels of government seemed hypocritical in light of the House of Commons debate on government spending, May 25, 1925. One of the items questioned was a bill for $7,500 (later amended to $7,800) for relief supplies to the Leeward Islands in the West Indies. In light of Mackenzie King's repeated refusals to send in relief to the starving citizens of Cape Breton, this verbal exchange in the House of Commons is worthy of repetition:

Mr Meighen: Are the Leeward Islanders the coal miners of Cape Breton? *Mr Low*: This is a grant for the people of Antigua, victims of a hurricane which swept the islands last August. *Mr Meighen*: What form did this request take? *Mr Low*: The Governor sent a cable to the Prime Minister. *Mr Woodsworth*: Why is it that our own native Canadians are discriminated against in favour of outsiders? If the Department of Trade and Commerce can give relief to the people of the Leeward Islands, why can this government not give relief to the Cape Breton Islanders? *The Chairman*: I do not think the question is relevant.

Dismissing the threat to use armed force, district president MacLeod notified Premier Armstrong on June 3 that he was withdrawing maintenance workers from the New Waterford central power plant. Pointing out the irony of Armstrong's willingness to spend from $100,000 to $200,000 on provincial funds to send in provincial police and soldiers, MacLeod reminded him that his government had for a long time refused to give anything to alleviate the suffering of thousands of women and children, but was now willing to spend huge amounts of money to protect the property of the British Empire Steel Corporation.

It has been our constant care to make every effort in the face of great provocation to prevent these natural and almost inevitable disorders which follow upon people reaching beyond a bearable state of hunger, and we have done so primarily to avoid a recurrence of the use of armed forces of the Crown to drive us to work in conditions of slavery, as has been done in the past. At the same time we have repeatedly pointed out that human nature is incapable of endurance beyond a certain stage. Now, when that stage is being reached, we receive from your government a threat.... There is too much sand in the miners of Nova Scotia to meekly submit to injustice imposed upon them by an incompetent and corrupt corporation, and when they are driven to it, they will arise and go over the top! [District 26, UMWA]

It was obvious to all that the strike was rapidly moving to a climax. Subsequent events were to show that men who had grown desperate as their families starved were not likely to heed the warnings for caution and forbearance that their union executive tried to instil in them. They had suffered too much.

12

"We Burned the Company Stores"

Prior to its amalgamation into the British Empire Steel Corporation, the Dominion Coal Company had effected great economies in the generation and distribution of electric power to its many coal mines throughout the Sydney coalfield. To eliminate the necessary power plant at each of its collieries, the company built two central power plants—one in the Glace Bay area and the other in the New Waterford area.

The New Waterford plant, which was located at Waterford Lake, some two miles to the west of the town, consisted of two substantial brick buildings. One contained high-pressure steam boilers, while the other contained electric generators of large capacity. The installation, considered the first and finest of its kind in North America, was, without doubt, the key element in the daily operation of Dominion's coal mines. Three Bettington boilers, each fed by coal slack, produced a steam pressure of twenty thousand pounds per square inch to rotate the turbine-driven generators in the adjacent building. Each of the generators in this building was capable of supplying two thousand kilowatts of high voltage electricity to power coal-cutting machines, haulage motors, lights, ventilation fans, and the massive water pumps in each of the mines it supplied.

In addition to the vital electrical power supplied to the company's mines, the Waterford Lake plant supplied fresh water from the lake to the town of New Waterford for the use of its citizens and fire department. Perhaps the first priority for the lake water was the town hospital, which had been converted from two semi-detached company houses.

With the union declaration of a 100-percent strike, maintenance workers were withdrawn from the collieries. An exception was made at the Waterford Lake power plant, where essential maintenance workers were allowed to remain on duty to maintain supplies of electricity and water to the town of New Waterford for the benefit of the citizens. At the same time, power output to the company's mines was reduced to discourage coal mining operations by supervisory personnel and imported labour.

The arrangement was not as one-sided as it may have appeared. Steam pressure had been reduced, but fires beneath the boilers had not been drawn. With an end to the strike, full power could be restored to the company's mines within a matter of hours to recommence pumping of water seepage, which threatened to flood the workings. But with Besco's refusal to negotiate under any terms, in spite of an offer of mediation by the federal Minister of Labour, the union executive ordered the last maintenance workers to withdraw from the Waterford Lake power plant on June 3, 1925.

Besco vice-president McLurg's refusal to negotiate under any terms had been accompanied by the arrogant statement "under conditions as they now exist, arbitration is not necesssary." The district executive of the union now became convinced that the main issue at stake was not an increase or decrease in wages, but the very existence of the union, which Wolvin seemed bent on destroying. If the workers could be starved into submission, they would be forced to return to work on the company's terms without the assistance of a federal arbitrator.

At a later date, when criticism was levelled at the union district executive for making the fateful decision to withdraw essential power plant maintenance workers, President MacLeod claimed he had only been following the advice of John L. Lewis who had ordered him to "prosecute a vigorous fight against Besco." Whatever the reasons behind the withdrawal, the decision was irrevocable; the union played its last card in a very weak hand, but the last card could quite possibly win the game. The decision to call out the vital maintenance workers and to disconnect electrical power to the mines was made only after long consideration and a good deal of soul-searching. It was a final, desperate move to end the strike quickly. McLachlan, MacLeod, and the district executive of the union were well aware of the consequences of an unconditional surrender. As in the past, miners would be rehired only on the company's own harsh terms. Their leaders would be permanently blacklisted and the union broken.

Time was the vital factor. The company knew it had a few weeks at most before its mines became unworkable. With power disconnected and the great pumps at each mine inoperative, workings would start to fill and then flood back through miles of tunnels and levels to the main deep shafts on the shoreline. After that, haulage ways would be ruined and pit props would collapse, leaving a mess that could take months to clear up before normal operations could be resumed. If the pumps remained inoperative for longer periods, many of the mines could be damaged beyond repair.

With the withdrawal of maintenance men from the Waterford Lake power plant, the union set up strong picket lines to prevent supervisory personnel or scab labour from entering the plant to recommence operations. But at dawn on June 4, the day after the union call for maintenance men to withdraw, a strong force of company police succeeded in overcoming union pickets to reoccupy the plant. Seven of the pickets were arrested after a brief struggle and lodged in the town jail after being charged under Section 520 of the Criminal Code of Canada, designed many years previously to protect mine owners from striking miners: "Everyone is guilty of an indictable offence and liable to seven years imprisonment who, with intent to injure a mine, or obstruct the workings thereof...."

Full power was again restored to the mines by supervisory personnel, but as a punitive measure, power and water supplies to the town of New Waterford were now cut off completely. Repeated appeals by the mayor, P.G. Muise, and his town officials, were ignored.

The coal company's action in cutting off life-giving supplies of water and electricity was a tragic mistake. Wolvin and McLurg had completely misjudged the character of the Cape Breton coal miner. Stubborn and determined, tenacious as bulldogs, they would not be bullied into abject surrender. This latest action by Wolvin and the British Empire Steel Corporation served only to stiffen their resolve and determination never to surrender. If they had to, they could live without electricity in their company homes and they could still obtain the life-giving water from wells in the area or from nearby lakes. At least, they thought they could.

In the Toronto *Sunday Star*, June 11, 1978, Alma Davies (now Mrs Pheiffer) recalled her efforts to obtain water after Besco had turned off the taps: "We would go up to a nearby lake for a bucket of water after the supply was cut off, and if we met the company police, they would catch us and dump the water out. They didn't even want us to have anything to drink."

Undaunted, a long line of sweating strikers and townsfolk formed a bucket brigade to pass water from hand to hand from one of the few wells in the area. The month of June 1925 was especially hot and dry. The hard-pressed staff at the New Waterford hospital had a large number of patients on their hands, some in critical condition. The majority were children suffering from a variety of ailments, including cases of advanced malnutrition, scarlet fever, diphtheria, typhoid fever, and tuberculosis. An adequate supply of cool, fresh water was vitally necessary if sick children were to be saved.

Unfortunately, the bucket brigade could not be continued indefinitely by men and women denied the bare necessities of life for so long. One by one, they were forced to rest and the precious flow of water slowed to a mere trickle and then stopped.

Again, the mayor appealed to Besco to restore his town's supply of fresh water to relieve the suffering, but his plea was ignored. Appeals to the provincial government also went unheeded. New Waterford was an incorporated town in Canada financed by taxpaying citizens. Its duly elected mayor and town council owed allegiance to the sovereign, the federal government of Canada, and the provincial government of Nova Scotia. Its inhabitants were law-abiding citizens subject to the due process of law and the courts, but a private company had seen fit to cut off its vital supplies of water and electricity to cause suffering and sickness.

Ludicrous and unbelievable it may have been, but a worse

crime was being perpetrated by the federal and provincial governments as they studiously ignored the plight of innocent citizens while condoning or turning a blind eye to the high-handed actions of a feudal coal baron. The provincial treasury was being rapidly depleted with the cutting of coal royalties, and politicians made no secret of the direction in which their immediate sympathies lay in the dispute. The federal government in Ottawa, headed by Prime Minister Mackenzie King, was being very careful not to override provincial jurisdiction. Like Pontius Pilate, they washed their hands of the whole affair with a solemn declaration that the crisis was strictly a provincial matter.

In desperation, Mayor Muise again pleaded with Besco to restore the town's water supply in view of the heat wave that was adding to the misery, but his request was ignored. The mayor then requested permission for an emergency pump to be used at Waterford Lake at town expense, but like all previous requests, permission was refused on the grounds that water from the emergency pump would have to pass through water mains owned by Besco to reach the citizens of New Waterford.

This final refusal to supply drinking water to the townspeople inflamed an already tense situation. Striking miners now began to realize that their only possible course of action was to take the law into their own hands. It had become obvious that the law of the land had become a mockery—a tool in the hands of unscrupulous entrepreneurs backed by all the power and majesty of a provincial government corrupted by its own longevity and invincible majority.

A meeting hurriedly convened in the ballpark at New Waterford was addressed by union leaders, who urged angry miners to take control of the water pumps at the power plant and give the town all the water it required. "The water did not belong to foreign corporations and absentee landlords" was the sentiment expressed by union leaders; "it had been provided by God for the benefit of all mankind."

At sunset, striking miners again succeeded in ousting company officials and police from the Waterford Lake power plant to restore the life-giving supply of water to New Waterford. Their victory was short-lived however—that same evening, a strong force of company police forced striking miners to vacate the plant. Many were placed under arrest, and water supplies were again cut off. The situation once more became critical.

It was a time for even stronger action. On the morning of June 11, hundreds of striking miners were called to a meeting on the school grounds at New Waterford. Before ten, the gathering swelled with miners from towns as far away as Glace Bay, Dominion, and Sydney Mines. Union leaders gave a brief summary of the events that had led to the present desperate situation, and resolutions were passed to contact both levels of government to demand immediate action and force the company to restore the water supply to suffering townspeople before it was too late.

Even at this late stage, it is doubtful if violence would have occurred if striking miners had not been goaded beyond endurance by a strong force of mounted company police bullies who had decided to teach them a lesson they would not easily forget. Charging down Plummer Avenue in a scene reminiscent of the 1923 Victoria Road atrocity in Sydney, these drunken louts knocked innocent people to the ground before beating them senseless.

Women and children were chased into their homes by other "specials" wielding clubs and whips as they shouted obscenities at one and all. Alma Davies Pheiffer continued her recollections:

> They even chased the kids around the school yards. It was terrible.... Those guys were just drunken bums with uniforms on. The company would hire anybody during a strike, they didn't care.... My knees were all cut from falling as I ran away from them. They were all on horses with big sticks and guns. They terrified all us kids, and they were laughing about it.... They had boasted that after the first shot, the miners would go under the bed to hide.

News of the outrage spread far and wide. By noon a great multitude had begun to march through the Cape Breton countryside towards the power plant at Waterford Lake, where it was reported the company bully-boys, headed by the hated Captain Noble, were celebrating their "victory" in a drunken spree. Miners came by car, bicycle, and on foot. At every street corner and crossroads, their numbers increased as long-suffering miners' wives and their children joined the ranks. Here and there, a grim-faced miner's wife could be seen pushing a perambulator packed to the brim with hungry, white-faced children, while on the outskirts of the march, scores of little boys raced excitedly back and forth, yapping mongrels at their heels, as they attempted to keep pace with their elders.

Many an old miner can still recall the battle of Waterford Lake. Ragged, gaunt, and hungry, they lacked all the trappings and accoutrements of a professional army, but marched with a disciplined step and a firm resolve that belied later company descriptions of an undisciplined rabble.

Jim McLachlan's rallying call to the workers of Nova Scotia was at last being followed. For many years he had told his followers they would have to be prepared to fight to gain a better standard of living and to wrest control of their destiny from those who sought to enslave them under the false banner of free enterprise. Henceforth, they would speak with one voice, and the coal companies would be wise to listen and to heed.

As they drew near the power plant, the smoke belching from the chimney told its own story. Full power was again being delivered to Besco's mines to break the strike.

Surrounded by a high barbed-wire fence, which had been erected some four hundred yards from the plant, the enemy stronghold appeared impregnable. From within, they could hear the sounds of drunken revelry, but any hopes of entering the stockade unobserved were rudely dashed when a strong body of mounted company police rode out to meet them head on. Initially, it seemed a very unequal contest as the company police, over a hundred strong, charged at full gallop into the ranks of striking miners. Mounted on fine black horses, belt buckles and spurs gleaming in the early morning light, the "cavalry" charge of heavily armed thugs was a display of martial strength designed to make even the stoutest heart quail. Known to have little or no scruples in their dealings with miners and their families, it seemed the confrontation could end only in bloodshed and defeat for striking Cape Breton miners.

As they clashed on the embankment, a pitched battle was

fought. The front row of striking miners collapsed in pools of blood as mounted police fired indiscriminately into their ranks. Those following appeared to give way before the bloody onslaught, but then, in a flanking movement worthy of military genius, they raced through the woods at either side of the embankment to surround their opponents and block their retreat back to the power plant. Charging horses were brought crashing to the ground with a cruel slash to forelegs or testicles. Bare fists and stones emptied many more saddles. One striker recalled many years after the battle, that the air was so full of stones and cinders that it seemed black with flights of starlings! Policemen unseated from their mounts were beaten unmercifully by the mob. Every company policeman represented the authority and cruelty of Besco, and every blow struck at them was a blow to the hated coal company and Roy "the Wolf" Wolvin, its absentee landlord.

Within minutes the police had been routed. Unhorsed and bloodied, many of them cowered behind a barricade of railway cars, fearful for their very lives as enraged miners, swearing vengeance, searched for each and every one of them. Other company police raced through the trees and brush trying to escape their pursuers while riderless horses screamed and reared, crashing their forelegs onto several luckless miners before they were calmed.

With the police put to rout, striking miners advanced through the barbed-wire fence to attack those entrenched in the powerhouse. From the rear, company police and officials escaped through windows to jump into the lake. Several could be seen swimming to the other side in a desperate bid to escape. With typical Cape Breton humour, one retired miner described how a certain company official ran across the lake in such panic and haste that his feet did not even get wet!

With victory in their hands, attention was paid to casualties. Several miners had suffered severe bullet wounds, one had been trampled by a horse, and one poor man, William Davis, had been shot dead! The Toronto *Sunday Star* reported that the deceased had been the father of nine children and that his widow was in an advanced state of pregnancy with the tenth. Jim Davis, one of his young sons, actually witnessed the shooting of his father:

I had seen this goon falling from his horse and my father went over to him. I'm sure he only meant to stop him from falling, but the guy just panicked and shot.... The bullet went right through Dad's heart, but I didn't know that at the time. When the shooting had started, some of the men had grabbed us kids and ran into the woods with us to get away from the bullets. When it was over, one man said, "Someone's been shot and 1 think he's dead." I asked who it was, and he looked away and said, "I think it's your father."

The *Sunday Star* reported that Davis' son had thrown himself across his father's lifeless body. Grief-stricken, he had cried to captured company police, "You killed my Daddy, now kill me!"

To add horror and pathos to the scene, a baby's bottle of milk peeped forlornly from the pocket of the slain miner to drip its contents onto the dirt road. His death had been a senseless one. He had not even been a participant in the raid; he had been making his way home with the bottle of milk, donated by a kindly neighbour, and had only wandered over to the scene of the disturbance out of curiosity.

Another miner, Gilbert Watson, a war veteran and father of six children, was shot through the stomach and reported in critical condition; another man was shot through the wrist, while yet another had been severely trampled by a horse. To even the score, three company policemen and one company official were injured after suffering severe beatings at the hands of enraged miners.

The Sydney *Post* reported the following day that murder was in the air. "The fact that any of the company police and maintenance people escaped with their lives was only due to the coolness and counsel of several miners who themselves risked the anger of the mob by pleading for mercy for them."

Old miners have testified that if it hadn't been for the intervention of a parish priest from nearby New Waterford, many of the captives would undoubtedly have been hung from the nearest tree. Bilked of their revenge, miners turned their attention to the power station, which had been the root cause of their misery and suffering during the strike. Machinery was smashed, windows and doors torn from their frames, and boilers, electrical generators, and switchboards damaged. Fortunately the damage was not irreparable.

The luckless prisoners—about thirty in number—were then forced to march back to New Waterford through a continuous gauntlet of kicks and blows. On arrival, they were dragged down Plummer Avenue, scene of the morning's outrage. Every step of the way, punishment was meted out by their captors, so that their final "debut" through the main thoroughfare of the town could only be described as ludicrous. As Alice Buchanan remembered it, gone were the fine uniforms, shiny buttons, spurs, and weapons; many who had been stripped naked hung their heads in shame as the jeers and taunts flowed over them, while the notorious commander of company police, Captain Noble, shuffled along, desperately hoping to avoid recognition and save his skin by acting like any other company policeman. At the rear of the column, in a scene reminiscent of the French Revolution, long-suffering miners' wives harried the prisoners along, using long hatpins as persuaders.

The battered and by now thoroughly cowed company police were thrown into the town jail to await their fate. Feelings were running at fever pitch and rioting miners were demanding that the hated company police be hanged from the nearest tree—others, more vengefully inclined, were suggesting that the jail be set on fire to roast the unfortunate inmates.

The long line of sorrowing miners filed past the body of William Davis as he lay at rest in the home of his mother-in-law to await a pauper's funeral, while his sorrowing widow and nine children grieved in the solitude of their humble company home.

According to *The Labour Gazette*, at two in the afternoon, Vice-president McLurg wired Attorney General O'Hearn in Halifax:

> There are twenty-five policemen and company officials locked in the cells of New Waterford Town Hall to protect them from the mob which is clamouring to take them out and lynch them.... There are three policemen in the hospital, one with a broken leg, one with a fractured skull and one badly cut about the face and head.

O'Hearn responded immediately. A train carrying five hundred troops and seventy-five recently recruited, special provincial police left Halifax within a matter of hours, bound for Cape Breton.

The necessary requisition had been signed by County Warden LeVatte and Judge Finlayson at Wolvin's request. To add substance to the requisition, a spokesman from the Nova Scotia Labour Department informed the press that miners in the strike-torn area were armed to the teeth and prepared to battle the forces of law and order. The Adjutant General in Ottawa was also notified that striking miners were in possession of a machine gun and that efforts were being made to procure ammunition for it. Both reports were completely false and without foundation, but they served to justify the requisition of armed troops to subdue workers.

It was an old familiar pattern, but this time, Premier Armstrong and Attorney General O'Hearn made a serious miscalculation. Striking miners in Cape Breton would not be intimidated by any show of strength. A grave injustice had been perpetrated against them and they were determined that the coal company was going to pay dearly for it.

Meanwhile, the prisoners shivered in their cells, awaiting death at the hands of the mob. Vice-president McLurg decided to act immediately to save their lives. The troop train could not be expected until the following day, and by then, rampaging miners could have carried out their threat to kill all their prisoners. With the assistance of certain town police sympathetic to the coal company, the prisoners were freed and rushed to Sydney in company limousines and then put on a special train bound for the safety of Halifax, the provincial seat of government.

When rioting miners were informed that the birds had flown, they rushed to Sydney to carry out their threat and lynch them before the train could leave, but again, they were prevented by priests who begged them to show mercy and await the course of justice. (The escaping company policemen were eventually brought to justice and charged with the murder and wounding of miners, but as expected, the charges were all dismissed due to "lack of evidence." The verdict was that the murdered miner, William Davis, had been killed by a stray bullet!)

Besco vice-president McLurg released a statement to the press shortly after the shootings to the effect that the company was blameless; Davis' death had not occurred, and the clash had been due to the irresponsibility of striking miners. A counter statement by miners' leaders was much simpler in tone and content; it called McLurg a liar!

With the news of the wounding and killing of miners, and of the subsequent request for troops and provincial police to break the strike, miners determined to strike back at the company. As expected, they turned their attention to coal company property. The government's action in sending troops served only to inflame an already dangerous situation. From one end of Cape Breton to the other, striking miners joined the rebellion and marched on the mining towns of Glace Bay, New Waterford, Reserve Mines, and Sydney Mines.

For months they had been denied food for their families. Under the circumstances, it was inevitable that their frustration and anger should be vented on the company stores, which had long been used as an economic weapon to keep them deeply in debt and in servitude to the coal company.

Within hours of the shootings at Waterford Lake, the washhouse at No. 12 mine in New Waterford was burned to the ground. It was the first of twenty-two burnings of company property and the opening of a reign of incendiarism, destruction, and looting spread over a three-week period costing half a million dollars.

With the power station destroyed, the town of New Waterford was left without electricity and water. From one end of the town to the other, hundreds of enraged miners roamed the darkened streets, shouting threats against the coal company and gathering strength for the next phase of the struggle.

The first raids on company stores took place shortly before midnight on June 11, 1925. The stores at No. 12 and 14 mines in New Waterford were cleaned out by a gang several hundred strong. Retired miner Dan "Dancer" MacDonald took part in the raid:

> The first raid on the company stores took place after dark.... The mayor, who was the vice-president of the union at the time, said, "For Jesus' sake,

boys, if you're going in, there are a lot of wooden buildings, be careful of fire or Waterford is finished." We had no water and no electricity to pump it. So we went in and cleaned them out, but we didn't burn them.

At New Aberdeen, a suburb of Glace Bay, rioters burned the screening plant before turning their attention to the company store. Again, thousands of dollars' worth of food and dry goods were looted and distributed to the poor. Unchecked, the looters next raided the company store at Reserve Mines. Windows were smashed, and over three thousand dollars' worth of goods stolen while company officials and their families sat shivering behind locked and barred doors, fearful for their very lives. Long after midnight, the coal company advised its managerial staff to leave their homes in the troubled mining areas and head for Sydney, where they would be protected by the authorities.

The troops, who arrived the following day, were met with a fusillade of stones thrown by a mob thousands strong. It was reported that when the crack regiment of the Royal Canadian Dragoons disembarked at Sydney Mines, a local girl quipped that the best-looking part of the force was the horses! Gone was the easy camaraderie between civilians and armed troops that had characterized the many previous entries of soldiers into the troubled Sydney coalfield. Long suffering and with the continuous trek to the cemeteries with the wasted bodies of their young had sapped any form of goodwill towards armed intermediaries who were regarded as nothing better than company bullies, ever ready to step into labour disputes on the side of the hated British Empire Steel Corporation.

With the arrival of the troops, the New Waterford police force put on a bold front—a quality noticeably absent during the previous day's riot—and proceeded to arrest numerous union officials on charges of inciting miners to burn company property. In turn, the labour-dominated town council sacked the arresting officers and ordered the release of union officials. A special peacekeeping force of striking miners was then sworn in to maintain order in the New Waterford area, and with the exception of an incident which followed three days later when the surface workings at

Number 12 mine were burned, no further damage was reported within the town's limits for the duration of the strike.

News of the shootings at New Waterford had travelled far and wide. Late Friday and early Saturday, thousands of men began to converge on Glace Bay from towns and villages all across the island of Cape Breton. The company's worst fears were about to be realized.

Saturday, June 13, 1925, was to be a Saturday unlike any other. From early in the morning to late afternoon, hundreds and then thousands of men roamed the streets of Glace Bay, gathering at street corners and on vacant lots when speakers retold the awful happenings of June 11 at Waterford Lake. As tensions mounted, the mayor and town council expressed concern and then alarm. The first contingent of troops arrived at Sydney Mines and Caledonia, but their numbers were few and the troubled area large. Bootleggers and "blind pigs" added their own contribution to the forthcoming riots by supplying copious quantities of illegal booze—much of it produced in local stills. By sundown, all were in the right frame of mind (with the aid of the "Good Spirit") for a rip-roaring evening of destruction. Retired miner Gordon MacGregor watched the influx of troublemakers on this fateful evening:

I can remember just how it happened. Everybody knew that the stores were going to be raided that night. I was living in No. 6 district. There used to be a train that ran from Donkin to Glace Bay on Saturday nights, forty cents return for an adult, twenty cents for a child, and young kids free. It used to leave Donkin at six o'clock in the evening and return from Glace Bay at nine-thirty. Well, I remember the train had just come in, and suddenly the great big window at No. 6 company store went smash! And that was that. There were at least five hundred men involved. Some had brought their families along, others had blackened their faces or put masks on. They cleaned out the store but the clerks had changed other merchandise for useless things. I saw one man—a great feller for MacDonald's Twist tobacco—crouched behind the Firemen's Parlour and we could hear him swear as he ripped off the box top. They'd switched the tobacco for clothespins!

An advance party of looters had broken into the company's central power station at New Aberdeen to disconnect electric power to the town of Glace Bay and its suburbs to allow rioting miners to operate in total darkness. The town police made themselves scarce at the first sign of trouble, but it should be emphasized that their absence from the riot scene was not due to a lack of courage or neglect of duty. The widespread malnutrition and suffering of the townspeople, followed by the more recent beatings and shooting of innocent workers and their families at the hands of company thugs, had made the police indifferent to the protection of coal company property, especially if the protection involved a very real risk of personal injury or worse at the hands of a drunken mob.

All through the night, company stores were looted. Caledonia, New Aberdeen, Donkin, Dominion, and Passchendaele—none were spared. Even the main company store supply depot was raided and thousands of dollars' worth of goods stolen. Until the break of dawn, Glace Bay residents were treated to an unforgettable display of riotous behaviour, looting, and burning. Hundreds of men could be seen dragging hogsheads of molasses, barrels of flour, or clothing, food, or even furniture through the streets of Glace Bay to hide in their homes or in some secret hiding place to be collected later when the hue and cry subsided.

Many were the stories, both humorous and pathetic, that were told after the raids. Ben Boone told of "Biscuit Foot" McKinnon, who was given the nickname by his workmates after he had injured himself in the raid:

He reached up to pull a big tin of biscuits off a high shelf and it fell onto his foot and crushed it; he was nicknamed "Biscuit Foot" ever after.

Then there was Big Frank McIntyre. Oh, he was a big powerful man that! The meat market was in a separate room at the back of the store and Big Frank, he just ripped off a few shingles and walked away with a big side of beef on his back. Then he rolled a fifty-gallon barrel of molasses down to the park and the guys were half paralyzed with drink they had stolen and people were coming with buckets for molasses from the barrel and the drunks got this little feller who was always messing his pants and they up-ended him and put him upside down in the barrel. And that was the end of the free molasses. Nobody would touch it after that!

And then there was Danny Turnbull, another big powerful man, who found some lemon extract upstairs in one of the company stores the night of the raid, and he got himself all loaded up on it—that stuff would flatten you! And other guys were drinking "Jamaica Ginger" and after-shave lotion, anything they could get their hands on to drink. And poor old Danny got a big chest of drawers on his back and stepped out of the loading doors on the second floor, not realizing he was up two storeys. There was a block and tackle on a girder outside the doors where they used to lower stuff down onto the loading dock. He never got over that fall, he was counter-sunk in the ground with the weight of the chest of drawers. He had a "Pluck-Me Back" ever after! Another guy had a huge roll of linoleum on his shoulder and he shouted, "Make way for a hungry man!" as he also stepped out of the same door.

Eric Scott of Dominion spoke of goods stolen in error:

I remember a man who went into the store and took what he thought was a bag of flour. In those days the bags were large and weighed ninety-six pounds. He put the bag on his back and walked down the railway tracks to Bridgeport, where he lived. He put the flour in the pantry and went to bed. His mother, who was nearly blind, got up early the next morning and mixed a batch of biscuits with the flour. The biscuits were not coming along very well so she took a look at the flour. It turned out to be a bag of hard wall plaster!

Hundreds of pairs of shoes and boots were stolen. But the joke was on the looters; all had been mixed so that a black, size-nine shoe lay in the same box as a brown size-six, etc. Many an old miner chuckles today when reminiscing about the shoes and boots they stole that night:

In the cemetery the next day, Sunday, scores of guys were swapping shoes and boots behind the gravestones where they thought they were safe from the cops. A guy would holler, "Who's got a black size-nine? I've got a brown size-eight I'll swap." And slowly they got it all sorted out. There was a peg-legged feller in Glace Bay who they said never had to buy another shoe from 1925 until the day he died. They gave him all the odd size-nine left shoes that were left over after the swapping session.

Ben Boone was only a young lad at the time of the raids on the company stores: "I was just starting work and just a kid when I went in the stores with the other guys, and this feller who was with me, said, 'Here's a suit that'll fit you,' and he gave me a whole bundle of suits!"

If the situation had not been so serious, it could have been described as hilarious. One man was seen carrying a large bag of potatoes in each hand while he kicked a huge round of cheese before him like a small boy with a wheel and stick. Another had loaded both arms from wrist to shoulder with circular black puddings, leaving his hands free to carry huge bags of flour. Furniture, rolls of linoleum, chests of drawers, even large double beds and down-filled mattresses, were rolled or dragged through the darkened streets to be hastily deposited in miners' homes.

Jim McLachlan may have warned in the past that miners facing starvation would eventually help themselves to food from company stores, but his strict Calvinistic upbringing and his natural honesty abhorred the looting and wholesale plundering of the company stores. His daughter, Eva Pemberton, told how a neighbour, Aloysius Gillis, an orphaned lad of eighteen, had offered a new pair of boots to her father. Knowing them to be looted from the company store, he refused to accept them. The same lad gave a box of what he believed to be chewing gum to her sister Jean, but when opened, the box of chewing gum turned out to be packets of dye! The clerks at the store had been busy indeed.

The final act in the drama took place after the stores had been cleaned out. From every point on the compass, the sky was tinged with red, as store after store was put to the torch. It was said afterwards that the company had been the guilty party, that the act of incendiarism had been carried out to collect massive insurance payments; no one could deny or substantiate the charge, but true or not, the national press placed the blame squarely on the shoulders of miners and "similar hoodlums." No one was ever apprehended or convicted of the crime.

The lootings and burnings continued the following evening, and two days later, on June 15, the rail-engine roundhouse and repair depot were burned in Glace Bay. Fortunately the British

Empire Steel Corporation was adequately covered by fire insurance. After the strike the Hartford Fire Insurance Company complained bitterly to the Duncan Royal Commission regarding the extent of its losses. Besco's claims had amounted to over half a million dollars for looted goods and burned buildings. Included in this gross figure was a claim for $120,000 for No. 11 bankhead, which was burned during the evening of June 29 in spite of the presence of hundreds of armed soldiers, barbed wire, machine gun pits, and searchlights.

This fire, the last major act of incendiarism to take place during the 1925 strike, was witnessed by McLachlan's daughters Eva and Mary. Eva Pemberton recalled:

> We had been strictly forbidden by Papa to go anywhere near the disturbances during the strike, but this night, Mary and I had been visiting our sister Esther and her husband, Murdock McKeighan. They had given us a bottle of homemade wine for my mother and we were hurrying home down Highland Street in Glace Bay, which is next to No. 11 mine, when we saw the mine buildings go up in smoke. Hundreds of people came out of their homes to see the fires, and then the soldiers came charging down the street on their great black horses and we ran for our lives, thinking we were going to be shot or trampled. The bottle of wine didn't appreciate the jogging up and down though, and the cork popped out with a loud bang and we were showered with warm red wine. Funny thing was, we thought we had been shot! We had many a good laugh over it afterwards, but we dared not tell Papa. He would have been very angry.

With the lootings and burnings, came more troops. In Ottawa, Defence Minister E.M. MacDonald explained the reinforcements. They had been sent at the urgent request of the Nova Scotia Attorney General after vicious assaults against coal company officials and police, he told the House of Commons, and they would be withdrawn as soon as the dispute had been resolved. But with the arrival of armed troops, Wolvin and McLurg now decided they were in a better position to dictate their own terms for settling the strike. On June 17, they announced that the company's original demand for a 10 percent wage cut remained the same. Four demands were added now that they were convinced the strike had been won and the miners beaten into submission. Checkoff union dues were to be abolished; men known to have engaged in disorderly conduct during the strike would not be rehired; union officers known to be communists would not be allowed to meet with company officials to discuss settlement terms; and maintenance workers were to be excluded from the union.

These "proposals" were made to James Murdock, federal Minister of Labour, who had been invited to Cape Breton by Besco to settle the dispute and persuade miners to return to work. Dutifully, Murdock wrote to President MacLeod, urging him to accept the company's punitive terms and end the strike:

> I learned during my visit to Sydney, that the company was not desirous of making any settlement and would let the situation go on indefinitely with 1,000 troops scattered throughout the territory, in the belief that finally the organization [union] would be dissolved and the workmen ready to work on the company's terms.... Your board is at liberty to indicate to your membership my personal view that more acceptable terms of settlement cannot be secured. [District 26, UMWA]

A similar letter was forwarded to John L. Lewis. Lewis replied promptly, with a stinging rebuke for the Minister of Labour for even suggesting that Cape Breton miners capitulate on the company's harsh terms. Since his visit to Cape Breton in April, Lewis had abandoned his sweetheart pact with Besco. The company's refusal to bargain on any terms but its own, the suffering and near starvation of Cape Breton miners and their families after credit was cut off at the company stores, and the bitter conference in Halifax with Vice-president McLurg had once again convinced Lewis that Besco was out to break the union.

Murdock returned to Ottawa to report to Prime Minister Mackenzie King, who then made the decision to make a direct approach to Wolvin to end the strike as soon as possible. But even when faced by the Prime Minister of Canada, Wolvin refused to modify his demands to the union, reiterating that Cape Breton miners were on the run and would be forced to return to work in the near future.

The attitude of the provincial government towards striking miners and the widespread famine in Cape Breton was amplydemonstrated by Premier Armstrong in a letter he wrote to a Saskatoon Methodist church that had asked him whether it should raise money to help miners' families. The letter was written on June 19, one week before the provincial election:

In my opinion, there has been nothing in the history of this country so exaggerated for political purposes as the situation in the mining districts of Cape Breton. I think practically every person in Nova Scotia has now agreed that one of the most pronounced hoaxes ever put upon a sympathetic people was that launched a few weeks ago by some over excited people in connection with this unfortunate matter. I do not believe that today one dollar could be raised in this province for this purpose. Further, I do not think it is needed. You have asked me a plain question and 1 can do no better than give you a plain answer.... When those who are fomenting this trouble see fit to accept money from the Red Internationale and to parade under the Red Flag in preference to the British Flag, it is time the public took notice, much more so the quarterly board of a Methodist Church!

Fortunately, the church elders saw fit to publish the letter via the Canadian Press before the Nova Scotia provincial election was called. Armstrong's callous indifference to the suffering of thousands of poor families living in the Sydney coalfield did not endear him to the electorate—particularly those who were suffering from malnutrition.

The Halifax *Herald* of Saturday, June 20, 1925, reported that the Montreal Trades and Labour Council had discussed the strike situation in Cape Breton and that President Foster of that organization had stated that Besco was not interested in settling the dispute except on its own terms, and that those terms meant the destruction of organized labour and the imposition of punitive wage rates stipulated by the company:

They have been on strike a long time and they have put up what is really a very fine battle. It was inevitable that the point would be reached when there would be trouble if it was incited.... I have every reason to believe the recent trouble there was incited for the express purpose of discrediting miners and those conducting the strike.... We might say something in criticism of a federal government which withheld financial assistance and declared it had no right to interfere and could not make any donations to relieve the sufferings of those people, and which is now prepared to face a tremendous cost to provide militia to protect what? The miners? No, the property of those who are depreciating the property down there when it could be operating at a profit.

In the end, it was the provincial election that terminated the strike. For forty-two years the Liberal Party had remained in power in Nova Scotia without a break, and now the citizens were making it plain that they favoured a change. The Conservative Halifax *Herald* wrote scathing denunciations of Armstrong's government in its June 20 edition. Pointing to the once prosperous town of Sydney Mines in Cape Breton, the editor told his readers the town was now silent and dead while the government dealt in unimportant trivialities. "Nero fiddled while Rome burned. Faced with one of the greatest and most ruinous industrial tragedies of late years, they play at building men of straw and then tear them down again. With the loss of jobs and mass blacklistings by Besco, our sons and daughters stream across the border never to return."

The Monday, June 22 issue of the *Herald* continued on the same theme. A large picture of an aging, careworn mother was captioned "To the Women of Nova Scotia":

In the provincial election in Nova Scotia on Thursday, the women of this province, the mothers, the wives and daughters, will vote to stop the exodus of fathers, sons, husbands who have been forced to leave their native province to earn a livelihood. The women of Nova Scotia will mark their ballots to *vote them back home*!

The Tories, led by the Honourable E.N. Rhodes, played on the province's labour problems, near civil war, and the suffering and privation throughout the Sydney coalfield. Laying the blame squarely on the shoulders of Armstrong and his scandal-ridden administration, Rhodes piously swore to settle the strike if elected. Further, he promised his first act as premier would be to come to Cape Breton and personally intervene in the dispute. He didn't specify what direction his intervention would take—for the company or the workers—but striking miners, bitter, disillusioned, and hungry, did not seek to question his promises; they grasped at the offer of mediation like a drowning man grasps at a straw, and thousands of them voted for a Conservative government while ignoring their own Labour candidates, Forman Waye, Dan Willie Morrison, Joseph Steele, and Emerson Campbell.

On Thursday, June 25, 1925, the Conservatives made a clean sweep, winning forty seats to the Liberals' three. All of the Labour candidates in Cape Breton County were defeated. The personal defeats of Armstrong and Attorney General O'Hearn must have afforded great satisfaction to the man they had persecuted and imprisoned on false charges, James Bryson McLachlan. But any sense of gratification was tempered with the distressing knowledge that once again, labour would be absent from the provincial government. From his knowledge and experience of labour history in Scotland and in Canada, McLachlan knew that Nova Scotia workers could expect little from a Conservative government, except promises. The truth of the matter was that the Conservatives were anxious to get rid of Wolvin. The promise of a settlement of the strike was a weapon they used not only against the Armstrong government, but also as a means of removing Wolvin's control of the British Empire Steel Corporation.

One of the successful Conservative candidates in the new government was Colonel G.S. Harrington, one of the barristers who had defended Jim McLachlan during his trial (many believed ineptly). A letter written by Harrington to President MacLeod of District 26 two months prior to the strike expressed this sentiment in no uncertain words:

> It will be satisfactory if the international (union) were to approve a policy of no reduction in wages. The announcement of such a stand would almost certainly have the effect of making it impossible for Mr Wolvin to finance, and therefore lead to control of the corporation passing to some group more favourably inclined to labour. [District 26, UMWA records]

The "group" obviously referred to members of the Conservative Party, which had just seized power in Nova Scotia, but whether they would be more inclined to favour workers in their fight for better working conditions, only time would tell.

The new premier, Edgar Nelson Rhodes, was sworn in on July 16, 1925. John C. Douglas, ex-mayor of Glace Bay, was sworn in as Attorney General of the province, while Colonel Harrington was handed the very controversial mines portfolio. The hated provincial police force was disbanded immediately, and the office of provincial purchasing agent abolished, with its incumbent, H.C. LeVatte, warden of Cape Breton County, dismissed.

Premier Rhodes arrived in Sydney on July 20, only four days after being sworn in. He was accompanied by his new Minister of Mines, Colonel Harrington. Without delay, talks were set up between District 26 officers and Besco management to try to hammer out an agreement to end the crippling coal strike. The talks lasted for five exhausting days, but no agreement could be arrived at. Besco was determined, as always, to slash miners' wages by 10 percent, and the miners were just as determined that no such wage cut would be put into effect.

Rhodes and Harrington returned to Halifax without resolving the strike, and then on August 3, they proposed a six months' contract with a wage cut of from 6 to 8 percent. In addition, if the contract was acceptable to both sides in the dispute, there would be a referendum under government supervision to decide if the checkoff for union dues should be continued or not. There would also be a full provincial enquiry into the Nova Scotia coal mining industry. Besco was to reinstate all workers on strike without forming a blacklist and the provincial government, in return, would rebate to the company one fifth of its coal royalties.

Besco immediately announced it would accede to all of these conditions provided that a pithead vote favoured a return to work. The vote was taken on August 5, and by a slim majority the men voted to return to work under the conditions outlined by the provincial government. The men were to be rehired on August 10, but no sooner was the rehiring commenced than it was found that Besco was refusing to take back over five hundred men who had been placed on a blacklist in contravention of the agreement. Union officers immediately suspended the rehiring until the provincial government could intervene. Rehiring was then resumed without further discrimination.

The troops left Cape Breton on August 15, after the District 26 executive announced the end of the strike. Wade's *History of District 26* says that the estimated cost of supporting and maintaining troops from June 12 to August 15, 1925, was a whopping $325,000. When added to the loss of coal royalties, the provincial government had lost the very considerable sum of $550,000 from the provincial treasury, not counting the many indirect and consequential losses, the amount of which would never be determined. Miners had lost over seven million dollars in wages, but Besco in comparison had lost only $1,505,430 in profits. To the holders of Besco securities, the loss meant little; a few dividends deferred or lost. Likewise, the loss of profits meant little to company officials, who received their normal salaries all through the crippling strike.

In contrast, the loss of wages to miners had deprived them and their families of any means of sustaining life. Besco had demanded a 10-percent wage cut, which had been refused by the men after a long, systematic program of reduced work weeks and the cutting of credit at the company stores. After five long months, the men had been forced to return to work and accept a slightly lower wage cut of 6 to 8 percent.

The provincial election in Nova Scotia and the defeat of Armstrong's government were followed by a federal election on October 29, 1925. The Nova Scotia Labour Party again nominated the people's champion, James Bryson McLachlan, but the deck had been stacked in favour of the other candidates. In an overt move, the retiring provincial government had ordered a redistribution of the Cape Breton ridings to prevent a Labour victory. The old riding of Cape Breton-South Richmond, which had included the working-class districts of Glace Bay, New Waterford, and Sydney Mines, was changed to Cape Breton South, with the north-side district of Sydney Mines—a hotbed of social unrest—replaced by the city of Sydney with its predominantly middle-class, anti-labour, anti-union electorate. The change represented a very substantial loss in working-class votes for McLachlan, who was once again unsuccessful in his bid for election as a Member of Parliament in Ottawa.

Towards the end of 1925, the new provincial government headed by Premier Rhodes set up a Royal Commission of Enquiry to investigate all aspects of the Nova Scotia mining industry. The chairman, Sir Andrew Rae Duncan, was invited from Great Britain, where his main contribution to the mining industry had been to direct the return of the state-controlled coal industry back to private ownership after World War I. With such a background, he was not expected to rule in favour of Nova Scotia miners. Assisting him in his task were two other commissioners, neither of whom were labour leaders nor had any experience of coal mining, the Reverend H.R. MacPherson, president of St. Francis Xavier University in Antigonish, and Hume Cronyn, K.C., president of the Mutual Life Assurance Company in Waterloo, Ontario.

The commission began its hearings on November 11, 1925, taking evidence from a large number of witnesses, including Besco president Wolvin, vice-president McLurg, District 26 president MacLeod, Jim McLachlan, Silby Barrett, and Bob Baxter. Expert witnesses in the form of medical doctors and municipal health inspectors told the commission of high infant mortality rates in all the mining communities controlled by Besco. Dr A.S. Kendall told of mass outbreaks of scarlet fever, diphtheria, smallpox, typhoid, tuberculosis, and even poliomyelitis. Poor sanitary conditions, lack of sewage disposal, open sewers, and contaminated milk were the main culprits, he maintained, but poor-quality company housing, with their leaky, drafty windows and doors, had also contributed to the poor state of health throughout the mining communities of Nova Scotia. Above all, prolonged malnutrition had weakened the body's natural resistance to disease and illness. The very young and the very old had succumbed and died in ever-increasing numbers while the strikes lasted. Drs. Sullivan and Hartigan confirmed Dr Kendall's testimony, adding their own horror stories to the evidence compiled by the commission.

Without doubt, the most entertaining period during the hearings was the verbal battle between McLachlan and Wolvin. McLachlan told how the Dominion Coal Company and the British Empire Steel Corporation had repeatedly refused to open their books for inspection to successive boards of enquiry and conciliation, although they had always tried to justify their demands for wage decreases by quoting the state of world markets and foreign competition while swearing on oath that they were making insufficient profits for their stockholders.

With a flourish, McLachlan produced a set of up-to-date balance sheets showing Besco's true profit and loss statements for the years 1922 to 1925. With an impish grin, he told the commission how a certain company employee (unnamed) had stopped him one day on a busy Glace Bay street to hand him a bundle of papers, which, he claimed, McLachlan had dropped.

Contrary to Wolvin's claim of insolvency for Besco, McLachlan was able to show conclusively that the company was in a very healthy financial condition and could easily afford an increase in miners' wages. But with wage cuts being enforced all over the world at this time, it was perhaps not surprising that the Duncan Commission recommended a 10-percent wage cut for Nova Scotia miners in spite of McLachlan's evidence.

District 26 miners were forced to return to work with a wage reduction only slightly less than that offered by Besco before the strike. They returned after they had been promised a full investigation and a fair, impartial settlement. The promises had been given by politicians anxious to obtain their votes in the provincial election. Now they were told they must accept what Besco had offered in the first place—before they had been forced to strike and suffer privations for five long months. With the district treasury exhausted, and international funds unobtainable, with coal miners all over the United States on strike, they had to wait for another opportunity when they regained their strength and their will to continue the fight against tyranny.

Commissioner Duncan stated there was ample justification for Besco's proposed wage cut of 10 percent based on the "inflated" wages of 1924. The commission recommended that in future wage negotiations between the union and the coal companies, wage rates should be tied to the ability of the industry to pay!

The British Empire Steel Corporation may have won the latest round in its continuing dispute with District 26, but the company itself did not emerge scot-free after the men had been forced back to work. President Wolvin and Vice-president McLurg decided to depart the scene late in 1925 when a reorganization took place in the corporate structure.

The news of their departure was not received with any feelings of regret by the downtrodden workers of Cape Breton, who had suffered greatly under their ruthless management.

The following year, 1926, when Besco published its financial statement, profits after depreciation on all Besco coal operations were shown as $2 million. Besco estimated the wage cut to be worth $1.5 million. Without the wage cut, Besco's coal companies would have earned roughly $1 million in 1925, which would have been ample to cover its bond interest of 5 percent and dividends on preferred shares at 7 percent.

So much for the fair, impartial investigation of the Nova Scotia coal mining industry.

On the positive side, the commission urged Besco to get rid of its company houses by selling them to its workers for a reasonable price. The provincial government was urged to make improvements to roads, sewers, and sanitary conditions and to uplift generally the living conditions of the mining communities in Cape Breton. But little action was taken in this regard. The houses remained under company control for another twenty years; toilet and sanitary conditions—especially open sewers, the cause of so much sickness and disease—remained more or less the same until the Depression of the 1930s when municipal authorities and governments were forced to allot public funds to put starving men to work building sewage plants and indoor toilets in workers' homes.

The commission's findings were published on January 11, 1926, just in time for Besco to impose the recommended 10-percent wage cut when the six-month contract proposed by Premier Rhodes ran out. The Duncan Commission had sought to justify its recommendation for a wage cut by arguing that reduced wages would actually increase annual wages of miners by making more working days through reduced costs of operation. It was a futile argument, and one without substance. All through 1926, Nova

Scotia miners were given only three to four days' work each week. At the same time, the cost of living continued to escalate, lowering their earning power and standard of living.

The company stores were not rebuilt after the looting and burnings. Although Besco was compensated in full, the decision was made not to enter into any further credit business with its workers. The end of the company stores closed out an era which in many ways had been detrimental to an independent way of life for miners and their families, and yet, when speaking of the old "Pluck Me Stores," many old miners remembered them with nostalgia and a strange sense of loss at their going. Gone were the bulk foods and full sides of bacon and beef, sacks of flour and sugar; gone, too, was the old potbellied stove, around which many of them had loved to gather during the long winter months to smoke a pipe of tobacco and swap yarns.

Gone too were the "Bob-tailed Sheets" and the evil system of extended credit that had held them in bondage to the company.

Perhaps Danny "Dancer" MacDonald should have the last word. He told *Cape Breton's Magazine*:

What you got at the company store was quality and quantity. A private merchant might cut a few ounces off, but there in the company store it was our own flesh and blood [working]—daughters and sons of miners. If there were any breaks you got it. And everything they had was first class. Clothes, furniture, grub was the best of everything. But we're better to have it out of our way, because it created a way of life that wasn't good. You know, there were men that died and still were owing to that store....

The company never tried to re-establish company stores after that. Never made a try. Now here's a peculiar thing. Do you know it took women a long time to get acquainted to go to stores with money? They were lost. When we went back to work we were paid cash, and we shopped where we wanted. Cash, but so much on that back bill that you still owed [to the company store]. They made sure their records weren't burnt.

13

The Death of J.B. McLachlan

With the change in corporate management came a change in the union. It came not through an election, but through a change in attitude—almost a change in sides—as President MacLeod and his District 26 executive board began moving to the right. Militancy was exchanged for compromise and a cosy relationship with coal companies at the expense of Nova Scotia miners.

McLachlan's left-wing supporters in the union executive were all defeated in the 1926 elections to be replaced by moderates or outright opponents of union militancy. Those elected to office quickly sided with the coal companies in the blacklisting of fellow union members who refused to toe the line and accept the new union policy of cooperation and compromise.

Men who had toiled at the coal face all their working lives now found themselves wearing a collar and tie as they sat behind a union desk. In many cases, the transition from a life of hard physical labour to a new pseudo-respectability, where intelligence was deemed more important than mere physical strength and muscle, proved detrimental. Inevitably some miners lost all thought of using militant tactics to regain lost wages and working conditions; it was far easier to accept things as they were and promote the new status quo among the rank and file membership of the union while assisting management to quell the few brave souls wishing to continue the struggle against insurmountable odds.

The new policy of compromise inevitably led to rebellion.

Keeping their silence, the true militants made their plans and consulted McLachlan at every opportunity.

With the swing away from socialism and the election of right-wing officers to the District 26 executive, the union now began to criticize McLachlan for his no-compromise approach to negotiations with the coal companies. In a total about-face, President MacLeod ordered all district locals of the union to cease funding of the *Maritime Labour Herald*, and within a year, McLachlan's gallant little newspaper had been forced to cease publication. McLachlan retired to his small holding at Steele's Hill and the management of Besco heaved a great sigh of relief. But their relief was short-lived. McLachlan had not been defeated. The forced "retirement" was only a breathing spell before the next round commenced. Hidden up his sleeve, he still had a card or two, but he waited for an opportune time to show his hand.

In 1928, President MacLeod was defeated by Dan Willie Morrison at the District 26 elections. With his defeat, MacLeod was appointed assistant superintendent of mines at Besco, thus joining other company "faithfuls" who had seen the light and lent their support to the company they had fought against for so many years.

Shortly after, it was announced that the British Empire Steel Corporation, which had been founded by Wolvin, was to be reorganized under a prominent English industrialist, Sir Newton Moore, and that, henceforth, the company would be listed on the stock exchange as Dominion Steel and Coal Corporation or Dosco. Any hopes that the new company would be more amenable to union demands were soon dispelled. In racing language, the new company was a "ringer"—the same horse with different markings. Its character remained the same.

Later that year, a provincial election was called by Premier Rhodes. The Nova Scotia Labour Party immediately selected James B. McLachlan and Forman Waye as its candidates. Since 1925, Labour had not been represented by a single member of the legislature, but now, an all-out effort was to be mounted to win one or more seats using the two most prominent Labour leaders in Cape Breton—McLachlan and Waye.

Conservative and Liberal campaigns against Labour candidates were based on the same old issues—communism and ungodliness. True to form, both parties that promised cushy government jobs and contracts, plus unlimited supplies of free rum and beer found plenty of willing listeners. Again "men of the cloth" thundered warnings of Bolshevik murders and revolution, and the voters listened and feared.

Ridiculous it may have sounded, but effective it must have been, for when the votes were counted, both Labour candidates had been soundly beaten and the Conservatives returned to power in Nova Scotia.

McLachlan's defeat did not deter him from future political aspirations. To the day he died, he believed implicitly in the principle of labour representation in government as a vital means of gaining a decent standard of living for the working class. His latest defeat did mark an important turning point in his life; from that time on, he determined to fight at the polls under a straight Communist Party ticket, not as a socialist or labourite. For twenty-six years, since his arrival in Canada from his native Scotland, he had fought tooth and nail for fellow workers in Nova Scotia, but now, with the decision to fight as a Communist, he turned his eyes to the west and determined to look after the interests of working men and women all across Canada, while not neglecting what he considered his primary concern—the miners and steelworkers of Nova Scotia. His decision was reached during a critical period in labour history. The years 1927 and 1928 had marked a distinct change in relations between governments and union organizations, with the Communist Party of Canada forced on the defensive.

It was a time of great unrest throughout the North American continent and all across the civilized world. To combat the rising tide of unionism and demands for political representation, financial institutions and controllers of industry were painting lurid pictures of the menace of communism, which was being expressed through demands for higher wages and shorter working hours.

Yet there was ample reason for the increasing trend toward socialism. As McLachlan and Silby Barrett had warned in 1919, "the best material for the making of a discontented man is a hungry man." All through 1929, unemployment had been growing steadily and it seemed obvious that both Canada and the United States were heading towards a total economic collapse.

On October 29, 1929, came the Wall Street crash, and stock markets all over the world plummeted downward in a sympathetic explosion that echoed through a capitalist system built on a rotten, unstable foundation. Factories closed by the hundreds. Thousands and then tens of thousands of workers were thrown on the streets to starve, and banks in every town and village were forced into bankruptcy as panic-stricken people withdrew savings or investments.

In Cape Breton, McLachlan launched a worthy successor to the twice burned-out *Maritime Labour Herald*. His new venture, *Nova Scotia Miner*, proved to be even more militant than its predecessor. Financed entirely through miners' contributions, it became the official organ and mouthpiece of the District 26 Left-wing Committee, as the militants styled themselves, and from the first day of publication on December 14, 1929, it became just that. McLachlan had never shown better form as in successive editorials, week after week, he lambasted John L. Lewis and his corrupt policy of working hand in hand with coal companies to the detriment of poorly paid miners. Politicians were not spared his biting vituperation, but his bitterest criticism was reserved for the District 26 executive and their collaboration with Nova Scotia coal companies.

In February 1930, negotiations for a new contract between District 26 miners and Dosco were halted when the new vice-president and general manager, H.J. Kelly, refused to allow any increase in wages, stating that the economic situation did not warrant it. After prolonged negotiations, Dosco finally offered a minuscule 3-percent increase for the lowest-paid miners, but allowed nothing for other miners even though their wages were almost 50 percent less than those received in 1921. To add insult to injury, the new contract was to be extended until January 31, 1932—a two-year contract in place of the traditional one year, without an increase in the pitifully inadequate wages paid to Nova Scotia miners.

Enraged at the settlement, McLachlan urged left-wing members to set up a new union, the Mine Workers Industrial Union of Nova Scotia, to replace the United Mine Workers of America and its right-wing District 26 executive. But the new, breakaway union was never fully recognized as a bargaining unit representing Nova Scotia miners, especially after a number of its more prominent advocates were expelled from District 26 on charges of dual unionism. The expulsions from the union were followed by firings and blacklistings from Dosco after a request had been received from union district president Morrison.

McLachlan's editorial in the *Nova Scotia Miner*, April 19, 1930, was headed "Herod and his Pals," and he poured scorn and ridicule on Morrison and his district executive for their punitive action. But in retrospect, it is difficult to picture the kindly Morrison as a Herod or class collaborator. Pressure from within the ranks forced Morrison to reinstate all of the expelled men some months later, but many felt his ruthless expulsion order had been promulgated out of fear. With vivid memories of suffering and mass evictions, he was trying to avoid a full-face confrontation with the powerful coal corporations during this period of the Depression. With millions unemployed all across Canada and the United States, Morrison believed, rightly or wrongly, that any work was better than none, whatever the restrictive wage policies of Dosco and other coal companies. In any case, his actions were governed by the international president of the union, John L. Lewis, who was pursuing the same policy of collaboration with American coal producers.

A federal election was called for July 28, 1930. Mackenzie King's Liberal government was under tremendous fire and criticism for the tragic unemployment situation. The Conservative opposition, headed by a bitter anti-socialist from western Canada, Richard Bedford Bennett, established its election platform on a new deal for Canadians, rich and poor alike. "Prosperity is just around the corner" was his favourite theme, and the working class, desperate for a word of hope with hundreds of thousands of unemployed walking the streets, believed him. King went down to defeat and Bennett took office as the Prime Minister of Canada.

Bennett's election platform had been based on economic recovery, but once in power, he showed little inclination or talent to forward imaginative programs to stimulate such a recovery. Even for those still employed, the situation was almost as bad. Many employers, taking advantage of the depressed economy, slashed wages while increasing hours of work. In the nation's sweatshops, thousands of poorly paid workers were forced to speed up production without an increase in wages, and tragically, the great majority of workers so affected had remained unorganized due to the myopic policies of the Trades and Labour Congress of Canada and the American Federation of Labor.

Three weeks after the Wall Street crash, the Workers' Unity League (WUL) was formed by the Communist Party of Canada to organize all of the so-called unskilled workers into a series of new "industrial unions" covering industries where workers had never belonged to a union. Under the protection of the WUL, workers belonging to the new industrial unions would be encouraged to fight the vicious trends of speedup, wage cuts, and increased hours of work.

With the catastrophic Depression, the leaders of the WUL also concentrated on the urgent problems of mass unemployment and relief from starvation. With breadwinners hopelessly unemployed, hundreds of thousands of families were in desperate need of assistance—a need that municipal, provincial, and federal authorities were reluctant to meet without immense pressure from labour groups and the Workers' Unity League.

As a candidate in one provincial and two federal elections, McLachlan had made his bid as an Independent Labour candidate, but with the Great Depression and the Conservative victory in 1930, the federal Independent Labour Party had ceased to exist as a political force representing Canadian workers. With its demise, the Communist Party of Canada now began to attract underpaid and unemployed workers by the thousands. Miners and steelworkers in Nova Scotia, suppressed for many years by both Liberal and Conservative governments, turned to the more radical movement to champion their cause and right their very real grievances. McLachlan's long fight for Nova Scotia miners, and the cruel repressive measures taken by coal companies, aided by the provincial government, had convinced him that workers' only hope of salvation lay in the overthrow of the capitalist-controlled state and a take-over by a workers' communist party.

Ever since the Communist Party of Canada had been launched

secretly in 1921, McLachlan had served as its District No. 1 representative, covering all of the Atlantic provinces. After his release from Dorchester Penitentiary in 1924, he had been invited by Tim Buck, general secretary of the party, to become more actively involved in the movement, and as a highly trusted party member and a martyr to the cause, he was eventually invited to be a member of the Central Committee. Regularly, from then on, McLachlan traveled back and forth to Toronto—a gruelling two-day journey each way by slow train—to attend meetings at Communist Party headquarters in the Labour Temple, 167 Church Street. All such journeys were made at his own expense, even though his income since his blacklisting from union office was primarily from his market garden holding at Steele's Hill and milk round in Glace Bay. His daughter, Eva Pemberton, told how he had often been forced to spend the night, after such a meeting, in the cold, inhospitable Union Station in Toronto, waiting for a train to carry him back to Cape Breton. Intensely proud and independent, McLachlan may have been too poor to seek the luxury of a hotel, but never by word or deed would he admit to any such embarrassment—not even to his closest friends and associates. Undoubtedly, the long journeys to Ontario and the severe discomfort suffered in cold, drafty waiting rooms aggravated his medical condition, which continued to deteriorate.

It wasn't difficult to recruit converts to communism. Hunger proved a more effective instrument than propaganda in convincing the unemployed and the destitute that their only hope was to follow the communist philosophy. In the mining and steel towns of Nova Scotia, the unemployment picture was reaching epidemic proportions. Even for those still employed, the picture was almost as bad, with the average miner only working two shifts a week, although a minimum of five shifts was necessary to support a family on a meagre diet. Nova Scotia miners were still being paid at a rate 60 percent lower than what they had received under the Montreal Agreement of 1920. With daily miners receiving the magnificent sum of $3.40 for an eight-hour shift and a weekly wage compressed into two shifts, only the gross sum of $6.80 was provided to feed a miner, his wife, and an average of five children.

Worst hit was the town of Sydney Mines, where it was reported the town's finances were in very bad shape after overdrawing at the bank. Only 5 percent of its miners were said to be working steadily. The remainder were unemployed or working only two shifts per week. With the town able to collect only 50 percent of its taxes, it was having difficulty in finding sufficient money to pay interest on its bonds and to keep its schools open. More than six hundred people were on direct relief during the month of January 1931, and the figure was expected to rise dramatically in the near future.

The same heart-rending story was being repeated in every community throughout Cape Breton. Miners' lives were now being governed by the whistle at the pithead at six in the morning. One whistle meant "Report to work," but two whistles meant another idle day without pay.

The Great Depression of the "Dirty Thirties" caused untold misery all across Canada. The Halifax *Herald* reported on July 30, 1931, that the need for relief in Cape Breton was real and desperate. Theatres in Glace Bay were closed for want of patrons. Thousands of tons of coal were said to be stacked in huge bankheads, unsold, while most of the mines worked part time. The *Herald* wrote:

> Two days' pay is but $6.80, which is not a living wage for the miner himself, let alone for his almost invariably large family. The wonder is that enough food has been obtained to keep them alive. Clothes they cannot buy, even though they are badly in need of them. A family of ten was found to have only one pair of stockings between them. They were shared by the mother and the eldest daughter. The rest of the family went barefooted. When the daughter went out, the mother took off the stockings for her to wear and vice versa.

Glace Bay, the largest town in Cape Breton, was reported to have paid out over $265,000 in relief to needy families, and the town's finances were being stretched to the limit. A letter written to Prime Minister Bennett by an observer reported signs of "Red" agitation among the mining communities. Undoubtedly, the stories were true. As the new, radical spirit of communism began to rear its head, all levels of government expressed concern. Fears of a possible uprising by the unemployed masses activated panic-stricken directions to police forces everywhere to quell gatherings of the unemployed—by force if necessary—and to jail communist organizers and agitators arranging such meetings.

Promising Conservative elements he would crush communists and the Workers' Unity League under an "Iron Heel," Prime Minister Bennett consulted with his Department of Justice before again declaring the Communist Party of Canada an illegal organization under Section 98 of the Criminal Code of Canada. On August 11, 1931, the Royal Canadian Mounted Police were ordered to carry out raids on Communist Party headquarters in Toronto and the homes of communist leaders all across Canada. Tim Buck, Malcolm Bruce, Tom Hill, John Boychuk, Sam Cohen, Tom McEwen, Mathew Popovic, Michael Gilmore, and Tom Cacic were all arrested and thrown into jail to await trial.

McLachlan left Canada in September 1931 to visit Russia. His trip was financed by Cape Breton miners and steelworkers who paid all the costs on a voluntary basis. McLachlan may have been deposed from the union office by Lewis, but the miners and steelworkers would always revere and respect him as their true leader. Now they were showing their gratitude by sending him on an expense-paid tour of Russia with the hope that firsthand knowledge of working conditions in the Soviet Republic would be relayed to them on his return.

During his absence, federal and provincial governments stepped up the campaign to suppress the Communist Party of Canada. Buck and his companions were tried and found guilty of sedition and conspiracy and were sentenced to a term of five years' imprisonment.

The Communist Party of Canada had just celebrated its tenth birthday.

In the midst of an economic depression, decreasing markets, and mass unemployment, the next round of wage negotiations opened between District 26, UMWA, and Dosco. It could hardly be described as the most propitious time to demand large wage increases but delegates to the union convention had listed many demands, including a 20-percent wage increase.

President Morrison presented the union's demands. Dosco

immediately countered with a demand for substantial wage cuts!

Answering Morrison's faint protests, vice-president and general manager H.J. Kelly of Dosco countered with the arrogant assertion that "in view of existing conditions, don't you think it only fair that your people should be taking a reduction at this time?"

The depressing news of wage-cut demands was followed by Dosco's announcement that it planned to close two of its largest mines—No. 11 at Glace Bay and No. 14 at New Waterford—followed by two other mines at a later date. Over two thousand miners would be thrown out of work, and with no possibility of obtaining alternative employment in Cape Breton, the island community faced a disaster of the first magnitude. Contract negotiations were broken off in December 1931, but work continued in the mines without any threat to strike. With close to one million workers already unemployed in Canada, a strike would have been doomed to failure before it began.

At this point, Premier Harrington of Nova Scotia intervened in the dispute. He asked both parties to allow the old contract to be extended until March 1, 1932, to allow another Commission of Enquiry to be set up and to make recommendations. The union and the company agreed and to nobody's surprise, Sir Andrew Duncan's services were again requested by the provincial government. The second Duncan report was published February 20, 1932 and, as expected, the commission had again ruled in favour of the coal company, recommending a 10-percent wage cut—almost what the company had demanded in the first place. In addition, the report concurred with the company's demand for the closing of four mines and the firing of the total labour force working them.

President Morrison and the District 26 executive expressed willingness to accept the commission's report in full, but the left-wing faction led by McLachlan, who had returned from Russia in January, decided to fight. A pithead vote on the commission's recommendations was set for March 14, 1932, and from all reports the rebellious majority would vote against acceptance. Company spies relayed the information back to Halifax, and on voting day the Sydney *Post* announced that Premier Harrington had secured an order for a million tons of coal, which would guarantee steady work of five shifts each week for all Nova Scotia miners and eliminate the necessity to close the four mines—*providing that Nova Scotia miners cooperate in accepting the recommended wage cut to lower the price of coal to a competitive level.*

To their everlasting credit, District 26 miners were not fooled for one minute by this cheap attempt to buy their votes and persuade them to accept the punitive recommendations contained in the second Duncan report. Known locally as "Harrington's Hoax," the false promise only served to make miners more determined than ever, and when the votes were counted, they had rejected the report out of hand.

Miners reporting for work the following day found that Dosco had posted the wage cuts.

The million-ton order for coal never did materialize, but the wage cuts did, thus continuing the pattern set by Besco and its successor Dosco. After receiving their only lucrative wage contract in 1920, Nova Scotia miners had been forced to accept a wage cut of 20 percent in 1922, followed by another 10 percent in 1925 and now a cut of 10 percent in 1932, in spite of the rising cost of living, which had more than halved the value of their take-home pay.

A Glace Bay citizens' committee led by Tom McLachlan, son of J.B. McLachlan, met with Premier Harrington and Sir Newton Moore, president of Dosco, to ask them to reconsider the mine closings, which would undoubtedly cause great privation in the communities affected. Tom McLachlan warned that the mass firings would also cause a drain on the provincial treasury because of relief payments to the unemployed. The young McLachlan's argument must have carried weight for, after the conference, it was announced that only two mines would be closed. But the company did not keep its word and the other two mines were closed a short time later.

In April 1932, a District 26 convention was held to discuss the enforced wage cuts and mine closings. Open rebellion was expressed by many delegates against the UMWA and Lewis' policy of collaboration with the coal companies at the miners' expense. Following the conference, a new miners' union—the Amalgamated Mine Workers of Nova Scotia—was formed as a breakaway union from the UMWA. The rebel Mine Workers Industrial Union of Nova Scotia, formed at an outlaw convention in 1931, was laid to rest.

After his return from Russia, McLachlan was asked to go on a speaking tour across Canada to tell struggling workers that Russian workers were better paid, better fed, and received better treatment than the great mass of Canadian workers. At this stage of the Depression, with almost a million unemployed workers across Canada, it wasn't difficult to convince his audiences that such was the case. From city to city, McLachlan spread the "gospel" and everywhere he went, he was received with great enthusiasm by the working class and something less than enthusiasm by business leaders and the forces of law and order. In Toronto, it was reported that a mass rally at the new Maple Leaf Gardens had been forbidden on orders issued by General Draper, the bitter anti-communist chief of police, and the city council. Undaunted, McLachlan held the meeting outside the Gardens instead.

In August 1932, labour and unemployed delegates gathered in Ottawa to attend the Workers' Economic Conference, held to parallel the Imperial Economic Conference of premiers from the British Empire countries. Mrs Eva Pemberton, daughter of J.B. McLachlan, told of his meeting with Prime Minister Bennett. Eva said:

When my father returned from Ottawa, he told us how he and four other workers' representatives were ushered into Prime Minister Bennett's office. He said he [Bennett] was sitting at a huge desk flanked by four officers of the RCMP in full uniform, red tunic, riding breeches, spurs, and all. My father said it was obviously staged to overawe the workers' deputation with a show of force and power! Little did he know my father. On one side of the huge polished desk lay an expensive box of chocolates into which Bennett delved at frequent intervals with plump, jewelled fingers. As the men in the group were introduced, Bennett nodded politely until my father's name was called, and then he bounced to his feet to hold out his hand, saying, "I've heard so much about you, Jim, it's a pleasure to meet you at last." And my father answered, "Mr Bennett, I am only called Jim by my friends, and you are no friend of the working class. There are thousands of hungry men outside which you should be taking care of. I would prefer you to address me as Mr McLachlan, just to keep the record straight!"

McLachlan returned to Glace Bay to address a mass rally of the unemployed. Eva Pemberton described the rally: "One of the men in the crowd shouted, 'I hear you shook the Prime Minister's hand, Jim.' And with a great big grin, my father held up his hand and shouted back, 'Yes, I did, and if you don't believe me, come up here and smell it!'"

With the founding of the Amalgamated Mine Workers of Nova Scotia shortly after McLachlan's return from Russia, and his repeated vitriolic attacks on John L. Lewis and the UMWA through the medium of his *Nova Scotia Miner*, the Communist Party of Canada began to attack McLachlan, especially after it had urged Nova Scotia miners to remain as a district within the framework of an international union. But with his cross-Canada tour, he was again restored to favour, although many of the party's remaining leaders distrusted him.

In 1933, Tom McEwen, first president of the Workers' Unity League, resigned to allow McLachlan to reign in his stead, and with his succession, a new phase opened up in his chequered career, although he continued to publish the *Nova Scotia Miner* and to add his support to the breakaway Amalgamated Mine Workers of Nova Scotia. His broader field of operations now encompassed the whole of Canada with its one million unemployed and its other millions of unorganized workers.

McLachlan's accession to the presidency of the WUL had occurred at a most opportune time. All across the country things were going from bad to worse. But it was under his masterful leadership that the same year marked a rapid increase in membership. Added to the WUL battle for industrial unionization was the continuing battle for adequate food and clothing for the destitute, relief money for unemployed families, political pressure on federal and provincial authorities to allot monies for works projects to employ the multitudes of unemployed, a comprehensive scheme for noncontributory unemployment insurance benefits, and the organizing of protests and active revolt against mass evictions and repossessions, which were taking place all across the country after default of taxes or mortgages by those denied work.

With McLachlan's appointment, Prime Minister Bennett and his Conservative government in Ottawa were faced with a worthy opponent who feared no one in the battle for the poor and the destitute. Threats meant little to him. He had survived the worst that industrial giants and government authorities could do to silence his voice. None had succeeded.

With the outlawing of the Communist Party in 1931, and the demise of the Independent Labour Party, concerned leaders of farmer protective organizations, social democrats, and prominent members of labour unions held a conference in July 1933 at Regina, Saskatchewan, to found a new political party that would represent workers and farmers in the House of Commons. Prominent during these early discussions was J.S. Woodsworth, Labour M.P. for Winnipeg, who was chosen to be the first leader of the party.

At this first national convention, delegates voted to name the new party the Co-operative Commonwealth Federation (CCF), and shortly after, the famous Regina Manifesto was published to outline the aims of the new party. In essence, many of the aims of the CCF were those long advocated by McLachlan in his lifelong struggle to elevate the working class to a comfortable standard of living and to replace the capitalist system with a new social order through political action—but the CCF did not promote revolution, as the communists and McLachlan himself had long preached. In the new party's first move to obtain long overdue social reforms, a total of nine candidates were chosen to run in the next general election.

One out of every two workers was now said to be out of work in Canada. In Cape Breton, unemployment was particularly bad. With the recent mine closings and a greatly reduced number of weekly work shifts for those still employed, many of the mining towns were facing financial disaster. To add to the overall picture of despair and suffering, the huge Sydney steel mills owned by the same company, Dosco, had been shut down after two years of reduced operation, throwing an additional thirty-eight hundred workers onto the streets to starve. With the closing of the steel mills, thousands of tons of coal were no longer in demand for the making of coke, and more miners were laid off as a consequence. Sydney, Glace Bay, and every town throughout the Sydney coalfield were forced to reduce wages for municipal workers, teachers, and officials in an attempt to stave off bankruptcy.

In August 1933, Premier Harrington was forced to call a provincial election. McLachlan again entered the fray—this time as a candidate for a new provincial labour party—the United Front—which he had helped create. But when the votes were counted, none of the labour candidates had won a seat in the legislature, although Harrington's Conservatives were ousted by a majority Liberal government led by Angus L. MacDonald.

On the national scene, evictions and foreclosures were on the increase. Through the Workers' Unity League, McLachlan and his colleagues had formed a new organization—the National Unemployed Workers' Association—to combat evictions and fight court orders confiscating household possessions. As the word spread, thousands more unemployed workers joined the association until eventually it developed into a mass protest movement with offices manned by militant organizers throughout Canada. Much of the activity on behalf of the unemployed was pure "McLachlanism," but as the WUL and the NUWA gained strength, opposition mounted. Everywhere heads were being cracked, demonstrations broken up, and picket lines steamrolled as police forces resorted to violence and intimidation. But the struggle continued.

In 1934 the number of unemployed and homeless had swelled to the terrifying figure of 1.5 million. It was hardly a favourable time to discuss wage settlements, but in Cape Breton negotiations were begun for a new contract between District 26 and the Dominion Steel and Coal Corporation. The rival Amalgamated Mine Workers of Nova Scotia was not invited in spite of its majority membership, which was now in the region of eight thousand.

Negotiations continued into 1935, with the final agreement giving a very small raise in wages to daily workers and nothing for contract workers. A pithead vote showed overwhelming approval for the agreement, but none of the eight thousand members of the Amalgamated were allowed to vote, even though their numbers greatly exceeded UMWA members.

The Communist Party of Canada was back in business. The tide of public opinion had swung far to the left, in favour of a new deal for the unemployed, and Bennett, a shrewd politician, was quick to sense the change and act accordingly. One by one, Bennett signed orders for the release of the leaders of the Communist Party. Tim Buck, general secretary, was the last to be released on November 24, 1934. But the party was still considered an illegal organization, forcing it to continue to operate underground.

The accession of Hitler and Mussolini, and the menacing rise of world fascism, once again raised the spectre of global war. Delegates to the seventh World Congress of the Communist International, held in Moscow, July 25 to August 20, 1935, heard Georgi Dimitroff, secretary of the executive committee, warn of a fascist offensive where totalitarian forces in Germany and Italy were planning an all-out war at the expense of workers all over the world. Dimitroff made an emotional appeal for a Workers' United Front to oppose world fascism.

On his return, Stewart Smith, leader of the Canadian delegation to Moscow, reported the text of Dimitroff's speech to the leaders of the Communist Party of Canada. The message was clear, he told Buck and assembled leaders of the party—to counteract the alarming spread of fascism, workers must be united in a common front, and the CPC must base future tactics through the trade union movement, especially through industrial trade unions, where the great mass of workers lay. Further, the party should support the merging of all industrial unions in Canada.

Then came the supreme act of betrayal—at least that is how McLachlan and other leaders of the labour movement saw it. As a further step towards workers' unity, Smith advised, the Communist party should support the merging of all industrial unions in Canada with American industrial unions which had recently been amalgamated into the new Committee for Industrial Organization (CIO), led by the president of the United Mine Workers of America, John L. Lewis.

In the cause of workers' unity to combat the rising menace of world fascism, the communist-sponsored Workers' Unity League, which had pioneered the growth of Canadian industrial unions under McLachlan's leadership, would have to be dissolved to force the leaders of Canadian industrial unions to join the American CIO, led by McLachlan's arch-enemy, John L. Lewis.

Little consideration was given to the wishes of the Canadian rank and file. The decision to disband the Workers' Unity League caused a great deal of bitterness and resistance from McLachlan, who had been deposed from office in the UMWA through the machinations of John L. Lewis, the man he was now being asked to support. His arrest and imprisonment on false charges had been welcomed by Lewis and his lieutenants. The Communist party ordered him to acknowledge Lewis as master.

Through the medium of his *Nova Scotia Miner* McLachlan continued to deride Lewis and the CIO. His bitter criticism was resented by the Communist Party of Canada, which had already made the decision to lend its full support to Lewis and the CIO. In the name of workers' unity, McLachlan was asked repeatedly to discontinue his attacks on Lewis, but he was firmly set on a course from which there was no drawing back.

As the criticism increased towards McLachlan, his faith in the Communist party leadership decreased, and as the criticism turned to open antagonism, he became a marked man. The Central Committee ordered Comrade Barker, District No. 1 organizer in the Atlantic provinces, to report on McLachlan's movements; within a short space of time, his every activity was watched and reported back to Communist Party headquarters in Toronto.

McLachlan, aware of the "watch and report," became increasingly bitter and disillusioned with the Canadian Communist Party for their defence of John L. Lewis—a man he considered a traitor to the working class.

Time had run out for the Conservative government in Ottawa. Parliament was dissolved on July 6, 1935, with an election date set for October 14. Prosperity still remained "just around the corner" with almost two million workers unemployed and crying for justice.

The Communist Party of Canada fielded six candidates in the election, even though it was still considered an illegal organization. Buck, Bruce, McLachlan, McEwen, Popovic, and A.E. Smith allowed their names to stand, believing the government would not dare disqualify them in the face of public opinion. McLachlan ran as the communist candidate for Cape Breton South. It was his sixth electoral attempt and it was to be his last. He was now sixty-five years of age.

Headlines in the newspapers screamed "King or Chaos!" while in Cape Breton McLachlan appealed to working men and women to send him to Ottawa as their champion—a workingman to represent workingmen. The Communist Party of Canada sent its heavyweights into Cape Breton to campaign for McLachlan, but he did not welcome their assistance. He had lost faith in the party leaders although he remained a true devotee of communist philosophy. Annie Buller, Sam Scarlett, "Moscow" Jack MacDonald, and Joe Wallace added their vociferous support to McLachlan's campaign, but support from such well-known radicals served only to repel a great many McLachlan supporters. There are many in Cape Breton today who maintain that the invasion of prominent communists during the election campaign was intended as a subtle means of making sure McLachlan was *not* elected. Many more remain convinced that if McLachlan had run as a Labour candidate instead of as a Communist, he would undoubtedly have won.

When the results were announced, McLachlan had been beaten by the Liberal candidate. None of the Communist candidates were successful, but Woodsworth's new CCF party had been given an unqualified stamp of approval by the Canadian people, with seven of the eight candidates elected to the House of Commons in Ottawa, along with a majority Liberal government headed by Mackenzie King.

McLachlan had done a sterling job of organizing industrial unions in Canada, but his past deeds were soon forgotten as plans were made to retire him from the labour scene. Many prominent members of the Communist Party considered him too old to be useful—or perhaps that was the reason given to shunt him aside like an old, worn-out horse. With what McLachlan considered the betrayal of Canadian industrial workers by the Communist Party of Canada, he became increasingly bitter, especially after receiving a series of critical letters from Tim Buck, general secretary of the party. The criticism was the result of a secret decision that had been made to rid the party of McLachlan the dissenter, who had dared question party policy. But the time was not yet opportune. "Old Jim" had many friends and supporters in the party.

In July 1936 McLachlan decided to cut all ties with the CPC, and regretfully he forwarded a letter of resignation to Buck, explaining his reasons. With his resignation, he had come full circle. Now he concentrated on the formation of a strong labour party as the only viable means of obtaining working-class representation in government. The shunting of Canadian industrial workers into an American industrial organization controlled by Lewis—a man he considered the arch-enemy of the working class—and the abolishment of the very successful Workers' Unity League had dealt him an all but fatal blow. His struggle for a worthwhile working-class movement continued with the building of a true labour party in Nova Scotia, a party that would work towards a better deal for workers without foreign pressure or domination.

With the amalgamation of both miners' unions in Nova Scotia, Lewis pressured District 26 miners into withdrawing their support for the *Nova Scotia Miner*, and in a short space of time, McLachlan was forced to cease publication. With the stopping of the presses, Nova Scotia miners lost the only dissenting voice in the affairs of the district, and with the demise of his beloved newspaper, McLachlan withdrew from active participation in union affairs.

Lack of support and financial backing may have forced the closing of the *Nova Scotia Miner*, but McLachlan continued his attacks on Lewis and the Canadian Communist Party through impromptu speeches at miners' meetings. In addition, he held regular meetings with many of his old labour comrades in his own home.

Eva Pemberton described one memorable meeting held on

the sun porch of her father's home when his most trusted lieutenants gathered to discuss the building of a new Cape Breton labour party.

They were all there—D.N. Brodie, Malcolm Link, Wes Bond, George Milley, Bob Stewart, and Alf Nash. I well remember the day. From his sick bed, my father told of the events which had led to his resignation from the Communist Party and of the sellout to Lewis, and then he concluded, "Well, boys, the Communist Party has had it as far as I'm concerned; they no longer represent the workers and the left; they've sold out to rightist elements at the expense of the working class.... We're going to have to start all over again with a new party to work in conjunction with Jim Woodsworth's group [CCF] in the west."

It was from this informal meeting on McLachlan's sun porch that the Cape Breton Labour Party was formed. Men previously considered right-wing leaders of Nova Scotia miners' unions, such as Silby Barrett and Dan Willie Morrison, hastened to join the new Cape Breton Labour Party along with left-wing radicals Forman Waye, Clarence Gillis, Bob Stewart, and D.N. Brodie.

As expected, the new labour party was enthusiastically endorsed by District 26 of the UMWA, but the enthusiasm was not shared by the Communist Party of Canada, which regarded the emergence of a new workers' party as a direct attack by McLachlan. In a move to discredit McLachlan, the CPC invited William Gallacher, a noted communist and British Member of Parliament, to speak to a mass meeting held in the Miners' Forum in Glace Bay in September 1936. For over an hour, Gallacher denounced McLachlan. Gallacher shouted, "And I ask you, where is McLachlan today?"

From the back of the Forum, where he had been deriving quiet amusement from his own character assassination, McLachlan rose to his feet to answer, "Here I am!" And then, as hundreds of miners and townspeople rose to their feet to give him a standing ovation, "Fighting" Jim McLachlan strode down the aisle to mount the stage. It was McLachlan's last public speech, and those who were present at this memorable confrontation swear it was his most magnificent. Spellbound, his audience listened as he gave them the facts about the Communist Party of Canada and his reasons for resigning. Point by point he hammered home the lesson: the dissolution of the Workers' Unity League by the Communist Party of Canada followed by the abandonment of many thousands of industrial workers all across Canada—the needleworkers, the truckers, the western miners, and scores of other unions and organizations that had all been left to their fate because the party had been told to follow the move to the right. He finished his speech with a rousing denunciation of John L. Lewis, a man he believed to be nothing more than a traitor to the working-class movement—an opportunist who was nobody's friend but his own!

As Gallacher began to speak again, Jim McLachlan climbed down off the stage to walk out of the Forum with head held high in great dignity.

Shortly after his last public appearance, Jim McLachlan suffered a major haemorrhage, which was diagnosed as advanced tuberculosis. The dread disease contracted during his ordeal in the Halifax County jail in 1923 had now reached the incurable stage, draining his strength and obliging him to rest for longer and longer periods each day.

But the fever that racked his body and weakened his limbs did not prevent him from exercising his fine brain and intellect. At the end of each week, McLachlan held council with old friends and colleagues, planning future strategy for the new labour movement, but even as he did so, he became increasingly aware of his approaching death. His sick bed was moved into a sun porch built by sons Tom and Jim with the help of many well-wishers. Jokingly, he had reminded them to provide a double entrance to the street to allow room for his coffin—a grim joke not shared with his wife and daughters as they prayed for a miracle. In the autumn of 1937, his condition worsened, leaving no doubt in the minds of family and friends that the end was near.

On the third day of November 1937, James Bryson McLachlan, friend of the workingman, died—his lifelong struggle over. The news of his death left shock waves reverberating from coast to coast with workers in every industry laying down tools to pay silent tribute to the man whose uppermost thoughts and ideals had been the advancement and well-being of the working class. Tributes began pouring in from people in every walk of life. Loved and respected by millions of workers, his passing was regretted by all. Though riches could have been his for the taking, he had taken the more difficult but more Christian course—the field of labour to fight the cause of the workers of the world, the downtrodden, the oppressed, and the underprivileged.

The casket lay amid a brilliant array of floral tributes banked all the way to the ceiling and around the walls of the sun porch. Every miners' local in Nova Scotia had sent a wreath, many in the shape of a miner's pickaxe; steelworkers from Sydney, railway workers, needle trade workers, unemployed workers' associations, all were represented along with hundreds of personal tributes from friends and labour colleagues. Scattered here and there among the noble wreaths and tributes, small bunches of wild flowers added their own contribution on behalf of miners' children.

For days prior to the service, thousands of mourners passed in single file before McLachlan's bier to pay last respects. Many stooped to kiss his stilled brow, many more wept bitter tears as they said goodbye to the man who had fought their battles and suffered martyrdom as a consequence. Now on the day of his funeral, many of them returned to follow old Jim to his last resting place.

The funeral cortege was led most appropriately by a miners' band from Dominion No. 6 colliery. Over five hundred miners, representatives from every union local in Nova Scotia, marched on foot. Steelworkers, members of the Unemployed Workers' Association, and hundreds of other workers all joined the cortege along with over two hundred cars carrying mourners from every walk of life—town councillors, shopkeepers, policemen, neighbours, and people from every corner of the land who wished to show their respect.

Several miles long, the funeral procession passed slowly through the silent streets of Glace Bay; thousands of townspeople and their children lined the sidewalks, heads bowed in sorrow. Traffic had been halted, streetcars removed from the streets, and all work brought to a standstill in silent respect for the man once considered a fiery "Red," a subversive, and a godless revolutionary who would surely lead the workers of Nova Scotia into armed insurrection.

The thousands of mourners withdrew, leaving Kate and her children to their own private sorrow. Jim McLachlan's voice was stilled, but his message would live on, and the struggle he had waged for so long would be continued by others. The epitaph on his tombstone, chosen by Kate, his lifelong partner, from *Proverbs* 31:9, read most appropriately: "Open thy mouth, judge righteously, and plead the cause of the poor and needy."

McLachlan was dead and Nova Scotia grieved. Within a matter of weeks, Dan Livingstone, deposed president of District 26 and lifelong friend of McLachlan's, also died, a victim, like McLachlan, of the tuberculosis contracted during their incarceration in the Halifax County jail. By 1939, Kate McLachlan had passed away. Incurably ill, she had kept the sad news to herself, not wishing to add to her husband's burden.

Jim McLachlan did not live to see his lifelong dream of political representation for the worker come true, but the founding of the Cape Breton Labour Party was a start. One year after his death, a by-election was held for the vacated seat of Cape Breton Centre, and a CCF candidate, miner Douglas MacDonald, emerged victorious after workers had added their support. When a federal election was called in March 1940, another CCF candidate, veteran miner Clarence Gillis, proudly took his seat in the House of Commons in Ottawa. At long last, Cape Breton's miners and steelworkers had succeeded in electing one of their own as their representative in the Canadian Parliament.

"Clarie" Gillis entered the mines at the tender age of fourteen to help support a large brood of brothers and sisters, but during the 1909–10 strike the family was evicted from their company house and spent the winter in a Bell tent. Gillis, Sr was blacklisted after the strike and forced to leave his family in Cape Breton to seek work in the United States. With such a background of suffering and want, Clarie Gillis, the new Member of Parliament for Cape Breton South, would strive to introduce legislation designed to protect all

Canadian miners and force unscrupulous coal companies to treat their workers more humanely.

Another progressive development of the time was the Antigonish Movement in eastern Nova Scotia—an effort launched by Father Jimmy Tompkins and Father Moses Coady of St. Francis Xavier University. (Ironically, part of the stimulus for this movement was the Catholic Church's concern over communism's influence on labour in Nova Scotia.) One initiative saw Cape Breton coal miners build Tompkinsville, said to be the first cooperative housing community in North America. Through a province-wide educational program, study groups were formed in every poor community and the people were encouraged to cultivate land to grow their own food, and to establish credit unions and co-op stores—achieving an independence never possible through company housing and the company stores.

With the necessities of life no longer controlled by ruthless corporations, workers could not be used as weapons in any future labour dispute. No longer would miners and steelworkers be faced with eviction in the depth of winter or suddenly find their credit cut off at the company store.

With their new political representation they could demand reform programs and insist on a living wage for miners and steelworkers. It would still be an uphill fight and the road was long and arduous, but McLachlan had shown the way when he had said:

> I believe in education for action. I believe in telling children the truth about the history of the world, that it does not consist of the history of kings, or lords or cabinets. It consists of the history of the mass of the workers. A thing that is not taught in the schools. I believe in telling children how to measure value, a thing that is not taught in any school.

Suggested Further Reading

We are grateful for the work of historians of Cape Breton labour, whose research and early reviews of *The Company Store* have served to make a good book better.

12,000 Men: Labour's War in the Cape Breton Coalfields. National Film Board of Canada, 1978.

Bentley, Capt. L.W., "Aid of the Civil Power: Social & Political Aspects 1904–1924," *Canadian Defence Quarterly*, Summer 1978.

Caplan, Ronald. *Views from the Steel Plant.* Wreck Cove: Breton Books, 2005.

Crawley, Ronald, "Class Conflict and the Establishment of the Sydney Steel Industry, 1899–1904," *The Island: New Perspectives on Cape Breton's History 1713–1990.* Fredericton/Sydney: Acadiensis Press/UCCB Press, 1990.

Earle, Michael, "The Legacy: Manipulating the Myth of McLachlan," *New Maritimes*, 6:4–5 (December 1987/January 1988).

Frank, David, "Class Conflict in the Coal Industry: Cape Breton 1922," *Essays in Working Class History.* Toronto: McClelland & Stewart, 1976.

——, "Company Town/Labour Town: Local Government in the Cape Breton Coal Towns, 1917–1926," *Histoire sociale/Social History*, 14:27 (May 1981).

——, "Contested Terrain: Workers' Control in the Cape Breton Coal Mines in the 1920s," *On the Job: Confronting the Labour Process in Canada.* Montreal & Kingston: McGill-Queen's University Press, 1986.

——. *J.B. McLachlan: A Biography.* Toronto: James Lorimer & Company Ltd., 1999.

——, "The Cape Breton Coal Industry and the Rise and Fall of the British Empire Steel Corporation," *Acadiensis*, 7:1 (Autumn 1977).

——, "The Miners' Financier: Women in the Cape Breton Coal Towns, 1917," *Atlantis*, 8:2 (Spring 1983).

—— & John Manley, "The Sad March to the Right: J.B. McLachlan's Resignation from the Communist Party of Canada, 1936," *Labour/Le Travail*, 30 (Fall 1992).

Fraser, Dawn. *Echoes from Labor's Wars: The Expanded Edition.* Wreck Cove: Breton Books, 1992.

Fraser, Rev. Fr John, "Fr Fraser Fights for the Miners, 1909," *Cape Breton's Magazine*, No. 59 (January 1992).

Gold, Sarah M., "A Social Worker Visits Cape Breton, 1925," *Cape Breton's Magazine*, No. 38 (January 1985).

MacDonald, Ned. *The Broken Ground: A History of Inverness Town 1803–1954.* Privately published, 1979.

MacEwan, Paul. *Miners and Steelworkers.* Toronto: Samuel Stevens Hakkert, 1976.

MacGillivray, Donald, "Cape Breton in the 1920s: A Community Besieged," *Essays in Cape Breton History.* Windsor: Lancelot, 1973.

——, "Glace Bay: Images and Impressions," *Mining Photographs and Other Pictures, 1948–68: a Selection from the Negative Archives of Shedden Studio, Glace Bay, Cape Breton*. Halifax: Nova Scotia College of Art and Design/Sydney: UCCB Press, 1983.

——, "Henry Melville Whitney Comes to Cape Breton: The Saga of a Gilded Age Entrepreneur," *Acadiensis*, 9:1 (Autumn 1979).

——, "Military Aid to the Civil Power: The Cape Breton Experience in the 1920s," *Acadiensis*, 3:1 (Spring 1974).

MacKenzie, Rennie. *BLAST! Cape Breton Coal Mine Disasters*. Wreck Cove: Breton Books, 2007.

McKay, Ian, "Strikes in the Maritimes, 1901–1914," *Acadiensis*, 13:1 (Autumn 1983).

——, "The Maritimes: Expanding the Circle of Resistance," *The Workers' Revolt in Canada, 1917–1925*. Toronto: University of Toronto Press, 1998.

Muise, Delphin A., "The Making of an Industrial Community: Cape Breton Coal Towns, 1867–1900," *Cape Breton Historical Essays*. Sydney: College of Cape Breton Press, 1980.

Pittman, Billy et al, "The 'Pluck Me': Life and Death of the Company Store," *Cape Breton's Magazine*, No. 3 (March 1973).

White, Mrs Arthur Gadd et al, "Mine Explosion in New Waterford, 1917," *Cape Breton's Magazine*, No. 21 (December 1978).

John Mellor's Bibliography

BOOKS

Akakumovic, Ivan. *The Communist Party of Canada*. Toronto: McClelland & Stewart, 1975.

Arnot, R. Page. *A History of the Scottish Miners*. London: George Allen & Co., 1955.

Ashton and Sykes. *Coal Industry of the 18th Century*. University of Manchester, 1924.

Bercuson, David Jay. *Fools and Wisemen, the Rise and Fall of the O.B.U.* Scarborough, Ontario: McGraw-Hill Ryerson Ltd., 1978.

Buck, Tim. *Thirty Years, 1922–1952. The Story of the Communist Movement in Canada*. Toronto: Progress Books, 1952.

Carlyle, Thomas. *Sartor Resartus*. London: J. M. Dent, 1833.

——. *Chartism*. London: Chapman & Hall, 1839.

——. *Past and Present*. London: Chapman & Hall, 1843.

Chaplin, Ralph. *Wobbly, the Rough-and-Tumble Story of an American Radical*. U. Chicago Press, 1948.

Coady, Moses M. *Masters of their Own Destiny*. New York: Harper & Bros., 1939.

Coats, R.H. "The Labour Movement in Canada," from *In Canada and Its Provinces*. Vol. IX, 1914, pp. 277–355.

Dubofsky, Melvyn. *We Shall Not Fail: History of the I.W.W.* Chicago: Quadrangle Books, 1969.

Forsey, Eugene. *Economic and Social Aspects of the Nova Scotia Coal Industry*. Toronto: Macmillan Co., 1926.

Fraser, Dawn. *Echoes from Labour's Wars*. Glace Bay, NS: Eastern Publishing, 1925.

Horn, Michael. *The Dirty Thirties*. Section 2E; Toronto: Copp Clark Publishing Co., 1972.
Hughes, H. Stuart. *Oswald Spengler*. London: Charles Scribner's Sons, 1952.
Jackson, Elva. *Window on the Past*. North Sydney, N.S.
Kealey, Gregory S., and Warrian, Peter. *Essays in Canadian Working Class History*. Toronto: McClelland & Stewart, 1976.
Lazarus, Morden. *Years of Hard Labour*. Ottawa: Ontario Federation of Labour, 1974.
Lipton, Charles. *The Trade Union Movement in Canada, 1827–1959*. Montreal: Canadian Social Publications, Ltd., 1966.
Logan, H.A. *Trade Unions in Canada*. Toronto: Macmillan Canada, 1948.
McLean, Iain. *Keir Hardie*. London: Allen Lane & Co., 1975.
Mill, John Stuart. *Autobiography*. Boston: Houghton Mifflin.
——. *Principles of Political Economy*. New York: Colonial Press, 1904.
——. *Utilitarianism*.... New York: Doubleday Ltd.
Morgan, Kenneth Owen. *Keir Hardie*. London: Weidenfeld & Nicolson, 1975.
Mother Jones. *The Autobiography of Mother Jones*. Chicago: Charles H. Kerr Publishing Co., 1925.
Myers, Gustavus. *A History of Canadian Wealth*. Toronto: James Lewis & Samuel, 1972.
Nef, John Ulric. *The Rise of the British Coal Industry*. Vol. 2, London: Frank Cass & Co., 1966. First published by George Routledge & Sons, 1932.
Rodney, William. *Soldiers of the International*. U. Toronto Press, 1968.
Ryan, Oscar. *Tim Buck, A Conscience for Canada*. Toronto: Progress Books, 1975.
Seymour, Edward E. *An Illustrated History of Canadian Labour, 1800–1974*. Ottawa: Canadian Labour Congress, Mutual Press, 1976.
Spargo, John. *The Bitter Cry of the Children*. Chicago: Quadrangle Books, 1968.
Stern, Gerald Emmanuel. *Gompers, Great Lives Observed*. Englewood Cliffs, N.J.: Prentice-Hall, 1971.
Stewart, Walter. *Strike*. Toronto: McClelland & Stewart, 1977.
Vernon, C.W. *Cape Breton, Canada, at the Beginning of the Twentieth Century*. Toronto: Nation Publishing Co., Provincial Archives, 1903.
Watson, Louise. *She Never Was Afraid: The Biography of Annie Buller*. Toronto: Progress Books, 1976.
Wechsler, James A. *Labor Baron: A Portrait of John L. Lewis*. New York: William Morrow & Co., 1944.
Williams, Jack. *The Story of Unions in Canada*. Don Mills, Ontario: J. M. Dent & Sons, 1975.

MAGAZINE ARTICLES, PAMPHLETS, ETC.

Anon., "A History of the Cape Breton Miners," June 1956.
Bagnell, Ken, "The Hobo Train," *Cape Breton Post*, January 12, 1976.
Barr, Rev. Robert, "Christ in the Coalfields," *Literary Digest*, June 18, 1927.
Bell, Tom, "Lewis Crucifies Nova Scotia Miners," *Labor Herald*, Magazine of The Trade Union Education League, Chicago, September 1923.
——, "Militant Miners Sent to Prison," *Labor Herald*, December 1923.
——, "McLachlan Released From Prison," *Labor Herald*, May 1924.
——, "Among the Coal Miners of Canada," *Labor Herald*, July 1924.
Braddock, John, "A Requiem," *Atlantic Advocate*, August 1967.

Browder, Earl R., "Lewis and Farrington Unite," *Labor Herald*, August 1923.
——, "Two Unaccepted Challenges," *Labor Herald*, September 1923.
Buck, Tim, "The Rise and Fall of The One Big Union," *Labor Herald*, October 1922.
——, "Rebels Come Back in Canada," *Labor Herald*, February 1923.
——, "The Struggle in the Maritime Provinces," *Labor Herald*, August 1923.
——, "Canadian League Eastern District Conference," *Labor Herald*, September 1923.
——, "Report of the Canadian District," *Labor Herald*, October 1923.
——, "The Movement for Autonomy in Canada," *Labor Herald*, February 1924.
Case, Henry Jay, "Mounted Police in the Coalfields," *Harpers' Weekly*.
Chanler, William C., "Civil Liberties in the Coalfields," Vol. III, No. 3853.
Craton, Ann Washington, "Facing the Family Line," *The Nation*, April 1928.
Debs, Eugene V., "How I Became a Rebel," *Labor Herald* (magazine of the Trade Union Education League, U.S.A. and Canada), June 1922.
——, "Getting Together," *Labor Herald*, April 1922.
Dimitroff, Georgi, "United Front Against Fascism," New Century Publishers, N.Y., 1935. (Speech delivered before Seventh World Congress of the Communist International, July 25, 1935.)
Dorsey, John, "How the Machine Beat Howat," *Labor Herald*, April 1922.
——, "Progressive International Committee of the U.M.W.A.," *Labor Herald*, March 1923.
——, "Alexander Howat," *Labor Herald*, April 1923.
——, "Coal Diggers Come Back Strong," *Labor Herald*, April 1924.
Editorial, "The Death of Sam Scarlett," *The Clarion* (bulletin of the Communist Party of Canada, Ottawa District), September 5, 1940.
Editorial, "The Curse of the Coal Towns," *The Nation*, March 4, 1928.
Flynn, Elizabeth Gurley, "How I Became a Rebel," *Labor Herald*, July 1922.
Foster, Wm. Z., "The Miners' Convention," *Labor Herald*, March 1924.
——, "The Progressive Miners' Conference," *Labor Herald*, July 1923.
Fox, Jay, "What is a Militant?" *Labor Herald*, April 1923.
Galsworthy, John, "Coal on the Dole," *Leading Affairs*, date illegible. Reproduced from Manchester *Guardian*.
Hapsgood, Powers, and Donovan, Mary, "Murdered Miners," *The Nation*, March 14, 1928.
Harrison, Caleb, "The Workers' Internationals," *Labor Herald*, September 1923.
Harrison, George, "Who's Who in Prison," *Labor Herald*, June 1923.
Husband, Joseph, "A Year in a Coalmine," *Atlantic Monthly*, November 1910.
——, "Fire in the Mine," *Atlantic Monthly*, December 1910.
——, "The Tragedy of the Mine," *Atlantic Monthly*, January 1911.
Johnstone, J.W., "Illinois Miners Vote for Howat," *Labor Herald*, June 1924.
——, "Push the Fight for Howat," *Labor Herald*, August 1924.
Kirchwey, Freda, "Miners' Wives in the Coal Strike," *Century Magazine*, n.d.
Legere, Ben, "Starving Nova Scotia's Miners," *The Nation*, April 1, 1925.
MacDonald, Colleen, "The Glace Bay Coal Strike of 1925," Acadia University, Nova Scotia, Soc. 210, March 8, 1973. Unpublished thesis.
MacDonald, Dan J., "Into the Mines as a Child," *Atlantic Advocate*, August 1967.
MacDonald, David, "A Coal Town Fights for its Life," *MacLean's Magazine*, March 15, 1954.

——, "Buried Alive at Moose River," *Reader's Digest* (date illegible).

MacDonald, Maurice, "Pioneers Built Well," *Cape Breton Post*, February 27, 1975.

MacGregor, Gordon (Educational Officer, Miners' Museum, G.B.), "The Seams, Collieries and Companies of Cape Breton." Unpublished account, Miners' Museum, Glace Bay, Cape Breton, N.S.

——, "Coal Mines of Nova Scotia"; "Power Plants"; etc. Unpublished accounts, Miners' Museum, Glace Bay, Cape Breton, N.S.

——, "Report of Dominion Coal Company's Mines in Cape Breton." Unpublished account, Miners' Museum, Glace Bay, Cape Breton, N.S.

Marsh, William H., "Farewell to Coal. Phase-In Please, Before You Phase-Out," *Atlantic Advocate*, August 1967.

Moe, Fred, "The Miner: His Outlook," *Labor Herald*, March 1923.

Murphy, J.T., "The Origin and Growth of the British Labour Party," *Labor Herald*, December 1923.

Myerscough, Thomas, "The Awakening Miners," *Labor Herald*, December 1923.

McCawley, Stuart, *The Agony of Cape Breton*. A series of articles originally published in the Halifax *Morning Chronicle* 1924–25: "The Check-off"; "A Splendid Chance to Get Together"; "The Future Miner"; "Cape Breton"; "A Brief Outline of the History of Dominion Coal Company in the Glace Bay District"; "Is Glace Bay Red?"; "Billions of Goods and No Buyers"; "One Hundred Percent Strike! What Does It Mean?"; "What Brought It All About?"; "They Don't Want to Settle"; "Who Will Win?"

McDonald, Jack, "Trade Unionism in Canada," *Labor Herald*, July 1922.

McLachlan, James B., "Letter of Resignation from Communist Party of Canada," June 13, 1934. McLachlan family archives.

Pretshold, Karl, "Who's Who in Prison?" *Labor Herald*, February 1923.

Raine, Norman Reilly, "Toilers Under the Sea," *MacLean's Magazine*, January 1, 1925.

——, "Cape Breton Folks," *MacLean's Magazine*, January 15, 1925.

——, "Miners Work and Play," *MacLean's Magazine*, January 30, 1925.

"Report of Industrial Strife in Nova Scotia Coalfields, 1922–25," *Canadian Annual Review of Public Affairs*.

Tippett, Tom, "Coal, The Miners' Story," *The Independent*, Vol. 115, No. 3926 (date unknown).

Zechariah, Chapee, Jr., "Company Town in the Soft Coal Fields," *The Independent*, Vol. 111, No. 3851 (date unknown).

NEWSPAPERS

Antigonish Casket, Antigonish, N.S., 1924

Bulletin (O.B.U.), Winnipeg, Man., 1913–24

Calgary *Herald*, Calgary, Alberta, 1918

Canadian Labour Leader, Sydney, N.S., 1912–18

Citizen, Halifax, N.S., 1923

Citizen, Ottawa, 1922–25

Eastern Chronicle, New Glasgow, N.S., 1923–25

Evening Palladium, Hamilton, Ont., 1886

Glace Bay *Gazette*, Glace Bay, N.S., 1909–25

Glace Bay *Standard*, Glace Bay, N.S., 1909–25
Globe, Toronto, 1909–30
Halifax *Herald*, Halifax, N.S., 1920–31
Highlander, Sydney, N.S.
Journal, Toronto, 1922–25
Leader, Regina, Sask., 1931
Left Wing, Toronto, 1924–26
Maritime Labour Herald, Glace Bay, N.S., 1921–26
Montreal *Gazette*, Montreal, 1909
Morning Chronicle, Halifax, N.S., 1909
Nova Scotia Miner, Glace Bay, N.S., 1929–32
Palladium of Labor, Hamilton, Ont., 1884
Sydney *Chronicle*, Sydney, N.S., 1899
Sydney *Post*, Sydney, N.S., 1909–25
Sydney *Record*, Sydney, N.S., 1909–29
The Worker, Toronto, 1922–30
Toronto *Daily Star*, Toronto, 1924
Workers' Unity, Toronto, 1931–32

ARCHIVAL MATERIAL

Department of Labour, Ottawa
Labour Organizations in Canada: Report of coal strikes in Nova Scotia, 1924 and 1925.
The Labour Gazette, February 1925. Coal strikes in Nova Scotia, 1925.

Library and Archives Canada
Correspondence and telegrams relating to 1922 slowdown and strike of Nova Scotia coal miners: Murdock, Minister of Labour, J.B. McLachlan, Prime Minister Mackenzie King, Members of House of Commons and mayors of mining towns in Cape Breton.
Criminal Code, Section 98.
Department of the Secretary of State: Remissions Branch. Release of J.B. McLachlan under "Ticket of Leave" terms, signed by Solicitor General and Governor General of Canada, Lord Byng of Vimy, February 27, 1924.
Militia Act. Regulations governing calling out of troops to prevent civil disobedience, insurrection, etc.
Report by F.A. Acland, Minister of Labour, on industrial conditions in Nova Scotia coalfields, 1909.
Royal Canadian Mounted Police, "Ticket-of-Leave" release of J.B. McLachlan, signed by various police officers, 1925–26.
The King v. *McLachlan*. Transcript of trial, 1923.
The Labour Gazette, 1900–11.

Nova Scotia Archives
Duncan Royal Commission report and recommendations, 1925.
Gillen Conciliation Board report and recommendations, 1921.
Journals and Proceedings of the House of Assembly of the Province of Nova Scotia, 1893. Granting of ninety-nine-year lease to Dominion Coal Co., and protest by George Forrest, M.P.P.

Journal and Proceedings of the House of Assembly, Province of Nova Scotia; report of mining disaster, New Waterford, 1917.
Morrison, Dr M.D., Glace Bay physician: Report of Polio outbreak in Glace Bay 1910–11, to St. Joseph Hospital, Glace Bay.
Nova Scotia Reports, 1923. Supreme Court of Nova Scotia. *The King* v. *McLachlan*. Appeal against conviction.
Nova Scotia Reports, 1924. Supreme Court of Nova Scotia. *The King* v. *McLachlan*. Appeal for permission to apply to Privy Council for retrial. January 29, 1924.
Nova Scotia Reports, Vol. LVI, Supreme Court of Nova Scotia. Application for bail under writ of *habeas corpus*, for J.B. McLachlan, 1923.
Report of MacKinnon Conciliation Board, Jan. 1920.
Report of MacKinnon Conciliation Board and recommendations, August 1922.
Report of Quirk Royal Commission on Nova Scotia coal industry and recommendations, September 20, 1920.
Report of Sessions, Provincial Government of Nova Scotia, 1925 and 1926. General Election.
Royal Commission Report on Nova Scotia coal industry and recommendations. Mr Justice A. Chisholm, Chairman, May 1917.
Wade, C.B., "History of District 26, United Mine Workers of America," n. d.

Provincial Archives of Ontario
Communist Party of Canada, Record Group 4: Section C3. Arrest of Tim Buck and other leaders of C.P.C. and provisions declaring C.P.C. to be an illegal organization.

University of Guelph
Children's Employment Commission, Vol. 1, 1842. An investigation into all aspects of child labour in factories and in coalmines in Britain during the early nineteenth century.

University of Waterloo, Government Publications Section
House of Commons Report of Parliamentary Debates, March 1922. W. Irvine, M.P., W. Carroll, M.P., J.S. Woodsworth, M.P., and James Murdock, Minister of Labour.
House of Commons Report of Parliamentary Debates, 1924. Speech by J.S. Woodsworth, M.P., regarding McLachlan release and Nova Scotia miners' dispute with Besco.
House of Commons Report of Parliamentary Debates, 1925. Speech by J.S. Woodsworth, M.P., regarding grants to Leeward Islands.
Report, Government of Canada, on Infantile Mortality Rates in Cape Breton and rest of Canada, 1920–24.

UNPUBLISHED THESES

Forbes, Ernest R., "The Rise and Fall of the Conservative Party in Nova Scotia," University of Waterloo (Waterloo, Ont.).
MacKenzie, Anthony, "The Rise and Fall of the Farmers' Labour Party in Nova Scotia," Dalhousie University (Nova Scotia), 1969.
Steele, Joseph, "The Big Strike 1909–10," St. Francis Xavier University (Nova Scotia), 1960.

John Mellor's Acknowledgements

In the writing of *The Company Store* I have been largely dependent on the historical research of many labour historians. The copious bibliography shows the extent of my debt, but it should be emphasized that this book was never intended as a definitive work on the controversial subject of District 26, United Mine Workers of America, and the tragic struggle of Cape Breton coal miners during the twenties. It is, however, a truthful and factual account checked and rechecked for its accuracy.

To add substance and credibility to my research, many survivors of the period have unselfishly provided memorabilia and personal accounts of the tragic happenings. Special mention must be made of the McLachlan family—Mrs Eva (McLachlan) Pemberton, Mrs Jean (McLachlan) Robinson, Tom McLachlan, and Jim McLachlan—retired miners Duncan Currie, Gordon MacGregor, Archie McIntyre, Billy Pittman, Stanley Michalik, Dan "Dancer" MacDonald, and Joe Nearing. For technical assistance I must thank the Cape Breton Miners' Museum of Glace Bay, the Beaton Institute of Cape Breton University, and the Provincial Archives of Nova Scotia; Mr Robert Kenny for his specialized knowledge of the Communist Party of Canada; Senator Dr Eugene Forsey for providing information through his learned treatise *Economic and Social Aspects of the Nova Scotia Coal Industry*; Mr Bill McNeil of the Canadian Broadcasting Corporation, who first sparked my interest through the medium of his programme, "Voice of the Pioneer"; and a special thanks to my Doubleday editor, Janet Turnbull, for helpful criticism and suggestions for the improvement and condensation of my book.

Without the generosity of the Ontario Secondary School Teachers' Federation and the award of the Dr G.W. Robinson Travelling Scholarship, the financial burden would have been intolerable and the completion of this book impossible. Without the intervention of my local Member of Parliament, Dr Peter Lang, and the Honourable Robert Kaplan, Solicitor General of Canada, the secret papers relating to the McLachlan trial and his release from prison by the Governor-General of Canada would have remained hidden from public view in the Public Archives of Canada, and history would be the poorer for its concealment.

Last and perhaps most important of the acknowledgements must be reserved for my family for their understanding and sympathy over the five long years it took to write this book. It has been said that a writer's life is a lonely one, but this is also true of a writer's family deprived of attention and companionship through the very nature and exigency of creative writing.

Publisher's Acknowledgements

Our thanks to the Board of Directors of the Cape Breton Miners' Museum in Glace Bay, Nova Scotia—with especial thanks to Chairman Angus MacMullin and Director Tom Miller—for their encouragement toward producing this new edition of *The Company Store*. Our thanks to Mora Devereaux, J.B. McLachlan's great-granddaughter, and to Jimmy McNeil, who took us to the grave of Catherine and J.B. McLachlan in the Greenwood Cemetery in Glace Bay.

Inside a Company Store

Index

As True As I'm Sittin' Here

200 CAPE BRETON STORIES

edited by Brian Sutcliffe & Ronald Caplan

COLLECTED BY ARCHIE NEIL CHISHOLM—laughs, comebacks, ghosts, fairies, put-downs, and all-round wit—from Dan Angus Beaton, Jim St. Clair, Sid Timmons, Hector Doink MacDonald, Annie the Tailor MacPhee, and many more.

Stories that shorten the road, lighten the work, and fill the pauses between tunes, throughout Cape Breton Island.

220 PAGES • $22.50 • ISBN 1-895415-58-6

The Cabot Trail in Black & White

VOICES & PHOTOS FROM NORTHERN CAPE BRETON

by Ronald Caplan

A FASCINATING AND TRIUMPHANT BOOK, filled with much laughter, community life, and down-to-earth daily work. Here are 40 chapters and 150 photos about the Cabot Trail and its people. From over 25 years of *Cape Breton's Magazine*.

144 PAGES • $19.95 • ISBN 1-895415-99-3

The Stud Horse Boy

MEMOIRS OF A HORSE BREEDER'S SON

by Darryll Taylor

FROM HIS ROOTS in the horse breeding world of rural Nova Scotia, Darryll Taylor carries the reader through a young man's amazing storied day with great good humour, shocking but realistic scenes, and a passionate respect for the dying art of breeding horses and the lovely countryside in which it all takes place.

144 PAGES • $14.95 • ISBN 978-1-926908-11-3

White Eyes

16 STORIES

by LARRY GIBBONS

WELCOME TO THE WORLD of Larry Gibbons. Brought to a Mi'kmaw First Nation reserve by a woman's love, and privileged to live there for ten years, Gibbons has written a rare and extraordinary batch of short stories. Sometimes he gets it right. Often he is the confused white man. But story by story, he delivers terrific reading—compassionate, often comic and absolutely unique.

176 PAGES • $17.95 • ISBN 978-1-926908-07-6

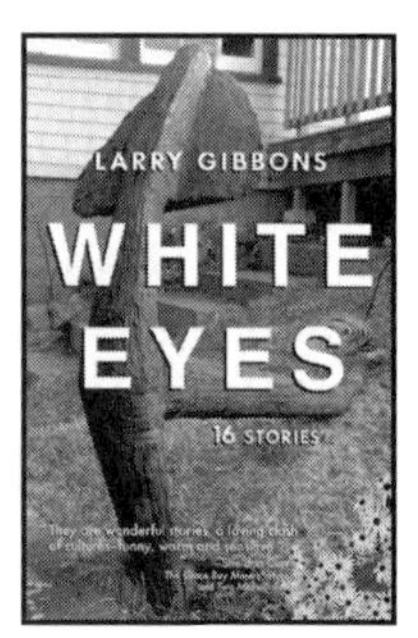

Breton Books

Wreck Cove, Cape Breton, Nova Scotia B0C 1H0

bretonbooks@ns.sympatico.ca • 1-800-565-5140

www.capebretonbooks.com